Natural Resources and People

Westview Special Studies

The concept of Westview Special Studies is a response to the continuing crisis in academic and informational publishing. Library budgets are being diverted from the purchase of books and used for data banks, computers, micromedia, and other methods of information retrieval. Interlibrary loan structures further reduce the edition sizes required to satisfy the needs of the scholarly community. Economic pressures on university presses and the few private scholarly publishing companies have greatly limited the capacity of the industry to properly serve the academic and research communities. As a result, many manuscripts dealing with important subjects, often representing the highest level of scholarship, are no longer economically viable publishing projects--or, if accepted for publication, are typically subject to lead times ranging from one to three years.

Westview Special Studies are our practical solution to the problem. As always, the selection criteria include the importance of the subject, the work's contribution to scholarship, and its insight, originality of thought, and excellence of exposition. We accept manuscripts in camera-ready form, typed, set, or word processed according to specifications laid out in our comprehensive manual, which contains straightforward instructions and sample pages. The responsibility for editing and proofreading lies with the author or sponsoring institution, but our editorial staff is always available to answer questions and provide guidance.

The result is a book printed on acid-free paper and bound in sturdy library-quality soft covers. We manufacture these books ourselves using equipment that does not require a lengthy make-ready process and that allows us to publish first editions of 300 to 1000 copies and to reprint even smaller quantities as needed. Thus, we can produce Special Studies quickly and can keep even very specialized books in print as long as there is a demand for them.

About the Book and Editors

The authors of this book provide an up-to-date assessment of research on human interactions with natural resource systems. Following an evaluation of long-term trends and the political and institutional settings, they assess the strengths and weaknesses of approaches designed to lead to a more holistic and interdisciplinary understanding. The social sciences, impact and risk assessment, and systems theory are considered in detail. The book concludes with a review of the limitations and barriers posed by disciplinary specialization and institutional fragmentation. It outlines the new approaches that will be necessary in order to better integrate concepts and data. Throughout the book, the authors pay attention to the interaction between theory and practice by including case studies and detailed examples involving specific natural resource systems.

Kenneth A. Dahlberg, professor of political science at Western Michigan University, is the author of Beyond the Green Revolution: The Ecology and Politics of Global Agricultural Development (1979). John W. Bennett is professor of anthropology at Washington University, St. Louis, and the author of The Ecological Transition: Cultural Anthropology and Human Adaptation (1976).

Natural Resources and People
Conceptual Issues in Interdisciplinary Research

edited by Kenneth A. Dahlberg
and John W. Bennett

Westview Press / Boulder and London

HC
59
N319
1986

Westview Special Studies in Natural Resources and Energy Management

All rights reserved. No part of this publication may be reproduced or
transmitted in any form or by any means, electronic or mechanical, including
photocopy, recording, or any information storage and retrieval system without
permission in writing from the publisher.

Copyright © 1986 by Westview Press, Inc.

Published in 1986 in the United States of America by Westview Press, Inc.;
Frederick A. Praeger, Publisher; 5500 Central Avenue, Boulder, Colorado 80301

Library of Congress Catalog Card Number: 85-13902
ISBN: 0-8133-7079-5

Composition for this book was provided by the authors
This book was produced without formal editing by the publisher

Printed and bound in the United States of America

 The paper used in this publication meets the minimum
 requirements of the American National Standard for
 Permanence of Paper for Printed Library Materials
 Z39.48-1984.

6   5   4   3   2   1

CALIFORNIA STATE UNIVERSITY, HAYWARD
LIBRARY

Contents

List of Tables and Figures ix
About the Contributors xi

INTRODUCTION--*Kenneth A. Dahlberg and
    John W. Bennett* 1

PART I: HISTORICAL AND INSTITUTIONAL TRENDS AND
         INFLUENCES

1 The Changing Nature of Natural Resources--
   Kenneth A. Dahlberg 11

2 Societal Constraints to Fisheries Management:
   A Peruvian Case Study--*Michael H. Glantz and
   Maria E. Krenz* 37

PART II: DISCIPLINARY APPROACHES

3 Geographical Approaches to Environmental
   Change: Assessing Human Impacts on Global
   Resources--*Leonard Berry and
   Douglas L. Johnson* 67

4 Anthropological Approaches to the Study of
   Human Impacts--*Emilio F. Moran* 107

5 Toward a Rural Sociology of Global Resources:
   Social Structure, Ecology, and Latin American
   Agricultural Development--*Frederick H. Buttel* . 129

6 Resources and People: An Economic
   Perspective--*Daniel W. Bromley and
   Ellen Szarleta* 165

PART III: MULTIDISCIPLINARY PROBLEM-ORIENTED APPROACHES

7   Range Management--Attempts to Build a
    Multidisciplinary Profession--*Fee Busby* 187

8   Desertification: Anatomy of a Complex
    Environmental Process--*Michael H. Glantz
    and Nicolai S. Orlovsky* 213

9   Impact Ecology: An Assessment Framework
    for Resource Development and Management--
    C. P. Wolf 231

PART IV: SYSTEMS APPROACHES

10 Systems Analysis and the World Food System--
    Donella H. Meadows 261

11 Ecosystems and Natural Resource Management--
    Frank B. Golley 281

PART V: PROBLEMS, NEEDS, AND PROSPECTS

12 The Idea of Disaster in a Technocratic
    Age and Natural Hazards Research--
    Kenneth Hewitt 303

13 Summary and Critique: Interdisciplinary
    Research on People-Resources Relations--
    John W. Bennett 343

14 Final Thoughts on Human Impacts on Global
    Resources--*Frank B. Golley* 373

Index 385

Tables and Figures

TABLES

7.1   Percentages of all federal land in three
      condition classes 205

FIGURES

2.1   Anchoveta catches, 1955-1983 39

2.2   Commercial pelagic fish landings 55

4.1   Model of socionatural systems 112

4.2   Soil maps of the Amazon Basin 115

4.3   Nested socionatural systems 121

6.1   Resource control centers 170

6.2   Resource control centers with sub-systems
      and feedback loops 173

9.1   Cultural ecology and impact analysis . . . 241

About the Contributors

JOHN W. BENNETT is Professor of Anthropology at Washington University, St. Louis. A long-time researcher in human ecology, his most recent books include The Ecological Transition and Of Time and the Enterprise: North American Family Farm Management in a Context of Resource Marginality. He is co-director of a recently funded three-year binational project to examine the development of culture history and agricultural development in the Northern Plains.

LEONARD BERRY is Professor of Geography, Provost, and Vice President for Academic Affairs, Clark University, Worcester, Massachusetts. In addition to numerous contributions to journals and books, he has authored or edited: Making the Most of the Least: Alternative Ways to Development (with R. W. Kates); Assessment of the Implementation of the Plan of Action to Combat Desertification in the Sudano-Sahelian Region; and African Environments (with L. Lewis, forthcoming).

DANIEL W. BROMLEY is Professor and Chairman of the Department of Agricultural Economics, University of Wisconsin, Madison. He has done international consulting, has served on advisory boards for various national agencies and commissions, and is editor of the journal Land Economics. He has co-authored two books and has published numerous articles on public decision making in the natural resource field.

FEE BUSBY is Associate Dean of the College of Agriculture and Director of the Agricultural Extension Service at the University of Wyoming, Laramie. Previously, he served as Head of the Department of Range Management. He has long been active at the state, national, and international levels in the Society for Range Management and will serve as its President in 1986.

FREDERICK H. BUTTEL is Associate Professor of Rural Sociology at Cornell University, Ithaca, New York. His publications include various articles on the political economy of agriculture, rural structures, and bio-technological issues. He has co-authored or co-edited several books, including The Rural Sociology of the Advanced Societies: Critical Perspectives (with H. Newby) and Environment, Energy, and Society (with C. R. Humphrey).

KENNETH A. DAHLBERG is Professor of Political Science at Western Michigan University, Kalamazoo. His book, Beyond the Green Revolution, was awarded the 1981 Harold and Margaret Sprout Award of the International Studies Association. He recently directed a two-year NSF/NEH project and edited the resulting book: New Directions for Agriculture and Agricultural Research. He has also consulted and published on global environmental and biological diversity issues.

MICHAEL H. GLANTZ is Head of the Environmental and Societal Impacts Group at the National Center for Atmospheric Research. His academic background is in political science. His research has focused on the politics of food, population, and climate. He has authored numerous articles and edited or co-edited Desertification: Environmental Degradation in and around Arid Lands and Resource Management and Environmental Uncertainty (with J. D. Thompson).

FRANK B. GOLLEY is Professor of Zoology and Environmental Design, and Research Professor of Ecology at the Institute of Ecology, University of Georgia, Athens. He has written numerous books and articles on the structure and function of ecological systems. He is a Past President of both the Ecological Society of America and the International Society of Tropical Ecology. He has also served as Secretary General of the International Association for Ecology.

KENNETH HEWITT is Professor of Geography at Wilfrid Laurier University, Waterloo, Ontario. He has had a long interest in human ecology and natural hazards research. He is currently involved in a collaborative research project on the snow and ice hydrology of the Upper Indus Basin. In addition to his many articles, he has edited or co-edited: The Hazardousness of a Place (with R. W. Kates) and Interpretations of Calamity from the Viewpoint of Human Ecology.

DOUGLAS L. JOHNSON is Associate Professor of Geography in the Graduate School of Geography, Clark University, Worcester, Massachusetts. His main research interests are in cultural ecology, arid land management, intensification in pastoral systems, and demographic history. In addition to numerous articles and contributions to books, he has authored The Nature of Nomadism.

MARIA E. KRENZ is a writer/editor in the Environmental and Societal Impacts Groups at the National Center for Atmospheric Research, Boulder, Colorado. She has edited several technical books on energy and other problems related to climate and society as well as numerous articles and book chapters on environmental matters.

DONELLA H. MEADOWS is an Adjunct Professor of Environmental Studies and Policy Studies at Dartmouth College, New Hampshire. She has served as a senior scientist at several international resource policy centers, including the International Institute for Applied Systems Analysis, Vienna. She has been involved in computer studies of global development, particularly The Limits of Growth, and has authored two retrospectives on computer modeling, Groping in the Dark and The Electronic Oracle: Computer Models and Social Decisions.

EMILIO F. MORAN is Professor and Chairman of the Department of Anthropology, and Professor in the School for Public and Environmental Affairs, Indiana University, Bloomington. His research interests include ecological anthropology, resource management, and agricultural development. He has authored or edited Human Adaptability, The Dilemma of Amazonian Development, and The Ecosystem Concept in Anthropology.

NICOLAI S. ORLOVSKY is the Deputy Director of the Institute of Deserts of the Academy of Science of the Turkmen SSR in the Soviet Union, and is a Candidate of Science in Geography. He was a member of the Soviet Delegation to the United States for the 1982 US/USSR Joint Agreement on the Protection of Arid Ecosystems and is author of numerous articles on arid-zone climatology and desertification.

ELLEN SZARLETA is a doctoral student in the Department of Agricultural Economics, University of Wisconsin, Madison. She recently returned from a 9-month stay in Burkina Faso (formerly Upper Volta) where she was conducting research on the behavior of grain-livestock farmers.

C. P. WOLF is Director, Social Impact Assessment Center, New York City. He has had a long-term interest in the development of social impact methodologies. In addition to many articles, he has co-edited three books: Methodology of Social Impact Assessment (with K. Finsterbusch), Social Impact Assessment Methods (with K. Finsterbusch and L. G. Llewellyn), and Accident at Three Mile Island: The Human Dimensions (with David L. Sills and Vivien B. Shelanski). He is President-Elect of the International Association for Impact Assessment.

Introduction

An evolving set of questions regarding the nature and need for interdisciplinary work in natural resources have shaped the form and content of this book. An initial set was posed and discussed at a workshop, "Social Sciences, Interdisciplinary Research and the U.S. Man and the Biosphere Program" (for the proceedings, see Zube, 1980). While the discussions started out with a review of the natural science origins of UNESCO's Man and the Biosphere Program (MAB) and its predominantly biome-oriented research, they soon came to focus on several key questions: Why was it so difficult to build bridges between the natural and social sciences, not only in MAB, but more generally? How might this be encouraged? Was it simply a matter of inadequate institutional mechanisms or of different conceptual approaches? And so on.

After extensive discussion, it became clear that in addition to a number of serious institutional barriers there were a host of theoretical, conceptual, and methodological gaps and differences which made effective collaboration difficult. Also, in terms of the substantive focus of U.S. (and UNESCO) MAB programs, it became clear that the larger regional and global population, resource, and environmental trends highlighted in the Global 2000 Report to the President (CEQ, 1981) had been neglected. The intellectual and practical implications were clear: that our understandings of resource and ecological systems were incomplete and fragmented, and that this, plus the lack of any systematic appreciation of longer-term and larger-scale trends, meant that the advice offered by MAB to governments, planning agencies, development assistance programs, and so on, however much better it might be than that based on a narrow disciplinary perspective, was itself in need of broadening and improvement. How to encourage this was less clear.

An ad hoc committee consisting of John W. Bennett (an anthropologist), Kenneth A. Dahlberg (a political scientist), and Frank B. Golley (an ecologist) was established to explore what might be done to address these issues within U.S. MAB and the larger academic community. The committee decided to organize a AAAS symposium, "Human Impacts on Global Resources: Disciplinary Approaches and Research," which included a representative mix of social and natural scientists, all of whom had experience in addressing interdisciplinary problems. In reviewing the symposium papers and discussions, the committee concluded that interdisciplinary attempts to assess human impacts on resource systems at a global level, important as they might be in raising issues and questions, had little to tell us directly about how better to understand and encourage interdisciplinary research. In addition to difficult analytic and data problems, it became clear that there was a fundamental conceptual problem: most of the research on natural resources tended to be narrow in focus and little of it was conceived of in systemic terms that included the major interacting social, environmental, and technological dimensions.

Reflection on these conceptual issues then led to a second set of questions. How have Western concepts of nature shaped our understandings of resources? To what degree have rationalistic approaches and utilitarian values led to biases in favor of exploitation over conservation? How have increases in technological capabilities interacted with the institutions and values of industrial society to shape our understandings as well as the use of natural resources? Has the disciplinary specialization upon which the modern university is built now become obsolescent? How have the institutions of the larger state system influenced research on natural resources? While realizing that these and other related questions could not be answered fully, the editors became convinced that a critical overview of the conceptual issues and interrelationships involved would help to provide a better foundation for interdisciplinary work. In addition, we wanted to include both examples of, and reflections upon genuine interdisciplinary research.

In pursuing these objectives, the editors requested revisions of the relevant symposium papers, commissioned several new papers, and sought out already published papers. In trying to illustrate the fundamental themes, issues, and questions, our approach has been selective, involving a smaller number of thoughtful and critical chapters, rather than a larger number of more descriptive ones. Thus, a number of disciplines and methodologies which might logically have been included are absent. Equally, we have not tried to impose intellectual order or coherence where little is currently apparent. Rather, we have organized the book so as to include the main approaches to interdisciplinary research as well as the questions and puzzles that emerged from the workshop and symposium.

Part I seeks to outline and discuss the larger historical, cultural, and institutional context within which work on natural resources has been developed and conducted. Chapter 1, by Kenneth A. Dahlberg, is an exploratory essay which cautions against assuming the universality of current concepts of natural resources by examining the broad changes in the nature and understanding of natural resources between hunting and gathering, agricultural, and industrial societies. Also, some of the major interactions between institutional specialization and centralization, increasing technological capabilities, and patterns of natural resource use (and abuse) are traced. Chapter 2, by Michael H. Glantz and Maria E. Krenz, employs a model which analytically separates factors operating at the individual, national, and international levels to do a detailed case study describing the social, political, and technological factors that have shaped the development and structure of the fisheries industry. While focusing on the Peruvian fishery, they show how it has been affected by both what happened in other fisheries and by the vagaries of El Nino. They thus conclude that traditional natural resource management approaches which stress concepts of maximum sustainable yield and focus on a specific fishery are not sufficient. International economic and technological trends, as well as national political and bureaucratic factors need to be included.

Parts II, III, and IV seek to provide a series of critical reviews and analyses of the strengths and weaknesses of the main approaches to interdisciplinary research and work. Rather than trying to develop a detailed typology, three broad approaches were identified--disciplinary approaches, multidisciplinary problem-oriented approaches, and systems approaches. Each can be seen to manifest certain holistic and integrative capabilities and conceptions, yet none of them can be said to be fully interdisciplinary. In part, this may be due to the institutional settings within which they operate--which clearly mitigate against interdisciplinary research or work. In part, this is also due to the particular cognitive "maps" with which they work. While each of the approaches borrows from the others, the disciplines generally explore the larger interactions of the problems they are exploring "from the discipline up." That is, they take the traditional academic division of labor as their starting point and then seek to build upon, expand, and reach out from that "slice" of the whole towards a larger understanding.

In contrast, there are what we have termed multidisciplinary, problem-oriented approaches. In focusing upon specific problems (such as desertification or range management) or types of problems (social impact assessments), they tend to draw upon data, concepts, and analytic procedures from the various disciplines relevant to their particular problem; they are thus multi-disciplinary. They are, in effect, putting together various disciplinary "slices" or pieces to form a mosaic depicting their problem area. However, unlike a mosaic, the pieces are more like those coming from a number of different jigsaw puzzles--with each piece having a shape and picture derived from its specific discipline. Thus, the resulting "mosaic" will have gaps and holes, as well as a conflicting mixture of component images. This analogy also helps to illustrate another characteristic of multi-disciplinary approaches: they tend to be more interested in testing their work in and against the real world, rather than employing the extensive theory- and model-building of the disciplines.

Systems approaches fall somewhere in between. Examples of two important, but rather different approaches are represented here: general systems theory and ecology. Each reflects a dissatisfaction with disciplinary approaches and clearly calls for a radical broadening of our theoretical approaches to understanding and dealing with natural resource problems. Yet neither really synthesizes either the traditional academic fields--the humanities, the social sciences, and the natural sciences--nor the three major constituent parts of natural resource systems--the technological, the environmental, and the social. Thus, while they offer stimulation and hope, their integrative theories and concepts are still largely in outline or prototypic form in terms of full interdisciplinary content; much of the rest--often admixed in curious patterns--still depends upon data and concepts generated by disciplinary or multi-disciplinary approaches. Thus, whatever approach is taken, each of us is left with the frustration of being able to see or speak of natural resource systems primarily through the parts. We have concluded that a better understanding of the intellectual and institutional roots of our divisions and separations is a prerequisite to making advances towards more holistic, integrated, and interdisciplinary research.

In Part II we asked each of the authors to reflect upon the strengths and weaknesses of their particular disciplines in terms of what they have and have not been able to tell us about natural resource systems, what levels of analysis are most fruitfully applied, what types of phenomena can be most clearly depicted, and so on. We also asked the authors to illustrate their assessments and concerns either by drawing upon case studies in which they have been involved or by integrating examples from selected resource management studies. In this way, we sought to include an interaction or dialectic between theory and practice. The disciplines chosen are all from the social sciences. This is both to counterbalance the historic emphasis on the natural sciences in work on natural resources and to illustrate what such approaches and perspectives can add. Thus, in terms of one of the primary needs identified in the initial MAB workshop, we have sought to encourage a redefinition and reconceptualization of resource and ecological systems so as to include human interactions with the environment.

Chapter 3, by Leonard Berry and Douglas Johnson, draws upon the long tradition of geography in seeking this same goal. As one of the original symposium papers, it does this both by reviewing various types of human impacts on resource systems--such as expansion and intensification of agriculture, desertification, and irrigation--and by giving an evaluation of the approaches geographers have developed to assess environmental change. They suggest the importance of integrating conceptually what they term livelihood systems into environmental and resource systems. Finally, they provide a number of practical suggestions regarding the monitoring and training needs required to better assess resource trends.

Chapter 4, by Emilio F. Moran, draws upon his extensive field work and research in Amazonia to evaluate anthropological theories and approaches and their strengths and weaknesses. He is particularly concerned about the limits of linear thinking and suggests the need for a clearer conceptual sorting out of what can be effectively analyzed at each level of analysis. To encourage this, he develops a model for human ecosystems research based on "nested" or hierarchically integrated concepts.

Chapter 5, by Frederick H. Buttel, reviews the development of rural sociology and its relationship to sociology. He also examines the various existing and emerging approaches that might be used to address natural resource issues, as well as their methodological and practical implications. His substantive focus is upon the social ecology of Latin American agricultural development and how rural sociology can help both to clarify the influence as well as the dynamics of the emerging international division of labor. Finally, he outlines some new development strategies based on agroecological theories and concepts.

Chapter 6, by Daniel W. Bromley and Ellen Szarleta, offers a formal model that explicitly includes interactions between ecosystems and social systems. In many ways critical of conventional economic approaches, it focuses on such issues as the choice of technique, the product mix, the processing choice, and the resource choices involved. By formally including ecosystems, they hope to improve our understandings of the economics of resource choices.

There is no one single focus--such as disciplines--in Part III. The multi-disciplinary problem-oriented approaches selected involve a cross-section. Chapter 7, by Fee Busby, represents what might be termed a multi-discipline. He provides a fascinating description of the early trials and errors of researchers in range management, where attempts to apply management concepts and experience from the temperate areas of Europe and the Eastern United States to the more arid West failed. There was little in the way of a scientific base, and federal and state programs (and the way they were shaped by private interests) pushed the field in particular directions. His tracing of the radical changes in the conventional wisdom of the field over the past half century should provide both caution and instruction to those working in newer problem areas.

One of these newer areas is desertification, which is discussed in Chapter 8 by Michael H. Glantz and Nicolai Orlovsky. The approach that they take is to examine all of the various concepts of desertification both in terms of their substance and in terms of how those concepts are shaped by external influences. Disciplinary and national and international agency influences are particularly notable. The authors organize their substantive review of the various concepts in terms of questions relating to how desertification occurs (What is the form of change? What is changed? Where does change occur? Is it reversible?) and why it occurs (Because of climate change? Drought? Overuse by humans? New technologies?). Finally, they argue for a broadened concept which goes beyond its current identification with arid and semi-arid zones.

Chapter 9, by C. P. Wolf, represents a somewhat different approach in that it examines the development of social impact assessment methodologies rather than focusing on specific resource systems. Also, it tends to emphasize the impacts of natural systems--as mediated through technologies, projects, and institutions--upon humans, rather than vice versa. Wolf reviews the different concepts of "resources" underlying the various assessment methodologies and seeks to develop a broader and more integrative framework--which he calls impact ecology. Part of this effort involves a consideration of different systems theories. Here again, there is more emphasis upon human systems and their causal patterns than upon natural systems.

Part IV deals explicitly with systems approaches. It includes provocative evaluations of two of the most important systems approaches which have been applied to natural resources. Chapter 10, by Donella H. Meadows, argues that formal systems modeling and analysis is as applied to the world food system have yielded meager results that are far below their potential. Meadows points to both methodological and conceptual weaknesses to explain this failure. Methodologically, there has been too much emphasis on the easily measurable and a tendency to draw upon existing data bases (often disciplinary in origin) rather than seeking to develop interdisciplinary data bases. Conceptually, there is often a failure to question assumptions and to explore genuine alternatives; i.e., most systems research in this area accepts current institutional and social structures. Questioning these and going on to ask the right questions for a complete systems analysis requires one to address the normative dimensions of world hunger, agricultural resource exploitation and sustainability, and so on.

Chapter 11, by Frank B. Golley, begins by reviewing two intertwined, but different approaches found in ecosystems studies: the "scientific" and the "philosophic" approaches. The former is more reductionistic and analytic, while the latter is based more on analogy, induction, and inference. In this chapter, Golley reviews the basic characteristics of scientific ecosystem studies and their application to natural resource management. In the final chapter of the book he explores the larger implications of the philosophical approach to ecosystem studies. There is a very careful review and evaluation of the methodology of scientific ecosystem studies here. Golley brings out both the analytic and institutional history of this relatively new approach. The magnitude of methodological and analytic problems in comparison to institutional resources (a problem not unique to ecology) has hindered the development of a completely adequate methodology. Even so, the methodology developed so far is shown to have significant value for analyzing both natural and social systems.

Concern with larger issues and questions characterizes Part V. In a sense the objective here is to evaluate where we are in terms of interdisciplinary research and practice, what our fundamental problems are, what the larger needs of society and the biosphere are, and how we might proceed. Chapter 12, by Kenneth Hewitt, offers an intellectual history and description of the idea of calamity and hazards in modern industrial society. The larger context which he portrays—where calamity and hazards are shown to be unexplainable symbolic and practical challenges to the technocratic paradigm—clearly has relevance to all natural resource research and work as well as to natural hazards research. Hewitt shows how the concerns and focus of natural hazards research have been strongly shaped by the larger needs of governments and agencies to appear to "control" hazards and risks (even though the programs they develop are often ineffective or even counterproductive in terms of encouraging resiliency in the systems they seek to "manage"). The larger cultural themes, institutional pressures, and analytic weaknesses depicted here need to be pondered by all working in the natural resources area.

Chapter 13, by John W. Bennett, reviews and critiques the other chapters. In doing so, he seeks to identify the underlying themes and models found in the chapters and to discuss how we might build upon them for the future. This provocative chapter challenges many of the concepts and institutions which underlie conventional scholarship. Bennett sees us as having developed a civilization with "a mindset which makes it extremely difficult to think clearly about such matters as time, change, responsibility, conservation, and causation." He argues that the disciplines--useful innovations in their day--are now outmoded, but kept alive through their institutional power. They do little to prepare us for the great debate over human and earthly survival which Bennett sees emerging. Besides the various analytic and theoretical suggestions he makes, Bennett stresses the need for a much greater normative awareness regarding both human and natural systems--an awareness that recognizes that "we treat Nature much as we treat each other."

In the final chapter, Frank B. Golley also stresses the importance of normative and philosophic matters in developing the "new science" that he argues will be required to deal with the larger questions and issues identified in this book. By seeking to view humankind from a global ecological perspective, he provides a balance to homocentric biases and assumptions. Yet the new science Golley calls for is one involving a deep concern for helping humankind learn to respect and evolve within the limits of the larger biological and physical systems upon which it is dependent.

The contributors to this volume hope that their efforts will help to build better foundations for interdisciplinary work. The range, depth, and rapid expansion of human impacts upon natural resource systems that are documented here certainly call for a significant increase in academic efforts to broaden our understandings of the complex interactions involved. Equally, decision makers, aid administrators, development planners, and others who increasingly will have to try to cope with such impacts will need a broader array of concepts, approaches, and detailed, but integrated studies to address them with. We hope that the new ideas and approaches presented here will stimulate other efforts to re-think and re-work current conceptual and institutional approaches to natural resources and people.

Kenneth A. Dahlberg and John W. Bennett

Part 1
Historical and Institutional Trends and Influences

1
The Changing Nature of Natural Resources

Kenneth A. Dahlberg

INTRODUCTION

It is commonplace to refer to the various ways in which technological innovations have changed the availability of natural resources. Indeed, the evolution and elaboration of modern industrial society has involved complex interactions whereby more traditional resources and fuels have been increasingly supplemented and overshadowed by newer ones made available through technological invention and innovation. Wood, fire, water, and windpower were gradually supplanted by the interacting capacities of coal and steam power. These in turn were modified, strengthened, and eventually overshadowed by mutually reinforcing petroleum, chemical, and metallurgical discoveries. Current developments and debates regarding the long-term place of nuclear power illustrate the expanding scale and complexity of resource-technological interactions. It is also common to refer to the intellectual and scientific developments and theories that either made possible or grew out of these technological developments. Much of the recent work on the history of science has sought to trace out such interactions in detail, although the corresponding impacts on, and changes in the resource base have received less analysis.

Less common are attempts to understand the changing nature of natural resources from a broad historical and cross-cultural perspective. That sort of overview is attempted here--both to place the remaining chapters of the book in historical perspective and to clarify our understanding of the changing nature of resources, past and present. Before beginning our broad historical overview, two important influences need to be discussed. First, we need to sensitize ourselves to the various ways in which Western cultural assumptions color our understandings of resources. Second, we need to review the institutional setting of the disciplines that help to shape our analytic and societal capabilities to respond to changing resource conditions.

A wide range of Western cultural concepts, beliefs, and attitudes--especially those regarding nature, progress, and science and technology--has been crucial to the development of modern industrial civilization. The concept of natural resources itself reflects these Western views and values and "is largely derived from our own society's ceaseless attempt at finding new and more intensive uses for the raw materials of nature" (Spoehr, 1956). Since every society's concept of nature is largely culturally defined, mediated through various rituals, and influenced by technological capacities, it is important that we become more self-aware of our cultural and industrial biases. For modern industrial man, "nature" is seen as largely separate, neutral in any spiritual sense, and subordinate. It is these perceptions which so distinguish modern concepts of "nature" from more traditional ones--where the realm of "nature" is seen to be larger (and often more threatening), more spiritual, and less subject to technological manipulation or control. The modern concept also sanctions much greater exploitation of nature (and often of other people).

Arguments against untrammeled exploitation have been primarily couched in terms of either utilitarian considerations, such as economic rationality or longer-term self-interest, or equity concerns involving questions of who should pay the costs and reap the benefits of resource exploitation. Of interest here are recent efforts to redefine or create a new moral basis for conservation.[1] Ecologists, environmentalists, and some religious groups are involved in seeking this new ethic, although it is not clear whether it is ultimately to be based on the survival of humankind as a species or on the survival of the biosphere--which can alternatively be conceived of as a complex and evolving ecosystem within the limits of which humankind must learn to live or as the ultimate manifestation of God's handiwork.

While the intellectual buttresses of modern industrial civilization--the universities and the academic disciplines--clearly have been influenced by Western cultural assumptions and beliefs, it is perhaps their adoption of, and the institutionalization of functional specialization that has most shaped their perspectives and capabilities. The long-term trend of increasing specialization has, of course, reflected and interacted with similar, and larger-scale trends in society itself. In the U.S., the rise of the land grant colleges, with their focus on the "agricultural and mechanical arts," represented an important innovation as well as a shift away from the classics, philosophy, and natural history stressed by the traditional Eastern universities. The expansion of industry and its requirements for engineering and science encouraged the spread of engineering and technical schools as well as the German university model for science. The latter stressed greater disciplinary specialization in the sciences--something that was soon carried over into the social sciences.

What has developed over the past century in the U.S. is a pattern of practical or professional schools linked to specific academic disciplines. One set relates broadly to natural resources (schools of agriculture and natural resources), while another relates to industry (schools of engineering and technology). Others, which may be seen to be service sectors, relate to medicine, law, business and finance, etc. These patterns have reflected the dual divisions seen to exist between the rural/agricultural and urban/industrial areas and sectors. Similarly, there have been two basic types of specialization in the field of natural resources, one involving an intellectual separation of natural resource systems from urban/industrial areas and problems, and the other involving disciplinary specialization.

These patterns generate a range of intellectual and practical problems. At the university level, there are tensions between those approaches and departments which are more practically oriented and those that are more theoretically oriented. Although often couched in terms of differences between "applied" and "basic" research, such tensions also reflect differences in approach and underlying rationale. These range from seeking what is directly useful to society in terms of society's definitions of utility on the one hand to seeking the truth, regardless of its implications for current societal norms and structures, on the other.

Academic work in natural resources has been strongly based on the natural sciences, although the tendency has been to separate out organizationally those aspects directly related to resource exploitation or conservation. Thus, there are departments of soil science, plant physiology, forest management, and so on. Equally, within the social sciences, the tendency has been to develop separate subdisciplines or departments of agricultural economics, rural sociology, economic geography, etc. Until very recently, there has been little attempt to involve or consider the humanities as they might relate to agriculture, forestry, or natural resources.

This sort of intellectual specialization and organizational separatism has led to a concern for how one might develop more integrated and holistic approaches. This book is an example of such concern at the intellectual and conceptual level. Other expressions of concern have included the creation of various multidisciplinary institutes both in and outside of universities and the creation of various taskforces and committees that are designed to bring a wide range of expertise to bear on a specific problem like arid lands, acid rain, or deforestation.

These intellectual and organizational developments can be seen as an attempt to try to deal not only with the problems of specialization, but with an increasingly important problem of industrial society--<u>the lead-time problem</u>. This problem results from the increasing scale and organizational complexity of industrial processes and is most visible in such large-scale industries as the automobile and steel industries. Both are highly productive, but gain that productivity through massive, centralized, and quite inflexible infrastructural and organizational patterns. A five to ten year lead time is required to make any basic changes in these industries. A failure to anticipate major changes in the larger operating environment--rising fuel prices, changing markets, etc.--can lead to severe economic disruption and painful social dislocations. In agriculture and forestry the lead times may be even greater and the consequences of failing to anticipate changes may be even more fundamental.

While a number of new institutes and interdisciplinary programs have been established in the universities, the difficulties of sustaining them--particularly in periods of tight budgets--suggest that the lead time required to bring about any significant changes in intellectual and budgetary priorities of universities is very great. This problem raises some basic questions about whether universities and the disciplines will be of much assistance to society in anticipating and outlining the implications of a wide range of changes and challenges facing modern industrial society.

For example, even though it appears that the various natural resource systems which have been the purview of the colleges of agriculture and natural resources are increasingly integrated into what may be called <u>industrial resource regimes</u>, there is neither an intellectual nor an organizational base available to describe, analyze, and evaluate linkages. The situation is complicated by the fact that the scale of operation of such industrial resource regimes is expanding from a national to a global scale. To give one example, a complex set of consumer demands (fueled by a sophisticated advertising and mass media system) places pressure upon the tropical forests of the world and their genetic endowments. The demands of the industrial countries for wood, paper, and furniture--as well as for rangeland to provide cheap beef for the mass hamburger chains--all add significant pressures to those already existing in the poor countries to cut down tropical forests. Thus,

while it is important to continue to develop better
understandings of the resources and forests in those
regions and to develop better techniques and programs
for managing them, a critical dimension is missed if one
ignores the total complex of pressures and demands,
trade and corporate patterns, and urban consumer values
and desires which so strongly influence the use of these
natural resources.

What is suggested by the above is that we need a
twofold rethinking of natural resource systems. First,
we need a major effort to develop better interdisciplinary concepts and methodologies to describe and understand the dynamics of natural resource systems. While
retaining the traditional focus on specific geographic
and environmental areas and regions, such an effort will
need to broaden current definitions to include human and
technological interactions with the environment. This
book should provide a foundation for such work, both
through its evaluation of current approaches and by
demonstrating in its case studies the extent of these
human and technological influences and interactions.
Next, we need to reconceptualize natural resource systems so that they are understood as increasingly integrated parts of progressively larger industrial sectors
and systems. While this goes beyond the scope of this
book, an awareness of these larger, less geographically
and enviromentally based systems should help researchers
start thinking about both the influence that a particular industrial resource regime may have on its component
natural resource systems and how one can begin mapping
out the various flows, demands, influences, and linkages. Both types of rethinking can benefit from a broad
historical overview of the changing balances between
resources, technology, and culture. What follows is a
preliminary attempt at such an overview.

CULTURAL EVOLUTION, RESOURCES, AND TECHNOLOGY

What will be highlighted here are the basic changes
and shifts between hunting and gathering, agricultural,
and industrial societies and the corresponding changes
in the balance and composition of their cultural,
resource, and technological components. The emphasis
will be on describing the "structural" differences
rather than the various theories of change and transition that have been put forth to try to explain how
these societies changed from one into the other. A much
fuller awareness of the range and depth of change
between these different types of societies would appear
to be a prerequisite to developing better theories of
cultural and social change and transition. Also, such
an awareness is needed as a corrective to many rather

simple-minded analyses which suggest we are in a transition to a "post-industrial society" (discussed below), even though they often assume a continuation of current industrial structures and values. Finally, by focusing on the ways in which the nature and conception of resources has shifted between these three types of societies, we will be in a better position to address the challenges sketched above.

The problems of academic specialization are manifest in the literature on these three types of societies. A great deal of detailed work has been done by anthropologists on a wide variety of hunting and gathering societies and how they evolved into prehistoric agricultural societies. This work is distinguished by the attempt to include the interactions of a culture with its environment, as mediated through technologies, rituals, and social structures, and how these may evolve. However much the historian might want to trace similar interactions in examining shifts from agricultural to industrial societies, the traditions, methods, and style of historiography have made this more difficult. Anthropologists have used contemporary ethnographic work with relatively small groups in the field to inform their historical researches about hunting and gathering peoples (see Lee and DeVore, 1968). Historians, however, deal with larger societies and have tended to focus on social and political factors more than on either environmental or technological factors. There are exceptions, and the work on the transition period called the "Middle Ages" has benefited from the holistic approaches of historians such as Ferdinand Braudel. Interestingly, the field that most systematically seeks to link the broad environmental, technological, and social trends of today's society is global computer modeling--although the social and institutional dimensions are far from being adequately integrated.

Culture, as anthropologists use the term, includes a group's world view, its patterned behavior and rituals, and its institutions and social structure. These obviously vary from group to group, but what has been of interest to anthropologists is to find whether there are certain common patterns or responses either to similar levels of technological development or to similar environmental settings. In addition, there is the question of how one distinguishes those cultural aspects which relate to the every day running and operation of a society from those which relate to helping it adapt to basic changes in its environment, technology, or culture. These adaptive aspects involve a combination of knowledge, wisdom, and guidance, the requirements of which will also vary from one type of society to another.

Resources are a part of a society's larger environment and are defined or understood both in terms of its culture and the levels of technology available and employed. Although there has been little systematic discussion of the matter, there does appear to be some sort of resource hierarchy present in any given type of society--a hierarchy which is linked both to the nature of the resources employed (and whether they are primarily based on natural or technological processes) and the social structures used to extract, process, maintain, and distribute them. The particular combinations determine which resources are generally available and which are "strategic" in the sense that the society will not be able to operate long without them.

Technologies are shaped by culture and environment and any particular technology must be understood in terms of its cultural history and environmental setting. This, plus the various scale demands and characteristics of specific technologies means that no technology is "neutral" and that the concept of "technology transfer" prevelant in the literature on economic development is a misnomer (for a full discussion, see Dahlberg, 1973 and 1979). What needs to be sorted out between the three different types of societies in this regard are the dominant technologies, the energy and resource systems that are related to them, and the range of functions they perform--which cover a spectrum from production to security to ritual.

How then has each of these societies been structured in terms of the above three components?

Hunting and Gathering Societies[2]

The culture and technologies of hunting and gathering societies are closely related to the resources found in their larger environment and to the basic survival needs of the group as well as the cultural values and goals they choose to pursue. In more specialized ecosystems, where species diversity is low, but where there are large numbers of individuals, the tendency is for more specialized forms of hunting and gathering to evolve--thus leading to what has been termed a "specialized economy" (Harris, 1969). In more species diverse ecosystems, where there are more species, but fewer individuals for each species--something generally found in transitional zones between biomes--more generalized approaches have evolved into "broad spectrum economies" (Harris, 1969 and Bender, 1975). The latter has been seen to be one of at least three prerequisites for evolution into an agricultural society (Flannery, 1969).

While the key resources are those found in the larger environment, it is important to recognize that they become useful only as a result of a great deal of very detailed and location-specific knowledge about the growing cycles of plants, their responses to various climatic conditions, the range and indicators of climatic variation, and how such plants can be treated, processed, or cooked to make them edible or useable for purposes of clothing or shelter. Similarly, with animals and fish, detailed knowledge is needed of the habitats, life-cycles, and daily habits of each species which is defined or selected as "useful." In his study of a contemporary foraging society, the !Kung, Lee (1979:455) has concluded that they "make no sharp dichotomy between the resources of the natural environment and the social wealth . . . they conceive of the environment itself as their storehouse." Their very detailed knowledge of their environment "is, in effect, a form of control over nature: It has been developed over many generations in response to every conceivable variation in climatic conditions."

The particular mix of hunting and gathering will vary between the different seasons of the year and also according to both periodic climatic variations and the general climate zone.

Generally, there appears to have been a sexual division of labor. "It is probable that a high proportion of these societies depended primarily on plant-foods. Hunting--and the hunters--probably got the kudos but gathering--usually the women's job--was more reliable" (Bender, 1975:3). Gathering among the !Kung is highly selective, with only a third of the potentially edible plants gathered, something requiring only some twelve to nineteen hours per week for those women who are involved (Lee, 1979). It may well be that the "surplus" generated from hunting and gathering societies was leisure--quite in contrast to still prevalent Hobbesian stereotypes.

The dominant technologies relate to hunting and gathering and the provision of clothing and shelter. Generally, the technologies were simple and unspecialized--most of which each household could manufacture for itself from locally available materials. Among the !Kung, Lee (1979:455-56) found that with a few exceptions, most of the basic household technologies, luxuries, as well as family shelters and bows and arrows were locally made and that their manufacture or construction involved a relatively small investment of time. Given the mobility of most of these societies, there was ample opportunity for trade in either luxury or "strategic" items, the major limitation being the total amount of goods which each household could easily transport. The energy systems associated with these resources and technologies were based primarily upon human and animal energy, supplemented by firewood.

The types of social structure and cultural values associated with hunting and gathering societies are related to the mobility required to take maximum advantage of the annual and life cycles of those plants and animals seen as resources. Equally, the advantages of sharing--both food within the group and access to food resources among groups--dictate values supporting food sharing on the basis of generalized reciprocity as well as reciprocal rules for access to the various land areas where food resources are present (Lee, 1979:117). A very flexible group structure is also encouraged, but one that has few social mechanisms for resolving strife among larger groups and gatherings (Bender, 1975:8). There is a strong egalitarianism, and leadership is often subtle and indirect, based upon the exercise of influence rather than on the exercise of power or authority. Mobility also influences such things as the spacing of births, where the average among contemporary nomads and foragers is three to five years between children--reflecting the fact that it is very difficult for women to travel carrying more than one small child at a time.

Among the !Kung and others, there is a collective, but not exclusive "ownership" of land and food resources. A loose territoriality is moderated by reciprocal rules for access to these lands and resources and by the limits to the accumulation of social wealth dictated by what one can actually transport during the household's annual round, which is some 2400 kilometers for the !Kung (Lee, 1979:118).

The knowledge, wisdom, and guidance required for the regular operation of this type of society are significant. As indicated above, much of it relates to very detailed knowledge of species and habitats and their responses to specific climatic variations. Effective assessment and behavioral response to the ever-changing balance of resource opportunities afforded by nature makes this process a continuous challenge. Prehistoric hunters and gatherers appear to have been generally successful in making such adjustments, since many of them were able to live in harmony with their environment and resource base for many centuries. Whether the main source for this was a culturally-based restraint or whether--given their simple technologies and the requirements for mobility--they were caught up in a type of "low-level equilibrium trap" is not clear (see Bennett, 1980, for a detailed discussion).

It is also not clear whether they were better equipped than other types of societies to adapt to macro changes in their environment. On the one hand, one can argue that their ability to adapt to micro and meso environmental changes, their mobility, and the lack of significant institutional and structural rigidities gave them an extensive adaptive capacity. On the other hand, one can argue that their lack of more powerful technologies and institutions limited their adaptive capacity. Perhaps it is best to understand these questions in contextual terms: each type of society has certain types of capabilities and weaknesses. Whether they are able to successfully adapt depends not only upon those, but upon the type and magnitude of change occurring in the larger environment. The question then becomes: what types of changes is a given society best and least able to adapt to? And correlary to that: what types of changes are most likely to occur in the larger environment?

Agricultural Societies

Very different cultural and technological patterns are associated with agricultural societies--where there is a more intensive use of a narrower range of the materials found in the environment. The pressures, adaptation, mechanisms, and modes of transition from hunting and gathering to agricultural societies is a matter of quite divergent interpretation (see Struever, 1971; Bender, 1975; and Smith, 1976 for discussions). Whatever the reasons for their evolution, the more intensive use of land through cultivation and the domestication of animals significantly increased the carrying capacity of a given region. The average carrying capacity for hunter-gatherers in the late Pleistocene has been estimated at 0.1 person per square kilometer, that for early dry farming systems at 1 to 2 persons per square kilometer, and irrigated agriculture at six times that number (Flannery, 1969). These increases are generally agreed to have required increases in the annual amount of work per capita and a corresponding decline in the amount of leisure. It is important also to recognize that prehistoric agricultural societies provided the base for the emergence of different historic agricultural societies ranging from tribal groups to chiefdoms to traditional kingdom states and trading empires to the great agricultural civilizations of the Orient.

The domestication of plants and animals and their more intensive use requires more manipulation of the environment (and thus different cultural definitions and understandings thereof) as well as more elaborate technologies and institutions. The basic nature of resources shifts to an emphasis on specific lands, seeds, root crops, animals and fish, and how climate variations interact with them. There is the shift in focus from a variety of landscapes and environments (and the mobility required to derive a living from them) to the specific area where the group is settled. Food preservation for the following seasons becomes a much greater concern, both for households and the larger village community. Also, as Smith (1976:47) has pointed out, territory, boundary consciousness, and restriction of access to these much more delimited resources becomes important.

The dominant technologies relate to the more narrow, specialized, and intensive nature of the food production system. In terms of direct food production they relate to cultivation, selective breeding, and irrigation; in terms of providing food for the entire year, they relate to food storage, and new preparation and preservation techniques; in terms of the more permanent nature of housing and shelter they relate to more specialized and elaborate construction techniques; and in terms of the increased security needs associated with more permanent settlements and heightened senses of territoriality they relate to the greater development of weapons. The energy systems that are associated with these technologies involve the more systematic use of human labor and the greater harnessing of animal power through various technological developments. All of these changes and developments increased the possibilities for, and the importance of trade--something that was elaborated on and expanded in historic agricultural trading empires and civilizations.

The social structures and cultural values associated with prehistoric agricultural societies are related to the more sedentary nature of these societies and to the technological requirements of food production. Some have seen the development of these food production systems as the beginning of serious attempts at the mastery of nature (Smith, 1976:37). In any case, their development involved shifts in conceptions of the relations of people to their environment as well as in regard to which natural materials are defined as resources. Also a distinction between natural resources and social wealth emerges because for agricultural peoples wealth comes more from careful husbandry, land improvement, and the creation of durable goods than directly from nature's storehouse (Lee, 1979:455). New sociopolitical forms are required to organize and legitimize the very different annual work cycle--where there are intense periods of activity (planting and harvesting) followed by periods of relative inactivity (Lee, 1979). Status tends to become more ascribed than achieved (Smith, 1976:48). Widely spaced births no longer have an advantage, so demographic patterns may shift (Bender, 1975:33).

Because agricultural peoples are at least one major technological remove from their environment and because of their more formally organized and structured social and economic patterns and beliefs, the functional requirements of knowledge, wisdom, and guidance needed

for the everyday operation of the society are different
than those in hunting and gathering societies. In addition to environmental variations--such as disease,
locusts, floods, and droughts--which must be watched
very carefully for their impacts on agriculture, there
are a number of new social, organizational, and technological adjustments which are also required. In terms
of adaptation to macro changes, lesser mobility may
reduce certain adaptive capabilities, while more powerful technologies and organizations increase others.

Just as there is no one clear set of characteristics to distinguish the range of hunting and gathering
societies from the wider range of prehistoric agricultural societies, it is even more difficult to fully distinguish prehistoric from the even wider range of historic agricultural societies, kingdoms, and civilizations.[3] Between hunting and gathering societies and
prehistoric agricultural societies, it perhaps makes the
most sense to talk about a point of irreversibility--
where either the habitat has been so modified or the
population so increased that a hunter-gatherer economy
is no longer sustainable (Bender, 1975:2). The one distinguishing characteristic of historic civilizations
appears to be a more formal organization of executive
power: "It is the crystallisation of executive power
which serves to distinguish the primitive world from the
civilized. . . Not the city but the state is the decisive criterion of civilisation" (Wolf, 1966:9).

The very wide range of socio-political structures
found among historic agricultural chiefdoms, trading
empires, and civilizations make it difficult to try to
devise any single classificatory or explanatory scheme:

> Above the level of simple tribal life, and in most
> cases evolving directly from it, there obviously
> existed a number of higher pre-industrial civilizations whose diversities can be ascribed only to a
> limited extent to technological features: stratified pastoral societies, hydraulic societies, the
> non-hydraulic and non-feudal agrarian societies of
> ancient Greece . . . and of republican Rome . . .
> the feudal societies of Europe (based on rainfall
> farming) and of Japan (based on small-scale irrigation); and perhaps some others that are less distinct typologically and less important historically
> (Wittfogel, 1955).

Wittfogel's work on the irrigation-based societies of
Asia, societies which typically developed into what he
called oriental despotisms (1957), is interesting in
several regards. He saw them as important challenges to
unilinear concepts of societal development because "in
contrast to the stratified agrarian societies of Medi-

eval Europe, they failed, of their own inner forces, to evolve beyond their general pattern" (1955). Also, by analyzing the organizational and societal consequences of developing huge, centralized irrigation regimes, he offers guidance for the type of analysis that is needed to understand the development of what we have called industrial resource regimes.

Industrial Societies

It is even less clear with industrial societies than agricultural ones how one might best categorize and understand them. In some ways, they represent quite a range of diversity--built as they are upon very different socio-political bases. On the other hand, there are some striking similarities and common themes. As indicated at the beginning, the idea of progress (and how it relates to an active science and technology), the increased secularism, the increased separation of man from nature, and explicit exploitative ideologies all derive from Western culture and institutions. Thus, rather than equating industrial societies with various major countries or regions, some argue that a world-system has been evolving over the past several centuries, one based on the expansion of Western industrial society. Those in the Marxist tradition tend to equate this spread with a particular economic system--capitalism--while others, like myself, tend to see it as linked to the large-scale, centralized, and functionally specialized infrastructural, institutional, and intellectual patterns associated with modern industrial countries--whether capitalist or socialist.

Without going into the complexities of the rise and development of industrial society in the West, one can point to a number of important influences. New technological capabilities plus beliefs in religious and cultural superiority helped drive the exploration and exploitation of the New World. These, plus the expansion of industrial production and trade encouraged colonialism. In terms of resources, colonialism can be seen as providing significant resource subsidies for the development and expansion of the metropolitan countries. Emphasis on rationality as a guide for societal development, combined with increased secularization and technological capacities provided fertile ground for the development of doctrines regarding the universality of science and its relation to progress.

The conceptualization of the work process--and ultimately society--in terms of functional specialization offers one of the most distinctive characteristics of industrial society. This mode of thinking assumes that:

> by analyzing and specializing work along functional
> lines--whether that work is to be done by man or
> machine--the most efficient use will be made of
> available resources. In this mode of analysis, the
> "factors of production" are all defined as part of,
> but subordinate to the total production process,
> and it is for this reason that men (labor) and the
> environment (resources) are molded to fit the pro-
> duction process rather than vice versa (Dahlberg,
> 1973:62-63).

The gradual institutionalization of this mode of analysis has been a slow and varied process:

> In the economic realm, it moved from separate
> machines like the printing press (16th century) to
> individual enterprises (17th and 18th centuries) to
> the establishment of national economics (19th cen-
> tury) to what is now called the world economy. In
> politics, its application (through the varied forms
> of bureaucracy) has roughly paralleled the changes
> in the economic realm, undoubtedly because of their
> many mutual links. In other areas (religious
> affairs, military matters, the academic world), its
> application has been more varied in time, place,
> and extent (Dahlberg, 1979:8).

These approaches are, of course, supported by a range of values associated with progress, rationality, and efficiency.

During the past several centuries, the importance of agriculture has shifted from the internal source of much of the capital and labor to fuel the rise of industry, to an important, but still largely autonomous economic sector, to a subordinate and underappreciated sector. The dominant technologies of industrial society have also shifted from those based on the development of iron and steel, to those based on chemicals, to those based on electronics. There is much speculation that the next "revolution" in industry (and agriculture) will be based upon genetics and genetic engineering. The energy sources upon which these technologies and industries depend have included such traditional ones as animal, wood, water, and wind (often taking on new forms through technological innovation) and the newer ones of coal, oil, chemical, and nuclear power. The explosive increase in the utilization of non-renewable fossil fuels is clearly one of the major factors in the rapid expansion of industrial society and is also the source of much debate and concern regarding the future of industrial society as the more easily available and cheaper to extract reserves are used up.

Turning to the changing nature of natural resources—and going beyond the technological and cultural sources of some of those changes mentioned at the beginning—we can examine changes that result from both institutional innovation and from the growing extent and impact of industrial society itself. Institutional innovations have often facilitated the growth of industrialism. The development of money and later of more sophisticated financial systems has encouraged the expansion of industrialism. The creation of the patent system encouraged inventors and entrepreneurs. The creation of the limited liability corporation in the 19th century removed a number of constraints to the operation and expansion of corporations. Increasingly complex forms of government-industry cooperation, support, and subsidy are a source of tension in the trading relations between major industrial powers.

Up through most of the 19th century, natural resources were seen to be there primarily for exploitation (Zimmerman, 1964:2-4). This was somewhat less the case in European countries where population densities and longer-standing communities and traditions encouraged earlier restrictions upon the impacts of industry than in the U.S. Only with the closing of the frontier and the massive impacts of mining, forestry, agriculture—as well as industry—was there the rise of the U.S. conservation movement, which called simultaneously for the preservation of wilderness areas and a more rational, long-term management of the natural resources owned by the federal government. The focus ever since, as indicated earlier, has been on the natural resource systems themselves, not upon their interlinkages with industrial and consumer demand, nor the expanding global networks of trade.

Some of the socio-political changes associated with the rise of modern industrial society have already been described. Others include the rise of a new class structure and the growth of mass political democracy and nationalism. Each of these had both technological and cultural roots. They often merged with developments in the security field—where the explicit territoriality of the modern state combined with new weapons systems to provide new forms and rationales for warfare. The creation by Napoleon of a mass citizens' army based upon nationalism transformed both the nature of warfare and the relations between states. The increasing integration and predominance of the military and weaponry in national and regional economies—the military-industrial complex of which Dwight Eisenhower warned—generates a range of pressures affecting not only resource definitions and use, but perhaps even the direction of industrial society through the types of technologies and research it supports and encourages.

As members of modern industrial society, it is hard for us to try to appreciate the nature and requirements of the knowledge, wisdom, and guidance which are needed for our society to be able to adapt to a range of potential basic changes in the larger environment. The major challenges will be discussed below but for now let us review some of the structural problems.

The progressive specialization of industrial society has meant that very few people are in either the intellectual or the organizational position to have a reasonably comprehensive overview of the society and its interacting components. Our technologies have removed us more and more from the daily pressures of the environment. Our institutions typically include elaborate filtering processes whereby leaders are exposed to only a limited range of individuals, opinions, journals, and technologies. The much maligned politician is one of the few who still must regularly meet and deal with more of a cross section of his community--although the impact of television upon campaigns and of data processing upon correspondence appears to be reducing this exposure. Finally, as hinted at in the beginning, our Western cultural views regarding both nature and technology may intellectually filter out increasingly important data regarding fundamental changes in both our natural and social environments.

NEW CHALLENGES AND NEW RESOURCES

Debates about the future of industrial society suggest a wide spectrum of possible scenarios and futures. Some of these are disaster scenarios involving such things as massive destruction caused by nuclear war; huge famines and epidemics as food production and medical systems collapse from resource shortages, pollution, and environmental degradation; or economic stagnation as fossil fuels run out. These disaster scenarios suggest not the development of new resources, but rather (and only after long periods of chaos and anarchy) a return to some earlier socio-technical form, perhaps modified by those bits and pieces of modern knowledge and science that might survive.

There are also a number of essentially "business as usual" scenarios, where the expectation is that industrial society will keep on expanding and developing along essentially current lines. Here, new resources would be related to normal patterns of technological innovation. Finally, there are two types of "transformation" scenarios. One is what has been termed the "hyper-expansionist" future (Robertson, 1979). It involves not only high technology approaches, but the expectation of major breakthroughs in such areas as energy (fusion reactors) and genetic engineering. It often includes dreams of humankind developing extensive extraterrestrial capabilities. The other stresses not new technological and spatial frontiers, but new cultural and socio-political adaptations to enable currently expanding, but hopefully stabilizing populations to live more resource-sparingly and ecologically. Both the "hyper-expansionist" and "conserver society" futures imply very different and new types of social structures and resources.

Curiously, it has been the question of whether industrial society can continue to expand even along "business as usual" lines that has generated the most intense debate about the limits to growth, the future of industrial society, and the shifting nature of resources. Let us examine each of these in turn.

The "limits to growth" debate is a much broader and more profound debate than its precurser, the Malthusian debate. Malthus focused on two major elements--food production and population growth--and explored the social and moral implications of what he saw to be their very different long-term growth rates. For some, the failure of Malthus' prediction of a return of the biblical "four horsemen" proved him to be wrong and showed that the food problem can be solved through technological innovation. For others, Malthus' failure to recognize the possibility of massively expanding the amount of land under cultivation or the importance of technological innovations has simply meant a delay in the day of reckoning. Global computer modelers have specifically tried to include estimates of land and resource availability as well as the possiblity of technological innovation in their projections. In addition, they have tried to include more elements or sectors, plus dynamic linkages between them operating either in terms of positive or negative feedback. The projections of these models--the most famous being the Limits to Growth (Meadows, et al., 1972), Mankind at the Turning Point (Mesarovic and Pestel, 1974), and the Global 2000 Report to the President (CEQ, 1981)--have challenged both disciplinary specialization and technological optimism and have been the subject of much controversy (see Cole, 1973 and Simon, 1981).

Others have approached the question of the limits of industrial society differently. Rather than seeking to develop global mathematical models, the accuracy and representativeness of which depends upon various assumptions, disparate and often incomplete data sets, and either global or regional averaging of impacts, they have sought to determine whether there are basic physical, biological, social, or organizational limits to the continued expansion of industrial society.

One of the most thoughtful analysts of the physical limits of industrial society (as well as of conventional modes of economic thought) is Nicholas Georgescu-Roegen. In a recent article (1981), he expands upon his earlier work on the entropy law (1971). Several important points are made. First, in addition to reviewing the energy limits imposed by the entropy law, he suggests a new law of thermodynamics, "which is that matter, like energy, continuously and irrevocably degrades from an available into an unavailable state. . . . One would like, of course to have a general entropy formula for matter, just as we have for energy. Unfortunately, this goal seems inachievable at this moment. Matter, unlike energy, is irreducibly heterogeneous, which is the reason that friction, elasticity, conductivity, and the like, differ from one substance to another" (198:17-18). This helps to explain why fossil fuels have been such a bonanza: they require relatively small amounts of matter for their supporting "scaffolds," while either of the two major proposed alternatives--nuclear power or large-scale solar systems--requires huge infrastructures and immense amounts of matter, something that ultimately makes it impossible for them to reproduce their own scaffolds.

Georgescu-Roegen is also skeptical that there will be a third basic innovation in energy conversion like the previous two which have so shaped history. The first, fire, where the chemical energy of combustible materials is converted into caloric power, led to the "wood age." The second, the invention of the steam engine, permitted the easy conversion of caloric power into motor power--leading to the fossil fuel age. From all of this, he concludes that:

> The only reasonable strategy . . . is conservation, so as to gain as great a time lead as possible to wait for the uncertain Prometheus III, or, alternatively, to change without great convulsions from the present high level of industrial activity to one probably analogous but not identical to that of the past wood age. (198:22).

Analogous concerns have been raised concerning the biological limits of industrial society. One area of concern relates to the question of how much pollution and environmental destruction the biosphere can endure before its basic biological systems suffer irreparable and irreversible damage. A wide range of global, regional, and national studies have been conducted to try to estimate the impacts of carbon dioxide buildups on climate, the impacts of acid rain on forests and soil, the problems of desertification, water pollution and salinization, pesticide dispersion, and so on.

Perhaps the most fundamental and tragic indicator of the biological consequences of the spread of industrial society is the increasing loss of species and such biologically important and species rich habitats as the world's tropical rainforests. The U.S. Strategy Conference on Biological Diversity (1982) stressed the value to the U.S. of preserving these resources. The World Conservation Strategy (1980) viewed these issues more in terms of ecological principles and concern for the developing countries and concluded that biological and genetic conservation would have to become a new and basic element in development planning. There are even more fundamental questions relating to survival and keeping our evolutionary options open which will be discussed later.

Discussions of the social consequences of the industrial revolution have a long history--going back to the discussions of alienation and the creation of a "manufacturing aristocracy" begun by de Tocqueville and continued by Marx. As the scale of organizations has increased and as there has been a progressive increase in the size of the formal sectors of society--with a corresponding reduction in the size of the personal and informal spheres--there has been increased risk of alienation at the same time that greater degrees of socialization have been sought. This is complicated by the fact that these large-scale organizations demand even greater amounts of "maintenance"--routinized support and service jobs simply to keep them operating. The hierarchies and specialized expertise required also generates serious tensions with egalitarian and democratic traditions. The wide range of alternative social movements and their radically different visions of the future suggest a significant degree of disaffection with industrial society.

The idea of social limits is closely linked to various organizational limits. It is not only the matter of size or scale mentioned above, but also the rigidities of large, centralized industries and institutions. As indicated earlier, they are slow to adapt to major shifts in their larger environment. Also, there are serious questions regarding how one analyzes and evaluates their efficiency. One must go well beyond economic criteria. What is really needed is a larger evaluation which would assess the efficiency of various units or industries (including the cost of all of their so-called externalities) in relation to system efficiency. The discontinuities between a number of what might be considered to be the most relevant "systems" complicate the problem. There is rarely much correspondence between the boundaries of ecosystems, resource regimes, corporate systems, and political jurisdictions. Not only are there many traditional intellectual and disciplinary limits to analyzing such discontinuities (many of which will be discussed in the following chapters), but there is emerging a fundamental political problem: precisely at a time when adaptability and flexibility are needed, the vested interests, power, and inertia of the major groups and organizations in industrial society are increasing. That, plus the insulation of elites from their local natural and social environments as well as from a full awareness of the operational impacts of their large-scale and geographically extensive organizations suggest that the road of adaptive change will be a very rocky one.

Whether one talks about avoiding disaster, providing for the ever-increasing demands of a "business as usual" industrial society, or trying to encourage some sort of basic transformation, it is clear that new types of resources as well as new forms of knowledge, wisdom, and guidance will be needed.

The new resources needed to avoid disaster and to keep industrial society going will involve a range of technological innovations to increase its overall energy efficiency (assuming no major breakthroughs in fusion or other energy sources) as well as to reduce the environmental impacts of its processes. Cultural and social changes will also be needed, including devising ways to neutralize the various threat systems and weapons systems that could destroy modern society (see Boulding, 1964 and 1978). How the structural and organizational trends associated with the expansion of industrial resource regimes, multinational corporations, and global telecommunications systems can be reconciled with persistent political fragmentation is not clear. The social and organizational limits discussed above make the prospects of developing more global social and political systems appear dubious without either major socio-political changes or the development of massive authoritarian control systems (Heilbronner, 1974).

The new resources needed for a transition to a hyper-expansionist society would be similar in many ways. A higher level of basic technological innovation would have to result from continued elaboration of high technology approaches. Developments in fusion energy and genetic engineering would have to be sufficient to overcome the basic energy and food production problems of an expanding global population. Such new technologies would have to be much more environmentally benign so that the pressures on the biosphere could be reduced as they are phased in. In addition, the new frontier of space is seen to offer an eventual "escape hatch" should we not be able to learn to live in harmony with our global environment and with each other. Cultural and socio-political problems are less seriously addressed in the hyper-expansionist scenario. When mentioned, it is often in hortatory terms, decrying the persistence of anti-scientific attitudes and narrow national loyalties. Also, the close interlinkages between modern industrial society, high technology, and continued arms races tends to be ignored. Thus, in terms of new resources, the focus is on rapid scientific and technological development, the social and organizational prerequisites for that development, and the resulting changes in resource definition and usage.

The new resources needed for a transition to a conserver society revolve around a very different set of questions than with the other two approaches. The underlying question of the business as usual approach appears to be: How do we keep on doing essentially what we have been doing while learning to avoid some of the more serious "side-effects?" The hyper-expansionist approach asks: How do we encourage scientific and technological breakthroughs which will enable us to leap over or escape from the dilemmas of industrial society? In contrast, the underlying question of the conserver society approach is: How do we encourage a transition towards a society which is based more on renewable resources and which is environmentally sound and socially just? New conceptions of resources, resource-use systems, and socio-political organization would clearly be required.

In this vein, a number of analysts and reports have argued that we must rework our culturally defined concepts of nature and once again seek to understand ourselves as being more fully interrelated with nature, not separate from it, and that we cannot afford to systematically undermine the basic ecosystems upon which we depend. The continued health of the world's basic ecosystems becomes fundamental as do the air, land, and water systems that sustain them. <u>This suggests that to keep its evolutionary options open humankind needs to shift the emphasis from those fossil fuels and minerals that are "strategic" to the operation of industrial society to the renewable ecological and genetic resources that are crucial to basic survival</u> (Dahlberg, 1983). This clearly would involve major cultural, social, technological, and organizational changes.

There would need to be not only some sort of cultural reintegration of humankind into nature, but a rethinking of linear and primarily material definitions of progress. New socio-political organizations would be needed as society moved from "through-put" approaches to structures and systems based on recycling. A greater degree of decentralization of both infrastructures and institutions is often suggested as a way to reduce energy conversion and transportation costs, to develop more environmentally harmonious systems, and to reduce many of the social costs of large-scale organization (see Lovins, 1977 and 1982, and Morrison and Lodwic, 1981). This would require a great degree of scientific, social, and technological innovation, the intimations of which can be found in the work and writings of people exploring alternate energy systems, appropriate technologies, and decentralist approaches.

Finally, new approaches to knowledge, wisdom, and guidance are needed, as well as greater attention to the traditional knowledge non-Western, small-scale societies have of their environments (see Altieri, 1983, and Klee, 1980). Perhaps even more than in previous ages, "knowledge is truly the mother of all other resources. . . . Freedom and wisdom, the fruits of knowledge, are the fountainhead of resources" (Zimmerman, 1964:12-13). Guidance involves bringing knowledge and wisdom to bear upon the direction of society, and thus an appreciation of, and the ability to employ a society's socio-political systems. While we might phrase the guidance function in more global and in more cybernetic terms today, de Tocqueville's understanding captures the core dimensions (1960:171):

> When, after many efforts, a legislator succeeds in exercising an indirect influence upon the destiny of nations, his genius is lauded by mankind, while, in point of fact, the geographical position of the country, which he is unable to change, a social condition which arose without his co-operation, customs and opinions which he cannot trace to their source, and an origin with which he is unacquainted exercise so irresistible an influence over the courses of society that he is himself borne away by the current after an ineffectual resistance. Like the navigator, he may direct the vessel which bears him, but he can neither change its structure, nor raise the winds, nor lull the waters that swell beneath him.

The kinds of intellectual and academic approaches which are required to simultaneously anticipate the crucial natural and social limits of industrial society while exploring and developing adaptive alternatives cannot be spelled out in any detail--for in many ways they still appear to be emerging. The need for holistic approaches is typically stressed. Also, interdisciplinary approaches are encouraged, although rarely in terms of bringing the natural sciences, social sciences, and the humanities together. Fewer still have sought alternative, more contextual modes of analysis to go beyond the weaknesses of universal-generalization and reductionist models (see Dahlberg, 1979). And while there is great need for institutional reform in universities and disciplines, it may be that it is just as important to develop new "invisible colleges" or networks of diverse groups of people working on adaptive approaches to the various problems reviewed above. Our willingness and capability to undertake new forms of intellectual and social exploration may be the key "new" resource for facing an uncertain future.

A number of the above themes and concerns run throughout the rest of the book, whether implicitly or explicitly. The reflections of this diverse group of scholars upon their own disciplines as well as upon the larger problems of analyzing natural resources should help not only to lay some of the foundations for understanding the traditional resource challenges of all societies, but the new challenges of contemporary industrial society as well.

NOTES

1. For a detailed discussion of the problems and dilemmas involved--as well as the need to recognize and find a basis for the preservation of "non-resources"-- see Ehrenfeld (1978), especially Chapter 5, "The Conservation Dilemma."

2. The generalizations in this section are based upon both archeological findings and research on contemporary tribal and nomadic peoples. Like anthropological theorizing on the same topic, the analysis may move back and forth between the past and present a bit too easily. The problems of ethnographic reconstruction are significant--as can be seen in the discussions reported at a major symposium on hunting and gathering peoples (Lee and DeVore, 1968). It is not clear, for example, how basic differences between the environments of prehistoric hunters (extensive and rich) and contemporary groups (isolated and harsh) both influence and weaken generalizations drawn from a comparison of what is known of each. The same difficulties apply to matters of population growth or stability.

3. It is important to recognize that it is a greater range of organizational complexity and distinctiveness that is being spoken of. In socio-cultural and biological terms, hunting and gathering societies are much more complex and diverse than their successors. It is perhaps the focus of historians, sociologists, and some anthropologists on formal organizations and institutions that has given the overall impression that each successive type of society has been more complex when in fact there has been a trade-off between a loss of socio-cultural and biological complexity and diversity and an increase in the complicatedness and productive capacity of formal organizations and institutions.

REFERENCES

Altieri, M. A. 1983. *Agroecology: the Scientific Basis of Alternative Agriculture*. Division of Biological Control. Berkeley: University of California Press.

Bender, B. 1975. *Farming in Prehistory*. New York: St. Martin's Press.

Bennett, J. W. 1980. "Human Ecology as Human Behavior: A Normative Anthropology of Resource Use and Abuse." In Altman, I., Rapoport, A., and Wohlwill, J. F. (eds.), *Human Behavior and Environment: Vol. 4, Environment and Culture*. New York: Plenum.

Boulding, K. E. 1964. *The Meaning of the 20th Century*. New York: Harper Colophon.

_____. 1978. *Stable Peace*. Austin: University of Texas Press.

Cole, H. S. D., et al., eds. 1973. *Models of Doom*. New York: Universe.

Council on Environmental Quality. 1981. *The Global 2000 Report to the President*. Washington, DC: U.S. Government Printing Office.

Dahlberg, K. A. 1973. "The Technological Ethic and the Spirit of International Relations." *International Studies Quarterly* 17, 1:55-88.

_____. 1979. *Beyond the Green Revolution: The Ecology and Politics of Global Agricultural Development*. New York: Plenum.

_____. 1983. "Plant Germplasm Conservation: Emerging Issues and Problems," *Mazingira* 7, 1:14-25.

Ehrenfeld, D. W. 1978. *The Arrogance of Humanism*. New York: Oxford University Press.

Flannery, K. V. 1969. "Origins and Ecological Effects of Early Domestication in Iran and the Near East." In Ucko, P. J. and Dimbleby, G. W. (eds.), *The Domestication and Exploitation of Plants and Animals*. Chicago: Aldine.

Georgescu-Roegen, N. 1971. *The Entropy Law and the Economic Process*. Cambridge: Harvard University Press.

_____. 1981. "The Crisis of Resources: Its Nature and Its Unfolding." In Daneke, G. A. (ed.), *Energy, Economics, and the Environment*. Lexington, MA: D.C. Heath.

Harris, D. R. 1969. "Agricultural Systems, Ecosystems and the Origins of Agriculture." In Ucko, P. J. and Dimbleby, G. W. (eds.), *The Domestication Exploitation of Plants and Animals*. Chicago: Aldine.

Heilbroner, R. L. 1974. *An Inquiry into the Human Prospect*. New York: Norton.

International Union for the Conservation of Nature and Natural Resources. 1980. *World Conservation Strategy*. New York: UNIPUB.

Klee, G. A., ed. 1980. *World Systems of Traditional Resource Management*. New York: Wiley.

Lee, R. B. 1979. *The !Kung San*. New York: Columbia University Press.

Lee, R. B. and I. DeVore. 1968. *Man the Hunter*. Chicago: Aldine.

Lovins, A. B. 1977. *Soft Energy Paths*. New York: Harper.

Lovins, A. B. and L. H. Lovins. 1982. *Brittle Power*. Andover, MA: Brick House.

Meadows, D. H.; D. L. Meadows; J. Randers; and W. W. Behrens. 1972. *The Limits of Growth*. New York: Universe.

Mesarovic, M. and E. Pestel. 1974. *Mankind at the Turning Point*. New York: Dutton.

Morrison, D. E. and D. G. Lodwick. 1981. "The Social Impacts of Soft and Hard Energy Systems: The Lovins Claims as a Social Science Challenge," *Annual Review of Energy* 6:357-78.

Robertson, J. 1979. *The Sane Alternative: A Choice of Futures*. St. Paul: River Basin.

Simon, J. 1981. *The Ultimate Resource*. Princeton, NJ: Princeton University Press.

Smith, P. E. L. 1976. *Food Production and Its Consequences*. Menlo Park: Cummings.

Spoehr, A. 1956. "Cultural Differences in the Interpretation of Natural Resources." In William L. Thomas, Jr. (ed.), *Man's Role in Changing the Face of the Earth, Vol.I*. Chicago: University of Chicago Press.

Struever, S., ed. 1971. *Prehistoric Agriculture*. Garden City: Natural History Press.

de Tocqueville, A. 1960. *Democracy in America, Vol. I*. Phillips Bradley (ed.). New York: Vintage.

U.S. Department of State. 1982. *Proceedings of the U.S. Strategy Conference on Biological Diversity*. Washington, DC: Department of State 9262.

Wittfogel, K. A. 1957. *Oriental Despotism*. New Haven: Yale University Press.

Wittfogel, K. A. 1955. "Developmental Aspects of Hydraulic Societies." In J. H. Steward (ed.), *Irrigation Civilizations*. Washington, DC: Organization of the American States.

Wolf, E. R. 1966. *Peasants*. Englewood Cliffs: Prentice-Hall.

Zimmerman, E. W. 1964. *Introduction to World Resources*. H. L. Hunker (ed.). New York: Harper & Row.

2
Societal Contraints to Fisheries Management: A Peruvian Case Study

*Michael H. Glantz
and Maria E. Krenz*

INTRODUCTION

A broad spectrum of societal factors influence the exploitation of marine resources, as is the case for most natural resources. Because of this, rational fisheries management cannot depend solely on biological, oceanographic and meteorological information. Its economic, political, cultural, and social aspects must be included as well. Thus, to understand how a particular fishery has been managed and how that management might be improved requires investigations by scientists of several of the social science disciplines as well as of the physical science ones.

The focus of this paper is on the exploitation of pelagic fish in general and on the Peruvian anchoveta in particular. Pelagic fish are relatively easy to locate and catch and with efficient gear, large quantities can be taken in short periods of time. While some species are used as food fish, others are of industrial value when reduced to fishmeal. The Peruvian anchoveta fishery grew quickly beginning in the early 1950s, and its history is relatively well documented. An analysis of natural as well as societal factors affecting the exploitation of the Peruvian anchoveta provides valuable insights into the management of fisheries based on similar stocks.

Coastal Upwelling, El Niño, and the Peruvian Fishery

With an increase, after 1945, in the worldwide demand for fishmeal as a poultry and livestock feed supplement, and with the failure of the California sardine fishery in the early early 1950s, U.S. interest in fisheries shifted to Peruvian waters (Boerema and Gulland, 1973). The Peruvian coastal upwelling ecosystem was rich in anchoveta which had great potential value as a commercial fishery. By the late 1960s, the Peruvian fishing industry had developed into one of the most productive in the world. By this time a relatively large number of people had become involved in or affected by the fishery. Thus, the possibilities for social dislocations resulting from a major oceanographic-meteorological event, such as that known as El Niño, were great.

El Niño has been defined as the occasional invasion of warm surface water into the region of upwelling (cold water) of the eastern Equatorial Pacific. Warmer sea surface temperatures can adversely affect both the primary productivity and the standing stock of the anchoveta, and ultimately the economy of Peru. El Niño events vary in intensity (with sea surface temperatures increasing from 3C° to 7C°), duration (lasting from a few months to more than a year), and geographic magnitude (extending from the coast of Peru to well into the Central Pacific). Thus, their ecological and societal impacts also vary (Paulik, 1971). The most recent El Niño, which began in early 1982 and continued to late summer 1983, has been referred to by scientists as the worst in the last century. The last major one before it occurred in 1972-73 and has been blamed for the near-collapse of the Peruvian anchoveta fishery and the resultant chronic poor condition of the Peruvian economy.

In fact, the high level of fishing activity and of fish landings in 1972 tended to obscure the poor state of the stock and the initial effects of El Niño on the standing stock. This eventually led to a sharp decline in the Peruvian catch and therefore in Peruvian fishmeal exports, and to unfavorable changes in Peru's balance of payments. Peru's anchoveta catch, on which its economy had to a large extent become dependent for foreign exchange, dropped from an all-time high of 12.4 million metric tons (MMT) (officially reported) in 1970 to less than 2 MMT in 1973 following the El Niño. In the next three years the anchoveta catch did not go above 4 MMT. The fishery was closed in the spring of 1977 and a ban was placed on fishing anchoveta for the rest of the year. Since 1977, the anchoveta catch has not surpassed the 2 MMT level (Figure 2.1) and in 1983 hit an all-time low of about 100,000 metric tons.

To what might the successes and failures of the Peruvian anchoveta fishery be attributed? One can find in the resource management literature views that relate the successes and failures of fisheries management in general and for Peru in particular either to activities at the international level ("international demands for fishmeal in combination with Peruvian import restrictions sparked the Peruvian construction of fishing boats"), to group behavior at the national level ("if

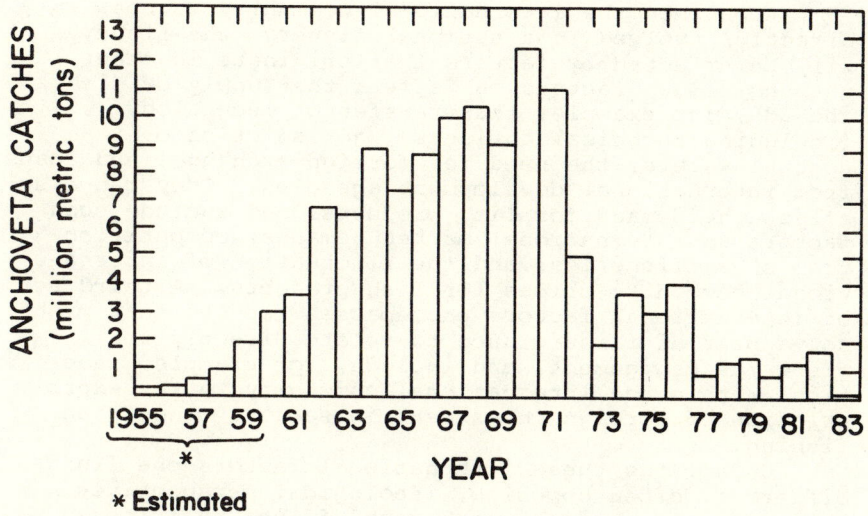

FIGURE 2.1 Anchoveta catches, 1955-1983

you allow an industrial fishery to begin, it will destroy the guano resource"), or to individual behavior ("fishermen want to sink every other boat but their own").

This paper uses three levels of analysis (the international, the state, and the individual) to examine three distinct categories of factors that can affect the management of a fishery. Such an approach encourages a broader consideration of potentially relevant factors for managing a fishery than considering just the fish population dynamics or oceanographic variables that are known to affect marine life. It seeks to identify the "less than obvious" factors that enhance or constrain the management strategies for the Peruvian anchoveta fishery. Its findings may be of value for the management of other pelagic fisheries within the eastern boundary current and more generally.

It should be noted that this paper does not attempt to present new factual information on fisheries and their management, but to present a new way of organizing and evaluating existing information. It applies an existing framework for analysis (Waltz, 1959) in order to improve our understanding of the different influences, stimuli, and constraints that can affect the management of a living marine resource such as the Peruvian anchoveta.

THE INTERNATIONAL LEVEL

Even when the international community is not directly involved in a national fishery, the fishery will be affected by factors that originate in other nations. Such factors can affect the supply of fish and include, for example, the transfer of technology (including technical advisers), jurisdiction over coastal waters, the need for foreign exchange, and loans from international development agencies. They can also affect the demand for fish products, and include such factors as international market demands, competition from other fisheries, and the fluctuation of international commodity prices for fish products. A third set of international factors encompasses aspects that might not appear at first glance to relate directly to fisheries management, and include, for example, reactions within the international community to the expropriation of foreign investment in sectors other than fishing.

Underlying these international factors one finds differing, often opposing, ideological perspectives about society through which each of them is filtered. While those with differing ideological perspectives may agree, for example, that a specific activity transpired, they often disagree about its causes or its consequences. Ideological considerations affecting the Peruvian anchoveta fishery will be discussed at the individual level of analysis.

Territorial Waters

Representatives of many coastal countries whose living marine resources have been subjected to high levels of exploitation have voiced concern that factory ships and long-distance trawlers would deplete their coastal living marine resources, long before they could develop a national fishing industry (see, for example, Gulland, 1979; Kaczynski, 1979). Factory ships can process, prepare, and store fish catches for several weeks before they return to port. Crutchfield and Lawson (1974, p. 14) suggested an hypothetical example of how devastating the fish harvesting technology of those ships could be: "a fleet of ten factory ships could harvest and process...the 1969 Peruvian anchoveta catch [9 million metric tons] in ten months."

Factory ships involved in fish reduction have been implicated in the demise of some important pelagic fisheries, such as the Californian Pacific sardine fishery (see Ahlstrom and Radovich, 1970; Radovich, 1981) and the pilchard fishery off the coast of Namibia (South West Africa) (Lees, 1969). They have also been blamed for the depletion of stocks in many other parts of the world, including the highly productive waters off the northwest coast of Africa (see Crutchfield and Lawson, 1974) as well as in the North Atlantic. Thus, factory ships as well as long-distance trawlers presented a clear danger to the survival of coastal living marine resources in various regions around the world, until the mid-1970s. Their sphere of operations, however, has been greatly curtailed with the adoption by many coastal states of the 200-mile extended economic zone.

In 1947, Peru (together with Chile and Ecuador) sought to protect itself from this important international aspect of fisheries exploitation by claiming 200-mile territorial waters and thus barring foreign factory ships from their waters. Although enforced by Peru, the 200-mile claim was rejected by the United States because, at that time, it, along with most states, claimed a 3-mile territorial limit and a 12-mile fishing limit. As a result, there were frequent international incidents when these South American governments, regardless of the ideological perspectives of the administration in power at the time, authorized their navies to capture vessels that violated their territorial waters. The fishing companies (or their flag countries) were then forced to pay large fines.

Outside the territorial waters which, until the mid-1970s, were still generally taken to be up to 12 miles (with the notable exceptions of Peru, Ecuador, and Chile), living marine resources were considered a common property resource and therefore beyond the jurisdiction of any single nation. Garrett Hardin (1968) popularized the concept of common property resources when he wrote about the "tragedy of the commons." In his article, which had been preceded by other papers on "the fishery commons" (e.g., Gordon, 1954), Hardin discussed how a resource could be destroyed when its preservation or protection is not the responsibility of any specific authority. Although his original discussion related directly to rangelands and livestock, the concept of the tragedy of the commons has been applied to other common property resources (see Hardin and Baden, 1977). Because Peru's coastal marine resources had been excluded from international exploitation, its yet-to-be-developed anchoveta fishery was spared from becoming another overexploited international common property resource. Thus, by declaring a 200-mile limit, a major, often troublesome, international aspect of fisheries management was avoided by Peru during the development of its anchoveta fishery.

The other side of this coin, however, was that Peruvian governments have (collectively) had to bear responsibility for the successes and failures of the management of their anchoveta fishery. When the near-collapse came in the early 1970s, Peruvian leaders could blame neither foreign factory ships nor neighboring countries for the overexploitation of their main stock of anchoveta off the central coastal area. They could only blame nature and, more specifically, El Niño events (Tantaleán, 1978, p. 250) as the primary cause of the reduced productivity of their anchoveta fishery.

Influence of Other Fisheries

The underlying conditions for the development of a food and/or industrial fishery in Peru had already been established in the early 1940s, when, for example, foreign assessments of biological productivity in Peruvian waters came up with extremely favorable results (Horna, 1968; Roemer, 1970). Another underlying international condition for any possible development of such a fishery was the rapidly increasing international demand for fishmeal as a feed supplement for poultry and livestock in the post World War II period.

An important international aspect of the development and management of the Peruvian fisheries relates to the origin of its fishmeal industry. The Californian Pacific sardine fishery had flourished for decades, since the early 1900s, and was at its peak in the 1930s. By the mid 1940s, however, it became apparent to all but the wishful thinkers that the continued productivity of that fishery was in question (Radovich, 1981). Its apparent decline was manifested in the quantity and quality, as well as the southward shift of commercial landings. Despite a brief increase in recruitment (i.e., fish entering the fishery) in the late 1940s, the fishery had essentially collapsed as a viable economic activity by 1952. As a result of the progressive collapse, California fishing industries were plagued with idle fleet and fish processing capacity, with no fish to catch or to process. Caravedo (1977), and others (Horna, 1968), suggested that the catalyst for development of the Peruvian anchoveta fishery came when the owners of the idle fishing vessels and fish processing plants in California decided to sell that capacity to Peruvian entrepreneurs, enticing them with extremely advantageous financial arrangements.[1]

This example suggests that it is important to dispel the belief that the collapse of one fishery is of little consequence (except in the marketing sector) to fisheries in other regions exploiting similar stocks. The historical record shows that the rapid development of the Peruvian fishing industry was spurred by the collapse of the Californian Pacific sardine fishery. The California collapse also provided a major impetus to the development of the Namibian (South West African) pilchard fishery. Today we see a repetition of that historical experience, only the roles of the actors have changed. Peru has recently been attempting to sell its idled surplus fleet and processing capacity to other fishing nations, and following the collapse of the Namibian (South West African) pilchard fishery in the late 1970s, South African entrepreneurs have become directly involved in the exploitation of Chile's pilchard stocks.

Technology Transfer

The implications of technology transfer in the exploitation of natural resources has stimulated a great debate for the past few decades on the role of technology in the development process in developing countries (Goulet, 1977). Clearly, there have been successes and failures (Farvar and Milton, 1972). In addition to describing successes in specific fisheries, Shärfe (1979, p. 53), for example, has commented that "unfortunately, there also have been a good number of costly and frustrating failures - mainly due to attempted introduction of overly sophisticated technology combined with a lack of understanding of local cultural, social and economic concerns." Technology, however, can be viewed as neutral. Whether its effects on society are favorable or adverse will depend on how it is used. Goulet (1977, p. 17) has referred to technology as a two-edged sword, suggesting that "although it brings new freedom from old constraints imposed by nature, tradition, or ancient social patterns, technology also introduces new determinisms into the life of its adepts."

There are many instances in which new technology has been incorporated into the Peruvian fishery. For example, the development of the nylon net has been cited by numerous authors as a major breakthrough for entrepreneurs wanting to invest in fisheries (e.g., Roemer, 1970; Horna, 1968). Nylon nets were more expensive than the cotton nets they replaced but they were also more durable. Thus, their use lowered the long-term costs of anchoveta fishing. Given the extremely favorable terms for the purchase of those nets that the Japanese and others offered, it became more attractive for Peruvians to buy into the fishery (Horna, 1968).

This particular technological input occurred at a propitious time for the fishery. The fishmeal entrepreneurs had recently won a major political victory defeating the efforts by the Guano Administration Company (the government agency responsible for the proper management and mining of guano[2] and the regulation of the industry), and more broadly of the agro-exporters, to block

the development of the fishmeal industry. The victory
was in part related to the fact that the prices of guano
and of agricultural commodities had fallen and, independent of that, there had been an increase in the price
and demand for fishmeal.

Other technological transfers that affected the
exploitation of the fishery include the power block,
echo sounder, purse seiner, and vacuum pump. Each new
additional input of technology increased the efficiency
of fishermen in capturing the anchoveta. Each addition
to plant or fleet capacity stimulated a desire, as much
as a need, for larger catches, which in turn required
greater efficiency in capture and processing
techniques.

Technical advice provided by foreign experts can
also be included as an element of technology transfer.
There have been successes and failures with technical
advice as well (Glantz, 1980a; Shärfe, 1979). Kasahara
(1979, p. 106) lamented the fact that

> [Developing countries] are swamped with advice,
> technical assistance, equipment selling, fishing
> agreement or joint venture offers, international
> funding proposals, etc. from various sources. A
> combination of these usually tends to result in
> over-capacities by building up a fishing fleet and
> shore facilities too rapidly since they appear to
> be cheap and sometimes free. The administrators of
> at least some of these countries are incapable of
> sorting out good advice and offers from bad ones.

One example of technical advice in the case of the
Peruvian anchoveta fishery was the establishment of an
institute for marine research. In 1960 the Marine
Research Institute of Peru began to study the fishery
and the biology of the anchoveta as a project supported
by the U.N. Special Fund and conducted by the U.N. Food
and Agriculture Organization. In 1964 the Institute was
renamed the Instituto del Mar del Peru (IMARPE).

An anchoveta stock assessment was undertaken (under
FAO/IMARPE sponsorship) in order to provide "the first
appraisal of the extent of the anchovy stock and of the
effects of fishery on this stock" (Boerema et al., 1965,
p. 1). Almost immediately, IMARPE scientists and
foreign consultants began to warn about the increasing
possibility of overfishing. For these scientists, the
task of aiding in the development of a management
strategy calling either for self-restraint on the part
of the fishing community or for restraints imposed by
government agencies on that community was extremely
difficult, especially in the absence of reliable and,
perhaps more important, generally visible indicators of
depletion of the anchoveta resource.

Foreign expert panels were convened on an ad hoc basis beginning in the late 1960s to advise on biological as well as regulatory aspects of fisheries management. In 1969, for example, IMARPE convened a panel of foreign economic experts to assess various regulatory schemes for the fishery (IMARPE, 1970). That panel concluded that the fishery was in great danger of collapse because of the excessive pressures on it from overcapitalization of the industry's fleet and plant processing capacity. Nowhere in the report, however, was there any mention of the potential impacts of an El Niño. Thus, the potential combined effect of overcapitalization of the fishing sector and the known variability of the environment was not considered by this panel.

Economic Development Policies

Another international aspect of fisheries management relates to Peru's policies toward economic development. Peruvian leaders, especially between 1948 and 1968, and once again after the 1980 election of Belaúnde Terry (whose government had been overthrown in 1968 by the military coup of Velasco), have, to varying degrees, favored a policy of export-led development. This development strategy is based on the export of primary resources (as opposed to manufactured goods) in order to earn foreign exchange which can then be used to finance economic development on a national scale.

An export-led development strategy can be categorized as a national level factor (to be discussed in the following section), if one assumes that the initiative for its implementation has been national as opposed to its having been imposed by other countries. This development strategy does, however, have important international aspects. For example, fishmeal exports are affected by foreign currency exchange rates (see for example, Brown, 1965) as well as by the variations in prices for fishmeal in the international marketplace (Kuczynski, 1977). Fishmeal exports are also affected by the availability of similar or substitutable exports from other countries with which they compete for markets (Vondruska, 1981). While Kuczynski (1977) recorded his belief that fisheries provided an unstable base on which to build a development program because of the highly variable nature of resource availability, another assessment (World Fishing, February 1978, p. 31) suggested that

> In developing countries there are good reasons why a particular fish resource may not be utilized as a source of food.... It is much more feasible to consider the establishment of fish meal industry

which will provide a basic earning power by the export of the product.

As a final example of international aspects it is important to note that some actions that appear to affect only one sector of the economy might be shown, upon closer scrutiny, to have international impacts on other, seemingly unrelated economic and social sectors. The Peruvian dispute with the American-owned International Petroleum Company (IPC) illustrates this point (see, for example, Kuczynski, 1977; Goodsell, 1974; Olson, 1975). The uncertainty that surrounded the outcome of an IPC settlement with Peru apparently led to the restriction of U.S. development assistance to Peru from 1962-1975.

Thus, it becomes quite clear that there are many linkages between the national development of a natural resource and the international community concerning when, how, why, and by whom that resource is exploited and managed.

THE NATIONAL LEVEL

There are many national-level activities that affect the management of marine resources. The issuance of government decrees related to fisheries or a strike in the fishing industry are obvious influences. Yet, there are many seemingly unrelated activities that have had an indirect influence on the fisheries; for example, government decrees related to agrarian reform, worker strikes in the mining sector, policies toward exchange rates (encouraging or discouraging foreign investment), government nationalization of foreign investment in, for example, extractive industries (oil, copper, iron). The fishing sector is only one subsystem embedded in a larger political system. In order to understand how the fishery is managed, it is necessary to be aware of that broader context.

In addition, there are political pressures with which leaders must constantly cope, such as the fear of a military coup or the lack of support of political groups, the legislature, or the press (Kuczyinski, 1977). These activities consume the attention of political leaders, and take time from other pressing issues, including the oversight of the management of the nation's coastal fishery.

This section focuses on (a) how conflicting objectives (goals, aims) pursued by various groups in society can affect fishery management, and (b) how political changes at the national level can affect fisheries management.

Objectives in Conflict

Competing interests (or objectives) of different national groups can adversely affect the management and viability of a fish population in which these groups have an economic, social, or political stake. It is necessary to recognize "that there are different classes of objectives - biological, economic, and social - as well as different time horizons over which objectives might be obtained" (FAO, 1979, p. 7). Each of these objectives or combination of objectives, if followed, could lead to a different pattern of harvest and exploitation.

One of the earliest conflicts over objectives related to the Peruvian fishery took place between those groups seeking to exploit the anchoveta and the Guano Administration Company's representatives, who saw a threat to their interests in any effort to exploit the anchoveta (see Murphy, 1954; and Kesteven, 1981). For decades, the Guano Administration Company had vigorously opposed any new attempts to establish a fishmeal industry because it would put the guano birds into direct competition for fish with an "insatiable predator"-- man. However, in the absence of scientifically-based stock assessments, there was little if any hard evidence on which to oppose the development of a potentially lucrative foreign-exchange-producing industrial fishery.

Different objectives in the exploitation of living marine resources also emerge from different approaches to economic development. If, for example, a government's objective is to improve the nutritional intake of its people, it may favor the development of a food fish industry either to increase domestic consumption of protein-rich fish products directly; or, in a country where fish is not a major source of protein for its people, a government must decide between making fish products acceptable to consumers within its country or selling those products in the international marketplace, and then using the foreign exchange to upgrade the population's nutritional intake (e.g., investment in those sectors of society that supply the people with their traditional protein needs).

A government might also decide to forego the development of a food fishery in favor of a reduction fishery; that is, the use of fish for industrial purposes, such as fishmeal. Fishing industries have developed around the world based on the production of fishmeal, which under favorable circumstances can command a high price in the international marketplace, thereby producing sorely needed foreign exchange. This has been viewed as an unholy choice by some observers. In 1927, for example, during a legal conflict between the Californian sardine canning industry and fish reduction interests, one observer commented that "It seems repugnant to every right-thinking citizen to see fresh fish used for any purpose other than human consumption" (Ahlstrom and Radovich, 1970, p. 186). This concern about the conflict between food and industrial catches extends into the present. For example, Popiel and Sosinski (1973, p. 228) have noted that "Rapidly expanding industrial catches along with steadily increasing fishmeal production in the last decades have been watched with anxiety by countries whose fishing fleets operate mainly for fish for human consumption." A few years ago, Mexico's Department of Fisheries decreed that its "sardine and anchovy industries must place the feeding of people before the feeding of animals" (Fishing News International, September 1981).

Another source of conflict involves government agencies with different jurisdictions that establish regulatory policies that tend to conflict with (and even cancel out) the policies pursued by other agencies. In the Peruvian case, tax credit policies formulated in the Finance Ministry tended to encourage an expansion in the fleet and processing capacity which contradicted the policies of those whose objective was the prevention of overfishing by the reduction of overcapacity. According to Hammergren (1981, p. 323), "fishing policy was not coordinated by any single office but was shaped by the diverse (and often conflicting) interests of the various agencies involved, agencies for which fishing policy was not a primary concern...." This was still true even after a separate Ministry of Fisheries was established in 1970 by President Velasco, who removed fishing from the jurisdiction of the Ministry of Agriculture, which at that time was preoccupied with land reform programs.

One can separate groups involved with the fisheries into those seeking to conserve the resource from those seeking to derive an immediate (short-term) benefit from its exploitation, with little regard to resource conservation. The aim of the former group is typified by an IMARPE (1970) report that noted that "The first objective of any system of regulation and management of the anchoveta fishery must be to ensure the continuation of the substantial contribution to the Peruvian economy."

The goals of the latter group have centered on the economic rewards derived from exploiting the anchoveta fish stocks directly by fishing or processing the catch or indirectly by building fishing vessels or supplying them with needed gear such as floats, nets, engines, etc. Industrialists, for example, may feel pressured to increase the level of exploitation of a fishery in order to reduce immediate monetary (economic) hardships giving little regard to the long-term effects of such an increase (Diegues, 1983).

Finally, not all interests in a society have the same political leverage at a given time. Often the views of some interest groups dominate the political process at a given time. For example, in Peru, the agro-export and guano interests dominated that of the anchoveta fishmeal interests for a long time only to have their positions eventually reversed. More recently, the fishmeal interests in Peru dominated the food fish industry interests only to have their positions later reversed. Gulland (1977, p. vii) has suggested that

> In practice management policies will have to be determined in each case <u>in the light of current objectives of society</u> [whoever determines what those might be], and of the scientific understanding of the stocks, bearing in mind that they will never be completely accurate. (insert and emphasis ours)

Scientific Uncertainty and Conflicting Objectives

A major problem for decisionmakers directly or indirectly responsible for fisheries management is scientific uncertainty. There is enough uncertainty in scientific information about living marine resources that whatever the recommendations of scientists, including foreign experts, the validity of their recommendations can be questioned by entrepreneurs, fishery managers, high ranking government officials, fishermen, as well as other scientists.

Such a lack of confidence in scientific research results has hindered the development of trust and credibility between scientists, fisheries managers, and policymakers. The general lack of confidence among these groups existed in Peru in the 1960s (Kuczynski, 1977) and in the early 1970s as well (Tantaleán, 1978), making it somewhat easier for the policymaker to give in to the pressure of the moment (political, economic or other) rather than to act in accordance with the scientific advice. Tantaleán Vanini, Fisheries Minister during the Velasco administration commented on how he viewed the role of IMARPE scientists (Tantaleán, 1978, p. 247):

> IMARPE is an organization to assess and recommend; the final decision of what has to be done has to be with the Chief of the Sector. For example, to determine the opening of the season, its ending, or the closures, first I listened to IMARPE's scientific recommendations, then looked to the

needs for foreign exchange, in coordination with the Ministry of Economy and Finance, and coordinated with EPCHAP, which was in charge of commercialization [of fishmeal], read the reports of the boat owners, analyzed the social factors and observed the activities of our neighbors.
Naturally, the recommendations of IMARPE should be followed but it should not be thought that the boat owners could not make good recommendations.

Changes in National Government

The national government is often the source of broad policy guidelines that establish ground rules by which various economic sectors in society, including the fisheries, operate. Changes in government often mean changes in policy. There have been a dozen changes of government in Peru from 1939 to 1984. Changes in government can also directly affect high ranking personnel in ministries related to the management of fisheries. On several occasions, especially in 1948, 1968, 1975, and 1980, new governments pursued policies affecting the fishery that involved major (if not drastic) changes from those of their predecessors. This helps to explain why the same resources in the same country may have been managed in different ways.

How changes in national government come about-- whether through free elections or military coups--may also be an important consideration for resource management. In 1945, for example, Bustamante was elected president and attempted to maintain a "controlled economy" that discouraged exports. His "experiment" was ended by a military takeover of government led by General Odría whose regimes (1948-50 and 1950-56) developed conservative economic policies that opened up the Peruvian economy to direct foreign investment and market-oriented policies. Odría favored a policy of export-led development, relying on the export of traditional primary resources such as copper, silver, zinc, cotton, coffee, and sugar. His changes in economic policies came at what seems in retrospect to have been the right moment for fisheries development: the Californian sardine fishery was on the edge of collapse (an international aspect), and there was an increase in demand for fishmeal as poultry feed (another international aspect). Thus, the takeover by the conservative military government in 1947 set the stage for the eventual development of the anchoveta fishery and the export of fishmeal.

The 1968 military coup by General Velasco brought to power a leftist military group that wanted to take control of the economy away from the established elites. In 1970, Velasco appointed General Tantaleán as head of the newly established Ministry of Fisheries. Hammergren, (1981, p. 333) commented on one of the effects of the establishment of this new ministry:

> From the Ministry's side several factors encouraged a larger catch. One was the inexperience of the new administrators and the inevitable disorganization following the creation of the new Ministry which meant that the catch was not closely monitored and that decision-makers were less sensitive than they would be later to the problems of resource conservation... A second factor encouraging large catches was the desire of the new Fisheries Ministry and its Minister to demonstrate their competence.

In the relatively short period of time that the fishing industry underwent very rapid growth (1952 to 1972), Peruvian governments and their policies (and ideological underpinnings) frequently changed, making difficult the formulation, let alone enforcement, of a long-term, acceptable, "wise" management strategy for their coastal fisheries. This is an aspect that is seldom addressed explicitly at technical meetings on fisheries management, in part because of the separation of science and politics in many countries.

THE INDIVIDUAL LEVEL

Individuals have different, often conflicting, perceptions of events that take place around them and those perceptions become their reality. While they may not prove to be accurate reflections of reality, the actions taken based on them will be real, as will be the consequences of those actions. Therefore, perceptions are an important element of the individual level of analysis. Three important considerations that relate to fisheries management at this level are as follows: (a) one's view of society's relationship to nature, (b) one's view of the renewability of living marine resources, and (c) one's ideological perspective.

Man-Nature Relationship

There are conflicting views about what the relationship between man and nature should be. These views, seldom made explicit, can in fact be spread across a continuum, with one extreme represented by the domination of nature by man and the other extreme represented by man's subordination to nature. Two major views relevant for the present day management of natural resources emerge: man-over-nature and man-in-harmony-with-nature (Kluckhohn and Strodtbeck, 1961).

A central theme of the man-over-nature view is that nature is (or should be) subordinate to mankind. It is man's obligation to devise ways to surmount natural obstacles in the path of human activities. One way to do this is through technology. Goulet (1977, p. 19) has commented on the cultural values associated with western technology, noting that "By definition technology is interested in getting things done; consequently, it breeds impatience with contemplation or harmony with nature." Supporters of man-over-nature contend that the environment is robust and therefore resilient in the face of those environmental problems or "insults associated with the use of technology." In other words, nature can absorb most, if not all, of the adverse impacts of human activities.

This belief in man over nature tends to foster the development and application of new technologies for the purpose of exploiting living marine resources. For example, the replacement of cotton nets with nylon ones, the use of purse seiners, power blocks, vacuum pumps, echo sounders, and so forth have all been developed to increase fish landings. These technological fixes, each in its own way, enable fishermen to outmaneuver fish, which, of course, do not have the capability to outmaneuver these new technological applications. For example, the shoaling behavior of pelagic fish apparently reduces the effectiveness of natural predators but at the same time has served to make such catch techniques as the purse seine more efficient. "With these techniques," noted Murphy (1977, p. 285), "man has so greatly nullified any advantage of shoaling with respect to protection from predation that these species are readily rendered extinct or near extinct by fishing."

The man-in-harmony-with-nature view is based on the belief that there are limits to exploitation of the natural environment and that those limits must be respected. In the absence of restraint, resources being overexploited will ultimately disappear. Because the advocates of this approach do not know with certainty what the limits of exploitation for a particular fishery might be, they tend to advocate a more conservative approach to resource exploitation, favoring, for example, such fishery management guidelines as safe yields (building in considerations of uncertainty) as opposed to optimum economic yield or maximum sustainable yield, which are based on theoretical calculations (see Clark, 1976; Edwards and Hennemuth, 1975). Supporters of the man-in-harmony-with-nature view tend to advocate the application of appropriate, as opposed to high, technology. Believers in either of the two contending views tend to oppose the other view.

Perceptions held by the various individuals or groups of individuals in a society are not equally influential in the policymaking process. Beliefs that national leaders hold about the relationship of man to nature constitute the dominant ideological perspective in a political system at a given point in time. Perceptions held by other individuals and groups in society can be considered subordinate. Changes of national leaders or of administrative personnel in relevant government agencies can bring about a change in the dominant ideology.

With respect to resource exploitation in Peru, the view of man-over-nature seemed to predominate. Peru's history has been one of rapid, almost sequential, development of several of its natural resources such as lead, zinc, copper, and cotton. At different periods of time during the past century, each one of these ventures could have been characterized as a boom-to-bust phenomenon.

The anchoveta fishery was the latest resource to be exploited by Peruvians. Fearing a rapid growth of the fishmeal industry, the Guano Administration Company hired an American scientist, Robert Cushman Murphy, to assess the potential impact of the development of a commercial anchoveta fishery on the guano birds' food supply, which is the anchoveta. Murphy (1954, pp. 226-27) explained his belief when he wrote that

> It is obvious that natural predators, such as fish, or birds or beasts, can never seriously reduce the number of their prey, because their very existence is determined by the abundance, including a dynamic surplus, of the food organisms. Predator and prey are in equilibrium. Man, on the other hand, is capable of depleting any readily attacked natural resource. Unlike a guano bird, man has no automatic checks and balances upon his operations. He is not directly dependent upon the tissues of his prey for the energy with which he executes his exploitation. A guanay must eat anchovetas in order to catch more anchovetas, but fishermen hunt with energy from a totally different source, such as petroleum. Only the slow and disastrous consequences of exhaustion and financial failure can end their campaign.

There is still controversy over why this fishery collapsed in the early 1970s. One group blames the environment (i.e., El Niño); another group blames poorly regulated fishing activities; and a third group blames the simultaneous occurrence of both of those events. This controversy is similar to others that continue to surround the collapse of scores of fisheries throughout this century.

Renewability

Most observers (optimists and pessimists alike) categorize fish as a renewable resource. This perception of renewability most probably stems from the fact that fish are self-generating, although it is recognized that some seasons are better than others with respect to reproduction.

There are many definitions of renewable and nonrenewable resources. According to Klee (1980), for example,

> Renewable resources would be those that can maintain themselves or be continuously replenished if managed wisely, such as soils, food crops and domesticated animals, land or open space, water (abiotic), freshwater (biotic), marine, wildlife, or forest resources.
>
> Nonrenewable resources are those not generated or reformed in nature at rates equivalent to those at which we use them, such as metals, fossil fuels, building materials, fertilizer chemicals, etc.

Pelagic fish resources such as the Peruvian anchoveta could conceivably fit into either of these categories, depending on one's assumptions about fisheries. For example, they could be considered renewable with proper management. If exploited, however, at rates faster than they can replenish their populations, pelagic fish could also be considered nonrenewable. These definitions suggest that a particular resource in a given place, over a period of time, can move from the renewable to the nonrenewable category, depending on how "wise" the management of the resource might be.

The following graphs (Figure 2.2) show commercial fish landings for three major pelagic fisheries; the Pacific sardine off the coast of California, the pilchard off the coast of Namibia (South West Africa) in the Southeast Atlantic, and the Peruvian anchoveta in the eastern Equatorial Pacific.

As the graphs suggest, each fishery collapsed or nearly did so. For each of these assessments of collapse or near collapse, there have emerged opposing schools of thought. Some observers suggest overfishing as the factor that led to the collapses. In the absense of heavy fishing pressures, they contend, the fish populations in the different regions would probably have been able to cope with fluctuations in their physical environment. Other observers contend with equal conviction, and often with equally convicing pieces of

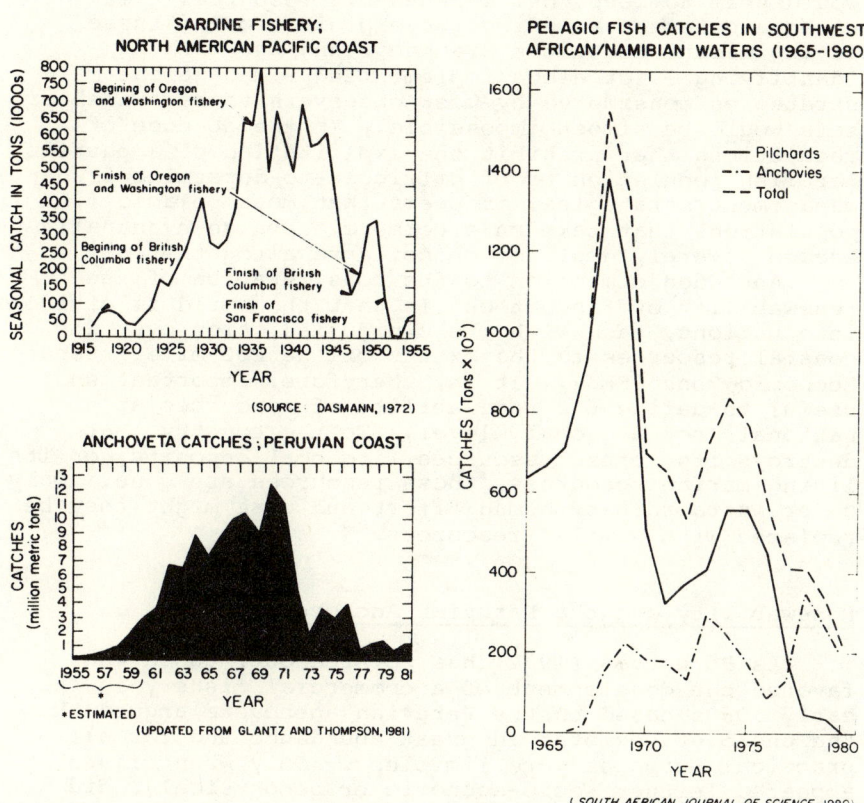

FIGURE 2.2 Commercial pelagic fish landings

scientific information, that the collapses of these fish populations resulted primarily from changes in environmental variables. While overfishing may have been implicated in each case, the environmental factors set the stage for, and were the major cause of, the demise.

Assuming that the view that environmental changes brought about a collapse of these fisheries is correct, would it then be valid to assume that fish populations in specific regions can appear and disappear regardless of the intervention of man? If so, might fish populations of a particular kind, in a specific region, and during a specified period of time, be considered nonrenewable resources? On the other hand, if the view that human intervention (for example, overfishing) was responsible for the collapse of these fisheries is correct, "wise" management of pelagic fish resources would seem to keep them a renewable resource. Yet the uncertainties surrounding the exploitation of these living marine resources are many, and the task of identifying - let alone implementing - management strategies considered by most observers to be "wise" or safe would be almost impossible. In the absence of regulations that prohibit the exploitation of a particular fish population or of difficult-to-determine prudent management strategies, it seems that most pelagic fish populations that take on a commercial value eventually become severely depleted or collapse altogether.

An added dimension to the consideration of the renewability of fish stocks is that the world is divided into nations, each with its own jurisdiction over its coastal resources to the extent of the 200-mile Extended Economic Zone (EEZ). It is, therefore, important and useful to define the renewability of resources at a national, not a global, level. To the country that destroys its forest resources, its coal deposits, or its living marine resources, those resources are gone. Only under extraordinary human effort and cost might they be replaced with similar resources.

Renewability and the Peruvian Anchoveta

As Borgstrom (1972) has pointed out, those who favored the development of a commercial fishery in the early 1950s based on the Peruvian anchoveta argued that the anchoveta existed in great abundance and for all practical purposes were limitless. Only when crises appeared (either socio-economic or geophysical), did Peruvians become concerned about the implications of treating the fishery as an unlimited resource. In 1965, as a result of a reduced supply of anchoveta and of scientific reports suggesting that the fishery was approaching its limit of exploitation, the government agency responsible for the fishery established its first closed season (veda). By the late 1960s it became abundantly clear that there were too many vessels competing with each other for what all came to realize was a limited resource. It was also at this time that the maximum sustainable yield (MSY) for the anchoveta fishery was calculated to be about 9.5 MMT per year, but that yield included the bird population's consumption of about 2 MMT per year. Nevertheless, the 1970 officially reported catch was 12.4 MMT. In 1973 it plunged to less than 2 MMT (see Figure 2.1).

Even in the period following the visible signs of overcapitalization of the industry and overexploitation of the resource, those involved with the fishery continued to be optimistic about the future availability of the resource. Much of this optimism appears to have stemmed from wishful thinking, and not from scientific fact. Despite continued optimism, the Peruvian anchoveta, in commercially desirable quantities, has remained "unrenewed," dropping to 0.1 MMT after the 1982-83 El Niño (NOAA, 1984).

Ideological Perspectives

The existence of opposing ideologies must be accepted, even if their particular content is not. A capitalist, for example, will have a view of the world that differs markedly from that of a marxist. Someone who believes in dependency theory (see, for example, Galtung, 1971) will have a worldview that could differ from either that of the capitalist or the marxist. As Bell (1962, p. 30) pointed out, "The most salient fact about modern life - capitalist and communist - is the ideological commitment to social change."

Ideological perspectives not only help to define the causes and consequences of certain actions related to fisheries management or to the management of other natural resources, but also come into play in the determination of strategies in response to those causes and consequences. It is therefore important to determine and analyze the ideological worldviews of the decision-makers involved directly or indirectly with fisheries. This applies as well to those observers whose views might be representative of various segments of society and who might, through their interpretation of history, influence activities in the fishing sector. In the reviews of a recently edited volume on coastal fisheries, there were several attacks made on the contribution of a self-avowed Marxist-Leninist oceanographer, while no comment was made in any of these reviews about the capitalist ideology implicit in the contributions of other scientists. Yet, the Marxist-Leninist perspective is an important one to know about, given that many in the Third World espouse socialist ideology.

CONCLUDING REMARKS

The Peruvian case study was chosen to highlight the societal factors that can directly or indirectly affect fisheries management because its fishery has been prominent in the scientific and popular literature since the middle of the 1950s. In the 1950s and 1960s it served as an example of how to develop the capability to exploit a natural resource, but in the 1970s it has been cited as an example of what to avoid in the development of a fishery. It seems, however, that examples of apparent success in fisheries management carry considerably more weight than examples of failures. Similarities are often cited when representatives of a fishery want to make a case for following the development path of an apparently successful fishery; while differences are usually highlighted when comparisons are made between their own fishery and a suggested analogous fishery that has collapsed.

To be sure, other fisheries might have been used as the case study of the management of shoaling pelagic fish, the notable ones being the Californian Pacific sardine fishery and the South African and the South West African/Namibian pilchard fisheries. There appear to be many similarities between these three cases that are worthy of additional research (see, for example, Glantz, 1980b).

The use of comparisons between fisheries based on similar species can be an extremely useful approach to develop an understanding of how coastal living marine resources are managed and why. The use of analogues in scientific research is not a new or recent phenomenon (see Culley, 1971; Troadec et al., 1980). With respect to understanding Eastern Boundary pelagic fish reproduction, scientists (Parrish, et al., 1983) have recently called for the use of analogies, noting that

> The four major eastern boundary current regions of the world ocean (i.e., the California, Peru, Canary, and Benguela systems) appear to involve similar environmental dynamics and contain very similar assemblages of important pelagic fish species. To the extent that corresponding species in different systems function as analogues, interregional comparative studies may yield information concerning environmental effects on reproductive success that could be difficult to derive from any single regional system alone.

Analogues could also be a useful methodological approach for an improved understanding of how societies interact with their physical and biological environments in general. Used with care, that is, identifying explicitly the strengths and weaknesses of particular analogues, they can be a source of new insights for resource managers as well as for political and economic development decisionmakers. It may be instructive to keep in mind the Chinese proverb: "To know the road ahead, ask those coming back."

NOTES

1. It is important to note that idle Californian fleet and plant capacity was also sold to South African entrepreneurs in the early 1950s, providing an impetus to the development of that fishery as well as to Peru's (see Diegues, 1983; Marx, 1981; Lees, 1969; Culley, 1971).

2. Guano is the excrement of anchoveta-consuming birds that inhabit the rocky barren islands along the Peruvian coast. It is a fertilizer that has been mined commercially since the 1840s and exported as well as used within Peru.

REFERENCES

Ahlsrom, E.H., and J. Radovich. 1970. Management of the Pacific Sardine. In A Century of Fisheries in North America, ed. N.G. Benson, 183-94. Washington, DC: American Fisheries Society Special Publication No. 7.

Bell, D. 1962. The End of Ideology. New York: The Free Press.

Borgstrom, G. 1972. Ecological Aspects of Protein Feeding - The Case of Peru. In The Careless Technology, ed. M.T. Farvar and J.P. Milton. Garden City, NY: The Natural History Press.

Boerema, L.K., and J.A. Gulland. 1973. Stock Assessment of the Peruvian Anchovy and Management of the Fishery. Journal of the Fisheries Research Board of Canada 30 (12): 2226-35.

_____, G. Saetersdal, I. Tsukayama, J.E. Valdivia, and B. Alegre. 1965. Report on the Effects of Fishing on the Peruvian Stock of Anchovy. Rome, Italy: FAO Fisheries Technical Paper No. 55.

Brown, W.B. 1965. Governmental Measures Affecting Exports in Peru, 1945-1962. Ph.D. Dissertation, Fletcher School of Law and Diplomacy, Tufts University, Medford, MA.

Caravedo Molinari, B. 1977. The State and the Bourgeoisie in the Peruvian Fishmeal Industry. Latin American Perspectives, Issue 14 4 (3): 103-21.

Clark, C.W. 1976. Mathematical Bioeconomics: The Optimal Management of Renewable Resources. New York: John Wiley and Sons.

Crutchfield, J.A., and R. Lawson. 1974. West African Marine Fisheries - Alternatives for Management. Washington: Resources for the Future.

Culley, M. 1971. The Pilchard: Biology and Exploitation. Oxford: Pergamon Press.

Dasmann, R.F. 1972. Environmental Conservation (3rd ed.). New York: John Wiley and Sons.

Diegues, A.C.S. 1983. Policies and Strategies for Fisheries Development. Discussion Paper for the Expert Consultation on Strategies for Fisheries Development, Rome, Italy, 10-14 May 1983. Rome: FAO mimeo.

Edwards, R., and R. Hennemuth. 1975. Maximum yield: Assessment and Attainment. Oceanus 18 (2): 3-9.

FAO (UN Food and Agriculture Organization). 1979. Interim Report of the ACMRR Working Party on the Scientific Basis of Determining Management Measures. Rome, Italy: FAO Fisheries Circular No. 718.

Farvar, M.T., and J.R. Milton, eds. 1972. *The Careless Technology*. Garden City, NY: Natural History Press.

Galtung, J. 1971. A Structural Theory of Imperialism. *Journal of Peace Research* 8 (2): 81-117.

Glantz, M. H., 1980a. Man, State and the Environment: An Inquiry into Whether Solutions to Desertification in the West African Sahel Are Known but not Applied. *Canadian Journal of Development Studies* 1 (1): 75-97.

_____. 1980b. El Niño: Lessons for Coastal Fisheries in Africa? *Oceanus* 23 (2): 9-17.

_____, and J.D. Thompson. 1981. *Resource Management and Environmental Uncertainty: Lessons from Coastal Upwelling Fisheries*. New York: Wiley-Interscience.

Goodsell, C.T. 1974. *American Corporations and Peruvian Politics*. Cambridge, MA: Harvard University Press.

Goulet, D. 1977. *The Uncertain Promise: Value Conflicts in Technology Transfer*. New York: IDOC/North America, Inc.

Gordon, H.S. 1954. The Economic Theory of a Common Property Resource: The Fishery. *Journal of Political Economics* 62:124-42.

Gulland, J.A. 1977. Goals and Objectives of Fisheries Management. Rome, Italy: FAO Fisheries Technical Paper No. 166.

_____. 1979. Developing Countries and the New Law of the Sea. *Oceanus* 22 (1): 36-42.

Hammergren, L.A. 1981. Peruvian Political and Administrative Responses to El Niño: Organizational, Ideological and Political Constraints on Policy Change. In *Resource Management and Environmental Uncertainty: Lessons from Coastal Upwelling Fisheries*, ed. M.H. Glantz and J.D. Thompson, 317-50. New York: Wiley-Interscience.

Hardin G. 1968. The Tragedy of the Commons. *Science* 162:1243-48.

_____, and J. Baden, eds. 1977. *Managing the Commons*. San Francisco: W.H. Freeman Press.

Horna, H. 1968. The Fish Industry of Peru. *Journal of Developing Areas* 2 (2): 393-406.

IMARPE (Instituto del Mar del Peru). 1970. Panel of Experts' Report on the Economic Effects of Alternative Regulatory Measures in the Peruvian Anchoveta Fishery. Lima, Peru: IMARPE Report No. 34. Reprinted in *Resource Management and Environmental Uncertainty: Lessons from Coastal Upwelling Fisheries*, ed. M.H. Glantz and J.D. Thompson, 369-400. New York: Wiley Interscience.

Kaczynski, W. 1979. Problems of Long-Range Fisheries. *Oceanus* 22 (1): 60-66.

Kasahara, M. 1979. Some Thoughts on Management. In Interim Report of the ACMRR Working Party on the Scientific Basis of Determining Management Measures. Rome, Italy: FAO Fisheries Circular No. 718.

Kesteven, G.L. 1981. Aid in Research into Fishery Resources: An Examination of Experience in Aid Projects Executed in Mexico, Peru, Chile, Argentina, Uruguay and Venezuela. In Working Party on the Promotion of Fishery Resources Research in Developing Countries. Rome, Italy: FAO Fisheries Report No. 251.

Klee, G.A., ed. 1980. *World Systems of Traditional Resource Management*. New York: John Wiley and Sons.

Kluckhohn, F.R. and F.L. Strodtbeck. 1961. *Variations in Value Orientations*. Evanston, IL: Row, Peterson and Co.

Kuczynski, P.-P. 1977. *Peruvian Democracy under Economic Stress*. Princeton, NJ: Princeton University Press.

Lees, R. 1969. *Fishing for Fortunes*. Cape Town, South Africa: Purnell.

Marx, W. 1981. *The Oceans: Our Last Resource*. San Francisco: Sierra Club Books.

Murphy, G.I. 1977. Clupeoids. In *Fish Population Dynamics*, ed. J.A. Gulland, 283-308. New York: Wiley Interscience.

Murphy, R.C. 1954. El Guano y la Pesca de Anchoveta (Guano and the Anchoveta Fishery). Official report of the Compañia Administradora del Guano to the National Government, Lima, Peru. Reprinted in *Resource Management and Environmental Uncertainty: Lessons from Coastal Upwelling Fisheries*, ed. M.H. Glantz and J.D. Thompson, 81-106. New York: Wiley Interscience.

NOAA (National Oceanic and Atmospheric Administration). 1984. The Latest Development in Latin American Fisheries. National Marine Fisheries Service, Foreign Fisheries Analysis Branch, 1FR-84/32.

Olson, R.S. 1975. Economic Coercion in Interntional Disputes: The U.S. and Peru in the IPC Expropriation Dispute of 1968-1971. *The Journal of Developing Areas* 9:395-414.

Parrish, R.H., A. Bakun, D. Husby, and S. Nelson. 1983. Comparative Climatology of Selected Environmental Processes in Relation to Eastern Boundary Current Pelagic Fish Reproduction. *Proceedings of the Expert Consultation to Examine Changes in Abundance and Species Composition of Neritic Stocks*, San Jose, Costa Rica, 18-29 April 1983. Vol. 3, 731-77. Rome: FAO.

Paulik, G.J. 1971. Anchovies, Birds and Fishermen in the Peru Current. In <u>Environment, Resources, Pollution and Society</u>, ed. W.W. Murdock, 156-85. Stamford, CT: Sinauer Press.

Popiel, J., and J. Sosinski. 1973. Industrial Fisheries and their Influence on Catches for Human Consumption. <u>Journal of the Fisheries Resource Board of Canada</u> 30:2254-9.

Radovich, J. 1981. The collapse of the California Sardine Fishery: What Have We Learned? In <u>Resource Management and Environmental Uncertainty: Lessons from Coastal Upwelling Fisheries</u>, ed. M.H. Glantz and J.D. Thompson, 107-36. New York: Wiley-Interscience.

Roemer, M. 1970. <u>Fishing for Growth</u>. Cambridge, MA: Harvard University Press.

Schärfe, J. 1979. Fishing Technology for Developing Countries. <u>Oceanus</u> 22 (1): 54-59.

<u>South African Journal of</u> Science. 1980. A Critique of "The Control of a Pelagic Fish Resource." 76 (October): 453-66.

Tantaleán Vanini, J. 1978. <u>Yo Respondo</u>. Lima, Peru.

Troadec, J.-P., W.G. Clark, and J.A. Gulland. 1980. A Review of Some Pelagic Fisheries in Other Areas. <u>Rapp. P.-V. Reun. CIEM</u> 177:252-77.

Vondruska, J. 1981. Postwar Production, Consumption, and Prices of Fish Meal. In <u>Resource Management and Environmental Uncertainty: Lessons from Costal Upwelling Fisheries</u>, ed. M.H. Glantz and J.D. Thompson, 285-316. New York: Wiley Interscience.

Waltz, K. 1959. <u>Man, State and War</u>. New York: Columbia University.

Part 2
Disciplinary Approaches

3
Geographical Approaches to Environmental Change: Assessing Human Impacts on Global Resources

Leonard Berry
and Douglas L. Johnson

Interest in human impacts on natural resources originates in two contradictory, yet complementary traditions: the earth science tradition of physical geographers and the "man-land" tradition of cultural geographers. The former approach stresses the importance of physical processes in the resource use equation, and is concerned particularly with the degradation of the physical resource base (soil, water, vegetation, etc.). The latter tradition emphasizes the role of cultural and livelihood systems in shaping their physical environment and is more interested in the impact of environmental change on human population (and the resources they represent) than on the diminution of the physical resources base per se. Both approaches provide valuable insights into resource management and regional planning, but only occasionally have been effectively integrated. In this respect, geography mirrors the communication gap between physical and social scientists that permeates much of contemporary science and development theory. The existence of this dialectic within one discipline, however, may provide a model for productive interaction, group research and problem solving, and fruitful dialogue across disciplinary boundaries.

The dichotomy between physical and cultural perspectives generates the current major issues that prevail in resource assessments. The purpose of this paper is to evaluate resource assessment issues and to indicate the way these perspectives influence the analysis of human environmental impacts. These major issues are discussed in the first part of the paper. A subsequent section reviews both assessment of human responsibility for environmental impact and approaches advocated for their solution. The chapter concludes with a discussion of the environmental monitoring and training needed to promote interdisciplinary perspectives on environmental change.

ASSESSING ENVIRONMENTAL CHANGE

Three major issues dominate contemporary geographic assessments of environmental change. These are: (1) stability and resilience in physical systems; (2) scale as a factor in resource use; and (3) integration of livelihood systems and environmental units into holistic structures.

Stability and Resilience in Physical Systems

A traditionally strong interest of physical geographers has been in physical processes and physical systems. In particular, these are strong research foci in Britain, in other parts of Europe and to a lesser degree in the United States. However, there has not been an even distribution of effort on the various physical systems. Most research has concentrated on: (1) diffuse and small scale water systems; (2) soil dynamics on slopes; and (3) intermediate scale vegetation systems. Nonetheless, some geographers have focussed on the issues involved with large scale water systems (White, 1977) and on macro changes in vegetation (Warren and Maizels, 1977).

Geographers have as a group emphasized the variability in stability and resilience of the physical systems with which they have worked. Geographers were widely involved in the global analysis done in preparation for the United Nations Conference on Desertification as well as much other work in arid areas. This and other work suggests that most arid ecosystems have substantial resilience in general (Noy-Meir, 1973, 1974, 1979) although some components of the system are very fragile and vulnerable (Warren and Maizels, 1977; Rapp, LeHouérou and Lundholm, 1976; Slaymaker, Dunne and Rapp, 1980). Key soil/vegetation complexes that have been shown to be fragile include fixed sand dunes found in more arid climates, stream margins and some forms of alluvial clays and their attendent vegetation. The _Acacia tortillas_ shrub complex, which is common in semi-arid areas of sandy and silty soils, is very resilient. This resilience is concentrated in soils and seeds, which are capable of rebounding from quite severe environmental shocks.

In the humid tropics the emphasis has been on the impact of the removal of much of the tropical rainforest. Tropical rainforests, long regarded as stable ecological systems because of their great species diversity, have now come to be regarded as possessing a high degree of fragility (Gómez-Pompa, Vázquez-Yanes, and Guevara, 1972). This recognition of severe stability-resilience constraints in the use of tropical ecosystems reflects a reappraisal of dominant temperate latitudinal perceptions of tropical productivity (Janzen, 1973). Traditional slash and burn agricultural systems have operated within the stability constraints of tropical rainforest regeneration. Basically, this has been possible because the scale of operation of such agro-ecosystems has been small. Temporary stress placed on one part of the system by small, localized social groups was followed by long periods of abandonment in which forest regeneration from nearby seed sources was possible. Promotion of large-scale colonization schemes has encouraged the removal of vegetation from substantial areas (Smith, 1981). Insufficiently detailed and careful planning has often resulted in the destabilization of forest landscapes and of the livelihood systems of the indigenous inhabitants (Gross et al., 1979).

This disruption of stability has had two major environmental consequences. The first is the replacement of forest with grassland (Denevan, 1973). The productivity of soils after the nutrients store of arboreal vegetation has been removed varies from almost zero to moderate/high, with impoverished soils being the more common. Second, the increase in run-off consequent upon removal of the forest cover has been considerable (Gentry and Lopez-Parodi, 1980), although the long-term impact of this development is uncertain.

The limitation of water resources and problems of their use and misuse have also received considerable attention. Although problems associated with the allocation of water among competing users of resource systems has long been recognized (White, 1960a), the full implications for the stability and resilience of resource use systems dependent on water have only recently become apparent. These issues are most acute in arid regions where the near total allocation of available water to meet human needs has taken place. The problem affects both industrialized and developing countries, and poses an immediate problem for planners in socio-economic settings as diverse as the Nile (Haynes and Whittington, 1981; Waterbury, 1979) and Colorado basins (National Research Council, 1968). The consequence is an increase in the salinity of available water which seriously affects both agricultural and urban sectors (Pillsbury, 1981; White, 1978a).

The general conclusions from this work are threefold. First, highly productive environments include some areas that are prone to severe degradation. Second, environments of low productivity tend to be more resilient at that low level, but can be rapidly destabilized when these resilience limits are exceeded. Finally, in most environments, there is considerable detailed variation in stability between different components of the major ecosystems.

Scale as a Factor in Resource Use

Societal concern regarding human impacts on natural resources tends to be concentrated at two main scales: that of the global commons and the scale of major ecosystems such as the topical rainforest. Geographers have joined the chorus of concern at these two levels, but have focussed most of their disciplinary research effort at meso and micro scales of investigation. A concern with detailed land use and resource management structures, including studies of related human settlement, have combined with a concentration of physical process studies at the local level. This has mirrored the approach of anthropologists with their focus on the local and the in depth field study. The traditional geographic interests in places, and the genre de vie of the inhabitants of those places, has encouraged a tradition of detailed studies of small to medium scale natural and social units. In France this pays tradition is particularly well developed (e.g., Buttimer, 1971), but comparable examples can be found in other national traditions (Mikesell, 1961; Nietschmann, 1973; Gómez-Ibáñez, 1975). This more micro-scale tradition is promoted by a tradition of field investigations, observation and data collection as well as a generic interest in regions. Although recent research trends have exhibited a more systematic approach that evaluates a specific management issue in a broader ecological zone (Ruthenberg, 1971; Manshard, 1979; Grigg, 1970), the methodological emphasis continues to stress the integration of environmental and physical process studies with human settlement variables.

Macro-scale studies that combine the knowledge learned from site specific investigations are, with a few notable exceptions, a recent phenomenon. Antecedents to this work can be found in earlier efforts to delimit world agricultural regions (e.g., Whittlesey, 1936) and carry out a world land-use survey. Much of the recent impetus for global scale integration has been provided by international organizations such as UNESCO and its arid zone research series, the United Nations and its environment, population, water and desertification conferences, and an alphabet soup of international scientific groups such as SCOPE, ICSU and COWAR. However, at a global scale the theoretical and methodological contributions of non-geographers such as Wallerstein (1973), Amin (1973) and the system dynamics modellers (Meadows, 1974) have probably had more impact on the development of theory if not on pragmatic decision-making.

Geographic concern with scale has produced five insights. The first stresses the concept of hierarchy in regional systems, and notes that regions exist at different scales. At each scale a certain range of goods and services can be found. These are generally concentrated in central places that are linked to hinterlands. From these central places an array of economic and environmental impacts flow. The level and spatial extent of impact is directly related to the size of the central place and its position in a regional framework of such places (Berry, 1967).

A second insight is the observation that there is an appropriate scale for most human activity. Irrigation systems provide a striking case in point. One conclusion that can be drawn from recent examination of the environmental impacts of irrigation (Worthington, 1977; White, 1978a) is that project scale is tremendously important. Many of the managerial factors associated with both large and small scale project operations are reviewed admirably by Bottrall (1978a). Large projects encounter managerial problems and experience unforeseen diseconomies if production schedules (weeding, spraying, harvesting, etc.) cannot be met. Conversely, small projects are characterized by diseconomies that reduce efficiency. But intermediate scale project units of approximately 10,000 ha can be integrated more effectively into indigenous managerial and technological capabilities.

Third, at whatever scale a project operates, it must interact with and relate to surrounding areas. These relationships often result in an internalization of benefits to project participants and the export of costs to off-project areas and populations. These exported impacts may produce both environmental and social changes that influence project success. Thus, the irrigation project that multicrops a riverine floodplain that traditionally produced only one crop denies dry season grazing resources to nearby pastoralists. Their animals must then be concentrated year round in rainy season pasture, which invariably causes overgrazing of pastoral resources. More bare soil surfaces increase soil erosion. The increased sediment loads in seasonal and perennial streams, in turn, contribute to accelerated siltation in project canals. The maintenance costs and infrastructure deterioration that result reduce project income and corrode its economic viability. Gainers and losers in environmental change frequently are spatially discontinuous, thus resulting in a variety of unassessed costs. These costs, in turn, may bring negative feedback to bear on the initiating project, with serious consequences for the success of the project as originally defined.

Fourth, the scale at which a system operates is also dynamic over time. For example, in the savanna zones of Sudan camel pastoralists, in part in response to climatic fluctuation and environmental deterioration, now spend the dry season much further south than in any previous recorded period. In some parts of the Sudan, they have penetrated into areas that a decade ago were the exclusive preserve of cattle herders (Hunting, 1980). Similarly, pastoral communities are no longer, if they ever were, isolated from global economic trends. Thus, inflation can force traditional pastoralists to sell animals in order to meet basic subsistence needs in a period when animals ideally should be retained to reconstitute drought-decimated herds. Such shifts in the terms of trade can have a devastating effect on the viability of pastoral communities (Swift, 1979; 1980), and in the long run can contribute to an acceleration in incentives to overstock rangeland whenever conditions permit. The consequence of this dynamism in the scale at which systems operate and interact precludes simplistic analyses based on homeostatic models.

The Khasm el Gherba irrigation scheme provides an excellent example of the operation of these scale factors (Sörbo, 1977; Hoyle, 1977; Murdock, 1979). The project was developed as a home for Nubian villagers dislocated by construction of the Aswan High Dam and as an inducement to nomadic tribes to become sedentary. The project, the second largest in Sudan after the Gezira scheme, allocated tenancies to people who either had no previous experience with irrigated agriculture or were accustomed to a much more independent, small-scale irrigation economy. Rigid managerial controls seemed necessary in such circumstances to insure that crops would be planted, tilled, irrigated, sprayed and harvested on schedule. Little provision was made for incorporation of animals into scheme tenancies, or for the cultivation of fodder to nourish them. As a result, Shukriya nomads, long accustomed to exploiting several pastoral and dry-farm agriculture niches simultaneously, found themselves at odds with the project managers. Nubians, who often sought non-agricultural employment off the scheme as a supplement to their tenancy, also found that their objectives contradicted those of management. Disagreement about the balance between cash crops (cotton and ground nuts) and traditional grains, such as <u>dura</u> (sorghum) and <u>dukhan</u> (millet), also sparked controversy. Yields, and therefore profits, seldom met managerial expectations. Overgrazing by herds owned by tenants occurred on the periphery of the project, and the pressure for incorporation of more animals into the project tenancies was always intense. From the standpoint of project management, irrational tenant behavior compromised project efficiency and resulted in a failure to achieve project goals. Disruption of the traditional grazing regime and an export of environmental costs onto adjacent rangeland went uncalculated in a project economy that appeared gloomy enough without conjuring up additional negative information. Conversely, participants viewed the project as a success because they could combine income from the tenancy with resources generated from animals held off scheme or skilled urban employment. Thus, although national scale economic objectives were not met, the individual tenant clearly benefited by maximizing the economic returns to himself and increasing personal security.

Finally, efforts are now being made to bridge the scale gap. These efforts involve linking micro, meso and macro data sets together. LANDSAT and other recent technological developments in monitoring from aerial platforms (Townshend, 1981) make practical regional scale overviews hitherto impossible to attain. Moreover, these monitoring systems can be integrated with more traditional assessment methodologies (Berry and Ford, 1977) to produce a diverse array of information at several scales. The potential contribution to land management of a monitoring system based on combining ground observations, aerial reconnaissance, and satellite imagery has been demonstrated by KREMU's monitoring work in semi-arid rangeland areas in Kenya (Croze, Norton-Griffiths and Gwynne, 1978). Equally necessary is the incorporation of data derived from human systems to compliment ecological observations. The indicators of environmental change used by indigenous farmers and herders often provide astute insights into system dynamics (Barker, Oguntoyinko, and Richards, 1977; Castro, Hakansson and Brokenshaw, 1981; Brokenshaw, Warren and Werner, 1980). The critical component in any monitoring system is the choice of indicators, for the indicators that satisfy scientists may not provide suitable data for pragmatic decision-making. Developing a matrix of critical indicators that elucidate at varying scales dynamic features of the ecological and human units under examination is a challenging intellectual exercise in applied science.

Integrating Livelihood Systems and Environmental Units

It is now an article of faith that adverse human impacts on the environment can be avoided by adopting holistic approaches to solving problems. Two truisms dominate contemporary thought. The first stresses the need to view human and environmental subsystems as part of a unified whole (White, 1980), a principle unfortunately as much honored in the breach as in the observance. The second tauts the development possibilities contained in indigenous knowledge systems (Brokenshaw, Warren and Werner, 1980), and advocates a bottom-up approach to development.

Both principles are a reaction to the four major problems that characterize much of contemporary resource management and economic development. The first is the prominence of segmental and sectoral development structures which typifies much of the development process. This tendency to compartmentalize development and land management responsibilities, which Baker (1976) calls the "administrative trap", often results in competitive actions and counter-intuitive environmental consequences. Thus, conversion of semi-arid pasture to mechanized farming schemes often results in a degradation of the remaining rangeland as grazing pressure is concentrated on a smaller total area. Inadequate administrative control and the use of soil-mining cultivation techniques can seriously erode yields and impoverish basic fertility (Thimm, 1979). Thus, agricultural development may well result in only short-term productivity gains, which are attained at the cost of lower pastoral productivity, diminished soil fertility and overgrazing.

Even when integrated development is achieved at a planning level, implementation frequently devolves to entrenched bureaucracies whose narrow priorities and immediate self-interest may run counter to project objectives. Since aid agencies must work with institutions as they exist, the tension between holistic objectives and implementation realities can be severe.

The problem is compounded by the frequent assertion that scientific knowledge is sufficient to manage resources, and that the only obstacles to successful application lie in cultural conservatism and inadequate extension design. This conviction was a basic rationale undergirding the Action Plan produced by the United Nations Conference on Desertification (UNCOD, 1977), and was a cornerstone of the United Nations University's Natural Resources Program (Mabbutt, 1979). This perspective reinforces segmental approaches, since it segregates technology and science both from the cultural milieu that produces it and from the social and environmental setting in which it is applied. The all too frequent tendency to involve social scientists in development project design after the major components have been decided is in itself a serious obstacle to successful development and is a prime cause of social and environmental maladjustments. An analogous failure occurs when inadequate time series data make it impossible to fully understand the variability and productivity of physical systems. Thus, management systems are designed that ultimately prove incapable of coping with random and unexpected fluctuations in local conditions.

Even when environmental and livelihood units are conceived in a holistic fashion, a second problem occurs. This is the general lack of coincidence between ecological units and the livelihood systems that exploit them. Most traditional resource use systems are based on exploiting several niches in a seasonal time/space framework (Carlstein, 1982). This enables individuals and groups to increase their security by spreading risk and investment across a number of different activities (Haalund, 1972). Pastoral nomads are a classic example of this pattern. Farmers also attempt to plant different crops in separate micro niches with varying soil characteristics, moisture regimes and degrees of risk due to drought, insect pests, floods and the like. Similarly, the fish on which flood-plain fishing cultures rely need seasonally inundated areas in which to spawn in addition to the between banks aquatic environment in which they spend the bulk of their life cycle. Conversion of the floodplain to perennial irrigation agriculture eliminates the seasonal spawning environment that is critical to the lifecycle of many riverine fish. The result is a rapid, often catastrophic, shift in the composition of the fish stock, and a consequent serious impact on available fish resources (Welcomme, 1979).

Thirdly, livelihood groups themselves often have overlapping ecologies. This means that resources not used by one group at one time of the year often are exploited by another group. Thus, pastoralists in the interior Delta of the Niger traditionally had legally assured access to delta areas during the dry season when agriculture was no longer possible (Gallais, 1975). The expansion of perennial irrigation threatens this access to critical seasonal resources and increases grazing pressures elsewhere in the area. Whenever management schemes exclude a livelihood system from a portion of the total habitat needed by that productive system, the consequence is social and environmental turmoil and decline.

Fourthly, management units often do not coincide either with livelihood systems or environmental units. National boundaries frequently cut across both, truncating pastoral migration patterns and disrupting established ways of using resources. At a micro-scale, development projects often exhibit the same tendency to carve out units of space and manage them as separate entities. These units seldom relate effectively to activities outside the project fence, and often are foci for the hostilities of groups not incorporated in the project design. A more consistent effort to plan at a regional level in order to balance out the conflicting priorities of ecological systems management and livelihood system sustenance is easy to conceive in the abstract but is difficult to achieve in practice.

This failure to achieve regional coordination results in serious boundary problems for environmental managers. The boundaries of the units in which evaluation and monitoring take place may encompass all of the system managed by a project, but they seldom encompass the entire system affected by a development scheme. As a result, it is relatively easy to identify the benefits that accrue from a given project, but it is frequently difficult to account for all of the costs. Participants within the project boundaries are gainers in the process, in part because losses are exported to populations and environments outside the scheme. These losers seldom figure into project assessments. Managers, understandably, are reluctant to acknowledge responsibility for events in areas outside their control. Yet, these impacts are very real and frequently represent a negative feedback loop that impairs, through erosion and other degradational processes, the effectiveness of the project itself.

Efforts to solve this administrative, boundary-setting dilemma need to incorporate several features. The first is the development of an interactive people-environmental model. This cultural-ecological model can serve as a fruitful focus for inter-disciplinary cooperation between the physical and the social sciences. Building this model up from local units to a regional framework is a second strategy. This does not preclude utilizing generalized systems models as part of the regional framework, but it does suggest that a critical component of the process must be an understanding of the detailed implementation units on the ground, and the way they interact with each other. Regional planning efforts in southern Kordofan (Hunting Technical Service, 1980) have followed this approach with great success in the project planning stage. Whether equal success can be attained in project implementation remains to be seen. A third requirement of a solution strategy is that the interactive model has to accommodate change. Too many models are based on concepts of homeostasis; only those models able to identify, measure and cope with change in both physical and social parameters promise to make a meaningful contribution. Finally, a people-environment model must be able to identify indicators of change which can be monitored. This is not an easy process, for many of the indicators of change that provide viable scientific data do not relate directly to policy and planning decisions. In spite of progress in identifying social indicators of environmental change (Castro, Hakansson and Brokensha, 1981), physical scientists are at present better able to specify indicators that lend themselves to reasonably accessible monitoring techniques (Reinig, 1978; Halldén, 1981). The need at present is to develop a matrix of indicators that can be monitored at several scales using a combination of technologies, and to do this in a way that incorporates both physical and social variables in a unitary framework.

HUMAN IMPACT ON RESOURCES

Assessment by geographers of the human impacts on resources has been based on an interactive people-environment model. This model rejects both environmentalism and cultural determinism and recognizes that not only do human systems modify their environment but also that natural fluctuations and rhythms impact upon people. The result is a complex, dynamic model that incorporates environmental change, human coping strategies, natural pulsations, and socioeconomic variables. The four areas researchers have had the most interest in are:

(1) desertification and dryland management;
(2) agricultural intensification and development;
(3) water resource use; and
(4) natural hazards.

Each of these areas is considered briefly below.

Desertification: The Degradation of Drylands

The degradation of dryland resources (desertification) is widespread in both industrialized and industrializing societies. Productivity loss in dryland resources results in more arid conditions as indicated by impoverished vegetation, increased soil erosion by wind and water, more saline soils in irrigated areas, and more stressful impacts on human populations (Dregne, 1977). This process is called desertification because, while little evidence exists for climate change reducing total available moisture (LeHouérou, 1977; Hare, 1977, 1983), land-use change commonly reduces the effectiveness of the moisture that is available. The result is the emergence of locally more desert-like conditions as a product of human-induced degradation (Ibrahim, 1978). The manifestation of desertification often comes as a result of a drought which dramatizes the underlying imbalances in resource care.

For example, concern about this problem captured popular attention when a prolonged drought afflicted Africa's semi-arid Sahelian zone during 1968-1973. Because the impacts of drought and land-use change affected environmental zones that transcended national frontiers, international coordination of both relief activities and remedial measures appeared essential. The United Nations Conference on Desertification was organized to marshal existing scientific knowledge about the process of dryland degradation and to develop a coordinated program to combat and reverse desertification.

Held in 1977, this Conference's official review papers summarized scientific awareness of dryland management problems and their causes. They also highlighted our poverty of knowledge in some areas. Global reviews of climate (Hare, 1977), ecological change (Warren and Maizels, 1977), and social impacts (Kates, Johnson and Haring, 1977) were authored by geographers. Geographers also were prominent among the senior UNEP consultants who supervised, and in part authored, the overview summary (UNCOD Secretariat, 1977). Comparative insight into the nature of arid land problems was advanced significantly. Not only did the conference serve to highlight existing research taking place (Rapp, LeHouérou and Lundholm, 1976; Hutchinson et al., 1977; Amiran & Wilson, 1973; IGU, 1976; IGU, 1980; Mabbutt, 1978; Glantz, 1976, 1977), but also it sparked both bilateral (e.g., U.S.-Mexico, USDI, [1980] and multinational (e.g., USAID, 1980) assaults on dryland development problems. Moreover, a significant number of these initiatives have been pursued since UNCOD, under MAB auspices. Particularly notable have been reviews of the obstacles and opportunities in dryland development (Pélissier, 1977), of the environmental impacts of irrigation (White, 1978), of research trends and applications of technology to arid zone development (Baker, 1979), and of basic productivity in the drylands (Bremen & de Wit, 1983). Less substantial progress has been achieved in dealing with these problems in the field (Berry, 1983).

Five salient features of the problem have been highlighted. The first is that industrialized countries as well as industrially developing states experience desertification. This fact is often obscured by the attention focused on Third World states. The United States is a good example. A recent Council of Environment Quality study reveals (Sheridan, 1981) significant overgrazing in the southwest, soil salinization in the San Joaquin Basin, depletion of groundwater in both rural (e.g., Texas High Plains) and urban (e.g., Tuscon) areas, and accelerating stress as a result of new mining, military and urban pressures. Concern both for decreased river water quality (Pillsbury, 1981) and competing uses for existing water resources has led the U.S. MAB IV (Arid Lands) Committee to sponsor a major conference to consider the economic, social and political issues associated with the problem (Engelbert with Scheuring, 1984).

A second aspect of the desertification problem is the differential distribution of degradational impacts. Less developed countries have greater difficulties coping with desertification because they have fewer resources to invest in remedial measures. Thus, the United States can apply high technology solutions to degradational problems. It can also subsidize management improvements by investing resources of finance and expertise generated elsewhere. The Vale rangeland improvement program is, for example, a success story in grazing resource management (Heady and Bartholome,

1977). Poor countries can seldom afford the luxury of investing scarce resources in the improvement of marginal lands.

The rash-like nature of desertification is a third insight into its character. The frontal expansion of desert margins is a figment of journalistic imagination. Desertification most commonly occurs in particular "spots" where pressures are greatest. Wherever people and their pastoral and agricultural activities concentrate, there often will desertification appear. Although improperly managed mechanized farming activities may strip the land of surface cover and result in soil erosion and decreased fertility over large areas (Thimm, 1979), concentrated activities usually produce the most severe disruption. Generally, it is the best portions of the environment that are most threatened. In the Gascoyne river basin of Australia, for example, the most degraded portions of sheep stations are those in the potentially most productive land system classes (Williams, Suijendorp and Wilcox, 1977).

Fourth, causal factors that produce such land deterioration are seldom simple or exclusively local. Rather, desertification is the product of social, economic and political factors operating at several scales in interaction with environmental fluctuation. Thus, drought may reveal a serious local overstocking causing long-term rangeland deterioration, which had been masked by a sequence of years characterized by better than normal conditions. Overstocking, in turn, may be more a response to economic opportunities in national and regional markets than a myopic desire to increase herd size regardless of environmental cost. Recent work in northern Kordofan, Sudan, suggests that where such disruption occurs in nomadic pastoral areas, it is invariably causal variables operating outside the control of local peoples that are responsible for environmental degradation (Viitanen, 1981).

Finally, most desertification is a result of inability to manage resource use. There is little evidence that any particular social formation has been successful in achieving the requisite levels of control to prevent desertification. The reasons for this are numerous, complex, and transcend simplistic notions of a "tragedy of the commons." Rather, explanations should be sought in the differential rates at which old management systems are replaced by new ones, the difficulties of communicating across cultural barriers, the way short term versus long term benefits and costs are weighed, the variable interests of managers at differing scales, the manner in which the boundaries of analytical systems are established, and the often inappropriate models and technologies that are applied to novel settings (Berry, 1983).

Most of these factors are found in the way water resources, and access to them, are managed throughout the Sahelian zone in Africa. Water development around El Khuwei, a small town in western Kordofan, Sudan, exemplifies the regional pattern. In the El Khuwei area, water development has produced ecological deterioration because effective land use controls do not exist. Traditional control mechanisms based on tribal authority have been eliminated, and new systems have proven ineffective (el-Arifi, 1979). Indeed, these new systems are susceptable to corrupt practices that favor certain herd owners over others and increase, rather than reduce, pressure on local resources. The record of water development, in consequence, has been counterintuitive. Designed to improve both quality of life and more uniform and rational exploitation of pasture, it has led to a concentration of people and animals that is seriously undermining the viability of basic land resources.

Coping with Environmental Change

Environmental changes due to human activity are seldom wanton acts of needless destruction. Most frequently they are the inadvertant, counterintuitive result of efforts to use resources. In many cases these efforts at intensified exploitation result in increased resource base productivity; these positive changes, in turn, alter carrying capacity in ways that support larger human populations.

Unfortunately, not all environmental changes are so benign. The record of the human experience is littered with the flotsom and jetsam of schemes gone awry and resources wasted. Examples of flawed interaction between nature, society and technology that produce adverse environmental change often are particularly serious because they consume the best, potentially most productive components of the resource base.

Concern about the human impact on environment has a long history in geographic studies. It draws its inspiration from the seminal work of George Perkins Marsh (1965), and is most convincingly summarized in the interdisciplinary symposium that examined Man's Role in Changing the Face of the Earth (Thomas, 1956). Geographers, in contradistinction to their discipline's initial deterministic perspective, have placed more emphasis on the role of humankind as a modifying agent than they have on a search for physical environmental influences on human life and livelihood. These studies possess four common features: (1) a predilection for micro-scale investigations; (2) a focus on the role of culture, and specifically technology, in promoting change; (3) an identification of change with the linkage of micro-scale systems into larger and more open systems; and (4) the increasingly explicit use of ecological concepts and methodology as well as systems analysis in study design and implementation. Particularly through the use of ecological concepts, geographers are employing language and constructs that readily link their research to work undertaken in other natural and social sciences. Many areas of active concern could be noted, but research on agricultural intensification and the management of water resources is singled out for particular attention.

Intensification and Development

Efforts to increase productivity and promote economic development have followed two paths. The first has involved the expansion of more intensive production systems into areas formerly devoted to extensive exploitation activities. The second practice has been to increase investments of labor and capital in presently cultivated zones. Major environmental changes have followed from each type of initiative, and many of these changes have been counterintuitive in nature.

Agricultural land in production in the Third World in particular has expanded by about 30 percent to deal in part with increases in numbers of agricultural producers. In many parts of the world, this expansion has been onto marginal land not previously used for agriculture. Formerly, exploitation was minimal because of constraints of quality, access, and other management problems. In semi-arid environments in Third World countries, much of this expansion has taken the form of introducing mechanized cereal cultivation into areas that previously were the domain of pastoral nomads. In Sudan, for example, this expansion has produced a short-term increase in yields and in profits for the entrepreneurs involved at the expense of long-term decreases in soil fertility (Thimm, 1979). Despite often heavy capitalization, these schemes seldom maintain their initial production levels. Both diminished soil productivity and the impact of episodic droughts, coupled with farmer unfamiliarity with the new resource conditions, results in serious environmental degradation. Moreover, pastoralists, denied access to the grazing resources alienated to cereal cultivation, overuse the remaining grassland (Rapp et al., 1976). The consequence is a ripple effect whereby often temporary gains in production in one segment of the resource base are offset by environmental damage exported to neighboring districts. The more marginal and pulsating these areas are, and the shorter the time span for which accurate environmental data is available, the more difficult it is to separate human from natural causation and short-term fluctuation from secular trend (Olsson, 1983).

The situation cited above is widely observed in micro studies of rapid cultural and technological change. Invariably it is an expansive, powerful, exogenous, introduced technology that is the culprit (Johnson, 1979). Kemp's (1973) analysis of Eskimo use of resources points out the unsettling impact of guns, motorboats and snowmobiles on a culture thought to exhibit a harmonic, I-thou relationship to the natural world. Nietschmann's (1973) study of Miskito Indian overexploitation of the turtle fishery demonstrates how a more efficient extractive technology, when combined with a seemingly limitless market demand, can threaten to drive an important local food source into extinction. Dickerson's (1974) examination of the Lake Itzabel fishery collapse is another example of how local resource use practices are conditioned and changed by external forcing variables of technology and economy.

In such circumstances, technology operates to remove constraints present in the local resource use system. This is beneficial in that it permits attainment of higher production levels. However, the new technology is also uncontrolled by local value systems. Essentially unfettered, it overrides negative feedback loops in local exploitation systems that served to slow the pace of change to a rate that could be accommodated and controlled. Because such negative feedbacks are often associated with traditional leaders and mores, they are consciously swept away by modernist exponents of change (el-Arifi, 1979). The incomplete integration of modern technology into changing local ways of knowing and doing is perhaps the single most important variable promoting undesired change.

Nonetheless, although expansion into marginal areas has been an important process, much of the increase in rural population, perhaps more than half, has taken place in a context that encourages an intensification of agriculture on land already under cultivation. The humid areas have seen the greatest increases in density of agricultural population in terms of numbers of people, but some drier areas have seen three-fold or more increases in numbers of people changing over from predominantly animal husbandry to predominantly crop farming.

Thus, the effects of agricultural intensification are in dispute, and examples of both improvement and decline can be cited. In many areas, there have been major increases in the total agricultural production even though technology has not changed much. For example, the high rainfall areas of central Kenya, northern Tanzania, Rwanda and Burundi all support twice as many people as they did two decades ago. Boserup (1965) argues that this is a normal process in which increased inputs of labor and natural fertilizer accompany the intensification of small-scale production. Stall-fed cattle replace range-fed, tree crops and field crops are intercropped and improved management is possible. The intensification and population pressure model appears to work well in a number of tropical agricultural subsistence cultures, although inclusion of subsistence and environmental factors increases the model's realism (Turner, Hanham and Portararo, 1977). Similar processes can be seen to have operated historically. A notable example can be identified in Mayan raised field agriculture (Turner, 1974; Harrison and Turner, 1978), whereby previously unproductive swamp ecosystems were developed into intensely managed agricultural systems capable of supporting large populations.

However, even with large increases in net production, per capita productivity has dropped in Africa as a whole as well as in some areas of small scale farming in southeast Asia. It is also not clear what the environmental costs of new levels of intensification are. In Kenya, there is growing national concern with the high level of soil losses from the high rainfall areas, and soil management has become an issue of great concern throughout the tropics.

The greatest problem with intensification seems to be in the somewhat drier areas of the tropics. As part of the process of population growth and intensification in the humid areas, there is a population movement outward to areas of lower and less reliable rainfall and to soils which have lower fundamental productive capacity. In some of these areas, population growth rates have approximated those of the cities, i.e., 6-8 per cent per annum.

This is only possible with a change to crop agriculture and a reduction in livestock numbers. Two problems arise. The first is the difficulty of maintaining productivity without large inputs of fertilizer, which many farmers cannot afford. Without such inputs, and in the absence of long fallow cycles, the result is loss of soil structure and soil by inappropriate agriculture (Bradley, 1977). Second, the impact of dry years on an environment supporting many more people than is traditional often is severe (Glantz, 1976). Basic land management problems obscured during good periods may be suddenly revealed (Warren and Maizels, 1977). Moreover, the number of people, national and international, at risk from drought, has increased drastically and the ability to deal with drought emergencies has not (Kates, 1980b). In consequence, the impact of environmental fluctuation, both on ecosystem productivity and stability and on the viability of society, seems to be increasing.

This has sparked interest in the long-term stability and resilience of societal adjustments. There exists an historical record of considerable population fluctuation over time in a number of areas. Waves, or greater than millenia cycles, of population growth and decay have afflicted Egypt (Butzer, 1976), Meso-America (Denevan, 1976; Sanders, 1976), Peru (Moseley, 1975; Ortloff, Moseley and Feldman, 1983), Iraq (Adams, 1965; Adams and Nissen, 1972; Adams, 1981), and China (Bilsky, 1980) to mention only representative cases. Although there is little evidence that climate change alone is responsible for such cycles (Bowden et al., 1981), it is credible that environmental fluctuations in combination with managerial inadequacies (Jacobsen and Adams, 1958; Gibson, 1974) could produce stresses that exceed the stability and resilience limits of existing resource use systems (Warrick and Bowden, 1981). Examination of such stresses in a simulation framework can provide insight into historical situations (Johnson and Gould, 1984) and man-environment theory, as well as serve as an interface area for fruitful interaction between ecology (Clark and Holling, 1979) and the social sciences (Kates, 1983).

Water Resources

The human impact on water resources in both quality and quantity has only recently been recognized as a global problem. To the extent that a United Nations conference is a measure of a problem's acceptance as an international concern, water issues have finally arrived (Biswas, 1978). However, interest in water resource issues is a long-standing concern. Although traditionally this interest was most intensive in arid areas where water is a limited good (White, 1960a; Baker et al., 1973; White, 1971), concern about finite limits to water supply in humid areas is widespread (Pereira, 1973). Interest is concentrated in three areas: (1) wise use of a limited resource; (2) interbasin water transfers and their environmental effects; and (3) the design and management of water resource systems, particularly in irrigation agriculture.

Water is now recognized as being a limited resource. Its wise use is essential if human livelihood systems are to continue in good health. The need to allocate water among competing uses requires both careful planning to achieve multiple objectives (Major, 1977; Maass et al., 1962) and the resolution of important societal conflicts in the political arena (White, 1960b). Aggressive development of ground water for irrigation purposes has had a serious impact on many areas. This is especially true in the High Plains of Texas where groundwater drawdown is threatening the viability of cotton production in many areas (Sheridan, 1981). More substantial still has been the environmental impact of nearly total use of water in many river basins. In the southwestern United States, the Colorado River's water is so heavily committed, and water withdrawal for agricultural activities is so extensive, that the salinity level of water in the river has reached alarming proportions (Pillsbury, 1981). In order to meet its treaty obligation to Mexico, the U.S. must desalt Colorado River water--an expensive proposition--before it is permitted to cross the frontier. With urban and industrial demand for water burgeoning in the southwest, it is likely that agricultural users of water who now account for the bulk of the water use, will face both rising costs and declining supply in the coming decade (Wilson, 1977; Engelbert, 1982).

Declining water supplies emphasize the need for water conserving policies and the wise use of existing resources. These might include greater attention to less water-demanding agricultural practices such as enclosed environment agriculture, control of water loss through seepage and evaporation during transfer, the development of salt tolerant crops, waste water reclamation, and the use of water efficient field application techniques such as trickle irrigation. Great potential for improvement in these areas exists in industrialized countries, although their applicability in the developing world is more likely to be limited by capital constraints.

Limitations on available water resources inevitably leads to pressure for interbasin transfers. Such transfer carry the tradition of concern for integrated river basin development into a totally new dimension and promise to be costly in both economic and environmental terms. Howe and Easter (1971) have concluded that such transfers in the U.S. are unlikely to provide enough economic benefits at the national level to justify investing resources in grandiose construction projects, and that attention to increased efficiencies in existing agricultural practices is more practical and is likely to result in fewer environmental problems. The ecological impacts of such transfers are difficult to predict, but they could be significant. To cite but one example, Soviet plans to transfer Siberian water, "wasted" in the cold-limited agricultural environment of northern Asia, to arid Central Asia (Gerasimov and Ginden, 1977) have raised concerns about possible global climate modification consequent upon alteration of the salinity levels of the Arctic Ocean (Gustafson, 1980).

A primary environmental impact of water development has been the salinization frequently associated with irrigation (Worthington, 1977). The record of water development in the developing world is generally recognized to have been a failure, for which managerial problems have been largely to blame (Bottrall, 1978b). Even technologically sophisticated industrial states such as the U.S. have encountered very significant problems.

Large, publically-operated surface systems have experienced the most problems. Inefficient, rigid, and remote management structures that fail to involve participants in meaningful and responsible ways are part of the problem. The scale at which large projects operate also mitigates against success. The larger the project, the more difficulties it encounters in delivering water, particularly to farmers at the tail of the system, and in organizing and maintaining adequate drainage. This latter is a critical problem, and is primarily responsible for widespread salinization in many projects. The Mussayib project in Iraq (UNCOD, 1977b) and the Mona project in Pakistan (UNCOD, 1977c) lost more than 20 percent of their area to salinization before drainage programs stabilized and revitalized them. So serious is the problem on a global scale, that for every unit of land brought into production a corresponding unit becomes inoperable (White, 1978a) due to salinization, waterlogging and other land management problems. Not only do such large scale schemes fail to achieve their economic objectives, but also they can adversely impact the health of project participants. The intensification of food and fiber production through irrigation has its unfortunate corollary in the creation of favorable habitats for the transmission of schistosomiasis (Obeng, 1978; McJunkin, 1975) and malaria. Similarly, efforts to improve domestic water quality has failed to achieve the expected improvements in health and in protection from cholera and other water-borne diseases (White, Bradley and White, 1972; Feachem, 1978). Indeed, for much of the world, in the absence of a comprehensive assault on water-related problems, the situation with respect to health and disease is probably worse now for a larger percentage of people than it was a decade ago.

Natural Hazards

The natural hazards posed by particular environments are closely related to human resource use systems. Extreme natural events such as drought, hurricanes, volcanic eruptions and floods occur as a normal aspect of the physical environment. These events are largely independent of the human use system. Biotic communities are able to adjust to these impacts or to recover quickly from the perturbations that they initiate. Natural event processes become hazards when they directly impact human populations that, by virtue of their location, are placed at risk. In the process of seeking to identify and use resources, people get in the way of natural events. The manner in which individuals and groups perceive and cope with such events and their impacts markedly affects the viability of their livelihood system.

For the last four decades the hazards posed by the physical environment have been the object of systematic study at a variety of scales (White, 1974), and increasingly the focus of attention has expanded to include those hazards that people themselves create (Burton, Kates and White, 1978). It is a vision of global environmental impacts that includes interactive man-nature systems that makes a brief review of natural hazards research appropriate.

Beginning with an interest in extreme geophysical events such as floods (White, 1945, 1961 and 1964) in the United States, interest in hazards has always been set in a resource use context, first in the floodplains exposed to risk (Burton, 1962; Kates, 1962, 1965) and then more generally. This has included both attempts to evaluate all of the hazards at a place (Hewitt and Burton, 1971) and to assess comprehensively particular hazards (Ward, 1978; Warrick, 1975) both in terms of perception (Saarinen, 1966) and the comparative impacts of comparable magnitude events (Kates, 1980a). Eventually a hazards research paradigm emerged that attempted cross-cultural comparison of human response to hazards and of the ways in which alternative adaptations to risk are chosen. Although the approach has not gone unchallenged (Waddell, 1977; see also the reply by White, 1978b), it has contributed useful insights into the nature of man-environment relations.

Of particular note is the observation that hazards are the result of an interplay between physical, biological and social forces. In this process, human actions more than physical events produce disasters. This results from the interplay between environments of opportunity and the risks that those locations contain. Transitional zones, where opportunity and risk are both concentrated, are often the settings with the greatest hazard potential. For example, it is the rich soils of volcano slopes that attract farmers despite the risk of catastrophic eruption.

Often the very remedial measures that society takes to reduce risk can be seen to increase hazards. Thus, the provision of levees and other physical structures designed to protect floodplains encourages increased, more intensive, and capital-demanding investment in the floodplain (Platt, 1976). The physical structures themselves confine the flood more rigorously, and can produce more damaging consequences from lower order of magnitude, more frequent events. The result is a rising cost in monetary damage in industrialized societies even though deaths decline. In contrast, both deaths and damages are on the increase in developing societies. This suggests that transitional societies are more at risk to hazards as traditional coping strategies are abandoned and new methods are only partially applied (Burton, Kates and White, 1978). It also implies that government intervention often makes matters worse by reducing, often inadvertently, the range of choice available to resource users. Overall, if present trends continue, White (1978b) concludes that less resilience and more exposure to risk is the fate of most developing economies. This conclusion is reinforced by the tendency in all societies for governments to select technological solutions to environmental problems rather than to promote improved land use (White and Haas, 1975). It is precisely because social, political and economic factors are so important, yet often seem so intractable and so slow of resolution, that preference for technological solutions to environmental hazards is so pronounced.

Conclusions

Research into human impacts in the global environment is diverse, and only a small portion is reviewed here. The emphasis is on work of geographers and others that share a spatial (geographic) perspective within a man-environment tradition. This research shares four features: (1) all of it addresses fundamental people-environment issues, and most work starts from the utilization components of the human system rather than from the characteristics of the physical system; (2) there is a strong international component to the research that links it to international organizations (UNEP, UNESCO, SCOPE, ICSU, among others); also, an international network of research collaborators is a feature of much of the research; (3) comparison of similar problems in both developed and developing countries is a common theme. In this sense there is a movement away from micro studies toward macro models and broad, comparative theoretical understandings; and (4) interest is increasing in applied as well as theoretical work. Although progress has been made, much remains to be learned. In particular, the relationship between theory and practice, that is, between fact and generalization, and between research and training in an interdisciplinary framework merits more attention than it has received in the past.

KEEPING TRACK OF RESOURCE TRENDS: MONITORING AND TRAINING

The record of research on environmental change is a substantial one; the extensive bibliography of this paper is one measure of that record. Yet the overwhelming impression gained from this review is one of ignorance. We still do not know a large part of what needs to be known to understand the major global, regional and local trends in resource use. We remain in basic ignorance of the fundamental causes of much environmental change as well as of the impacts of those changes. Therefore, we are not able, in many cases, to establish priorities in our attack on the problems involved or to avoid repeating mistakes made in previous problem-solving efforts.

For example, assessment of the soil erosion problem in an area as environmentally diverse as East Africa is based largely on two sets of studies (Rapp et al., 1973; Dunne, 1977) and some general observations (Eckholm, 1976; Kjekshus, 1977). But these data are better than most that exist for much of the rest of the vast African continent. Data on the rates of reduction of tropical forests are based on a few Landsat interpretations. Water pollution information for much of the developing world is not available. Despite this lament, much information is available in unpublished form, stored on Landsat tape, in roughly bound files in regional offices and in the minds of people experienced in particular areas and topics.

It is an important challenge to change this state of affairs. Two approaches seem to tackle such a challenge: (1) the development of soundly based, low cost information and monitoring systems for key resource trends; and (2) the radical revision of current training and educational approaches to resource matters.

Monitoring

The word monitoring tends to suggest sophistication. There should be sophistication in our approach to monitoring resource trends. However, the sophistication should come through the skills needed in identifying and establishing priorities for monitoring rather than through excessive reliance on high technology surveillance systems.

The task of identifying and analyzing change itself can be controlled with a wide variety of tools. Some of these utilize relatively sophisticated technology, such as air photography and other imagery (Townshend, 1981; Adrien and Baumgardner, 1977). Use of platforms such as airplanes and satellites can provide useful monitoring data on matters as diverse as rangeland carrying capacity (Crowze, Norton-Griffiths and Gwynne, 1978) or the identification of fossil drainage patterns (Haynes, 1982; McCauley, et al., 1982). Other methodologies are relatively simple, for example land observation of vegetation trends. This usually requires both isolation of test areas from use for control purposes as well as detailed knowledge of local flora and land use conditions in order to interpret trends (Novikoff, 1976; Boudet, 1975). Monitoring technology in varying degrees of sophistication and of scale can be combined into a unified information system. Berry and Ford (1977) outline a global approach towards monitoring desertification, while the Environmental Training and Resource Management for Africa (ETMA) program (Johnson, 1981) is in the process of developing a prototype monitoring program specifically for the dry areas of Sudan.

Experience with developing monitoring systems indicates that several ingredients are likely to be important. First, there is a need to build time-series information in order to separate long-term trends from recurrent events. Both an adequate baseline and consistent monitoring of critical indicators are necessary if this is to be accomplished. Few areas possess information that is sufficient for the task, since few researchers are able to acquire funding to study the same area for several decades. Thus, data adequate for planning purposes is seldom available. Even in Sudan, where several teams of Sudanese, Americans, Swedes, Germans and British scholars are involved in monitoring activities (Andrawis and Khidir, 1980; Helldén and Olsson, 1982; Mensching and Ibrahim, 1977; Shakesby and Trissbach, 1982), much work remains to be done before a coherent picture of the causes and consequences of environmental change can emerge.

Second, the use of remote sensing techniques is essential, but these methodologies are no substitute for ground level monitoring. The most sophisticated remote sensing data collection and processing system is utterly dependent on detailed familiarity with the characteristics of local physical environmental systems if imagery is to be analyzed and interpreted accurately (Helldén, 1978). The need for data collected from the ground is particularly apparent in all aspects of environmental change that involve social indicators. Without careful examination of the local context, Viitanen (1981) might easily have attributed environmental change in northern Kordofan to the single factor of overstocking rather than to the complex set of variables, such as an expanding dryland agriculture and water development policy, that play a determining role. Similarly, changes in some aspects of the human environment such as settlement pattern can be observed from extra-terrestrial platforms, but most indicators are too subtle to be identified in this fashion and must be assessed through other, more direct, methodologies (Grant, 1978).

Third, highly quantitative data collection systems and models are probably inappropriate, particularly for most developing countries. Such systems work well in the industrialized world, where rigid property boundaries and continuity in ownership guarantee interannual statistical comparability. The United States Department of Agriculture's area sampling frame is an example of a quantitatively sophisticated data gathering methodology (Houseman, 1975) that enables planners to predict yields and the impact of environmental fluctuation with considerable confidence. However, in areas where tenure is communal or insecure, where field boundaries are imprecise, where fallow cycles are long, and where indigenous patterns of time-space allocation differ from the industrial world, such systems are likely to be inappropriate. Even if the data could be collected and calibrated, it is not clear that decision-making structures can either absorb or act upon the information.

Rather, what is needed are simple indicators capable of qualitative assessment. A prototype system of this type has been proposed to accompany a well-drilling project in eastern Kordofan (Mohammed, El Sammani and Shadad, 1982; El Tayeb, 1981). Based on careful scientific baseline studies, it identifies several simple indicators of change that require ground level monitoring. When these changes are observed, structured feedback to local and regional leaders should initiate remedial land management measures. To the extent that change indicators can be linked to the indicators that local resource users themselves employ, the system will increase in significance and usefulness. These ethnoscience indicators have received considerable attention (Johnson, 1977; Brokensha, Warren and Werner, 1980). Oguntoyinbo and Richards (1978) have demonstrated the existence and relevance of ethnoscience indicators among Nigerian farmers. Nonetheless, despite their sensitivity to environmental change, folk knowledge is not a substitute for, but is an essential complement to, the measures employed by technoscience systems (Johnson, 1979). The ability to integrate indigenous folk and educated elite in a common monitoring system would also keep the skilled manpower requirements of any monitoring system within reasonable bounds.

Finally, links to regional planning and on-going project evaluation are essential for successful environmental monitoring. This is a vitally important feature of any monitoring system, but one that is all too often neglected (O'Riordan and Sewell, 1981). Only by building evaluation and monitoring components into development projects can the effectiveness of the project and its impact on the surrounding, traditional environment be assessed (Adams and Howell, 1979; Carruthers, 1977; Howell, 1977). The information produced must have as its primary justification its practical relevance to decision-making rather than its theoretical sophistication. The potential use and users of the data produced by a monitoring system are in many ways more important than the specifics of the system itself.

Monitoring of resource trends can be a precursor to action at many different levels. At the local level the observer, through involvement in the process, may become much more aware of the dynamics of the situation and perhaps much more aware of the need to develop responses. At regional, national, and global levels, the monitoring process should also be geared to supply information which leads to specific analysis, increased understanding of the situation and the development of appropriate responses. UNEP as well as many national bodies and independent institutions are all involved in developing approaches to this task, but a great amount of careful work is required before functional monitoring systems can be established.

Training

Earlier in this paper we emphasized the global nature of many of the basic problems we discuss, although their impact may be very different in differing ecological and economic systems. A similar observation applies to training programs in resource management. This is a field (or set of fields) where training in a single discipline often provides too narrow a focus, and where interdisciplinary approaches can often fail to provide the detailed understanding that is needed. In some ways the problem is analogous to that of business schools--how do you train managers?--whether they are to manage companies or the environment. The solution may be similar to those favored by many business schools: a case study approach in formal learning and a large amount of on the job training.

Training for resource professionals and paraprofessionals is still very much based on specific fields or disciplines. Most often, agriculture, forestry, ecology, geography, hydrology and soil science are the basic specialties of the professionals involved, all of whom find in their work that they are called on to deal with much broader issues. So, too, are the monitoring systems that have been suggested to deal with specific environmental problems such as drought (Sandford, 1979; Hinchey, 1979). A basic problem is that of linking together the sets of expertise represented by the various parts of the scientific enterprise so that solutions can be sought for complex interaction problems. Individuals or systems that can bring a range of resource issues into one informational framework are still very few.

As Berry and Renwick (1980) point out, an integration of resource knowledge often occurs in the mind and practice of the local resource manager. He or she, knowing the territory, can apply an integrated approach to the management of that territory. This knowledge is not often written and is not often used by professionals with larger system viewpoints.

However, with the growing efficiency of remote sensing, we now have new ways of viewing resources as an integrated system. There is some hope that by using the image as a meeting place for different professionals more coordination will be possible. Training in resource management must at least for the time being start from the disciplinary perspective, the reality being that this is the way most people are trained. From that beginning we need to develop case-study approaches using small groups of professionals who work on the ground and with remotely sensed information. This will allow us to develop and disseminate our approaches to resource management.

As resource issues interlink in places on this earth and as the combined impact of those issues is felt by people, it becomes more and more urgent to develop a more coordinated information and analysis system and corresponding patterns of training and information gathering. In particular, there is a critical need for monitoring and training systems that produce communicators. These information facilitators must be able to bridge the ethnoscience-technoscience communication gap. This yawning gulf separates the indigenous resource user from the western educated professional, and is a major factor in environmental degradation.

REFERENCES

Adams, Martin E. and John Howell. 1979. Developing the Traditional Sector in the Sudan, Economic Development and Cultural Change 27:505-18.

Adams, Robert McC. 1965. Land Behind Baghdad: A History of Settlement on the Diyala Plains. Chicago: University of Chicago Press.

_____. 1981. Heartland of Cities: Surveys of Ancient Settlement and Land Use on the Central Floodplain of the Euphrates. Chicago: University of Chicago Press.

Adams, Robert McC. and Hans J. Nissen. 1972. The Uruk Countryside: The Natural Setting of Urban Societies. Chicago: University of Chicago Press.

Adrien, Pierre-Marie and Marion F. Baumgardner. 1977. Landsat, Computers, and Development Projects, Science 198 (No. 4316; 4 November):466-70.

Amin, Samir. 1973. Unequal Development: An Essay on the Social Formations of Peripheral Capitalism. New York: Monthly Review.

Amiran, David H. K. and Andrew W. Wilson, eds. 1973. Coastal Deserts: Their Natural and Human Environments. Tucson: University of Arizona Press.

Andrawis, Amazis Samuel and Mohamed Osman Khidir, eds. 1980. Proceedings of Sudan Symposium and Workshop on Remote Sensing. 2 vols. Brookings, S.D.: South Dakota State University, Remote Sensing Institute.

el-Arifi, S.A. 1979. Some Aspects of Local Government and Environmental Management in the Sudan, in J.A. Mabbutt (ed.), *Proceedings of the Khartoum Workshop on Arid Lands Management*. Tokyo: The United Nations University. Pp. 36-39.

Baker, Randall. 1976. The Administrative Trap, *The Ecologist* 6:247-51

_____. 1979. *Trends in Research and in the Application of Science and Technology for Arid Zone Development*. MAB Technical Notes 10. Paris: UNESCO.

Baker, T. Lindsay, Steven R. Rae, Joseph E. Minor and Semour V. Connor. 1973. *Water for the Southwest: Historical Survey and Guide to Historic Sites*. ASCE Historical Publication No. 3. New York: American Society of Civil Engineers.

Barker, David, Julius Oguntoyinko and Paul Richards. 1977. *The Utility of the Nigerian Peasant Farmer's Knowledge in the Monitoring of Agricultural Resources*. London: Monitoring and Assessment Research Center.

Berry, Brian J.L. 1967. *Geography of Market Center and Retail Distribution*. Englewood Cliffs, N.J.: Prentice-Hall.

Berry, Leonard. 1983. *Assessment of Desertification in the Sudano Sahelian Region 1977-1984*. Worcester, MA: Clark University for the United Nations Sudano Sahelian Office (UNSO).

Berry, Leonard and Richard B. Ford. 1977. *Recommendations for a System to Monitor Critical Indicators in Areas Prone to Desertification*. Worcester, MA: Clark University.

Berry, L. and H. Renwick. 1980. Environmental Information: Integrating Knowledge, in Leonard Berry and Robert W. Kates (eds.), *Making the Most of the Least: Alternative Ways to Development*. New York: Holmes and Meier. Pp. 183-200.

Bilsky, Lester J. 1980. Ecological Crisis and Response in Ancient China, in Lester J. Bilsky (ed.), *Historical Ecology: Essays on Environment and Social Change*. Port Washington, N.Y.; London: National University Publications, Kennikat Press. Pp. 60-70.

Biswas, Asit K., ed. 1978. *United Nations Water Conference: Summary and Main Documents*. U.N. Water Conference, Mar del Plata, 1977. Oxford; New York: Pergamon.

Boserup, Ester. 1965. *The Conditions of Agricultural Growth: The Economics of Agrarian Change under Population Pressure*. Chicago: Aldine.

Bottrall, Anthony. 1978a. Technology and Management in Irrigation Agriculture, *ODI Review* 2-1978: 22-50.

Bottrall, Anthony. 1978b. The Management and Operation of Irrigation Schemes in Less Developed Countries, in Carl Widstrand (ed.), Water and Society: Conflicts in Development. Part I. The Social and Ecological Effects of Water Development in Developing Countries. Water Development, Supply and Management, Vol. 7. Oxford: Pergamon. Pp. 309-32.

Bowden, Martyn J. et al. 1981. The Effect of Climate Fluctuations on Human Populations: Two Hypotheses, in T.M.L. Wigley et al. (eds.), Climate and History: Studies in Past Climates and Their Impact on Man. Cambridge: Cambridge University Press. Pp. 479-513.

Bradley, P.N. 1977. Vegetation and Environmental Change in the West African Sahel, in P. O'Keefe and B. Wisner (eds.), Landuse and Development. African Environment Special Report 5. London: International African Institute. Pp. 34-54.

Breman, H. and C.T. de Wit. 1983. Rangeland Productivity and Exploitation in the Sahel, Science 221 (No. 4618; 30 September): 1341-47.

Brokensha, David W., D. M. Warren and Oswald Werner. 1980. Indigenous Knowledge Systems and Development. Lanham, Md.: University Press of America.

Burton, Ian. 1962. Types of Agricultural Occupance of Flood Plains in the United States. University of Chicago, Department of Geography, Research Paper No. 75.

Burton, Ian, Robert W. Kates and Gilbert F. White. 1978. The Environment as Hazard. New York: Oxford University Press.

Buttimer, Anne. 1971. Society and Milieu in the French Geographic Tradition. Association of American Geographers Monograph Series No. 6. Chicago: Rand McNally.

Butzer, Karl W. 1976. Early Hydraulic Civilization in Egypt: A Study in Cultural Ecology. Chicago: University of Chicago Press.

Carlstein, Tommy. 1982. Time Resources, Society and Ecology: On the Capacity for Human Interaction in Space and Time. Vol. 1. Preindustrial Societies. London: George Allen and Unwin.

Carruthers, Ian. 1977. Applied Project Appraisal: The State of the Art, ODI Review 2-1977:12-27.

Castro, Alfonso Peter, N. Thomas Hakansson and David Brokensha. 1981. Indicators of Rural Inequality, World Development 4:401-27.

Clark, W.C. and C.S. Holling. 1979. Process Models, Equilibrium Structures, and Population Dynamics: On the Formulation and Testing of Realistic Theory in Ecology, Fortschritte der Zoologie 25:29-52.

Croze, Harvey, Michael Norton-Griffiths and Michael Gwynne. 1978. Ecological Monitoring in East Africa, New Scientist 77 (No. 1088; 2 February): 283-85.

Denevan, William M. 1973. Development and the Imminent Demise of the Amazon Rain Forest, Professional Geographer 25:130-35.

_____, ed. 1976. The Native Population of the Americas in 1492. Madison: University of Wisconsin Press.

Dickinson, Joshua C., III. 1974. Fisheries of Lake Izabal, Guatemala, Geographical Review 64:385-409.

Dregne, Harold E. 1977. Desertification of Arid Lands, Economic Geography 53:322-31.

Dunne, Thomas. 1977. Studying Patterns of Soil Erosion in Kenya, Soil Conservation and Management in Developing Countries. FAO Soils Bulletin No. 33. Rome: FAO. Pp. 109-20.

Engelbert, Ernest A. 1982. Competition for California Water: Alternative Resolutions. Berkeley: University of California Press.

Engelbert, Ernest A., editor, with Ann Foley Scheuring. 1984. Water Scarcity: Impacts on Western Agriculture. Berkeley, Los Angeles, London: University of California Press.

Eckholm, Eric P. 1976. Losing Ground: Environmental Stress and World Food Prospects. New York: Norton.

Feachem, Richard. 1978. Domestic Water Supplies, Health and Poverty, in Carl Widstrand (ed.), Water Supply and Society: Conflicts in Development. Part I. The Social and Ecological Effects of Water Development in Developing Countries. Water Development, Supply and Management, Vol. 7. Oxford: Pergamon. Pp. 351-62.

Gibson, McGuire. 1974. Violation of Fallow and Engineered Disaster in Mesopotamian Civilization, in Theodore E. Downing and McGuire Gibson (eds.), Irrigation's Impact on Society. Tucson: University of Arizona Press. Pp. 7-18.

Grant, James P. 1978. Disparity Reduction Rates in Social Indicators: A Proposal for Measuring and Targeting Progress in Meeting Basic Needs. Monograph No. 11. Washington, D.C.: Overseas Development Council.

Hare, F. Kenneth. 1977. Climate and Desertification, in UNCOD, Desertification: Its Causes and Consequences. Oxford: Pergamon. Pp. 63-167.

_____. 1983. Climate and Desertification: A Revised Analysis. World Climate Programme No. 44. Geneva: World Meteorological Organization/United Nations Environment Programme.

Harrison, Peter D. and B.L. Turner, II. 1978. Pre-Hispanic Maya Agriculture. Albuquerque: University of New Mexico Press.

Haynes, C. Vance, Jr. 1982. Great Sand Sea and Selima Sand Sheet, Eastern Sahara: Geochronology of Desertification, Science 217 (No. 4560; 13 August):629-33.

Haynes, Kingsley E. and Dale Whittington. 1981. International Management of the Nile-Stage Three, Geographical Review 71:17-32.

Heady, Harold F. and James Bartolome. 1977. The Vale Rangeland Rehabilitation Program: The Desert Repaired in Southeastern Oregon. USDA Forest Service Resource Bulletin PNW-70. Portland, Oregon: Pacific Northwest Forest and Range Experiment Station, Forest Service, U.S. Department of Agriculture.

Helldén, Ulf. 1978. Evaluation of Landsat-2 Imagery for Desertification Studies in Northern Kordofan, Sudan. Rapporter och Notiser No. 38. Lund: Lunds Universitets Naturgeografiska Institution.

_____. 1981. Satellite Data for Regional Studies of Desertification and its Control--Approaches to Rehabilitation of Degraded Ecosystems in Africa. Rapporter och Notiser 50. Lund: Lunds Universitets Naturgeografiska Institution.

Helldén, Ulf and Katarina Olsson. 1982. The Potential of Landsat MSS Data for Wood Resources Monitoring: A Study in Arid and Semi-Arid Environment in Kordofan, The Sudan. Rapporter och Notiser No. 52. Lund: Lunds Universitets Naturgeografiska Institution.

Hewitt, Kenneth and Ian Burton. 1971. The Hazardousness of a Place: A Regional Ecology of Damaging-Events. University of Toronto, Department of Geography, Research Publication No. 6.

Hinchey, Madalon T., ed. 1979. Proceedings of the Symposium on Drought in Botswana. National Museum, Gabarone, Botswana, June 5th to 8th, 1978. Gabarone: The Botswana Society in Collaboration with Clark University Press.

Houseman, Earl E. 1975. Area Sampling Frame in Agriculture. SRS No. 20. Washington, D.C.: Statistical Reporting Service, United States Department of Agriculture.

Howe, Charles W. and K. William Easter. 1971. Interbasin Transfers of Water: Economic Issues and Impacts. Baltimore: Johns Hopkins Press for Resources for the Future.

Howell, John. 1977. Administration and Rural Development Planning: A Sudanese Case, Agricultural Administration 4:99-120.

Hoyle, S. 1977. The Khashm el-Girba Agricultural Scheme: An Example of an Attempt to Settle Nomads, in P. O'Keefe and B. Wisner (eds.), Land-use and Development. African Environment Special Report 5. London: International African Institute. Pp. 116-31.

Hunting Technical Services. 1980. South Kordofan Central Districts Indicative Development Plan. Herts.: HTS; Khartoum: Democratic Republic of Sudan, Ministry of Agriculture, Forestry and Natural Resources.

Hutchinson, Joseph, A.H. Bunting, A.R. Jolly, and H.C. Pereira, organizers. 1977. Resource Development in Semi-arid Lands. London: The Royal Society.

Ibrahim, Fouad. 1978. Anthropogenic Causes of Desertification in Western Sudan, GeoJournal 2:243-54.

International Geographical Union, Working Group on Desertification in and around Arid Lands. 1976. Desertification: A World Bibliography. Tucson: University of Arizona, Office of Arid Lands Studies.

International Geographical Union, Working Group on Desertification in and around Arid Lands. 1980. Desertification: World Bibliography Update 1976-1980. Compiled and edited by Patricia Paylore and J.A. Mabbutt. Tucson: University of Arizona, Office of Arid Lands Studies.

Jacobson, Thorkild and Robert McC. Adams. 1958. Salt and Silt in Ancient Mesopotamian Agriculture, Science 128 (No. 3334; 21 November):1251-58.

Janzen, Daniel H. 1973. Tropical Agroecosystems, Science 182 (No. 4118; 21 December):1212-18.

Johnson, Douglas L. 1973. The Response of Pastoral Nomads to Drought in the Absence of Outside Intervention. New York: United Nations, Special Sahelian Office (ST/SSO/18).

_____. 1979. Management Strategies for Drylands: Available Options and Unanswered Questions, in J.A. Mabbutt (ed.), Proceedings of the Khartoum Workshop on Arid Lands Management. Tokyo: The United Nations University. Pp. 26-35.

_____. 1981. Monitoring Environmental Change: Thoughts on Physical and Social Indicators in the Sudan. ETMA - Sudan Working Paper No. 1. Mimeo.

Johnson, Douglas L. and Harvey Gould. 1984. The Effect of Climate Fluctuations on Human Populations: A Case Study of Mesopotamian Society, in Asit K. Biswas (ed.), Climate and Development. Dublin: Tycooly International Publishing. Pp. 117-138.

Johnson, Kirsten. 1977. Disintegration of a Traditional Resource-Use Complex: The Otomi of the Mezquital Valley, Hidalgo, Mexico, Economic Geography 53:364-67.

Kates, Robert W. 1962. <u>Hazard and Choice Perception in Flood Plain Management</u>. University of Chicago, Department of Geography, Research Paper No. 78.
_____. 1965. Industrial Flood Losses: Damage Estimation in the Lehigh Valley. University of Chicago, Department of Geography, Research Paper No. 98.
_____. 1980a. <u>Drought Impact in the Sahelian-Sudanic Zone of West Africa: A Comparative Analysis of 1910-15 and 1968-74</u>. Office of Evaluation Working Paper No. 32. Washington, D.C.: USAID; reprinted as Background Paper No. 2. Worcester, Mass.: Clark University, Center for Technology, Environment and Development.
_____. 1980b. Climate and Society: Lessons from Recent Events, <u>Weather</u> 35:17-25.
_____. 1983. Nature, Society and Technology: Theories of the Human Environment, Paper presented at the Conference on Nature, Culture and Technology, Hasselby Castle, Stockholm, Sweden, 12-14 September, 1983.
Kates, Robert W., Douglas L. Johnson and Kirsten J. Haring. 1977. Population, Society and Desertification, in UNCOD, <u>Desertification: Its Causes and Consequences</u>. Oxford: Pergamon. Pp. 261-317.
Kemp, William B. 1973. The Flow of Energy in a Hunting Society, <u>Scientific American</u> 225 (September):104-15.
Khalifa, A.H. and Morag C. Simpson. 1972. Perverse Supply in Nomadic Societies, <u>Oxford Agrarian Studies</u> 1:46-56.
Kjekshus, Helge. 1977. <u>Ecology Control and Economic Development in East African History: The Case of Tanganyika 1850-1950</u>. London: Heinemann.
LeHouérou, H.N. 1977. Biological Recovery versus Desertification, <u>Economic Geography</u> 53:413-20.
Maas, Arthur, Maynard M. Hufschmidt, Robert Dorfman, Harold A. Thomas, Jr., Stephen A. Marglin and Gordon Maskew Fair. 1962. <u>Design of Water Resource Systems: New Techniques for Relating Economic Objectives, Engineering Analysis and Government Planning</u>. Cambridge, MA.: Harvard University Press.
Mabbutt, J.A. 1978. The Impact of Desertification as Revealed by Mapping, <u>Environmental Conservation</u> 5: 45-56.
Mabbutt, J.A., ed. 1979. <u>Proceedings of the Khartoum Workshop on Arid Lands Management</u>. The University of Khartoum-The United Nations University 22-26 October, 1978. Tokyo: The United Nations University.

McCauley, J.F. et al. 1982. Subsurface Valleys and Geoarcheology of the Eastern Sahara Revealed by Shuttle Radar, Science 218 (No. 4576; 3 December): 1004-20.

McJunkin, Frederick E. 1975. Water, Engineers, Development, and Disease in the Tropics: Schistosomiasis Engineering Applied to Planning, Design, Construction and Operation of Irrigation, Hydroelectric and other Water Development Schemes. Washington, D.C.: Agency for International Development, Department of State.

Major, David C. 1977. Multiobjective Water Resource Planning. Water Resources Monograph 4. Washington, D.C.: American Geophysical Union.

Manshard, Walther. 1979. Tropical Agriculture: A Geophysical Introduction and Appraisal. London: Longman.

Marsh, George Perkins. 1965. Man and Nature: Or, Physical Geography as Modified by Human Action. Ed. by David Lowenthal. Originally published in 1864. Cambridge, MA.: The Belknap Press of Harvard University Press.

Meadows, Dennis L. 1974. Dynamics of Growth in a Finite World. Cambridge, MA.: Wright-Allen.

Mensching, Horst and Fouad Ibrahim. 1977. The Problem of Desertification in and around Arid Lands. Applied Sciences and Development 10:7-43.

Mikesell, Marvin W. 1961. Northern Morocco: A Cultural Geography. University of California Publications in Geography, Vol. 14. Berkeley and Los Angeles: University of California Press.

Mohammed, Yaqoub Abdalla, Mohammed Osman El Sammani, and Mohammed Zein Shadad. 1982. Baseline Survey and Monitoring Programme for North Kordofan Rural Water Supply Project. Khartoum: Institute of Environmental Studies, University of Khartoum for CARE.

Moseley, Michael E. 1975. Chan Chan: Andean Alternative of the Preindustrial City, Science 187 (No. 4173; 24 January):219-25.

Murdock, Muneera Salem. 1979. The Impact of Agricultural Development on a Pastoral Society: The Shukriya of the Eastern Sudan. A Report Submitted to the Agency for International Development. Mimeo. Binghamton, N.Y.: Institute for Development Anthropology.

National Research Council. 1968. Water and Choice in the Colorado Basin: An Example of Alternatives in Water Management. Publication 1689. Washington, D.C.: National Academy of Sciences.

Nietschmann, Bernard. 1973. Between Land and Water: The Subsistence Ecology of the Miskito Indians, Eastern Nicaragua. New York: Seminar.

Novikoff, G. 1976. Traditional Grazing Practices and Their Adaptation to Modern Conditions in Tunisia and the Sahelian Countries, in A. Rapp, H. N. LeHouérou and B. Lundholm (eds.). Can Desert Encroachment Be Stopped? A Study with Emphasis on Africa. Ecological Bulletins No. 24. Stockholm: SIES and UNEP. Pp. 55-69.

Noy-Meir, Imanuel. 1973. Desert Ecosystems: Environment and Producers, Annual Review of Ecology and Systematics 4:25-51.

_____. 1974. Desert Ecosystems: Higher Trophic Levels, Annual Review of Ecology and Systematics 5:195-214.

_____. 1979. Stability in Arid Ecosystems and the Effects of Man on it, Proceedings, International Congress of Ecology, The Hague. Pp. 220-26.

Obeng, Letitia E. 1978. Starvation or Bilharzia? - A Rural Development Dilemma, in Carl Widstrand (ed.), Water Supply and Society: Conflicts in Development. Part I. The Social and Ecological Effects of Water Development in Developing Countries. Water Development, Supply and Management, Vol. 7. Oxford: Pergamon. Pp. 343-50.

Oguntoyinbo, Julius and Paul Richards. 1978. Drought and the Nigerian Farmer, Journal of Arid Environments 1:165-94.

Olsson, Lennart. 1983. Desertification or Climate? Investigation Regarding the Relationship Between Land Degradation and Climate in the Central Sudan. Lund Studies in Geography, Series A Physical Geography No. 60. Lund: University of Lund, Sweden, Department of Physical Geography/C.W.K. Gleerup.

O'Riordan, Timothy and W.R. Derrick Sewell. 1981. Project Appraisal and Policy Review. New York: John Wiley.

Ortloff, Charles R., Michael E. Moseley and Robert A. Feldman. 1983. The Chicama-Moche Intervalley Canal: Social Explanations and Physical Paradigms, American Antiquity 48:375-89.

Pelissier, P. 1977. Development of Arid and Semi-arid Land: Obstacles and Prospects. MAB Technical Note 10. Paris: UNESCO.

Pereira, H.C. 1973. Land Use and Water Resources in Temperate and Tropical Climates. Cambridge: Cambridge University Press.

Pillsbury, Arthur F. 1981. The Salinity of Rivers, Scientific American 245 (No. 1):55-65.

Platt, Rutherford H. 1976. The National Flood Insurance Program: Some Midstream Perspectives, American Institute of Planners, Journal, 42:303-13.

Rapp, Anders, Len Berry and Paul Temple. 1973. *Studies of Soil Erosion and Sedimentation in Tanzania.* [Dar es Salaam, Tanzania]: Bureau of Resource Assessment and Land Use Planning, University of Dar es Salaam.

Rapp, A., H.N. LeHouérou and B. Lundholn, eds. 1976. *Can Desert Encroachment Be Stopped? A Study with Emphasis on Africa.* Ecological Bulletins No. 24. Stockholm: UNEP/SIES.

Reining, Priscilla, ed. 1978. *Handbook on Desertification Indicators Based on the Science Associations' Nairobi Seminar on Desertification.* Washington, D.C.: American Association for the Advancement of Science.

Ruthenberg, Hans. 1971. *Farming Systems in the Tropics.* Oxford: Clarendon.

Saarinen, Thomas Frederick. 1966. *Perception of the Drought Hazard on the Great Plains.* University of Chicago, Department of Geography, Research Paper No. 106.

Sanders, William T. 1976. The Agricultural History of the Basin of Mexico, in Eric R. Wolf (ed.), *The Valley of Mexico: Studies in Pre-Hispanic Ecology and Society.* Albuquerque: University of New Mexico Press. Pp. 101-59.

Sanford, S. 1979. Towards a Definition of Drought, in M.T. Hinchey (ed.), *Proceedings of the Symposium on Drought in Botswana.* Gabarone: The Botswana Society and Clark University Press. Pp. 33-40.

Shakesby, R.A. and A. Trilsbach. 1982. Irrigation is the Desert's Secret Agent, *Geographical Magazine* 54 (No. 2):77-83.

Sheridan, David. 1981. *Desertification of the United States.* Washington, D.C.: Council on Environmental Quality.

Slaymaker, Olaf, Thomas Dunne and Anders Rapp, eds. 1980. *Geomorphic Experiments on Hillslopes.* Zeitschrift für Geomorphologie Supplementband. Berlin: Gebr. Borntraeger.

Smith, Nigel J.H. 1981. Colonization Lessons from a Tropical Forest, *Science* 214 (No. 4522; 13 November):755-61.

Sorbo, G.M. 1977. Nomads on the Scheme: A Study of Irrigation, Agriculture and Pastoralism in Eastern Sudan, in P. O'Keefe and B. Wisner (eds.), *Landuse and Development.* African Environment Special Report 5. London: International African Institute. Pp. 135-50.

Swift, Jeremy. 1979. The development of livestock trading in nomad pastoral economy: The Somali case, in *Pastoral Production and Society*. Proceedings of the International Meeting on Nomadic Pastoralism - Paris 1-3 December, 1976. Cambridge: Cambridge University Press; Paris: Editions de la Maison des Sciences de l'Homme. Pp. 447-65.

_____. 1980. *The Economics of Traditional Nomadic Pastoralism: The Twareg of the Adrar N Iforas (Mali)*. D. Phil. thesis, University of Sussex (Great Britain).

El Tayeb, Shorahabeel Ali. 1981. *The Impact of Water Points on Environmental Degradation: A Case Study of Eastern Kordofan, Sudan*. Environmental Monograph Series No. 2. Khartoum: Institute of Environmental Studies, University of Khartoum.

Thimm, Heinz-Ulrich. 1979. *Development Projects in the Sudan: An Analysis of Their Reports with Implications for Research and Training in Arid Land Management*. Tokyo: The United Nations University.

Thomas, William L., Jr., ed. 1956. *Man's Role in Changing the Face of the Earth*. Chicago: University of Chicago Press.

Townshend, John R.G., ed. 1981. *Terrain Analysis and Remote Sensing*. London: George Allen and Unwin.

Turner, II, B.L. 1974. Prehistoric Intensive Agriculture in the Maya Lowlands, *Science* 185 (No. 4146; 12 July):118-24.

Turner, II, B.L., Robert Q. Hanham, and Anthony V. Portararo. 1977. Population Pressure and Agricultural Intensity, *Annals of the Association of American Geographers* 67:384-96.

United Nations Conference on Desertification, Secretariat, ed. 1977a. *Desertification: Its Causes and Consequences*. Oxford: Pergamon.

UNCOD. 1977b. *Case Study on Desertification: Greater Mussayeb Project, Iraq*. Nairobi: United Nations Conference on Desertification.

UNCOD. 1977c. *Case Study on Desertification: Mona Reclamation Experimental Project, Pakistan*. Nairobi: United Nations Conference on Desertification.

USAID. Sahel Development Program. 1980. *Annual Report to Congress*. Washington, D.C.: AID.

U.S. Department of the Interior. 1980. *Desertification in the U.S.: Status and Issues*. Working Review Draft.

Viitanen, Erkki. 1981. *Nomadism and Desertification: A Case-Study of Northern Kordofan, Sudan*. University of Helsinki, Department of Geography, Development Geography Pro Gradu Thesis.

Waddell, Eric. 1977. The Hazards of Scientism: A Review Article, Human Ecology 5:69-76.

Wallerstein, Immanuel M. 1973. The Modern World System: Capitalist Agriculture and the Origins of the European World Economy in the Sixteenth Century. New York: Academic.

Ward, Roy. 1978. Floods: A Geographical Perspective. New York: John Wiley.

Warren, Andrew and Judith Maizels. 1977. Ecological Change and Desertification, in UNCOD, Desertification: Its Causes and Consequences. Oxford: Pergamon. Pp. 169-260.

Warrick, Richard A. 1975. Drought Hazard in the United States: A Research Assessment. Boulder: The University of Colorado, Institute of Behavioral Science.

Warrick, Richard A. and Martyn J. Bowden. 1981. The Changing Impacts of Droughts in the Great Plains, in Merlin P. Lawson and Maurice E. Baker (eds.), The Great Plains: Perspectives and Prospects. Lincoln: Center for Great Plains Studies, University of Nebraska - Lincoln. Pp. 111-37.

Waterbury, John. 1979. Hydropolitics of the Nile Valley. Syracuse, N.Y.: Syracuse University Press.

Welcomme, R.L. 1979. Fisheries Ecology of Floodplain Rivers. London: Longman.

White, Gilbert F. 1945. Human Adjustment to Floods: A Geographical Approach to the Flood Problem. University of Chicago, Department of Geography, Research Paper No. 29.

_____. 1960a. Science and the Future of Arid Lands. Paris: UNESCO.

_____. 1960b. Alternative Uses of Limited Water Supplies, Impact of Science on Society 10:243-63.

_____. 1961. Papers on Flood Problems. University of Chicago, Department of Geography, Research Paper No. 70.

_____. 1964. Choice of Adjustment to Floods. University of Chicago, Department of Geography, Research Paper No. 93.

_____. 1971. Strategies of American Water Development. Ann Arbor: University of Michigan.

_____, ed. 1974. Natural Hazards: Local, National, Global. New York: Oxford University Press.

_____, ed. 1977. Environmental Effects of Complex River Development. Boulder, Colorado: Westview Press.

_____. 1978a. Environmental Effects of Arid Land Irrigation in Developing Countries. MAB Technical Notes 8. Paris: UNESCO.

_____. 1978b. Natural Hazards and the Third World--A Reply, Human Ecology 6:229-30.

White, Gilbert F. 1980. Environment, Science 209: (No. 4452; 4 July):183-190.
White, Gilbert F., David J. Bradley and Ann U. White. 1972. Drawers of Water: Domestic Water Use in East Africa. Chicago: University of Chicago Press.
White, Gilbert F. and J. Eugene Haas. 1975. Assessment of Research on Natural Hazards. Cambridge, MA.: The MIT Press.
Whittlesey, Derwent. 1936. Major Agricultural Regions of the Earth, Annals, Association of American Geographers 26:199-240. Reprinted in M.W. Mikesell and P.L. Wagner (eds.), Readings in Cultural Geography. Chicago: University of Chicago Press, 1962.
Williams, O.B., H. Suijdendorp, and D.G. Wilcox. 1977. Gascoyne Basin (Case Study on Desertification). An associated case study presented by the Government of Australia to the United Nations Conference on Desertification. Nairobi: UNCOD/UNEP, 1977.
Wilson, Andrew W. 1977. Technology, Regional Interdependence, and Population Growth: Tucson, Arizona, Economic Geography 53:388-92.
Worthington, E.B. 1977. Arid Land Irrigation in Developing Countries: Environmental Problems and Effects. Oxford: Pergamon.
Wright, Robert A., ed. 1978. The Reclamation of Disturbed Arid Lands. Albuquerque: University of New Mexico Press.

4
Anthropological Approaches to the Study of Human Impacts

Emilio F. Moran

INTRODUCTION[1]

Anthropological interest in the study of human impacts goes back to the earliest ethnographic descriptions of the subsistence activities of human populations. For most of this century, such studies have been characteristically micro-level, more concerned with the impact of the State on community-level societies than vice versa, and guided by a holistic perspective. Since anthropology was born in reaction to the environmental and racial determinism coming from vulgar forms of anthropo-geography (cf. reviews of the literature in Moran 1982:24-8; Glacken 1967; Thomas 1925), anthropology during its early decades seemed bent on proving that environment was not very important to the ways societies were constituted (cf. Boas 1896:901-8; Goldenweiser 1937). It did not take long for anthropologists to return to a more whole-systems orientation and to turn their attention to the interaction between people and habitat.

Largely as a result of the writings of Julian Steward (1938; 1955), anthropologists began to get away from treating environment and culture as if they were totalities in complete interaction. Steward's approach, which he labeled cultural ecology, noted that human societies did not interact with total environments but only with particular features of it. In turn, he noted, behavior and ideology seemed to be primarily guided by the need to obtain subsistence. Human organization for subsistence orders individuals in a society in such a way that other aspects of social and cultural life must contend with the requirements of labor organization for obtaining resources from the environment.

The result of this postulated relationship was the development of a sub-area within anthropology known variously as cultural ecology, ecological anthropology and human ecology (Netting 1977; Hardesty 1977; Moran 1982). The immediate impact of Steward's ideas was restricted to the fields of archeology and social anthropology. During the 1930's and 1940's very little interest in adaptation, the environment, or ecology was expressed by physical anthropologists (Little 1981). Archeologists and social anthropologists undertook studies in the 1940's and 1950's using the cultural ecological research strategy. This research led to major changes in our ideas about adaptive systems. Hunter and gatherers are no longer understood to live at the margin of survival but, rather, as having complex adjustments achieved through stabilization of population size, low levels of input for extracting resources, and systems of exchange that vary with resource availability (cf. Lee and DeVore 1968, 1976; Lee 1980; Damas 1969). Cultural ecologists also changed our views about shifting cultivation, beginning with the study of Conklin (1957) among the Hanunoo; Geertz (1963) in Indonesia; and Netting (1968) among the Kofyar. The result has been to treat shifting cultivation no longer as a general category with commonly shared practices but as constituting a variable set of adjustments to specific environmental, agronomic, demographic, and cultural constraints (cf. the review in Netting 1974).

By the late 1950's not only was cultural ecology flowering as an anthropological pursuit, but so were alternative approaches to the study of human interaction with environment coming to the fore. During this period the "new physical anthropology" made its appearance through its interest in the study of adaptation to environment (Washburn 1951; Coon, Garn and Birdsell 1950; Montague 1951; Baker 1958; Roberts 1953). The new physical anthropology focused on studies of body morphology and composition, physiological response to environmental stress, demographic and health parameters of adaptation, and genetic attributes of populations (Harrison et al. 1964). These interests crystallized around the study of human biology, generally, and human adaptability in particular (cf. the excellent review in Little 1981).

Whereas the majority of archeologists and social anthropologists continued to benefit from the approach of cultural ecology in their investigations, during the 1960's a number of social anthropologists began to find in biological ecology a more useful basis for their study of human systems. What they proposed was the use of the ecosystem concept as a unit of analysis and the treatment of human populations within the total ecological system (cf. Geertz 1963; Rappaport 1967). Little and Morren succinctly stated this new research strategy:

> We are concerned with those cultural and
> biological responses, factors, processes, and
> cycles that affect or are directly connected
> with the survival, reproduction, development,
> longevity or spatial positions of people. This
> set of questions, rather than the traditional
> division of scientific labor defines the subject
> matter.
>
> (Little and Morren 1976:5)

The new research strategy was initially called ecological anthropology to emphasize its foundations in ecological rather than anthropological theory. During its early applications, researchers found it useful to be guided by the use of energy as a common currency. Then current ecological systems theory suggested that flows of energy led to clearly defined trophic structure, biotic diversity, and material cycles (E. Odum 1971:8). Energy seemed to be, at the time, the only measurable common denominator that structured ecosystems and could serve to define its functions (H. Odum 1971). Rappaport (1971), Kemp (1971), Thomas (1973), Moran (1973), Little and Morren (1976), and others made use of energy flow analysis to organize their studies of human adaptability.

What these studies demonstrated was the descriptive usefulness of energy flow studies both before, during, and after field investigations. What they also proved--after a decade of efforts--was that the forcing functions of ecosystems varied from site to site and that it was naive to postulate energy as a constraint that served to organize all human or "natural" ecosystems. For example, the flow of water is a more determining force in the structure and function of desert ecosystems than is energy (Noy-Meir 1973, 1974).

The research of the new physical anthropologists found a home in the International Biological Program (IBP) which began ca. 1964. A Human Adaptability section was included in the IBP, intended to cover "the ecology of mankind" from the perspectives of health and welfare; environmental physiology, population genetics, developmental biology and demography (Weiner 1965). What is notable about these important studies was their exclusion of social/cultural anthropologists from the study of human adaptability (Little 1982).

The reasons for this omission are not, however, difficult to infer from IBP documents. At the time the IBP was formulated, disciplinary compartmentalization did not permit easy communication even between allied areas like aquatic and terrestrial biology. The gap between the biological and the social sciences was even greater, with little in common in either method or theory (Worthington 1975). Of all the branches of anthropology, only physical anthropology, especially in the areas of physiological adaptation and population genetics, was ready in 1964 to fully participate in what was an anbitious biological program (Baker and Weiner 1966). But even in the 1964 scientific symposium at Burg Wartenstein doubts were expressed about the omission of the social component in the IBP (Weiner in Worthington 1975:16).

Perhaps more than any other project could have done, the IBP began the process of bringing scientists together to communicate about problems which were clearly interdisciplinary, international and fundamental to our long-term survival. During the period of the IBP the process did not advance to the point that a paradigm for such work was produced but, at least, an increasing recognition developed in many quarters that the rigid sectional structure of IBP mitigated against truly interdisciplinary pursuits (Worthington 1975:xix).

Before the IBP officially ended in 1974, already the UNESCO-sponsored Man and the Biosphere Program (MAB) had started. MAB was conceived as a scientific program that would develop a scientific basis for the rational use and conservation of resources. It was guided by the structure and the lessons from the IBP. Thus, it continued the use of biome units for many of its projects, guided by the optimism prevalent at the time in the productivity of studying "natural ecosystems." On the other hand, MAB included the recognition that some resource management problems existed across environments and were particularly significant for human welfare. It, thus, included in addition to seven biome-oriented projects, six topic oriented projects--two of which had particular relevance to the study of human adaptive strategies.

MAB is now into its thirteenth year and it is composed of nearly 1000 field projects in some 77 countries. Unlike the IBP, MAB has more limited goals and funds (Worthington 1975; diCastri 1976). MAB does not aim at generating comprehensive biome models. Rather, its aims are more site-specific--recognizing that resource management problems are human problems and subject to the particularities of social, political, historical, and other factors that filter the interpretation of what the ecosystem is that is to be managed. How well integrated the social and ecological projects are depends on the directorates in each country or site. Some have clearly chosen to design the projects in ways that allow for the linkage between the biological and the social (Moser and Peterson 1981), whereas other projects are notable by the conspicuous absence of serious social analysis of management constraints and characteristics of the human population (Andersson 1981).

Bennett (1980) recently summarized the characteristics of MAB reports and found that they fell into three categories: human acts cast in biological garb; human acts cast in economic garb; and integrative studies. By and large, the bulk of the reports fall in the first two categories and treat humans with very little knowledge of social organization and the role of ideology in directing human management decisions. The closest studies to the integrative type are the reports on island ecosystems. None have been produced, according to Bennett (1980), that really fulfill the lofty goals of MAB interdisciplinary research. Social activities are viewed as impacting Nature, rather than being the characteristic way in which humans define Nature for their own ends. Bennett has advocated the use of "socionatural systems" (1976, 1980) as a conceptual way to turn thinking around from a linear model to one that is truly interactive (see Figure 4.1). Since humankind is an all pervasive modifier of so-called "natural" systems, it behooves research on the human biosphere to begin by selecting problems recognized by human populations and studying them in whatever biome they may appear. In the rest of this paper I will deal with recent ecological, anthropological, and agronomic research in the Amazon Basin with a view to showing the constraints of past approaches to the study of human impacts on this important biome and make some tentative suggestions that build on Bennett's concept of socionatural systems.

RESEARCH ON TROPICAL RAIN FORESTS

From the outset, MAB Project 1, on the impact of human activities in tropical forest ecosystems, was given high priority due to the perceived danger that such areas of the tropics faced due to development activities initiated by Third World countries. A number of projects were started, among them the San Carlos de Rio Negro Project in the Venezuelan Amazon; the East Kalimantan Project in Indonesia; and the Tai Project in Ivory Coast. These projects contrast in how they approached their research goals and what variables they tried to integrate. The San Carlos de Rio Negro Project was designed as a study of the nutrient cycling of a rain forest based on comparative plot studies (Uhl 1980). By contrast, the Kalimantan and Tai Projects chose areas that were under serious human pressure due to logging and farming penetration into the forest. The Tai project began by anthropological studies of the traditional populations' forms of resource use and contrasted them with those of the immigrants to the

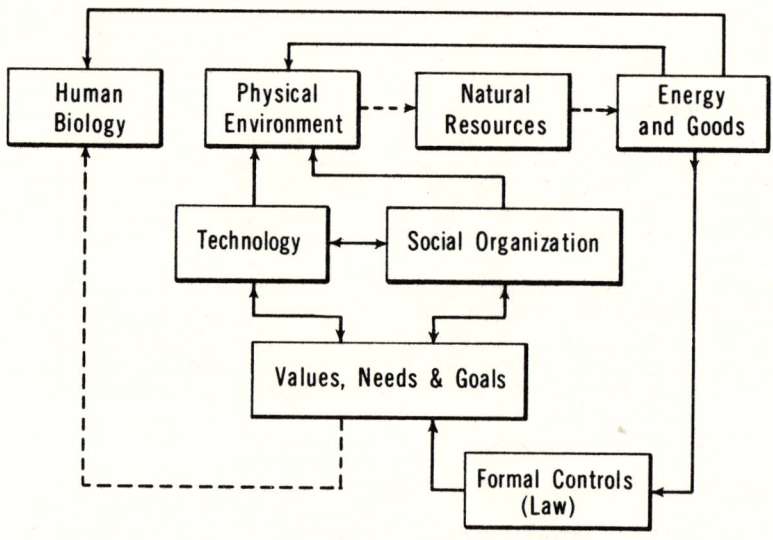

FIGURE 4.1 Model of socionatural systems
(after Bennett)

region. From these studies they were able to establish the need to control the immigrant flow and to reduce the impact of practices by the immigrants that were not sensitive to the forest's regenerative capacity (Dosso et al. 1981). By contrast, the Kalimantan Project has shown that when plots given to immigrants are too small the impact can be even greater. Given an inadequate land base for food production, the Kalimantan immigrants have become a willing labor force for logging companies and have subjected the rain forest to even more severe stress (Kartawinata et al. 1981). These two studies with their emphasis on the <u>problem</u> of the inevitable entry of pioneers into the tropical rain forests due to the inequitable distribution of land in regions of origin, population growth, and the need to appropriate some of the resources of the forest for goals defined by policy-makers reflect the greater "development" pressure felt in these two countries than in the Venezuelan Amazon.

Thus far there have been few holistic studies in the Amazonian rain forest. Research has been highly site-specific--with no systematic sampling of habitat types, the impact of various technologies per habitat type, or representative aggregate data for major social, ecological or economic indicators. To a large extent, research priorities are a function of government actions that seek to exploit areas of the Amazon even when no research exists to evaluate possible impacts. Scientists have been put in the uncomfortable position of choosing sites not because they are "representative" but because they are locales experiencing immediate impact. This is true for the research of anthropologists (Moran 1975, 1981); geographers (Smith 1976, 1982), and ecologists (Fearnside 1978, 1980; Herrera et al. 1978; Goodland 1980; Falesi 1972). Perhaps the most systematic sampling has been carried out by agronomists and climatologists in Brazil. Even these efforts, however, face the serious sampling problems posed by the diversity and high degree of endemism in Amazonia (Sombroek 1966; Falesi 1972; IPEAN 1974; Salati et al. 1978; Tillman, personal communication 1982).

Much of the available data on the Amazon does not constitute a coherent body of individual studies. What we have for the Amazon thus far are a relatively small number of micro-level studies that can only explain the internal dynamics of those sites. While even extrapolations from weak data sets can increase the probability of success in reducing negative impacts of development interventions, caution must be exercised to limit the scope of conclusions arrived at by this "salvage" approach to ecological analysis. Macro- or <u>biome-level generalizations require aggregate data from a broad and representative sample of the universe in</u>

question which are not yet available for the Amazon. Studies have treated sites as if they represented the universe that is the subject of human impacts. Such site-specific studies do not represent, and may not be validly extrapolated to, other sites nor to how they will be structurally or functionally affected by human impacts of various magnitudes. Site-specific studies, for example, cannot address issues of social evolution, explain changes in the economic structure of society or predict the species composition of forest following various kinds of clearing. To arrive at such predictions it is necessary that research be guided by representative sampling of sites under realistic conditions of human/habitat interaction. The great difficulties of such a task should not prevent us from undertaking them, or reducing the claims made from site-specific studies.

LEVELS OF ANALYSIS AND AMAZONIAN RESEARCH

The relevance of these considerations about the specificity of each level of analysis and the scale of sampling appropriate to answering given questions about human ecosystems helps shed light on some of the major questions we are confronted with regarding the impact of current human activities in the Amazonian rain forest.

The problem of scale emerges at the outset as one of the fundamental problems in the ability of both scientists and farmers to differentiate between Amazonian soils. Most soil maps available are, at best, at a scale of 1:100,000 to 1:5,000,000. These macro-scale maps show the soils of the Amazon to be primarily oxisols (latosols) with a small area of inceptisols (alluvial soils) along the floodplain (cf. National Academy of Science 1972, and the map of the Basin in Figure 4.2). Discussions of human use of these soils, guided by these maps in making their interactive analysis of human/habitat components, emphasize that the practice of long fallow swidden cultivation is based on the poverty of the oxisols for sustaining any other form of cultivation (Meggers 1971; Goodland and Irwin 1975). A great many of our notions about the potential of the Amazon as a habitat for man comes from this biome level of analysis based on non-representative sampling.

When one changes the scale from the Amazon as a whole to specific sub-regions, the soil homogeneity evidenced in the macro-scale maps yields to increased variability. Instead of only two soil types, at least three to five are noted. Not only is there increased detail in visible soil types but even the areal extent of soil types may be misjudged (Ranzani 1978). The RADAM aerial survey of the Amazon mapped the Marabá

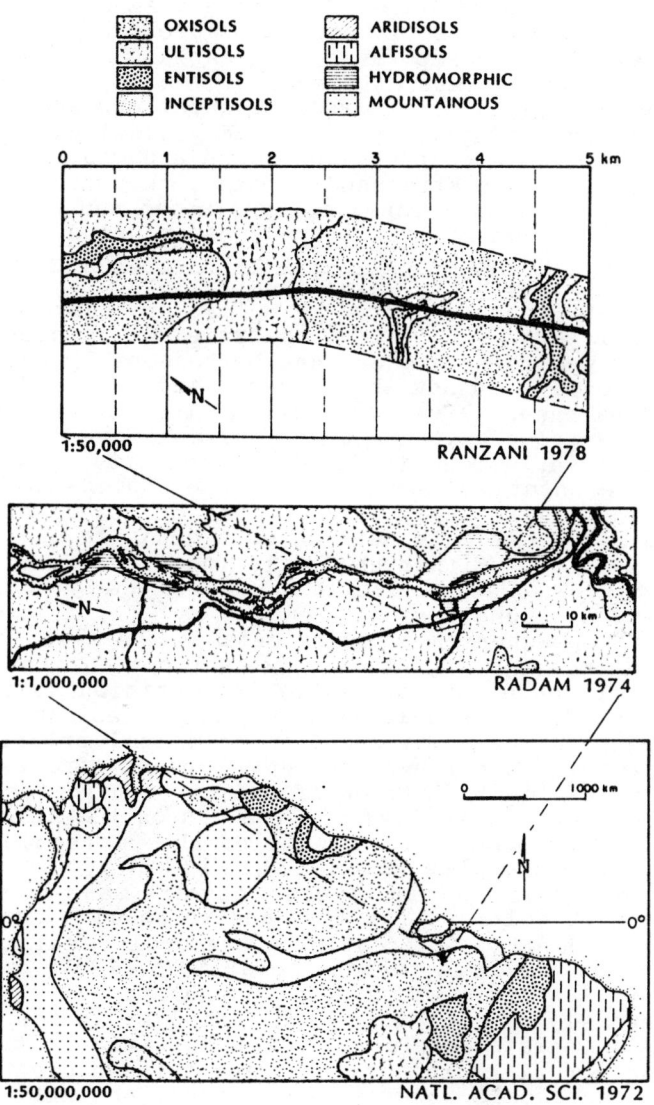

FIGURE 4.2 Soil maps of the Amazon Basin

region near the Tocantins River as being composed predominantly of ultisols. However, a ground-level study by Ranzani (1978), at a scale of 1:10,000 rather than the 1:100,000 of RADAM, identified the ultisols to compose only 13% of the soils in the area in question (see middle and top soil maps in Figure 4.2).

Scale is very important when variability is present. Whereas maps at a scale of 1:100,000 and above may be useful in addressing questions about geologic history, geomorphology and general questions about the relationship between soils and biotic productivity, speciation and climate, they are of little use in addressing questions about human use of resources. In short, <u>for the purpose of studying human impacts, one needs to nest micro-level site-specific studies within a hierarchically-structured representative sample of sites</u>. This procedure allows one to know at what level of analysis one is operating and what types of processes can be reasonably addressed at that level--and how the current study fits into the total data base. Given the current lack of a coherent sampling approach, it has been easy for investigators to dismiss variations in findings from site to site as "non-representative" and to have more confidence in either their site study than in that of others or to trust macro-scale data sets as more accurate and representative. Either choice is incorrect from the point of view of areal sampling and its analytical implications (Duncan et al. 1961).

The consequences of using data at the macro-level for development planning can have serious environmental and social consequences. While the decision to focus government-directed colonization along Brazil's Transamazon Highway was based on political priorities, the focus of attention of the development effort was based on the identification of medium to high fertility alfisols west of the town of Altamira on the Xingu Basin (IPEAN 1967). As a result of the extrapolation of a few soil samples taken within 17 km. of Altamira to the region as a whole, decisions were made to settle thousands of colonist families and to spend large amounts of capital in creating a regional development pole in the Altamira region (Moran 1975, 1981; Smith 1976, 1981). Since soils were thought to be homogeneously of medium to high fertility in the region, colonists were placed on all available land, the same cereal crops were promoted through credit schemes, and goals were set for production that assumed high yields from the unexpectedly fertile land base (Ministerio da Agricultra 1972). Later site-specific studies demonstrated that soils in the area were a patchwork with radical differences in nearly every kilometer (Moran 1975; Smith 1976; Fearnside 1978). The soils of Altamira were later assessed to be made up

of only 8% alfisols, scattered in small patches
throughout, and that the dominant soil type were the
proverbial oxisols. Soil data from Fearnside's study
has shown the need for large sample sizes if the
masking effect of random differences between locations
being compared is to be penetrated (1980). If
development planners had recognized that road-side soil
sampling cannot be extrapolated to regional-level
design of human settlements in heterogeneous
environments, perhaps the tremendous social and
environmental cost of the Transamazon Highway could
have been reduced (cf. the critiques in Bunker 1983;
Cardoso and Muller 1977; Wood and Schmink 1979). A
similarly scaled colonization project is currently
attracting settlers to Rondonia, Brazil. It remains to
be seen if implementation of planned safeguards are put
into effect (Moran, 1984).

Before we, as scientists, can become complacent in
our insights into the problem, it is important that one
recall how scientific projects are often flawed in like
manner. The IBP biome-level projects chose their
research sites according to where work was going on or
could go on, by interesting features of the sites, or
in response to the impending impact of government
programs on the area.[2] The important nutrient-cycling
studies in the oligotrophic black water river basin of
the Venezuelan Rio Negro were guided by curiosity into
the extreme poverty of that ecosystem, the relative
absence of human activity in that area, and the
Venezuelan government's intentions to develop the area
(Herrera et al. 1981; Golley, personal communication).
Publications seem to imply that the nutrient cycling
mechanisms of that forest occur throughout the tropical
rain forests of Amazonia. Yet, the Rio Negro is poorer
than white or clear water ones in the Amazon, the soils
are extremely poor and sandy spodosols are estimated to
constitute only 3% of the Amazon's soils (Nicholaides
et al. 1983), and the area has attracted significant
populations only recently, due to the relative poverty
of its floodplains. Whereas it has been estimated that
the floodplains of white water rivers supported as many
as 28 persons/km^2 before 1492, the black water basins
probably supported less than 2 persons/km^2 (Denevan
1976). The studies of the Rio Negro Basin demonstrate
the fragility of the Rio Negro Basin and the need to
design policies to encourage regional planning
assigning to that region an important role in
conservation through forest reserves. The studies tell
us very little about how to deal with human activities
in other areas of the Amazon. The Altamira and
Rondonia areas of the Brazilian Amazon are more
heterogeneous, with patches of fertile soils alongside
a large array of low to medium fertility soils, and
with little evidence of the nutrient conservation

adaptations noted in the Rio Negro (i.e., above-ground root mat, trans-location of certain nutrients from the leaf to the branch before shedding, high polyphenol content of leaves to reduce herbivory, etc.). The conclusions from the Rio Negro studies, that only swidden cultivation at low levels of population density are possible, hold for the Rio Negro but may not hold for Rondonia and Altamira. The focus of research in the latter sites should be on identification of the better sites for settling human populations in plot sizes adequate for sustainable production, while protecting the less fertile sites from deforestation leading to subsequent abandonment, erosion stress, and habitat degradation. Such an approach was recently recognized in the new plan for forest reserves in the Brazilian Amazon.

Next I want to propose a Model for Nested Research on Human Ecosystems that is responsive to the patchiness of Amazon rain forest ecosystems.

Bennett's (1976) concept of socionatural systems provides a provocative starting point for the development of an operational model for studying human impacts on resources. In village-level societies the territory or effective environment may be defined by myth and traditions in the present and over time in given localities (Rappaport 1967). These societies, like our own, are continually transforming Nature to appropriate its resources, and in the process changing their natural systems. To understand village-level societies, what is needed is to discover their "cognized environments" encapsulated in ritual and myth (Rappaport 1967). However, there are hardly any truly isolated village-level societies left on earth. Some would argue there have been few of them at any time. All communities are now linked to other systems. As soon as human populations begin to be organized above the village-level, an investigation must deal with the political domain that sets boundaries to the human ecosystem, and to increasing levels of variation from village to village in how communities respond to their surroundings.

Human beings as members of social systems do not interact or impact natural systems directly. Rather, cultural propositions encode information about Nature, in ways that reflect past experience and new information. Human language tends to follow a binary form of logic and is an imperfect representation of the more complex analogic and multiple feedback loops of ecological systems.[5] As a result of this apparent lack of fit between linguistic propositions about reality and the operation of natural systems, cultural systems also tend to include non-binary forms of logic based on analogic processes that mimic the complexities of Nature through the use of metaphor and symbol. Human systems, thus, include both a directional and a random component aimed at balancing the need to arrive at decisions through the relative simplicity of binary logic and the need to provide a "transformational image" of Nature sensitive to the processes of environmental change and adaptation in ecosystems.

Conscious purpose and its expression in propositional language is an efficacious form of short-term response to material needs but may be exceedingly destructive if not compensated by the corrective action of "unconscious," non-linear feedback loops (Bateson 1972). The logic of optimization models is an inadequate representation for the structural relations that permit the stability of natural systems through time or human adaptation. Efficiency is not the only measure that is selected for in adaptation, effectiveness can be just as important in the survival of organisms and ecosystems. If we are to understand how to devise systems that are sensitive to the imbalances created by linear/binary thinking, we must begin by looking for the cultural forms embodied within specific human systems that embody the non-linear feedback loops that maintain viable socionatural systems (Slobodkin 1968).

A number of studies in anthropology suggest that non-linear models of human/habitat interaction exist. Reichel-Dolmatoff (1971), Harner (1973), and Rappaport (1967) have shown that ritual and myth embody postulates in a hierarchy of meaning which reflects the levels present in natural systems and how human societies intersect with Nature. One level is that of "high-level propositions," such as those found in ecology in the definition of an ecosystem: "composed of all living and non-living components in a given environment through which flow energy, matter and information." Corresponding to it in Desana Culture is the concept that "men and animals share the same pool of energy." A second level is more concrete and divides up the world into "structural oppositions" that include both humans and animals. This is usually the level of culture which is widely shared within a region such as the Vaupés in the Amazon. This level is comparable to the population level of analysis in ecology. A third level, corresponding to the individual level in ecology, finds its analogue in specific cultural responses to specific features of the environment within which a human population finds itself. It is at this level that the general postulates of the previous levels are transformed into conduct and where we find such a wide array of responses even within a relatively "homogeneous population." Within a given cultural area, postulates are transformed into acts sensitive to local environmental and socio-historical conditions.

In all societies one can find individuals and/or institutions that serve to articulate these transformational rules of Culture into a pattern of action towards Nature. In village-level societies, this role appears to have been played by shamans who could, for example, declare hunters taboo and thereby reduce hunting pressure. Bastien (1978) has discussed the provocative notion that the Andean use of the mountain metaphor serves to maintain the articulation between the altitudinal zones of the Andes and as a viable adaptive system to the limited ecological breadth of each zone. Whereas the research from the IBP human adaptability section was able to show the logical sense or efficiency of the systems of exchange across vertical zones in the Andes (Thomas 1973; Baker and Little 1976), it overlooked the role of metaphor in Andean ritual as of fundamental import in the explanation of the persistence of this system until now, as well as the conditions under which it might be destroyed. An understanding of the energy flows of a human ecosystem tells us how efficiently the population uses energy at each trophic level. It cannot tell us the transformational rules generated by the human systems (from within or without) that lead to change and evolution.

An evolutionary biology model of an ecosystem must include the study of the non-linear forms of logic within human Cultures, the propositions used to make decisions about Nature, and the level of articulation between those propositions and the management of the environment. It seems quite clear from recent psychological and farm-level studies that human beings simplify the inputs to decision making by pre-attentive (unconscious) simplification of alternatives into binary choices guided by language (Gladwin & Murtaugh 1980). March (1982) notes that human actions seem often to be based on "a different logic," that information is remarkably independent of decisions made, and that decision outcomes are only partly explained by what we have come to know as "rational" decision-processes. What we have not yet studied is the role of metaphors and analogic thinking in reducing the infinity of inputs to a binary set. It also seems that we make minimal changes in adaptive strategies and that we return to past strategies as soon as the cause of stress is over (Morren 1980). While we like to think that in contemporary urban-industrial settings we are significantly different in these matters than village-level populations, it appears that the same processes of unconscious simplification, preference for routinized behavior, and the dual presence of binary and analogic processes in decision-making are to be found in all human systems.

What this rather extended discussion brings us to is the need for a "nested approach" that recognizes the

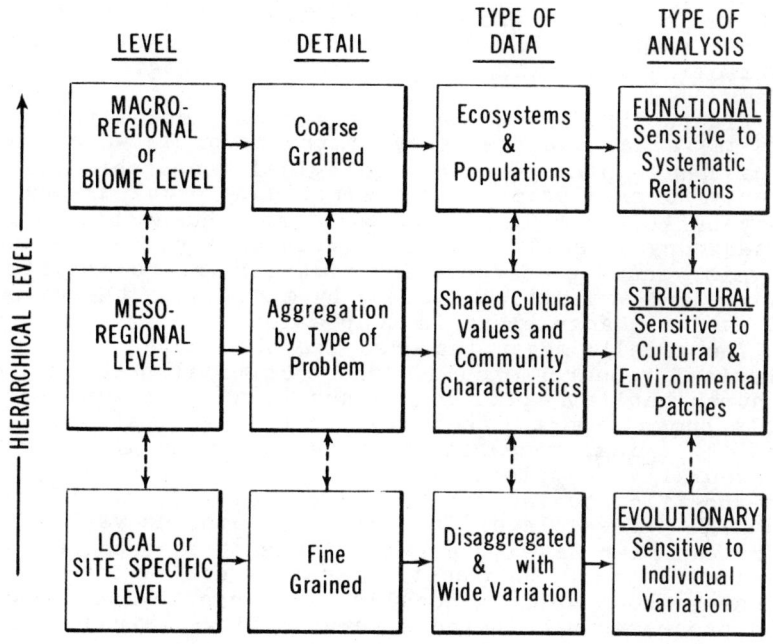

FIGURE 4.3 Nested socionatural systems

discrete limits of various levels of analysis and how they articulate with the human populations which transform Nature for their ends, and in turn transform themselves in the very act of appropriating Nature. Future research on human impacts on global resources generally, and in the Amazon in particular, needs to be guided by greater attention to the informational processes operative at each level of analysis. Just as samples from sites are nested in regional systems which in turn may be nested in biome and "continental" systems, in the same manner cultural forms of cognition about the ecosystem are nested in hierarchies of response with variable logic, and variable effectiveness in mimicking the analogic processes of biological systems.

Figure 4.3 illustrates a preliminary model that seeks to reduce the frequency of the problems which in the past have plagued human ecological research: the tendency to give primacy to disciplinary problems and theory-building while trying to address human impacts; the tendency to shift levels between data gathering and analysis; and a preference for reducing the complexity of human and ecological systems by minimizing the role that random change plays in adaptation.

The model's major features are that human ecological research should address critical problems in the human/habitat equation, rather than questions of little human import. Secondly, that directorates of human ecological research begin by designing a representative sample of sites so that the eventual site-specific studies can be understood in terms of the variation present in all micro-ecosystems, as well as generate higher level generalizations at the regional and biome level. Such nesting keeps track of the processes about which generalizations can be made, and which processes are indeed site-specific. Thirdly, that both social and natural aspects of socionatural systems be included at the start of projects and that choices be based on the ability of scientists in dealing with the complex socionatural system--rather than with simply one or the other. For this task, there are now significant numbers of scientists, thanks to the IBP and MAB Programs, with sufficient knowledge to give hope that future research formulations can address not simply ecosystems in which man is absent, or isolated tribes, and that will stop considering all that is social as a negative impact. Rather, the study of nested socionatural systems places human beings where they belong, as the major force in the transformation of Nature. We cannot understand what is happening to Nature--and what to do about it--until we understand how we make the decisions that we do. It is this process of environmental perception, cultural transformation, and human action which lies at the heart of our so-called environmental crisis. There are fundamental contradictions between the requisites, goals and effects of operation at different levels of analysis. The task for anthropology and the other social sciences is to work closely with biological scientists in order to understand how those impactful decisions are made, and how each one leads to different transformations at different hierarchical levels. If we cannot incorporate non-binary, non-linear logic into contemporary human decision making, we may be studying the steady running down of the biosphere by a dominant species which has refused to acknowledge the need to balance optimization and efficiency with effectiveness in adjusting to its ever-changing environment.

NOTES

   1. I wish to thank Dennis Conway, William Denevan, Jim Eder, Roy Ellen, Frank Golley, Ivan Karp, and R.E. Tillman for comments on earlier versions of this paper. An earlier version of this paper appeared in E. Moran, ed., The Ecosystem Concept in Anthropology. Washington, D.C.: AAAS, Selected Symposia Series, No. 92, 1984.
   2. Recent studies of decision-making suggest that the framing of a decision strongly influences the outcome. In experiments even research psychologists failed to base their decisions on their knowledge of probabilities, but rather underestimated the size of the sample required in experiments, and were affected by the framing of choices.
   3. I wish to acknowledge my debt to Mr. David Crum, a graduate student in the Department of Anthropology at Indiana University, for some of the provocative ideas raised in this section. His recent research paper on the role of hallucinogenic ritual in Amazonian cultural ecology inspired my own excursions into the role of pre-attentive choice simplification in resource management--and the dangers of marginalizing non-optimizing forms of communication. I am also indebted to Professor Christina Gladwin for her provocative research on decision-making and our discussion of how to study this process.

REFERENCES

Andersson, F. The Swedish Coniferous Forest Project. Ambio 10:126-9, 1981.
Baker, P.T. The Biological Adaptation of Man to Hot Deserts. American Naturalist 92:337-57, 1958.
Baker, P.T., ed. The Biology of High Altitude Peoples. Cambridge: Cambridge University Press, 1978.
Baker, P.T. and J.S. Weiner, eds. The Biology of Human Adaptability. Oxford: Clarendon, 1966.
Baker, P.T. and M. Little, eds. Man in the Andes: A Multidisciplinary Study of High Altitude Quechua. Stroudsburg, PA: Dowden, Hutchinson and Ross, 1976.
Bastien, J. Mountain of the Condor. St. Paul, MN: West Publishing Company, 1978.
Bennett, J. The Ecological Transition. New York: Pergamon, 1976.
———. Social and Interdisciplinary Sciences in US/MAB: Conceptual and Theoretical Aspects. In E. Zube, ed., Social and Interdisciplinary Research and the U.S. Man and the Biosphere Program. Washington, D.C.: MAB/Department of State, 1980.
Boas, F. The Limitations of the Comparative Method in Anthropology. Science 4:901-8, 1896.
Blair, W.B. Big Biology: The US/IBP. Stroudsburg, PA: Dowden, Hutchinson and Ross, 1977.
Conklin, H. Hanunóo Agriculture. Rome: FAO, 1957.
Coon, C.S., S.M. Garn, and J.B. Birdsell. Races: A Study of the Problems of Race Formation in Man. Springfield, IL: Thomas, 1950.
Damas, D. Environment, History, and Central Eskimo Society. In Contributions to Anthropology: Ecological Essays. D. Damas, ed. Ottawa: National Museum of Canada, 1969.
Denevan, W., ed. The Native Population of the Americas. Madison: University of Wisconsin Press, 1976.
diCastri, F. International, Interdisciplinary Research in Ecology: Some Problems of Organization and Execution. Human Ecology 4(3):235-46, 1976.
Dosso, H., J.L. Guillaumet and M. Hadley. The Tai Project: Land Use Problems in a Tropical Rain Forest. Ambio 10:120-5, 1981.
Duncan, O., R. Cuzzort, and B. Duncan. Statistical Geography: Problems in Analyzing Areal Data. Glencoe, IL: Free Press, 1961.
Falesi, I.C. Os Solos da Rodovia Transamazônica. Belem: IPEAN, 1971.
Fearnside, P. Estimation of Carrying Capacity for Human Populations in a Part of the Transamazon

Highway. Ph.D. dissertation, University of Michigan, Dept. of Biological Sciences, 1978.

──────. Land-Use Allocation of the Transamazonian Highway Colonists of Brazil and Its Relation to Human Carrying Capacity. In Land, People and Planning in Contemporary Amazonia. Barbara Scazzocchio, ed. Cambridge: University of Cambridge (UK) Centre of Latin American Studies. pp. 114-138, 1980.

Geertz, C. Agricultural Involution. Berkeley: University of California Press, 1963.

Glacken, C. Traces on a Rhodian Shore. Berkeley: University of California Press, 1967.

Gladwin, H. and M. Murtaugh. The Attentive-Preattentive Distinction in Agricultural Decision Making. In Agricultural Decision Making. P. Barlett, ed. New York: Academic Press, 1980.

Goldenweiser, A. Anthropology. New York: Crofts, 1937.

Goodland, R. Environmental Ranking of Amazonian Development Projects in Brazil. Environmental Conservation 7(1):9-26, 1980.

Goodland, R. and H.S. Irwin. Amazon Jungle: From Green Hell to Red Desert? Amsterdam: Elsevier, 1975.

Hardesty, D. Ecological Anthropology. New York: Wiley, 1977.

Harrison, G.A., J.S. Weiner, J.M. Tanner, and N.A. Barnicott. Human Biology. Oxford: Oxford University Press, 1964.

Herrera, R., C. Jordan, E. Medina and H. Klinge. How Human Activities Disturb the Nutrient Cycles of a Tropical Rainforest in Amazonia. Ambio 10:109-114, 1981.

IPEAN. Contribuição ao Estudo dos Solos de Altamira. Belèm: IPEAN, circular No. 10, 1967.

──────. Solos da Rodovia Transamazônica: Trecho Itaituba-Rio Branco. Belèm: IPEAN, 1974.

Jamison, P., S.L. Zegura, and F.A. Milan, eds. Eskimos of Northwestern Alaska: A Biological Perspective. Stroudsburg, PA: Dowden, Hutchinson and Ross, 1978.

Kartawinata, K., S. Adisoemarto, S. Riswan, and A.P. Vayda. The Impact of Man on a Tropical Forest in Indonesia. Ambio 10:115-19, 1981.

Kemp, W. The Flow of Energy in a Hunting Society. Scientific American 224(3):104-15, 1971.

Lee, R.B. The !Kung San. Cambridge: Cambridge University Press, 1980.

Lee, R.B. and I. DeVore, eds. Man the Hunter. Chicago: Aldine, 1968.

──────. Kalahari Hunter/Gatherers. Cambridge: Harvard University Press, 1976.

Little, M. Human Ecology and Adaptation. Paper presented at 50th annual meeting of Amer. Assoc. of Phys. Anthro., Detroit, MI, 1981.
──────. Human Biology and the Development of an Ecosystem Approach. Paper presented at Amer. Assoc. for Adv. of Sci., Washington, D.C., 1982.
Little, M. and G. Morren. Ecology, Energetics and Human Variability. Dubuque, IA: W.C. Brown, 1976.
March, J.G. Theories of Choice and the Making of Decisions. Public Lecture presented on January 5 at the Annual Meeting of the AAAS in Washington, D.C., 1982.
Meggers, B. Amazonia. Chicago: Aldine, 1971.
Ministerio da Agricultura. Altamira 1. Brasilia, DF: Min. da Agric./INCRA, 1972.
Montague, M.F. An Introduction to Physical Anthropology. Second edition. Springfield, IL: Thomas, 1951.
Moran, E.F. Energy Flow Analysis and Manihot esculenta Crantz. Acta Amazonica 3(3):29-39, 1973.
──────. Pioneer Farmers of the Transamazon Highway. Ph.D. dissertation, University of Florida, Department of Anthropology, 1975.
──────. Developing the Amazon. Bloomington: Indiana University Press, 1981.
──────. Human Adaptability. Boulder: Westview Press, 1982. Originally published in 1979 by Duxbury Press.
──────. Colonization in the Transamazon and Rondonia. In Frontier Expansion in Amazonia. M. Schmink and C. Wood, eds. Gainesville: University of Florida Press, 1984.
Moran, E.F. and J. Hill. Subsidy and Resource Use in the Rio Negro Basin, Venezuelan Amazon. Paper presented at the annual meeting of the Amer. Ethnol. Soc., Washington, D.C., 1981.
Morren, G. The Rural Ecology of the British Drought, 1975-76. Human Ecology 8(1):33-63, 1980.
Moser, W. and J. Peterson. Limits to Obergurgl's Growth. Ambio 10:68-72, 1981.
National Academy of Science. Soils of the Humid Tropics. Washington, D.C.: NAS, 1972.
Netting, R. Hill Farmers of Nigeria. Seattle: University of Washington Press, 1968.
──────. Agrarian Ecology. Annual Review of Anthropology 3:21-56, 1974.
──────. Cultural Ecology. Menlo Park, CA: Cummings, 1977.
Noy-Meir, I. Desert Ecosystems: Environment and Producers. Annual Review of Ecology and Systematics 4:25-51, 1973.

_____. Desert Ecosystems: Higher Trophic Levels. Annual Review of Ecology and Systematics 5:195-214, 1974.
Odum, E. Fundamentals of Ecology. Third edition. Philadelphia: Saunders, 1971.
Odum, H. Environment, Power and Society. New York: Wiley, 1971.
PRORADAM. La Amazonia Colombiana y Sus Recursos. Bogotá: PRORADAM, 1979.
Ranzani, G. Alguns Solos da Transamazonica na Região de Marabá. Acta Amazonica 8(3):333-55, 1978.
Rappaport, Roy. Pigs for the Ancestors. New Haven: Yale Univ. Press, 1967.
_____. The Flow of Energy in an Agricultural Society. Scientific American 224(3):116-32, 1971.
Reichel-Dolmatoff, G. Amazonian Cosmos. Chicago: University of Chicago Press, 1971.
Roberts, D.F. Body Weight, Race and Climate. Amer. J. of Phys. Anthro. 11:533-58, 1953.
Slobodkin, L.B. Toward a Predictive Theory of Evolution. In R. Lewontin, ed. Population Biology and Evolution. Syracuse: Syracuse University Press, 1968.
Smith, N. Transamazon Highway: A Cultural Ecological Analysis of Settlement in the Lowland Tropics. Ph.D. dissertation, Univ. of California, Berkeley. Dept. of Geography, 1976.
_____. Colonization Lessons from a Tropical Forest. Science 214:755-61, 1981.
Sombroek, W.G. Amazon Soils. Wageningen: Centre for Agric. Public. and Docum., 1966.
Steward, J. Basin Plateau Aboriginal Sociopolitical Groups. Washington, D.C.: Smithsonian Institute Bulletin 120, BAE, 1938.
_____. A Theory of Culture Change. Urbana: University of Illinois Press, 1955.
Thomas, F. The Environmental Basis of Society. New York: Century Co., 1925.
Thomas, R.B. Human Adaptation to a High Andean Energy Flow System. University Park, PA: Penn State Univ., Dept. of Anthropology, 1973.
Uhl, C. Studies of Forest, Agricultural and Successional Environments in the Upper Rio Negro Region of the Amazon Basin. Ph.D. dissertation, Michigan State University, Dept. of Botany and Plant Pathology, 1980.
Washburn, S.L. The New Physical Anthropology. Transactions of the New York Academy of Science. Series II, 13(7):298-304, 1951.
Weiner, J.S. IBP Guide to the Human Adaptability Proposals. London: ICSU, special committee for the IBP, 1965.
Worthington, E.B., ed. The Evolution of IBP. Cambridge: Cambridge University Press, 1975.

5
Toward a Rural Sociology of Global Resources: Social Structure, Ecology, and Latin American Agricultural Development

Frederick H. Buttel

INTRODUCTION

Rural sociology, perhaps the most longstanding speciality in U.S. sociology, has not survived for and grown over nearly 80 years due to its innovativeness alone. Indeed, rural sociology has long been viewed as a laggard subdiscipline, late to adopt and elaborate on scholarly innovations in sociology and other social science disciplines. While this reputation for scholarly mediocrity clearly persists, it is important to note that rural sociology pioneered in many aspects of the subject matter that is the subject of this volume. Environmental sociology was in a strong sense born within rural sociological circles in the late-1960s, and the contemporary leaders in the field of environmental sociology still continue to be dominated by persons with rural sociological training, rural sociology department affiliations, or other connections to the subdiscipline of rural sociology.

That rural sociologists were at the center of an emergent ecological viewpoint in the larger discipline of sociology no doubt had many origins. However, the most influential factor was the fact that rural sociology's distinctive subject matter foci--particularly the primary sector industries of agriculture, forestry, fisheries, and mining--had continued to remind its practitioners of the crucial importance of the material bases of social life. The appearance of an exceptionally talented cohort of young rural sociologists during the rise of the late-1960s environmental movement arguably played a role as well. Rural sociologists, nevertheless, tended to take more seriously the environmentalist arguments and claims that dominated the mass media in the wake of Earth Day than did the bulk of "nonrural" sociologists (Humphrey and Buttel, 1982:Chap. 1) or social scientists in general (Catton and Dunlap, 1978a; Dunlap and Catton, 1979).

The late-1960s and 1970s thus found rural sociologists at the forefront of arguing for ecologically-informed analyses of social structure and social change. The outcome of this intellectual movement was by no means a united front. Controversies emerged rapidly and still persist (see, for example, Catton and Dunlap, 1978b; Buttel, 1978; Schnaiberg, 1980; Sandbach, 1978, 1980; Humphrey and Buttel, 1982). Nevertheless, ecologically-informed analyses kindled the innovative and critical spirit among rural sociologists and gave a long-overdue shot in the arm to a subdiscipline that had been on the verge of scholarly obscurity for over two decades.

The purpose of this paper will be to discuss the applicability of an ecologically-oriented rural sociology to the understanding of socioeconomic impacts on global resources. As will become apparent in the discussion that follows, sociology is an extremely diverse social science, and rural sociology exhibits comparable theoretical and methodological differentiation. Thus, the present paper must be taken as a rural sociological perspective on global resource problems, and other rural sociologists would no doubt use very different concepts and make different social policy assessments than I would.

The principal focus of the paper will be on agricultural resource use in low-income countries, primarily in Latin America. However, at certain junctures I will comment on ostensibly nonagricultural uses of natural resources--for example, the use of fuelwood for cooking--although the connections of these uses of natural resources to agriculture are generally direct and unambiguous. The paper is intended to be neither a "management manual" (e.g., to provide agricultural policymakers and planners with firm guides as to the design of agricultural development and conservation programs) nor a theoretical treatise. Instead, my goal will be to elaborate on socioeconomic trends that have influenced and will continue to influence agricultural resource use and on concepts that can help policymakers and academicians connect the macro forces of social structure and change with the pragmatic experiences of agriculturalists, other rural populations, and those charged with devising policies to enhance the public good. However, before turning to the central issues of concern in this paper I will provide several comments on the nature of the larger discipline of sociology and of the subdiscipline of rural sociology that undergird the analyses that follow.

THE NATURE OF SOCIOLOGY AND RURAL SOCIOLOGY

Sociology, as noted above, is a most diverse social science. This diversity has two major origins. First, like its kindred disciplines of economics, political science, and anthropology, sociology is pervaded by the theoretical, methodological, and philosophical disagreements that normatively parallel the differences of interest manifest in stratified societies. Thus, sociology exhibits familiar theoretical controversies among Marxist and critical theorists on one hand, and functionalists and behaviorists on the other. Sociology is also cleaved by controversies over normative versus positive science, over the proper levels or units of analysis (i.e., macrosociology versus microsociology), and over the very purposes of social analysis (i.e., a framework for scholarly understanding versus schemas for policymaking and other forms of social intervention). Moreover, these differences of viewpoint are taken very seriously by sociologists and are meaningful points of debate within the sociological community (in contrast to, for example, the nearly complete hegemony of the neoclassical viewpoint within contemporary U.S. economics).

A second source of diversity in sociology has resulted from its very raison d'etre as a social science: its promise of being an overarching or integrative social science. Each of the other major social sciences has been premised on a principal focus on either specific institutional complexes (e.g., the economy, the polity, or culture) or, in the case of psychology, on a specific unit of analysis (the individual). Sociology, in fact, emerged historically as a critique of the other major social science disciplines--principally in reaction to the utilitarianism of economics, the reductionism of psychology, the environmental determinism of geography, and the tendency of anthropology to focus primarily on prehistorical and preindustrial cultures. Sociology's founders (especially Comte and Durkheim) self-consciously fashioned the discipline to be an overarching perspective for understanding the interrelations among social institutions and among the social forces that operate at disparate levels of analysis (ranging from the individual and organizational to the institutional, societal, and global or geopolitical). As C. Wright Mills (1959) pointed out nearly 25 years ago, the promise of sociology is to understand the intersection between biography and history--that is, to grapple with the macroscopic or global forces of change in conjunction with the processes by which individuals and groups affect and are affected by these larger social forces.

The performance of the sociological enterprise in fulfilling the promise of sociology has been mixed. Two disciplinary trends highlight the unevenness of this performance. First, as noted by Mills (1959; see also Gouldner, 1970), there has been a strong tendency for sociology to gravitate toward either "grand theory" or "abstracted empiricism." By grand theory, Mills referred to highly abstract, generally macrosociological formulations which tended toward unidirectional determinism and neglect of the role of human agents of change. By abstracted empiricism he meant a sociological style of utilizing micro units of analysis (usually individuals from whom data were collected from sample surveys) combined with structural concepts operationalized as variables pertaining to these microsociological units. Abstracted empiricism, in Mills' view, tended to presume that social structure was the sum or distribution of individual characteristics and that social change could be adequately depicted in terms of changes in these distributions or in the statistical relationships among individual characteristics.

A second indicator of the unfulfilled promise of sociology as an overarching social science is the extreme fragmentation of the discipline, especially as it has developed since the disintegration of Parsonian and Mertonian functionalism (Parsons, 1951; Merton, 1968) as unifying theoretical influences.[1] It would be no exaggeration to suggest that contemporary U.S. sociologists identify themselves with subdisciplinary labels representing some 100 specialties. Rarely do theorists now bother to make the pretense that their work is an exemplar for the entire discipline. Sociological theory has been replaced by political sociological theory, world-systems theory, development theory, human ecological theory, and so on. There has been a virtual disappearance of individual celebrities whose work is familiar to sociologists regardless of specialty or interests.

Rural sociology has been shaped by the same centrifugal forces that have characterized the larger discipline. But perhaps an even more fundamental influence on rural sociology has been its close articulation with the land-grant college system. Rural sociology as an identifiable subdiscipline (although not necessarily as a substantive area of inquiry) was a U.S. phenomenon. Rural sociology emerged in the wake of President Theodore Roosevelt's Country Life Commission in 1907-1909. Members of the Commission, headed by Cornell University's Dean of Agriculture, L. H. Bailey, urged colleges of agriculture to form rural sociology departments to help foster a technological "revolution in the countryside" while preserving the rural "Gemeinschaft-like" values that made agricultural communities desirable places to live. Using broad criteria, roughly 25 rural sociology programs have been created in the U.S., some, however, have as few as two faculty.

The vast majority of self-identified rural sociologists in the U.S. were trained in land-grant universities and are employed in comparable institutions. It is generally recognized that rural sociological research has been closely shaped by its land-grant institutional milieu (Friedland, 1979; Newby, 1980; Newby and Buttel, 1980; Buttel, 1983). Rural sociology has tended to be highly applied and to a degree aloof from the major theoretical controversies in the larger discipline. To a considerable degree this separation of rural sociology from its parent discipline has been reinforced by the "practical" and public-service orientation of land-grant institutions. Another pervasive influence of the land-grant institutional milieu of rural sociology was the pressure to acquire the trappings of science, which has been manifest in the highly quantitative cast of rural sociology over the past 25 years. Also, the subdiscipline until quite recently has shown little tendency to take a critical posture toward the technological mission of its parent institutions or of their siblings--the international agricultural research centers in the Third World.

I noted earlier that rural sociology was a U.S. phenomenon, nurtured within the land-grant college system. However, those who frequently travel to Third World countries will note that rural sociology programs are quite commonplace in agricultural colleges and universities in other countries. The diffusion of rural sociology to underdeveloped regions (and, to a lesser degree, to other advanced industrial countries) was largely the result of the activities of a small handful of U.S. rural sociologists (especially T. Lynn Smith, Robert Polson, Eugene A. Wilkening, Charles Loomis, and Herbert Lionberger) who, in almost messianic fashion, labored to sow the seeds of rural sociology across the globe. A good share of Third World rural sociologists were trained in U.S. institutions, and U.S. influence on Third World rural sociology remains strong, especially in Asia and Africa. (Latin America has over the last 20 years begun to develop its own indigenous sociological perspective, which has been generally hostile toward U.S.-style rural sociology.)

For all the influence U.S. rural sociology has had on Third World institutions of higher education in agriculture, the position of international research in contemporary U.S. rural sociology faculties remains weak and tenuous. Less than five departments have sufficient critical mass that they can claim to have a graduate training program in international rural and agricultural development (Koppel and Beal, 1982, 1983). The graduate program at my own institution, Cornell University, is the only one purporting to have major emphasis on international topics. The reason for the fragile state of international research and graduate training is quite obvious: The state agricultural experiment stations are primarily supported by state government funds, and land-grant administrators tend to be hesitant to devote these funds to activities that are not of clear benefit to residents and firms in the state. Moreover, the lead-time from project initiation to preparation of publishable papers is much longer in international than in domestic research. Thus, younger faculty who might otherwise be interested in doing internationally oriented research are discouraged from doing so by a reward system that usually fails to take account of the special circumstances surrounding data collection in Third World settings.

While the institutional conditions for innovative rural sociological research into human impacts on global resources have not been entirely propitious, the past 15 years have witnessed a number of accomplishments that form the basis of this paper. The increasing relevance of rural sociology to an ecologically-based analysis and more effective facilitation of agricultural and rural development was largely prompted by two interrelated phenomena of the late 1960s and early 1970s, both of which were largely external to rural sociology. The first, as noted above, was the environmental movement and increased recognition of the limits of renewable and nonrenewable resources. The second was the widespread critique of the Green Revolution, particularly the socioeconomic dislocations and inequities that resulted from the diffusion of high-yielding varieties (HYVs) in the context of inegalitarian agrarian systems (see especially Griffin, 1974; Lipton, 1977; Pearse, 1980; Cleaver, 1972; Frankel, 1971). The issues raised by the environmental movement and by the critics had a significant common thread: One of the weaknesses of the typical HYV "packages" originally developed by the international centers—usually centering around inorganic fertilization, synthetic pesticides, and sometimes irrigation—was that they were energy- and resource-intensive. In fact, many critics of the Green Revolution (see, for example, Perelman, 1977, and, in a different vein, Dahlberg, 1979) have argued that its principal limitation is its long-term ecological unsustainability.

These external impetuses were seized upon by a talented cadre of young, dynamic rural sociologists. Two papers (Havens and Flinn, 1975; Saint and Coward, 1977) can be noted as exemplars of the reorientation of rural sociology over the past decade. The first, by Havens and Flinn, demonstrated through the use of panel data from Colombia that the diffusion of Green Revolution coffee varieties had led to socioeconomic differentiation. This finding was, of course, hardly novel. What was distinctive about the Havens-Flinn approach was their having pointed out that the characteristics of technologies--in this case, the long lead-time before new coffee plants bear beans--are crucial in shaping the socioeconomic impacts of their deployment. The differentiating impacts of HYV coffee were especially surprising given the fact that large-scale or plantation agriculture was almost totally absent from coffee production in the early 1960s (during the first wave of the panel study), but was well on its way only 10 years later.

The Saint and Coward (1977) article in a sense takes off from the experience of the Green Revolution and summarizes "emerging orientations" in "behavioral science" as applied to agricultural development. The "emerging orientations" discussed by Saint and Coward represented sharp departures from both the traditional practice of sociology and of agricultural development institutions. The article has worn surprisingly well after eight years, since the perspectives emphasized in this paper (ecological systems approaches, farming systems research, the analysis of traditional agricultural practices, limiting factors analysis, the sociology of technology development systems, and so on) remain fashionable if not important up to the present time.

One of the legacies of the intellectual turmoil of the past 10 years was an institutionalized foot-in-the-door for rural sociological input into agricultural development programs. Rightfully or wrongfully, many of the limitations of traditional Green Revolution programs were ascribed to the lack of "social scientists" (generally a euphemism for rural sociologists, although the category at times includes anthropologists) on project teams. Rural sociological input has now become obligatory for many types of projects, especially those funded under Title XII of the Foreign Assistance Act. Rural sociologists can no longer complain about being outsiders to the processes of technological innovation and deployment. However, as I will point out below, formidable challenges face social scientists who wish to lend their expertise to agricultural and rural development projects so as to avoid the mistakes often attributed to Green Revolutionaries.

THE APPLICATION OF RURAL SOCIOLOGY TO THE ASSESSMENT OF HUMAN IMPACTS ON GLOBAL RESOURCES: DISCIPLINARY OR INTERDISCIPLINARY PRIMACY?

It is widely recognized, by ecologically-oriented social scientists at least, that the mainstreams of the major social science disciplines are somewhat inhospitable to a holistic and dynamic consideration of the interrelationships among social structures, human groups, and natural resources. The classical traditions of sociology, economics, political science, and anthropology all carry methodological conventions emphasizing the causal primacy of "social" forces.[2] These legacies largely derive from the social milieus in which 19th century classical theory was written. The classical social theorists had two major "determinisms"--psychological reductionism and geographical or environmental determinism--to contend with. Once these determinisms were disposed of intellectually, the dominant thrust of classical social theories was a preoccupation with the social causes of social facts; social psychology replaced psychological reductionism, and natural resource phenomena ceased to be relevant explanatory or contextual factors or variables. Anthropology has been a partial exception. There has long been a rich tradition of ecological anthropology which has focused explicitly on the interrelations between environment and cultural behavior (see, for example, Vayda, 1969; Bennett, 1976a, 1976b). However, this tradition has been of limited use as an exemplar for other social sciences for three major reasons: (1) its tendency toward functionalist or neofunctionalist explanatory schemes (see Bennett, 1976b; Orlove, 1980; Vayda and McCay, 1975),[3] (2) its tendency to focus on esoteric academic issues and to study preindustrial (if not prehistorical) peoples, and a corollary unwillingness to become actively involved in applied development work, and (3) its lack of theoretical or empirical attention to one of the key institutions that affects development and change: the modern state.[4]

Designing and executing socioecological analyses have proven to be formidable and controversial tasks, a conundrum which has found me alternatively as a partisan critic (Buttel, 1978; Humphrey and Buttel, 1982) and as a subject of equally strident criticism (Catton and Dunlap, 1978b; Dunlap and Martin, 1983). During the course of the debate, I have found myself altering my own views and being haunted by my previous published work which I would do quite differently now had I the opportunity.

There are essentially three strategies for utilizing the social sciences in an ecologically-grounded fashion. The first, what I call <u>socio-ecological systems</u> approaches, involves the partial if not entire discarding of conventional social scientific disciplinary concepts and their presumed patterns of interrelationship. These concepts are typically eschewed in favor of a set of concepts deriving from "systems theories" or from other highly abstract formulations generally of nonsocial scientific origins. Such attempts are as common among nonsocial scientists (see, for example, Odum, 1971) as among social scientists (see, for example, Norgaard, 1981). The outcome, as Vayda (1982) has pointed out, has generally tended to be a sterile set of highly abstract, poorly articulated concepts and theories that contain little predictive power. Socioecological systems approaches are not really theories, since it is only with the greatest difficulty that one can deduce from them specific, falsifiable hypotheses. They are and should remain sensitizing devices to draw one's attention to some parallels in the dynamics of social and ecological systems. However, it is my view that attempting to superimpose categories from the natural sciences on social scientific inquiry is likely to be unproductive.

The second major social scientific approach to ecological analysis, that of <u>disciplinary primacy</u>, is for all intents and purposes, to retain fully the identity of social scientific theory and to articulate this theory to ecological phenomena in one of two ways. The first subapproach treats ecological phenomena (e.g., soil erosion rates, energy consumption) as dependent variables to be explained qualitatively or quantitatively with conventional social scientific concepts. A second subapproach is for a social scientist to work on an interdisciplinary team in which the social scientist and his or her nonsocial science colleagues work from disciplinary premises and frequently "compare notes." Social and nonsocial scientists may even jointly coauthor publications, but the disciplinary kinship of their results will tend to be so transparent that either specialist could unhesitatingly submit his or her work to a disciplinary journal. Both subapproaches are thus characterized by minimal alterations of disciplinary viewpoint--representing, at the extreme, social scientists who "just happen to be studying ecological phenomena," and who could as easily and willingly shift their attention to the analysis of political development, industrial location, balance of payments problems, or landlord-tenant relationships.

A third framework is an analogue of what Vayda (1982) has referred to as <u>progressive contextualization</u>. Vayda's conceptualization of progressive contextualization essentially involves an incremental process of working back and forth between social science and ecological knowledge in which an understanding of man-environment relationships is continually redefined vis-a-vis levels of social science analysis and comparative insights from other settings. Thus, research designs would include no <u>a priori</u> designation of the most relevant levels of analysis or units of observation and measurement. Vayda's view is that such a methodological posture can best be implemented by persons who are trained as specialists at the interfaces between social and ecological systems. To put the matter in my own terms, social scientists need to be well trained in and conversant with their own disciplines as well as with relevant natural science disciplines (e.g., ecology, agronomy, forestry) that lie across the interface. Some of this knowledge of natural science disciplines can be picked up as on-the-job-training. For example, if a sociologist studying agricultural resource use in the Ecuadorian Sierra is struck by the importance of reciprocity among peasants across diverse ecological zones, the sociologist could be trained by an ecological colleague or through self-directed education about the nature and properties of these ecological zones. Nevertheless, progressive contextualization is an approach to human-environment relations which retains disciplinary concepts and insights but which strives to understand social and ecological dynamics on their own terms and to move the focus of analysis back and forth across social-natural interfaces.

The progressive contextualization approach as depicted above represents an ideal which will be difficult to live up to fully. Nonetheless, such an ideal reaffirms the primacy of disciplinary analysis while placing primary emphasis on "interfaces" and on understanding the analytical and explanatory schemas of the disciplines across the interface on their own terms. The door is not closed, of course, to conceptual modification as a result of this form of interdisciplinary research. But attempts to develop universal vocabularies across the social and natural sciences are certain to fail, and the retention of fully disciplinary approaches will inevitably result in communications and knowledge gaps.

In the remainder of this paper I will in a sense fail to practice what I preach. I will first set forth some methodological principles for understanding the impact of humans on global resources and then

illustrate these points with materials pertaining to
Latin American agricultural development in the context
of the changing international division of labor. However, I will fall short of the ideal of placing
coequal emphasis on ecological processes and the
social-natural interface. This is because my goal is
to develop a framework for analyzing the major social
forces that impinge upon agricultural development in
Latin America and lead to the degradation of agricultural resources.

METHODOLOGICAL PRINCIPLES

The framework to be elaborated upon below is
premised upon four major methodological principles,
all of which are at least partially deducible from the
notion of progressive contextualization just discussed. These four principles, briefly put, are: (1)
placing major <u>emphasis on the economic and political
transformations</u> currently underway throughout the
world (i.e., "<u>development</u>"), (2) considering the
<u>reciprocal interactions between social structures and
ecosystems</u>, (3) <u>reserving the notion of "adaptation"
for the actions of individuals and groups</u> (rather than
applying this notion to societies or other levels of
social organization that do not engage in purposive
behaviors or actions), and (4) <u>examining the impacts
of social forces both external and internal to "societies</u>." Each will be discussed in turn.

Virtually all individuals and groups, no matter
how remote from urban-industrial locations, are now
affected by two major dynamics that operate essentially at a global scale. The first such force is the
international division of labor. The notion of an
international division of labor refers to more than
trade linkages, although trade is a vital component of
this division of labor. What is most crucial about
the world-economy is that the development of any
country within this division of labor is conditioned
by the development paths undertaken by other countries. As will be discussed in more depth below,
Third World industrialization is constrained by its
technological inferiority vis-a-vis the advanced
industrial societies; to be competitive on the world
market, most low-income countries must purchase industrial capital goods abroad--something which has vital
implications for Third World economic and agricultural
policies. Likewise, the advanced industrial societies
have recently been highly affected by the low wage
rates and living standards that prevail in low-income
countries; the "capital flight" of multinational
corporations has involved the transfer of industrial

jobs to Third World countries where unions are weak and wages are low (Bluestone and Harrison, 1982; de Janvry, 1981). These global economic interrelations are approaching universality in the mid 1980s as international markets penetrate directly or indirectly virtually every peripheral region on the globe. Even remote "societies" of indigenous peoples are becoming effectively incorporated within the sphere of international economic relations (Barlett, 1980). They may maintain their traditional cultures, but their material fortunes are substantially intertwined with how their "host" society is implicated in the international division of labor.

The second global force, one which is given only minimal treatment in this paper, is the dynamics of the international political arena and its competition and culture. Historically, international political competition in the form of colonialism has left its imprint on virtually all contemporary low-income countries. The world wars, the most widespread and violent expressions of this competition, have also had notable impacts. But the international political arena is characterized not only by centrifugal forces such as international conflict and competition through diplomacy (e.g., negotiations over protectionism vs. "free trade"), but also by centripetal forces. Perhaps the most important global centripetal political force is the essentially universal desire expressed by Third World political elites to "modernize" and "develop" their countries, particularly in the direction of industrial development. To be sure, economic development is, in a sense, an economic imperative in a changing world-economy; the very ability of a nation to protect itself requires technologically sophisticated armaments, which in turn dictate some minimal level of industrial development (or an export-oriented economy to generate the foreign reserves to purchase such armaments). But the "development impulse" is a more basic cultural phenomenon. The virtually universal desire for higher standards of living has led to a widely shared political culture which dictates emulation of the industrial mass consumption economies of the developed countries.[5] It can be said that during the past 10 years only a small handful of eccentric Third World political leaders (Idi Amin of Uganda and Jean-Claude Duvalier of Haiti) did not wholeheartedly orient their government policies toward economic (generally industrial) development (irrespective of how ill-advised many of these policies have been).

The pervasiveness of the global political-economic forces affecting Third World countries, from capital city to remote hinterlands, suggests that an ecological rural sociology (or anthropology, economics, and so on) must be articulated with the theories and issues of "development." The specific theoretical approach need not be one of the postures (modernization theory, world-systems theory, dependency theory, modes of production theory, and so on) that is conventionally identified as a variety of "development theory." However, the approach should be contextualized by a consideration of how the global forces of economic division of labor and political conflict and culture affect the setting under study.

The second methodological principle is that interaction between social structure and natural environment should be viewed as reciprocal and mutually interrelated. The ecological concept of coevolution captures the essence of this principle at a metaphorical level. It was noted earlier that the social scientific imagery of social structures and human institutions affecting natural resource utilization and environmental quality has been utilized frequently. (The other direction of causality, which was most crudely expressed as environmental determinism in turn-of-the-century geography, has also had a long history.) However, the reciprocal and interactive relationships between social institutions and the natural environment have rarely received systematic attention. A useful exception, albeit with certain flaws, is Franke and Chasin's <u>Seeds of Famine</u> (1980). Franke and Chasin explore both the socioeconomic roots and institutional consequences of the Sahelian drought and famine of 1968-73. (The Franke and Chasin book is also an outstanding example of integrating ecologically-oriented social science with the global dynamics of economic change.) The study exhibits a creative diachronic method in which social structure and ecology are seen to coevolve during the course and aftermath of the drought.

The third methodological principle relates to the logical status of the notion of "adaptation" in socio-ecological analyses. The use of the notion of adaptation as applied to individuals and purposive social groups is a useful procedure (see especially Barlett, 1980). The notion that individuals and groups seek to adapt to environmental changes and perturbation is sociological common sense, although it should be recognized that these adaptations may be only partial from the vantage points of human welfare or ecological sustainability. Utilizing the notion of adaptation to understand the course of social change in nonpurposive groups (especially "societies") is, however, sociologically problematic. At its extreme (e.g., Rappaport's, 1967, interpretation of the "latent functions" of ritual among the Tsembaga), societal adaptation as a conceptual framework represents patent teleology. Societies do not act; the people within them do. Social structural factors have close connections to societal sustainability and adaptability to ecological change and perturbation. However, adaptation is not a "functional imperative," and the course of change in contemporary societies will just as frequently be viewed as maladaptive as it is adaptive.

A useful example of the caution that must be exercised in applying the notion of adaptation to non-purposive groups was reported in Boserup's <u>The Conditions of Agricultural Growth</u> (1965). Boserup noted that a typical societal consequence of population pressure on limited agricultural resources was increased human fertility. Fertility often increased in the wake of overpopulation-induced ecological scarcity as families had more children to increase the labor available for an intensified or involuted agricultural system. Larger families may be adaptive in the narrow sense for individual families, but the societal reflection of these familial responses would otherwise tend to exacerbate population pressure on ecological resources at some later point--hardly an adaptive or self-regulatory societal mechanism. The degree to which social change is adaptive is thus an empirical question--and an inherently contentious one, since what is "adaptive" to one observer may appear to be "maladaptive" to another.

The final methodological principle is that one must be attentive to forces both internal and external to societal or subsocietal groups. This principle was partially implicit in the first relating to the global context of political-economic transformation. But as necessary as it is to place socioecological interactions in the global context of development, it is important to pay comparable attention to internal dynamics. While this principle is, in a certain sense, obvious, it has been repeatedly ignored in many styles of social research. For example, the traditional practice of ecological anthropology has almost always tended to ignore external socioeconomic forces. Likewise, analysts working out of dependency theory (see, for example, Frank, 1980; Wallerstein, 1979) have largely neglected social forces internal to societies and subsocietal structures (Chilcote, 1984: Chap. 6; Roxborough, 1979). While social problems and policy responses will tend to be conditioned by global economic and political forces, the outcomes may vary dramatically across different societies and regions because of variations in internal social organization and culture.

EXTERNAL "DEVELOPMENT" FORCES: THE DYNAMICS OF THE
CONTEMPORARY INTERNATIONAL DIVISION OF LABOR[6]

It has been widely recognized that the past 15
years have witnessed a crisis of conventional development theory. Although a detailed analysis is beyond
the scope of this paper (but see Chilcote, 1984;
Young, 1983; Roxborough, 1979, and Long, 1977, for
convenient summaries), it can be noted that prevailing development theories of the 1950s and 1960s
(e.g., Hirschman, 1958; Rostow, 1963; Hoselitz, 1960)
were largely based on analyses of the social forces
that shaped the development of the presently advanced
industrial societies. However, it has become increasingly apparent that there are a number of factors that
render the Western experience essentially nonreplicable in most areas of the contemporary Third World (de
Janvry, 1981).

Present underdeveloped countries experienced
colonial pillage and often face major overpopulation
problems. They must contend with protectionism and
trade monopolies, and compete in world markets from a
position of technological inferiority. These conditions generally did not plague the development of the
now-advanced industrial societies, especially those in
Western Europe. The most crucial disjunction between
the development milieus of contemporary Third World
countries and those of advanced industrial societies
during their industrial "take-off" stages is Third
World technological inferiority and the capital-
intensive character of modern industrial technology,
which absorbs relatively little labor. With few
exceptions, the present developed nations began their
industrial and larger economic take-offs during the
eighteenth and nineteenth centuries, using primitive,
labor-intensive industrial technologies and facing
little competition in the world market from established industrial powers. (The U.S. was a partial
exception, given its technological inferiority and
subjection to trade monopolies in the late eighteenth
and portions of the nineteenth century.) Contemporary
Third World countries, on the other hand, must utilize
relatively modern industrial technologies which are
capital-intensive and which have little labor absorption capacity; this imperative is a reflection of the
need for Third World producers to be competitive on
the world market already dominated by major industrial
countries. These technologies are extremely capital-
intensive by comparison with those used by the
contemporary developed countries during their "industrial revolutions." But the industrial technologies
used by Third World countries also tend to be

inferior, especially with regard to labor productivity, to those technologies now monopolized by the major industrial powers and their corporations.

The technological inferiority of low-income countries leads to two crucial consequences. First, capital goods must be imported from the advanced industrial societies, creating the need to generate foreign exchange through exports to repay loans. The foreign exchange problem is compounded if foreign loans are necessary to develop the infrastructure (e.g., transportation, electrical generation) necessary to support industrialization. Finally, the need to service foreign debt will typically dictate economic policies which subsidize the export sectors (both primary and secondary) over sectors primarily oriented toward the internal market. The second concomitant of technological inferiority for low-income countries is that they must compete against the firms of advanced industrial societies which have the very latest and most efficient technologies in the world market (Frobel, 1980; Evans, 1979). They tend to do so on the basis of their cheap labor, since low wage scales are the principal means for compensating for low labor productivity. Third World governments thus tend to orient their public policies toward minimizing labor costs. Policies supporting low wage scales are varied, but include public subsidies of workers' consumption costs (e.g., transportation and other services) and, most importantly for the purposes of this paper, policies that ensure low food prices.

The tendency for Third World governments to enact policies which result in low food prices has been widely recognized (see, for example, Schultz, 1978; Lipton, 1977; Bates, 1981; de Janvry, 1981). Cheap food policies are pursued in direct fashion (e.g., manipulation of currency exchange rates, food export restrictions, importing of foodstuffs) and indirectly through ensuring cheap agricultural labor. A major example of the latter aspect of food policy is the initiation of integrated rural development programs aimed at retaining peasants in the countryside, but at a sufficiently low level of subsistence so that they are available as a cheap labor force for the large farm or estate sector (Galli, 1981).

The structural imperative for developing countries to restrain food costs tends to have a relatively common set of impacts on agrarian structures. At the most basic level, cheap food requires inexpensive agricultural labor. The mechanisms by which agricultural employers and government officials restrain agricultural labor costs vary greatly among Third World countries. In the Latin American context,

the heightened international interdependence following
World War II was superimposed on highly unequal landholding structures typified by the precapitalist
hacienda and patron-client relationships. Commercial
penetration typically led to the commercialization and
transformation of the hacienda. In some cases,
tenants were expelled from resident plots on the
estate as rising land prices dictated intensification
of production; landlords thus found it more cost-
effective to evict their tenants and hire them for
temporary periods as wage labor. Other contexts
(e.g., the Ecuadorian highlands) witnessed landlords
selling part of their lands to well-situated peasants
(or to the government for land reform schemes), with
landlords either farming the remaining land more
intensively and/or transferring their capital to urban
industry (Waters, 1985). Labor for the estate sector
(and for the "kulak" or "middle" peasant sector) would
be provided by peasants unable to purchase sufficient
land to meet family needs from the minifundio (see
Goodman and Redclift, 1982:Chapter 4).

Land concentration in Latin America, which was
largely a legacy of its colonial heritage and its preindustrial development up to World War II, has decis-
ively shaped the trajectory along which agricultural
labor has been cheapened. Land concentration and the
latifundia-minifundia complex ensured the availability
of cheap wage labor by blocking widespread peasant
access to land and creating the need by landless and
near-landless peasants to seek out wage employment.
There has, in fact, been a strong tendency for Latin
American landholding systems to become increasingly
bi-modal or dualistic--characterized by simultaneous
growth of the large estate and of the postage-stamp-
sized minifundia (Roberts, 1978). Peek (1978) has
reported data on 11 Latin American countries which
reveal a strong trend in the direction of "re-
peasantization"--that is, the reinforcement of peasant
numbers on small, "subfamily" plots. For example, in
Brazil, farms under 10 hectares increased from 34 to
51 percent of total farms from 1950 to 1970. During
this same time period, the average size of Brazilian
farms under 10 hectares decreased from 4.25 to 3.61
hectares. Most Latin American countries exhibited
comparable trends, with the tendency toward re-
peasantization being strongest in those countries
(Brazil, Ecuador, and Colombia) with the greatest
degree of land concentration.

Thus, although there are notable exceptions
(Goodman and Redclift, 1982:Chapter 4), there has been
a general pattern in Latin American agriculture for
the estate sector to be functionally related to the
subsistence, smallholder, or "subfamily" farming

sector through members of smallholder families working for wages (either cash or, decreasingly, in-kind) on neighboring large farms. This pattern is frequently referred to as "functional dualism" or "semiproletarianization" (de Janvry, 1981; Galli, 1981). This tendency toward functional dualism can be explained by the high (albeit often only seasonal) labor demand of the estate sector and the imperative faced by these large farmers to produce on an economically competitive basis in an interdependent national and world economy. Labor costs for the latifundista can be reduced through perpetuation of the subsistence sector. This is because functional dualism between the modern estate and traditional subsistence sectors enables large farmers to pay their hired workers a wage which is lower than the cost of maintaining the worker, since part of the subsistence costs of the hired laborer is provided by unpaid family workers who labor on small subsistence plots.

Before returning to socioeconomic and resource issues pertaining to Latin American agriculture, it is useful to underscore a crucial consequence of the dynamics of Third World insertion in the contemporary international division of labor. It was noted earlier that the constraint of technological inferiority creates tendencies toward cheapening both industrial and agricultural labor. One aggregate or social structural consequence of these tendencies is stagnation of internal markets as a lever for economic growth and development. A mass of poorly-remunerated peasants and urban dwellers constricts the internal market and encourages large farmers and industrial firms to seek foreign customers for their products. The search for export markets will, of course, help to alleviate balance of payments problems. Reinforcement of the import-export linkage, however, deprives the domestic economy of multipliers of economic activity. These multipliers are transferred to the foreign countries which manufacture capital goods and other inputs, and process the raw materials or market the industrial goods produced in the Third World. The limited domestic market and lack of economic multipliers in turn tend to constrain internal investment that would provide employment opportunities for marginal rural and urban populations. To be sure, there has been a mass influx of rural migrants into Latin American cities, motivated largely by the desire to escape oppressive rural poverty (Roberts, 1978). Their destination--typically oppressive urban poverty--offers little improvement, although the prospects for mobility are arguably greater there than in the countryside. Nevertheless, high rural fertility (which, as will be noted later, is intimately related to re-peasantization and semiproletarianization) has been sufficient to place increasing demographic pressure on the resources of subsistence minifundia despite the exodus of peasants to the cities.

The forces that have affected Latin American agricultural development have by no means been wholly external in origin.[7] As noted above, external forces have been mediated by the longstanding latifundia-minifundia complex. The degree to which the penetration of international market forces has transformed traditional patron-client relations and the hacienda has varied greatly between and within Latin American countries.[8] Government policies, as discussed below, many of which have been shaped primarily by domestic political structures, have greatly affected the social structure and ecology of Latin American agriculture.

THE SOCIAL ECOLOGY OF LATIN AMERICAN AGRICULTURAL DEVELOPMENT

Latin American agricultural development has generated two dominant forms of human-environment relations. The first, dependence on nonrenewable energy resources, is most characteristic of the estate sector (Redclift, 1984). The second, degradation of land resources, is induced by population pressure, land fragmentation, and socioeconomic marginalization and typifies the subsistence-semiproletarian sector (de Janvry, 1981). These ecological problems are, of course, not neatly confined to the sectors they are identified with above. Land destruction occurs in the estate sector (e.g., in cattle ranching in the Amazon; Bunker, 1985), and many smallholders have begun to depend on purchased petrochemical inputs (Redclift, 1984). Nevertheless, the correspondence is quite high and will serve to organize the discussion that follows.

The Latin American nations are generally characterized by moderate use of petrochemical inputs to agriculture by comparison with the developing countries of Africa and Asia. For example, average fertilizer consumption in Latin America tends to be roughly 25-50 kg/ha of arable land per year, while most developing market economies in Asia consume in excess of 50 kg/ha and most African countries less than 25 kg/ha on an annual basis (Wortman and Cummings, 1978:68). This pattern can be largely explained by Latin American's lower emphasis on agricultural development and greater land resource endowments by comparison with Asia and its far greater level of industrial and overall economic development relative to Africa. But as in many other developing country contexts (see, for example, Griffin, 1974; Pearse, 1980), fertilizer use in Latin American countries is largely accounted for by the estate sector (and in some settings, by the "middle peasant" or "kulak" sector), with this disparity in fertilizer consumption having increased along with the transformation of the hacienda and the reinforcement of peasant numbers on small subsistence plots. Nevertheless, aggregate growth in fertilizer consumption in Latin America over the past 15 years has been in excess of 10 percent per annum, with these growth rates tending to be highest in tropical South America (especially Venezuela and Colombia) and Brazil, and lowest in the Southern Cone countries (especially Chile, Argentina, and Paraguay) (Lynam, 1981; Ashby, 1981).

The growth of the petrochemical trajectory of agricultural development in the estate sector has been largely due to the activities of the international agricultural research centers, especially CIMMYT in Mexico and CIAT in Colombia. The international centers in conjunction with developed country (especially U.S.) scientists have diffused the HYV and petrochemical trajectory to the national agricultural research institutes in Latin American countries. The attractiveness of petrochemical inputs was also enhanced by the extremely low world fertilizer prices that prevailed in the 1960s (Perelman, 1977). Moreover, governments in Latin America tended to subsidize the prices of petrochemical inputs in the late 1960s and early 1970s in an attempt to stimulate agricultural production, to reduce imports and hard currency outflows, and to constrain food price increases. These subsidies were especially important in countries (Colombia, Brazil, Peru, Chile) where organizations of large "modernizing" landowners became influential in shaping government agriculture and agricultural research policies (Crouch and de Janvry, 1979). Finally, use of modern petrochemical inputs was generally accompanied (and largely preceded) by mechanization, the combination of which greatly increased energy consumption in the estate sector (Castro and Buttel, 1980).

The pattern of resource use in the estate sector depicted above exhibits substantial variations across a region so socially, culturally, and ecologically diverse as Latin America. For example, fertilizer use tends to be much greater in the tropical Latin American countries with high population densities than it is in the temperate Southern Cone countries which have more abundant land resources. Agricultural production also tends to be more energy-intensive in economically dynamic regions than in economically stagnant regions (Castro and Buttel, 1980), largely because more thorough market penetration and higher land values and wage rates in these more dynamic regions have induced farmers to substitute energy for land and labor inputs. Moreover, many regions in Latin American countries still have significant amounts of arable lands which are either unutilized or farmed very extensively (e.g., as pasture for cattle). While a significant amount of Latin America's agricultural output growth over the past 15 years has been accounted for by rapid increases in HYV and corollary energy inputs, expansion along the extensive margin--that is, incorporation of new lands and more labor into agricultural production--remains significant in several countries that have agricultural frontiers (especially Brazil). Nevertheless, the general pattern of the estate sector dominating in the use of energy intensive inputs and becoming rapidly more dependent on the use of these inputs characterizes the bulk of Central America, the Caribbean, and South America.

The increased use of petrochemical and mechanical inputs has several crucial socioeconomic and ecological concomitants. First, Latin American agricultures have become more dependent on imported inputs (especially petroleum, manufactured fertilizers, and machinery) and more vulnerable to energy price increases (Buttel, 1981). While the petroleum price shocks of the mid- and late-1970s have subsided as a result of the decline in OPEC solidarity, global recession, and energy conservation in the developed countries, nitrogen fertilizer prices have continued to ratchet upwards. This has occurred as a result of decontrol of natural gas prices in the U.S. (the world's major fertilizer producer and a prime supplier of imported nitrogen fertilizer for Latin America), which has led to rising relative prices for natural gas and for manufactured products for which natural gas is a feedstock.

Second, increased mechanization has tended to increase the specialization of latifundias in the production of one or a small number of crops. Increased specialization and monoculturing have potentially significant ecological consequences depending upon local agroecological conditions. Mechanization has also tended to confine the demand for hired workers to a highly seasonal basis. For example, sugar cane producers in the Cauca Valley of Colombia have mechanized land preparation and planting to a degree comparable with that of advanced industrial societies. However, harvest is only partially mechanized, with the bulk of cane cutting done manually by hired workers.

Third, increased estate sector dependence on nonrenewable energy inputs has, contrary to the plans of architects of the Green Revolution, begun to lead the estate sector away from staple crop production and toward production of agro-export commodities, luxury foods, and industrial raw materials (e.g., soybeans, cattle, poultry, and sorghum). The shift from staple to agro-export and related commodities has been conditioned by several factors in addition to rising energy input prices. One key factor has been government food policies aimed at constraining price increases in staple wage foods for the industrial working class, as noted above. Lagging prices for staple wage foods have thus encouraged the estate sector to seek out other crops for which the source of demand is more dynamic or has a high income elasticity of demand. High income inequality in Latin America has made the affluent urban strata an attractive source of demand for commodities such as meat and dairy products (Waters, 1985). Export-oriented economic policies of the Latin American governments have stimulated production of commodities such as soybeans and sorghum (Graziano Neto, 1982). These shifts have exacerbated the constraints on feeding the Latin American population from its otherwise abundant agricultural resources. Agricultural output in Latin America from 1950-1978 increased by 3.4 percent per annum, well above the rate of population growth (Lynam, 1981). Daily per capita calorie production in 1975-77 was 2,542, well above the average per capita requirement of 2,380. Yet for roughly two-thirds of Latin American countries, in excess of 30 percent, and sometimes as high as 60 percent, of the population receives less than 90 percent of recommended caloric levels (Pachico and Lynam, 1981).

It was noted earlier that the principal socioecological relation in the estate sector is its increased dependence on nonrenewable energy inputs. However, it should also be noted that the diffusion of Green Revolution-type production practices into staple and agro-export commodity systems has proven to be ecologically destructive under many local conditions, particularly in tropical areas (Graziano Neto, 1982). This is not to imply that tropical ecosystems are uniformly vulnerable to modern monocultural practices or that all tropical soils are too fragile for sustainable agricultural production. Nevertheless, large-scale, monocultural, energy-intensive agriculture has proven to be ecologically destructive in many areas of tropical Latin America. This destruction, however, appears to have had minimal impact on estate or plantation systems, since land abundance facilitates movement of these systems to frontier locations if land destruction becomes severe.

For the vast majority of the Latin American rural population, however, human survival, let alone survival as a self-provisioning or commercially-oriented peasant, represents a protracted struggle with extant socioeconomic and ecological conditions. Data for Brazil and Ecuador (Lynam, 1981) effectively illustrate the contrasts between the estate and sub-family-subsistence sectors in Latin America. In 1975, Brazilian farms with less than five hectares represented roughly one-fourth of the country's total farms but accounted for only 1.2 percent of the total land in farms. These small minifundia absorbed 27.9 percent of the total agricultural labor input in Brazilian agriculture. By contrast, Brazilian farms with more than 1,000 hectares accounted for 42.9 percent of land in farms but only 3.3 percent of total labor input. Ecuadorian data for 1974 reveal a similar pattern. Minifundia with less than five hectares accounted for 6.7 percent of land in farms and 52.9 percent of total labor input. Farms in excess of 1,000 hectares represented 20.1 percent of land and only 2.4 percent of labor input in Ecuador (Lynam, 1981:34).

Peasant adaptive strategies in a milieu of land concentration and dependent capitalist development are multifaceted and dependent upon a variety of factors such as size and quality of the family plot, the nature of household labor resources, availability of off-farm employment opportunities, and the structural requirements for cash (see Barlett, 1980). Most minifundias are too small to feed a family and generate sufficient cash income to pay taxes and debts and to purchase commodities that cannot be produced on the farm. Given such a circumstance, a crucial family labor allocation decision will be the degree to which the household's land and labor will be devoted to producing subsistence or cash crops and the amount of labor that will be allocated to off-farm wage work. Production of subsistence crops such as cassava, maize, and beans, with traditional production practices, involves relatively little risk and can account for the majority of a family's consumption needs; however, subsistence crop production generates little cash and must be accompanied by off-farm employment, typically on a seasonal basis for low wages on a neighboring plantation or estate. Cash crop production introduces significant risks (e.g., of indebtedness, market downturns, or crop failures) but will generate cash and may increase labor productivity. However, peasant producers of cash crops will tend to be at a competitive disadvantage with their more heavily capitalized estate sector neighbors (de Janvry, 1981).[9]

In practice, these decisions tend to be highly constrained. The data noted earlier on the allocation of labor to the Brazilian minifundia sector indicate that when land is scarce, households may have no alternative to devoting long hours of family labor to intensive production on the minifundia and to wage work off the farm. Labor productivity on the minifundia tends to be extremely low, partly because, to use a neoclassical economics expression, labor has very little opportunity cost in the rural economy and additional production may be valuable despite its large labor requirements. Family survival thus hinges on the ability to deploy large amounts of labor to some combination of on-farm and off-farm work. Although Latin American rural population growth rates have declined perceptibly over the past 10 years, these fertility rates remain high because of the fact that children as young as six years of age are valued for their potential contributions to subsistence production and later to cash income. It was noted earlier that the Latin American agricultural economies have generally experienced a process of "re-peasantization" over the past decades in conjunction with the expansion of commercial estate sector agriculture. This trend should not be construed as a renaissance of the traditional independent peasantry. It was emphasized above that this re-peasantization trend was based on demand for poorly-remunerated wage labor in the estate sector and on the lack of employment opportunities in urban-industrial regions. Moreover, these trends indicate a fragmentation of minifundia and a marginalization of the economic status and living standards of the peasantry. This is partly a reflection of the demographic dynamics just discussed, in which large families eventually lead to the subdivision of already small plots. The marginalization of the peasantry has also been caused by the extension of market relations which tend to incorporate peasants into a competitive struggle with the more heavily capitalized estate sector. The trend toward increasing numbers of smallholding peasants thus should not obscure the fact that economic competition and risk often lead to peasants being evicted from the plots they farm as tenants or being squeezed off the land because of their inability to repay loans. The contemporary peasant economy is thus dramatically different from a self-sufficient "natural economy." The differentiation and marginalization of the peasantry thus make peasant survival and livelihood closely dependent upon agroecological dynamics and the ability to derive sustenance from a small plot on a sustainable basis.

Overall, then, the demographic explosion, caused by the attractiveness of children as a source of labor (and by traditional cultural values), and the marginalization of the peasantry are leading to ecological changes that threaten to undermine the smallholder sector. Increases in population press up against the limits of land resources, leading to consequences such as fuelwood shortages and deforestation and to the shortening of fallow periods in swidden agriculture. The marginalization of the peasantry in many areas of Latin America, especially the Andean countries, is reflected in their dislocation to marginal (often hilly, high altitude) lands in which traditional production practices lead to massive soil erosion and land destruction.

Under certain circumstances the marginalization of the peasantry causes smallholders to withdraw from commercial production, due to the lack of credit worthiness or to the fact that closeness to the margin of survival prohibits assumption of the risks of borrowing money to purchase manufactured inputs with which to improve productivity. The low quality of land--for example, its slope, altitude, or aluminum toxicity to plants--may also prohibit the production of cash crops. Other sets of circumstances have led marginalized peasant households to abandon traditional production practices in favor of more intensive ones based on purchased petrochemical inputs. For example, Barlett's (1976) study of the impact of population pressure on traditional swidden agriculture in Costa Rica indicated that the demographic explosion resulted in shortened fallow periods and reduced soil fertility. Deterioration of soil fertility eventually led to the more intensive system being adopted because it maximized caloric returns to labor.

Ecological changes induced by the reinforcement of peasant numbers on progressively smaller and marginal plots have important implications across the human-ecosystem interface. Declines in nutritional status have been frequently documented, and despite overall improvements in health status resulting from the penetration of urban-industrial forces, nutritional deficiencies appear to be responsible for increasing the susceptibility of certain age groups (especially the young and elderly) to disease. Also, there is an increasing recognition that peasants' exposure to toxic pesticides in their wage labor activities in the estate sector may have dire health consequences (Redclift, 1984). Declines in health and nutritional status no doubt have further impacts across the human-ecosystem interface. For example, deterioration of nutritional and health status decreases family labor resources and may reinforce Boserup's (1965) "law of least effort" (see also Barlett, 1976, 1980) such that peasant adaptive strategies are heavily determined by their perceived or actual returns to labor.

AGROECOLOGY AND AGRICULTURAL DEVELOPMENT STRATEGIES

It was noted earlier that the 1970s were a decade of ferment in development theory and practice, largely because then-prevailing development strategies gave scant attention to the types of problems just discussed with regard to the smallholder sector. The mid-1970s to the present have witnessed dramatic changes in development rhetoric and some actual changes in practice (Chambers, 1983). Notions such as "integrated rural development," "basic needs development," "appropriate technology," and many others have become a part of the official vocabulary of development agencies in both the First and Third Worlds (see, for example, Galli, 1981) since they were codified by Saint and Coward (1977) and others.

Perhaps the most useful of these notions, many of which have unfortunately been reduced to faddish slogans by those seeking to repackage traditional development thrusts, is "farming systems research" (see Whyte and Boynton, 1983). Farming systems research is an approach that seeks to understand the farm as an integrated system of crops, animals, and humans, with emphasis generally given to smallholder or subfamily farms. Thus, in contrast to the typical experiment station approach initially adopted by the international centers and most national research institutes, the research process involves on-farm data collection and the interaction of multidisciplinary teams of scientists and extension workers with smallholder peasants. The general goal of farming systems research is to enable smallholding peasants to utilize new technologies with minimal disruption to traditional farming systems. Initial on-farm research is aimed at understanding the dynamics of the farming system(s) and enabling scientists to simulate farm conditions at the experiment station. One or more technical options for introducing new practices within the context of traditional farming systems are extended to peasant farms and evaluated by a multidisciplinary team. Refinements are made as needed based on peasant experience. The results of on-farm field trials and the "fine-tuning" process are then introduced into extension channels to enable the broader diffusion of the new technology.

Social scientists, usually rural sociologists and economists, have become increasingly involved in farming systems research, partly due to mandates to this effect in U.S. foreign technical assistance legislation. Many ecologically-oriented social scientists have seen farming systems research as a rubric for employing the micro "ecological systems" approaches that have become increasingly common in ecological anthropology. Moreover, farming systems research can serve as a lever for incorporating social science insights into research and extension policy.

The potential benefits of farming systems research have become increasingly recognized, but this approach should not be seen as a panacea for the socioecological problems of the Latin American smallholder sector. A key but often only implicit assumption of farming systems research is that if smallholders are the focus of research and technical change, they will be able to capture the benefits of increased productivity. A corollary assumption is that the "farming system" is a self-contained entity in which the variables that affect peasant decision-making are largely endogenous to that system (e.g., soil resources, animal inventories, climatic constraints, the nature of household labor resources). Both assumptions, however, are only partially applicable to the latifundia-minifundia functional dualism of rural Latin America. At the extreme, in which peasants are more wage workers than they are agriculturalists, productivity improvements on minifundia may merely reinforce the role of the subsistence sector in subsidizing the costs of agricultural wage labor; the widespread socioeconomic and ecological rationalization of minifundia under these circumstances would over time benefit the estate sector more than the smallholder sector by enabling large farmers to further depress the wages of hired laborers (see Flinn and Buttel, 1983). Put somewhat differently, for farming systems research to lead to significant benefits for smallholder peasants, their plots must be sufficiently large that the farm is capable of meeting household subsistence needs <u>and</u> producing a marketable surplus so that wage labor can be significantly reduced in importance as a component of household income (Garrett, 1982).

These comments should not be construed as dismissing the very real potential of the farming systems approach as a research and public policy strategy. But its limitations must be recognized so that the further diffusion of farming systems approaches does not become viewed as the ultimate solution to the problems of the Latin American smallholder.

SUMMARY

Rural sociology has played a pioneering role in introducing ecological variables to sociological analysis. The land-grant context of rural sociology and the influence of the centrifugal forces of the larger discipline on rural sociological research have constrained the subdiscipline in making greater contributions to ecological analysis. But rural sociology's longstanding concern with development problems (both domestic and international) has been extremely useful in anchoring its ecological research in the realities of the international division of labor and of the production and consumption problems of Third World peasants. Rural sociological contributions to the literature have not been dominant (although many have been innovative or pathbreaking efforts), mainly because the U.S. rural sociologists working in the field discussed in this paper probably number fewer than 30. Of these 30, the majority work outside of academic milieus and have limited access to scholarly publication outlets.

The major thrust of this paper is that ecological analysis will bear the most fruit if it takes seriously the promise of sociology articulated by C. Wright Mills (1959) and given wide lip service since that time: understanding society through the intersection of biography and history. Sociology must grapple with macrosocial and microsocial dynamics and their interrelations, and as well must do so in ways that are sensitive and responsible to human concerns. Moreover, comprehensive ecological analysis must recognize the reciprocal patterns of causality across human-environmental interfaces.

This chapter has illustrated such an approach by examining the general parameters of the social ecology of Latin American agricultural development. The analysis has attempted to articulate the macrosociology of the development of the world-economy, the microsociology of estate and peasant sector "adaptive strategies," and the ecology of the Latin American agricultural regions. Given the limitations of space, the discussion of certain topics has been more comprehensive than that of other topics. These limitations notwithstanding, it is hoped that the analysis both illustrates the virtues of a holistic ecological approach in rural sociology and illuminates the complexities of the development task in rural Latin America.

NOTES

1. The demise of functionalism as the unifying focus of American sociology after 1965 was incredibly rapid. The intense attack on functionalism, spearheaded by Gouldner's (1970) The Coming Crisis of Western Sociology, led, in particular, to Talcott Parsons' falling from his pre-1965 position as the dominant figure in contemporary sociology to a situation at present where Parsons' influence is negligible.

2. But it should be noted that the three major classical sociological theorists (Marx, Weber, and Durkheim) did pay considerable attention to natural resource issues and that the classical theorists remain influential, albeit indirectly, in contemporary environmental sociology (Humphrey and Buttel, 1982:Chapter 1).

3. Much ecological anthropology has been limited in its applicability to resource problems in contemporary complex societies because of its typical argument that societies tend to be ecologically self-regulating (or "adaptive") systems. See the section below on "methodological principles."

4. This is not to imply that anthropologists have neglected the study of the state. However, the traditional emphasis in anthropological theorizing about the state has pertained to the emergence of the state in preindustrial societies. Only recently have political anthropologists become involved in theoretical controversies over theories of the modern state in contemporary capitalist societies.

5. This is not to imply that industrial-led development is the only possible course for improving living standards in low-income countries. Indeed, there has been growing attention to notions of rural and agriculturally-led development as alternatives to the industrial development strategies that have predominated since World War II (see, for example, Chambers, 1983).

6. This section is based on Buttel (1981) and Flinn and Buttel (1983).

7. Roxborough (1979), in fact, emphasizes the tremendous diversity among Third World countries and suggests that general development theories

have tended to be insensitive to variations in internal social structures.

8. Goodman and Redclift (1982) is an excellent source on the diverse patterns of agrarian transformation in Latin America that have resulted from the penetration of international economic forces since World War II.

9. Smallholder peasants tend to be at a competitive disadvantage with large producers with regard to both scale economies and government subsidization of inputs and agricultural research. Thus, de Janvry (1981) notes that smallholders will tend not to produce the commodities that are produced in the estate sector.

REFERENCES

Ashby, J. 1981. Fertilizers. Latin American Agriculture: Trends in CIAT Commodities. Cali, Colombia: Centro Internacional de Agricultura Tropical.

Barlett, P. F. 1976. Labor efficiency and the mechanism of agricultural evolution. Journal of Anthropological Research 32 (2):124-140.

Barlett, P.F. 1980. Adaptive strategies in peasant agricultural production. Annual Review of Anthropology 9:545-573.

Bates, R. H. 1981. Markets and States in Tropical Africa: The Political Basis of Agricultural Policies. Berkeley: Univ. of Calif. Press.

Bennett, J. W. 1976a. Anticipation, adaptation, and the concept of culture. Science 192:847-853.

Bennett, J. W. 1976b. The Ecological Transition. Chicago: Aldine.

Bluestone, B., and B. Harrison. 1982. The Deindustrialization of America. New York: Basic Books.

Boserup, E. 1965. The Conditions of Agricultural Growth. Chicago: Aldine.

Bunker, S. A. 1985. Underdeveloping the Amazon. Urbana: Univ. of Illinois Press.

Buttel, F. H. 1978. Environmental sociology: a new paradigm? The American Sociologist 13 (November):252-256.

Buttel, F. H. 1981. Energy, agrarian structure, and food production. Cornell Rural Sociology Bulletin No. 122, August.

Buttel, F. H. 1983. The land-grant system: a sociological perspective on value conflicts and ethical issues. Eds. R. Haynes and R. Lanier. Agriculture, Change, and Human Values Vol. II. Gainesville: Humanities and Agric. Program, Univ. of Florida.

Castro, L. M. B., and F. H. Buttel. 1980. Social organization and agricultural technology in Brazil: a sociological analysis of Minas Gerais municipios,

1950-1970. Paper presented at the Fifth World Congress for Rural Sociology, Mexico City, August.

Catton, W. R., Jr., and R. E. Dunlap. 1978a. Environmental sociology: a new paradigm. The American Sociologist 13 (February):41-49.

Catton, W. R., Jr., and R. E. Dunlap. 1978b. Paradigms, theories, and the primacy of the HEP-NEP distinction. The American Sociologist 13 (November):256-259.

Chambers, R. 1983. Rural Development. London: Longman.

Chilcote, R. H. 1984. Theories of Development and Underdevelopment. Boulder: Westview Press.

Cleaver, H. M., Jr. 1972. The contradictions of the Green Revolution. Monthly Review 24 (June):80-111.

Crouch, L., and A. de Janvry. 1979. The class basis of agricultural growth. Working Paper No. 70. Berkeley: Dept. of Agricultural and Resource Economics, Univ. of Calif., Berkeley.

Dahlberg, K. A. 1979. Beyond the Green Revolution. New York: Plenum.

de Janvry, A. 1981. The Agrarian Question and Reformism in Latin America. Baltimore: Johns Hopkins Univ. Press.

Dunlap, R. E., and W. R. Catton, Jr. 1979. Environmental Sociology. Annual Review of Sociology 5:243-273.

Dunlap, R. E., and K. E. Martin. 1983. Bringing environment into the study of agriculture: observations and suggestions regarding the sociology of agriculture. Rural Sociology 48 (Summer):201-218.

Evans, P. 1979. Dependent Development. Princeton: Princeton Univ. Press.

Flinn, W. L., and F. H. Buttel. 1983. Socioeconomic constraints on the transfer and adoption of agricultural technologies in low-income countries. Eds. J. Molnar and H. Clonts. Transferring Food Production Technology to Developing Nations. Boulder: Westview Press.

Frank, A. G. 1979. Dependent Accumulation and Underdevelopment. New York: Monthly Review Press.

Franke, R. W., and B. H. Chasin. 1980. **Seeds of Famine: Ecological Destruction and the Development in the West African Sahel**. Montclair: Allanheld, Osmun & Co.

Frankel, F. 1971. **India's Green Revolution**. Princeton: Princeton Univ. Press.

Friedland, W. H. 1979. Who killed rural sociology? Paper presented at the annual meeting of the American Sociological Assoc., Boston, August.

Froebel, F. 1980. **The Current Development of the World Economy**. Tokyo: United Nations Univ.

Galli, R. E., ed. 1981. **The Political Economy of Rural Development**. Albany: State Univ. of NY Press.

Garrett, P. 1982. Farming systems research: an appreciation and a critique. Paper presented at the annual meeting of the Rural Sociological Society, San Francisco, September.

Goodman, D., and M. Redclift. 1982. **From Peasant to Proletarian: Capitalist Development and Agrarian Transitions**. New York: St. Martin's Press.

Gouldner, A. W. 1970. **The Coming Crisis of Western Sociology**. New York: Avon.

Graziano Neto, F. 1982. **Questao Agraria e Ecologia**. Sao Paulo: Ed. Brasiliense.

Griffin, K. 1974. **The Political Economy of Agrarian Change**. Cambridge: Harvard Univ. Press.

Havens, A. E., and W. L. Flinn. 1975. Green Revolution technology and community development: the limits of action programs. **Economic Development and Cultural Change** 23:469-481.

Hirschman, A. O. 1958. **The Strategy of Economic Development**. New Haven: Yale Univ. Press.

Hoselitz, B. 1960. **Sociological Aspects of Economic Growth**. Glencoe: Free Press.

Koppel, B., and G. Beal. 1982. Graduate education for international development: a first report on a study of American rural sociology. **The Rural Scoiologist** 2 (November):346-355.

Koppel, B., and G. Beal. 1983. Graduate education for international development: a second report on a study of American rural sociology. <u>The Rural Sociologist</u> 3 (January):2-10.

Humphrey, C. R., and F. H. Buttel. 1982. <u>Environment, Energy, and Society</u>. Belmont: Wadsworth.

Lipton, M. 1977. <u>Why Poor People Stay Poor</u>. Cambridge: Harvard Univ. Press.

Long, N. 1977. <u>An Introduction to the Sociology of Rural Development</u>. Boulder: Westview Press.

Lynam, J. K. 1981. Growth in Latin American agriculture: a cross-country analysis. <u>Latin American Agriculture: Trends in CIAT Commodities</u>. Cali, Colombia: Centro Internacional de Agricultura Tropical.

Merton, R. K. 1968. <u>Social Theory and Social Structure</u>. New York: Free Press.

Mills, C. W. 1959. <u>The Sociological Imagination</u>. New York: Oxford Univ. Press.

Newby, H. 1980. Rural sociology: a trend report. <u>Current Sociology</u> 28 (Spring):1-141.

Newby, H., and F. H. Buttel. 1980. Toward a critical rural sociology. Eds. F. H. Buttel and H. Newby. <u>The Rural Sociology of the Advanced Societies</u>. Montclair: Allanheld, Osmun & Co.

Norgaard, R. B. 1981. Socioeconomic and ecosystem coevolution in the Amazon. <u>Journal of Environmental Economics and Management</u> 8:238-254.

Odum, H. T. 1971. <u>Environment, Power, and Society</u>. New York: Wiley-Interscience.

Orlove, B. S. 1980. Ecological anthropology. <u>Annual Review of Anthropology</u> 9:235-273.

Pachico, D., and J. K. Lynam. 1981. Food supply and malnutrition in Latin America. <u>Latin American Agriculture: Trends in CIAT Commodities</u>. Cali, Colombia: Centro Internacional de Agricultura Tropical.

Parsons, T. 1951. <u>The Social System</u>. Glencoe: Free Press.

Pearse, A. 1980. <u>Seeds of Plenty, Seeds of Want</u>. New York: Oxford Univ. Press.

Peek, P. 1978. Agrarian change and rural emigration in Latin America. ILO Working Paper, World Employment Research Programme. Geneva: ILO.

Perelman, M. 1977. *Farming for Profit in a Hungry World*. Montclair: Allanheld, Osmun & Co.

Rappaport, R. A. 1967. *Pigs for the Ancestors*. New Haven: Yale Univ. Press.

Redclift, M. 1984. *Development and the Environmental Crisis*. London: Methuen.

Roberts, B. 1978. *Cities of Peasants*. London: Edward Arnold.

Rostow, W. W. 1963. *The Stages of Economic Growth*. Cambridge: Cambridge Univ. Press.

Roxborough, I. 1979. *Theories of Underdevelopment*. Atlantic Highlands: Humanities Press.

Saint, W. S., and E. W. Coward, Jr. 1977. Agriculture and behavioral science: emerging orientations. *Science* 197 (19 August):733-737.

Sandbach, F. R. 1978. The rise and fall of the limits to growth debate. *Social Studies of Science* 8:495-520.

Sandbach, F. R. 1980. *Environment, Ideology, and Policy*. Montclair: Allanheld, Osmun & Co.

Schnaiberg, A. 1980. *The Environment*. New York: Oxford Univ. Press.

Schultz, T. W., ed. 1978. *Distortions of Agricultural Incentives*. Bloomington: Indiana Univ. Press.

Vayda, A. P., ed. 1969. *Environment and Cultural Behavior*. Garden City: Natural History Press.

Vayda, A. P. 1982. Progressive contextualization: a method for integrated social and biological research in the Man and the Biosphere (MAB) Program. Proceedings of the Workshop on Ecological Bases for Rational Resource Utilization in the Humid Tropics. Faculty of Forestry, Universiti Pertanian Malaysia, Serdang, Selangor, Malaysia.

Vayda, A. P., and B. J. McCay. 1975. New directions in ecology and ecological anthropology. *Annual Review of Anthropology* 4:293-306.

Waters, W. F. 1985. Access to land and the form of production in the Central Ecuadorian Highlands. Ph.D. diss., Cornell University.

Whyte, W. F., and D. Boynton, eds. 1983. *Higher-Yielding Human Systems for Agriculture*. Ithaca: Cornell Univ. Press.

Wallerstein, I. 1979. *The Capitalist World-Economy*. Cambridge: Cambridge Univ. Press.

Wortman, S., and R. W. Cummings, Jr. 1978. *To Feed This World*. Baltimore: Johns Hopkins Univ. Press.

Young, F. W. 1983. *Interdisciplinary Theories of Rural Development*. Greenwich: JAI Press.

6
Resources and People: An Economic Perspective

*Daniel W. Bromley
and Ellen Szarleta*

INTRODUCTION

    Economics, as the science of choice, is fundamentally concerned with the study of the way in which humans decide to do this rather than that, or to use this resource in a certain way as opposed to a slightly different way. Or, why humans use one resource and not another. In this discussion we propose to develop a conceptual view of the choice process central to the way in which humans interact with the natural environment. Throughout we will be attempting to focus on particular resource-human interactions. We also will be concerned with the relationship of our conceptual approach to resource management issues "on the ground."
    At the outset it is important to point out that the perspective we will present is not part of the mainstream of resource economics. That more usual approach tends to focus on natural resources as mere inputs into a production process that includes labor and man-made capital. The economic problem is considered to be one of determining the most efficient level of use of the factors of production--of which natural resources are but one type. Interesting complications are introduced by admitting that some natural resources are non-renewable and so the problem becomes transformed into one of determining the optimal intertemporal path over which the resource is driven to economic---if not physical--depletion. A second aspect of the conventional approach would be to view natural resources as the receiving medium for by-products of human activity. Here, the economic problem becomes one of weighing the benefits and costs of certain levels of discharge into the natural environment.
    In contrast, our view draws one away from considering the optimal rate of use of natural resources--a question about which there is a great deal of analytical and emotional literature. Neither are we here concerned with the economically efficient level of discharges into the natural environment. Our purpose

is, rather, to highlight the structure of man's interaction with the natural environment. We intend to develop a model of the structure within which humans make economic (and other) calculations of the sort that have been extensively analyzed in the conventional literature.

Let us then start with the obvious; man must eat, and must have access to certain materials and tools to facilitate that need, as well as to provide a range of creature comforts. It also is--or at least ought to be--obvious that man is a cost minimizer. That is, work has an implicit cost (called an opportunity cost) in the form of foregone leisure. The cost of laboring in the fields is, at bottom, the gain that could be derived by engaging in the next most preferred pastime--be it conversation with friends, or sitting alone under a tree. But of course the cost of leisure is seeing one's family ill fed and ill housed. Few choices are costless since each action we take possesses a correlate for which certain benefits and costs exist. If I do A, I may not do B; the benefits of A must be considered against its costs, plus the costs of not doing B. And the costs of not doing B are the benefits that could be enjoyed from B had it actually been undertaken, net of the costs of doing B and the costs foregone by not doing A.

While this all seems rather formidable, it is necessary to keep in mind that we make such choices daily, though we are often not conscious of the sorts of tradeoffs described above.

The second aspect of man is that change has its own costs--call it the psychic costs of the unknown. If doing A has been the tradition (habit) then switching to B will carry some costs--at least initially. The concept of a learning curve captures this notion of the costs of change. We start from the position that to consider choices is to consider change from the status quo, and that this process carries a special cost that must be considered.

A less uncontroversial aspect of our premise-- though one that is reasonably secure--is that man makes explicit choices on the basis of information at his disposal. And if presented with exactly the same bundle of information and states of nature at two discrete points in time would make the same choices, assuming that preferences remained the same. This is rationality in its starkest form. If state of nature I exists and an individual chooses to do A, then rationality simply requires that when presented with the same state of nature an instant later the individual would not choose B. Finally, bounded rationality is simply a reflection that information to the decision maker is not unbounded, nor perfect, nor is it costless. There is an economically efficient level of information and we daily calculate whether or not an extra unit of information is worth the costs. To decide to seek no more information and to act on the basis of the available data (and to make the same choice when faced with the same data) is bounded rationality.

Let us be clear that rationality says nothing at all about man's relentless pursuit of profit. Rationality simply speaks to consistent behavior in the face of constraints (including information) as guided by an individual's utility (or preference) function. One individual may lie awake nights scheming to make more income, while another may engage in the same thought process to avoid as much work as possible (shirking). Both are rational given their preferences, though the latter may go hungry from time to time.

These behavioral assumptions are necessary for us to begin to construct a conceptual framework of how man interacts with an ecosystem in his daily pursuit of food and materials. The ultimate goal of any inquiry of this sort should be to derive testable hypotheses about the structure of institutional arrangements that govern: (1) control of natural resources; (2) the level and the incidence of the benefits of that use; and (3) the level and the incidence of the costs of that use. Ultimately, our interest lies in the interrelations between a social system and an ecosystem.

THE MODEL

A natural community is one in which undomesticated species of plants and animals evolve in some serial progression towards a climax ecotype. The very essence of man's interaction with an ecosystem is the process of arresting that progress so that the ecosystem produces those things of economic value to man; where "economic" does not mean to sell for profit, but means instead that as man economizes on that which is scarce (labor, information, and energy) he is able to extract from the ecosystem valuable objects. A climax community is one with very little interest to man in a direct material sense--though it may be quite nice to view as a tourist, and it may contribute significantly to long-run ecological stability.

Man comes into these natural plant and animal communities and begins to use a very small part--two or three of the hundreds of plants are edible and nutritious, and several of the animal species can be harvested at a net gain (yield in nutrition and material more than they cost to harvest). Of course, the ultimate extreme in this chain of events is when man finally eliminates much of the natural plant community and replaces it with a few species that have acquired--because of conditions to be developed in more detail below--tremendous economic value. Corn, wheat, and soybeans in the American midwest have virtually replaced a large number of plant species. Once that substitution has occurred, it too must be assiduously maintained--else nature will "take back the land."

Let us start with the idea of a "resource." This term is prominent not only in academic circles, but in practical management discussions as well. The adjective "natural" is often added, though there is often confusion about how much processing is required before a resource ceases to be a "natural" resource. But the more pertinent issue for us concerns the exact meaning of a "resource." In simplest terms, a resource is something with value to man--directly or indirectly. Coal and wood are resources, but so is solar energy, though it was only recently (since the advent of solar collectors) that it has been considered to be a natural resource that we can manage. However, plants are solar collectors and so we use solar energy embodied in plants.

The second aspect of a natural resource is that it can be controlled by humans. That is, man could control solar energy through its manifestation in plants, but he could not control the solar energy directly. So solar energy has always had tremendous economic value to man, but it was not a natural resource in the sense that it could be controlled (its access denied until the payment of a fee was offered). Now with marketable solar collectors it is possible to harvest and sell the sun's energy directly rather than as the embodied energy in a tree. Once this happens we begin to think of solar energy as a natural resource in the same category as energy from coal (former plants), or from wood (plants). In a sense, solar energy trapped by a collector represents a future source of energy as wood or as coal. Although it is not particularly scarce, such rays collected on one's roof means that a possible tree is without that energy.

This discussion is intended to make the point that a resource is defined by two aspects of the particular society under study--its technology, and its institutional structure. Gravel was not a building resource for the native Americans because the technology (knowledge and tools) for making concrete did not exist. Solar energy was not a natural resource for us in the direct sense until the technology appeared to make its capture and use on demand possible; and until the institutional arrangements for controlling it became common. These institutional arrangements, by the way, are still evolving; city zoning laws regarding the

blockage of a collector by a neighbor's trees are under
consideration. The demand for the technology and the
institutional arrangements has been stimulated by the
apparent economy of solar energy vis-a-vis more conventional energy sources. This brings us to the third
aspect of a resource.

Natural resources, because they do not exist
outside of a particular technical and institutional
milieu, are not defined once and for all, but rather
"become" as institutional and technical conditions
change (see Chapter 1). As new things become scarce
and valuable, it becomes economical to change the way
we do certain things. Part of the process of change is
the recognition that new inputs are available. When
those inputs become defined in such a way that they can
be controlled, then a new natural resource has been
created.

For completeness, we must consider those things
that have not yet assumed economic value (that is, have
not yet become resources), and those things that have a
negative economic value (that is, are negative resources). We will call the first non-resources, and
the second neg-resources. In a community of plants and
animals, certain plants provide sustenance to the
animals, and others are of no account to the animals.
If man relies upon the animals for sustenance and
materials, then not only are the animals a resource,
but so are the plants that sustain those animals. Man
manipulates the plant community to provide for himself
directly, and for himself (indirectly) through the
animals.

Those plants with economic value to man as processed by the animals are resources as much as are the
plants that man uses directly. But there are some
plants that are quite incidental to both man and animal; these are the non-resources. It could very well
be the case that over time a non-resource could become
a resource. Gravel, as mentioned previously, would be
an example. Likewise, sand became a resource for
making glass once that technology became known.

Let us now consider neg-resources. A neg-resource
is something with negative economic value to the human
enterprise--either directly or indirectly. Malaria and
schistosomiasis are neg-resources, with the intense
search for cures (preventative measures) at least
having neutralized the impacts of the former. Indirect
neg-resources would be plant diseases and animal diseases, or plants that are poisonous to valuable
animals. A great deal of human energy is devoted to
the enhancement of the contribution of resources, and
to minimizing the contribution of neg-resources.

Before proceeding, it is worth discussing, if only
briefly, the delicate balance that often exists between

something being a resource (having positive value) and something being a neg-resource. If we leave aside momentarily the ground water implications of snow, it is a useful part of the ecosystem with which to make our point. In some parts of the world where snow falls, we see a human activity having evolved that creates considerable enjoyment for the participants (winter sports of various kinds), and considerable income for those who have managed to capture the economic rents from that enjoyment (ski-lift operators, other service establishments). Institutional arrangements exist such that only a few fortunate individuals can obtain a franchise to haul people up mountains, to groom ski trails, and to cater to their food and lodging needs. The franchise allows the capture of income streams from a naturally occurring physical entity (snow); snow is surely a resource.

But snow can also be a significant neg-resource. The amount of human time and financial resources devoted to its removal--and the social costs of accidents arising from those who try to walk or drive on it--mean that it is a neg-resource of some moment. Hence, we see that the same item, depending upon its location, amount, and human use, can be both a resource and a neg-resource. The distinction is seen to lie in the human effort that evolves to both benefit from it, and contend with it.

This recognition of the positive and negative attributes of the same basic physical object allows us to introduce the concept of "control centers." A control center is the locus of individual and collective choice exercised with respect to the use of a resource; we will see that there are a number of control centers in an economic system. The first of these will pertain to technical choices made with respect to the use of either plant or animal resources; we will exclude other types of natural resources (including snow) from the present discussion to permit a more streamlined explanation. That is, if we start with a restricted set of resources (plants and animals) we could develop the following:

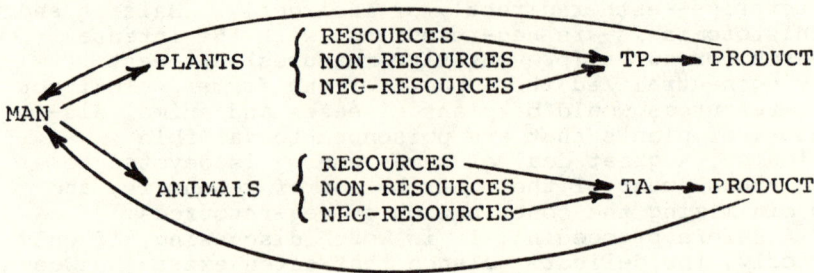

FIGURE 6.1 Resource control centers

Here we see the social system receiving the products of both plants and animals, with the control being exercised over both domains in terms of attempting to enhance the value of the resources, and minimize the impact of the neg-resources. The products that result are the outcome of a conscious choice process regarding the particular resources to be used, the particular neg-resources to be controlled, and the means for doing both. The means include both the technical aspects as well as the institutional aspects; we will refer to this as the techno-institutional structure. Let us consider an example. Working groups of the Arapesh in New Guinea that tend the sago palm are characterized by a particular institutional structure that determines work responsibilities, as well as the distribution of the harvest among a number of non-workers. We would say that this choice resides in control center TP. The hunting parties of traditional societies possessed extensive rules regarding responsibilities in the hunt, as well as rights to share in the kill. Here, we are concerned with control center TA.

Figure 6.1 is much too simple for the reason that it does not permit product flows to be redirected back to the resource base from whence they came, nor to a counterpart resource base. That is, man faces the choice of directing the product: (1) back to the same subsystem; (2) to the other subsystem; (3) to his direct use; or (4) as an intermediate input into a further production process. Consider the following examples. In the plant subsystem, leaves can be taken from the forest for fodder for livestock, in which case they become a direct input into the animal subsystem. It is also possible that the leaves might be cooked in water to make tea for direct human consumption. Or, the leaves might be used as fuel for a fire with which to cook other items. Finally, the leaves can be left in the forest to provide organic matter--which implies that they are an input back into the same subsystem from which they came.

In the animal subsystem, animal products such as milk can be consumed directly by humans, it can be used as an input to make a different product (cheese), or it can be fed to other animals (calves). Other animal products (dung) can be left on the land as an input to the plant subsystem, it can be used directly to "paint" a mud hut, or it can be burned to cook other foods. How the members of a social system choose to allocate the products of both the plant and animal kingdoms is determined at two separate control centers. On the plant side, there is an initial choice between allocating the product to the animal subsystem or reintroducing it into the plant subsystem. If it is to be taken

out of the ecosystem, the choice must still be made
whether or not it will be used directly--that is, is it
a final good--or will it be processed in some way prior
to human use (an intermediate good). We show this
control center as P1 in Figure 6.2. On the animal side,
a product can be returned to the animal subsystem, it
can be directed to the plant subsystem, or it can go to
man for either final or intermediate use. This control
center is shown as A1 in Figure 6.2.

Also shown in Figure 6.2 are two other control
centers (P2 and A2). For those product flows that are
for intermediate use rather than for final use, it is
possible for the product to be directed either back to
the same subsystem from whence it came, or to man for
further processing prior to ultimate use.

We have also labeled product flows in Figure 2 to
illustrate the contribution from each resource. FPM+
represents the plant products destined for man's direct
(final) consumption. Examples are berries, fruits, and
plant materials used directly for, say, building construction (thatch). The flow of plant products for
intermediate use can either be returned to the plant
community (wood for a fence to control grazing use) or
the flow can go to man for further processing (wood for
conversion into cut lumber). The former flow is labeled IPP+, while the latter is labeled IPM+.

From the animal subsystem FAM+ represents the flow
of animal products for man's direct (final) consumption. As indicated above this could be meat, milk, or
hides for clothing. But certain products from the
animal subsystem can be taken by man and directed
selectively back into the animal subsystem (IAA+). An
example would be animal products such as milk given to
selected young animals, or it could be young animals
themselves retained as part of the breeding herd. This
choice is made at control center A2. Part of the
intermediate product flow (IAM+) returns to man for
further processing. An example of this flow would be
animal products that are processed into leather and
glue.

We have focused on positive flows from the plant
and animal subsystems, but we must recognize that there
are negative flows as well. One example of a negative
flow is that arising because man manipulates the
ecosystem (at TP or TA) to realize a greater product
and by so doing creates negative impacts for the plant
or animal systems (PA- and AP-). An example of a
negative flow from the plant side of the system would
be the destruction of habitat for crop production that
then causes negative impacts on certain wildlife (PA-).
Likewise the reliance on certain animal outputs
(choices made at TA) causes a negative flow to certain
parts of the plant subsystem (AP-). Overgrazing could

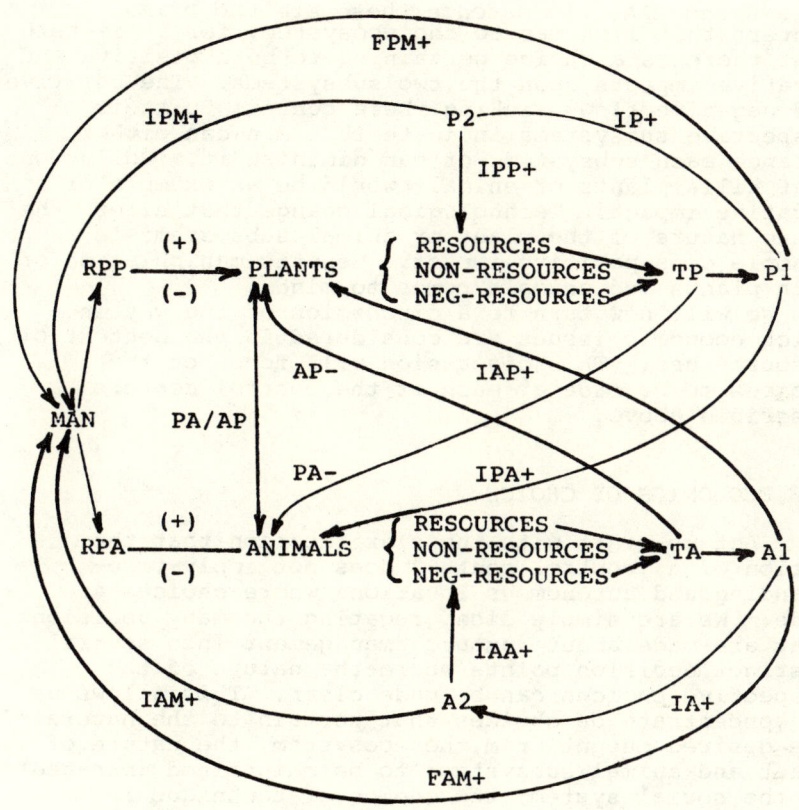

FIGURE 6.2 Resource control centers with
sub-systems and feedback loops

be an example of this effect, but so would the specific choice of animal species that used only a portion of the plant subsystem.

Notice in Figure 6.2 the relation PA/AP (plant-animal/animal-plant). In essence this link represents the natural ecosystem before man's influence is brought to bear. That is, in terms of the figure, man's influence in the natural system is to control the vertical linkage between the plant and animal subsystems and to divert that linkage into an horizontal one monitored and manipulated at the various control centers.

The final control centers in Figure 6.2 are noted as RPP and RPA. In essence these are two primal centers that link man to the ecosystem, for it is here that there is a choice pertaining to both positive and negative impacts upon the two subsystems. The positive and negative flows linking these centers to their respective subsystems indicate that man can either enhance each subsystem, or can diminish it. Pollution that kills plants or animals would be an example of a negative impact. Technological change that alters the basic nature of the plant or animal subsystems is an example of a positive impact. Genetic manipulation of both plants and animals comes to mind.

We will now turn to a discussion of the way in which economic issues are considered in the context of resource use. This discussion will focus on the choices to be made at each of the control centers described above.

THE ECONOMICS OF CHOICE

Let us start with the clarification that the notion of a "control center" does not imply free-standing and autonomous locations where choices are made. We are simply disaggregating the many decisions that are made about resource management into several distinct decision points where the nature of the respective choices can be made clear. This allows us to concentrate on choices that pertain to the nature of the desired output from the ecosystem, the nature of plant and animal subsystems to be maintained (managed) by the social system, the choice of technique in utilizing those subsystems, and the choices regarding the degree of processing applied to the various products.

It is essential to recognize that the control centers being considered here are at an intermediate level in the institutional structure of the hypothetical society--they are subsidiary to the basic institutional structure, and they are above the level of choice at the individual household level. That is, any society consists--at the highest and most abstract level--of a constitution that specifies the general structure of interpersonal relations; who counts (one individual vis-a-vis other individuals), the individual vis-a-vis the state, and the rules (procedures) for changing the rules. The constitution and ancillary rules define individual rights, duties, obligations, privileges, and exposure to the rights and privileges of others. It is within this level that entitlements (property rules and liability rules) are specified and given protection [Bromley, 1978].

It is at this level that the broad outlines of political and economic power are specified. The rights of landowners to choose cropping patterns and labor-use arrangements are detailed at this level. The eminent domain clause in the U.S. Constitution protects the vegetable farmer from the taking of her land for an airport without compensation. But where is the protection for the displaced farm laborers? The Constitution recognizes only those income streams arising from land and capital equipment on that land--not from the possession of labor power.

Against this backdrop of basic social rules and conventions then, we come to a second level of institutional arrangements. The structure of ownership of land, input supply firms, marketing firms, futures markets, commodity exchanges, public land management agencies, and the like, define yet another component in the specification of the operating environment for firms and households. To the extent that this structure defines income and wealth positions for individuals, then it also is instrumental in specifying certain aspects of the demand for products--which then becomes a derived demand for particular resources. Consider the following example. If choice cuts of beef are the desired diet of the rich, then this creates a demand for a livestock industry that must rely on certain types of land. If this land is devoted to beef production instead of the production of corn and beans for the masses then this structure of demand will have a profound impact on resource (land) use patterns and prices.

In simple/traditional economies and social systems, these same forces are present, although the degree of social stratification is usually less pronounced than in more "advanced" capitalist systems. In the traditional setting each group/band/tribe is both a consuming and a producing unit, and the several control centers depicted in Figure 6.2 are not well differentiated. As the family supplants the group as the prime decision unit, there becomes some distinction that will eventually show up in more articulated control centers. Eventually, some families control land (and the plants and animals thereon), while other individuals control the availability of technology, and yet others regulate or control the positive and negative effects on the resource base indicated by RPP and RPA in Figure 2.

In the Swiss Alps we find family control of some lands (the valley land) and group control of the summer pastures. This institutional articulation is not some historical accident but rather grows out of a conscious choice given the physical and economic facts of the situation (Netting).

In Figure 6.2 we can make reference to the fact that as an economic system moves from the more traditional to the more "modern," a greater degree of control is exercised over the resource system (the ecosystem) and the flows PA/AP become of less significance. Part of this diminution shows up as less of the product of the two subsystems going to the other subsystem--going instead to (or through) the economic system. But another dimension is that there is less randomness in the PA/AP flow and more purposiveness. That is, as humans exercise ever more control over the ecosystem, the flows PA/AP become residuals that exist for a specific purpose.

Of course we must recognize that the apparent control over the ecosystem may be just that--apparent. The current debate over the sustainability of monocultures is focused on this question of the costs-- and the certainty--of control. Only time, and more research, will settle the question.

The resource economist would be concerned with two crucial aspects of choice at each of the control centers: (1) the structure of incentives--i.e., the relative "prices"--that influence choice; and (2) who is able to make, or substantively influence, the choices. Let us turn to that consideration.

The Choice of Technique

Given that land is to be plowed, is it to be done by oxen or by tractor? Are plant and animal pests (neg-resources) to be controlled by chemicals, by natural predators, or by brute force? Is the harvesting to be by machine, or by hand? Are animals to be herded off of cliffs, to be trapped in nets, to be shot, or to be raised in confinement? Are fish to be caught with nets, with hooks, or to be brought to the surface with dynamite? While these alternative choices of technique seem rather stark as comparisons at any moment in time, the social system has options for structuring choice such that one approach is "efficient" while others are not. The choice of technique problem also entails the diversion of resource flows away from the PA/AP avenue and towards human use. And, at this point, there is a choice to be made regarding control of the other subsystem so as to enhance the productivity of the one under study. The flows PA- and AP- depict this influence.

The Product Mix

At the next step in the decision process, there is a conscious choice within each subsystem regarding the nature and extent of the contribution that will go to the other subsystem directly (IPA+/IAP+), the nature and extent of the contribution to go back to the subsystems indirectly (IPP+/IPA+), and the nature and extent of the contribution to go to humans directly (FPM+/FAM+) or indirectly (IPM+/IAM+).

The basis of this choice will be the nature of the contribution to one destination versus the nature of the contribution to its next best destination; opportunity cost again. If we eat the seed corn it cannot become the basis of next year's crop. If we drink the milk of the cow (FAM+) then it is unavailable to nourish the young animals in the herd and IAA+ is diminished accordingly. If plants are used by man then they become unavailable for animals and the flow PA is diminished accordingly. If cow dung is used by man to cook his food then it is unavailable to fertilize the fields and the flow AP is diminished accordingly.

At each control center, choices are made on the basis of apparent advantage at the moment, dictated in the large (and over the longer run) by the basic institutional structure in place that determines, for the most part, the relative "prices" attached to each possible use of a resource, a neg-resource, and a particular product. Another set of prices is, of course, relevant; the prices that attach to particular technical choices. Here we have in mind the relative cost of labor vis-a-vis tractors, or the relative cost of chemical control of pests versus the labor-intensive method. If labor is abundant and chemicals are scarce, then their respective prices will dictate the "efficient" choice. We emphasize the adjective efficient to remind the reader that efficiency is a concept without independent meaning; it is a function of the distribution of income and rights (Bromley, 1982b).

The Processing Choice

As indicated earlier, any economic system faces a choice in terms of the degree of processing to be applied to its products. That choice is here depicted at P2/A2 and it involves a decision about relative values of products going forward for human use as opposed to being returned to the subsystem as a positive contribution. The attractiveness of one particular choice vis-a-vis another will depend upon the comparative costs and gains from that allocation. Since, over time, those relationships change, we should expect to find shifts over time reflecting these changes. It also bears mention that new knowledge acts to reduce the costs of choice and so over time, as our knowledge of particular ecosystems increases, it becomes easier to make adjustments that are beneficial to humans.

The Resource Choice

Although we here discuss it last, the basic question to be addressed by the social system is the particular aspects of the plant and animal subsystems that will be used, and how those subsystems will be treated. Humans now obtain approximately 80 percent of their food supply from just 11 plant species (Loomis, 1976). Similarly, only a small fraction of the animal subsystem is used either by hunting wild species, or relying on domesticated ones. The economics of this choice is most complex, but it surely reflects the interplay of tastes, needs, and the ability and willingness to forego other things (opportunity cost again) to obtain certain parts of each subsystem. This is the demand side. On the supply side we have the ecological conditions that dictate what is available, but also the technical infrastructure (including knowledge) that indicates what it is economical to utilize.

The other dimension of the broader "resource policy" choice at RPP/RPA concerns social norms regarding the less positive impacts visited on the two subsystems from general economic activity. With more advanced technical knowledge the economic system can now deposit on both plant and animal communities a large number of debilitating and toxic residues that hold important implications for resource flows reaching TP/TA and Pl/Al, and ultimately man.

The nature of the choices made at RPP/RPA are fundamental to general resource policy, and yet they reflect embedded entitlements that convey privileges, rights, duties, and exposures. The idea that there is an efficient level of pollution control is simply an admission that under the prevailing structure of property relations regarding whose interests count when it comes to the use of air and water, then one configuration of waste disposal will be considered "efficient" and all others will be "inefficient." The control center merely takes that institutional structure as given and becomes the locus of choice with the relative prices taken for granted.

By way of summary, it is important to distinguish between the static problem of choices regarding resource use at all four of the control centers on a "daily" basis, and those conscious social choices that influence the more basic institutional structure on which relative prices rest. For instance, a land reform movement, by gaining control of that resource from one small subset of society, would permit a quite different set of plant and animal resources to be produced. This would call forth a whole new constellation of prices, and would imply a quite different technical configuration.

The economist must be equipped to work in the static world of daily choice, but also to recognize the dynamic aspects that will influence relative prices and costs. The institutional structure as defined by the constitution and the more operational rules and conventions concerning resource control will provide the foundation (and rationalization) for the specific sanctions and incentives that define the daily environment for choice; what the economist would call opportunity sets of firms and households, individuals and groups.

THE ECOSYSTEM AND THE SOCIAL SYSTEM

In essence, resource management is the manipulation of the ecosystem via control centers such that a certain output bundle is achieved. Norgaard makes the point that economic "development" is, in large part, the process of making the ecosystem less complex, and of making the social system more complex (Norgaard, 1981). Geertz (1962) refers to this effect on the social system as "involution." In the transition from hunter/gatherer to sedentary agriculturalist, and then to modern industrial society we have become more dependent on non-renewable resources (coal, minerals), and less dependent on renewable resources (wood). We have also found it necessary to direct the nature of ecosystem transition into one in which diversity gives way to uniformity; complexity is replaced by simplicity. The reason for this is that the human enterprise seeks to minimize the transaction costs of interacting with the ecosystem. A highly diverse ecosystem such as found in the Amazon can be represented as a highly "scattered" or "chaotic" ecosystem that demands great effort by man to channel its diverse elements and embodied energy to his advantage. A piece of land with a large number of different plant and animal species requires considerable diversification of the economic system to use and process this physical diversity. It is much more "efficient" to consolidate species so that a large piece of land is devoted to species A, another to species B, yet another to species C, and so on. Then, we can build the man-made counterpart to the ecosystem to use these locally uniform plant and animal resources. Corn can be grown here, and we can have the physical infrastructure to handle corn and its products. Cotton can be grown over there and again we can localize the special infrastructure for handling cotton and its products. Since the economic system demands the specialization of function in both man and machine, we find it "efficient" to force the ecosystem to specialize as well. The economic concept of regional comparative advantage is built on this imperative.

This process of molding the ecosystem to fit the imperatives of an economic order is not as innocent as the foregoing paragraphs seem to imply. This is especially so when, as history shows us, it is often an external colonial power whose economy is being served by the ecosystem transformation (Brockway, 1979; Bromley, 1982a; Kent, 1983). Again the concept of efficiency as used by the economist is meaningless without reference to a specific institutional structure. Put somewhat differently, there are an infinite number of efficient solutions--each one dependent upon the initial structure of property arrangements and wealth.

In a static sense the types of choices made at the respective control centers are quite marginal in nature. However, over time, the very choices made at the control centers will change. That is, modernization expands the choice set available at any of the control centers. At RPP it was only recently that herbicides, insecticides, and new genetic material were available. Prior to that time man simply selected from among the set of available species. The introduction of the cow at RPA held important implications for the social system (and the ecosystem) that absorbed it.

The colonial legacy throughout much of the world can be considered in Figure 6.2 as the introduction of a stronger social system overlaying the indigenous social system. This then introduces an entirely new set of tastes and preferences for parts of the native ecosystem and can upset not only the ecosystem, but the indigenous social system as well. The advent of plantation crops (banana, rubber, coffee, tea, sisal, and pineapple) in the tropics was a particularly striking form of this intervention. The colonial power forced important land-use changes on the indigenous social system, and also required a particular form of social organization (indentured servitude) to assure that the crops could be planted and harvested at exactly the correct time.

Much of colonial history focuses on the crops and animals that were developed, and ignores the social aspect in the colonial country and in the colonized country. Monetization of the local economy came with colonization and this change alone introduced important changes further encouraging manipulation of the native ecosystem.

Because this volume is concerned with the relationship between man and the environment it is essential that we understand the structure within which choices about that relationship are made. The foregoing discussion is intended to present a particular method of viewing man's interaction with (and dependence upon) the ecosystem. The emphasis has been on disaggregating that relationship into only two parts of the ecosystem (plants and animals), and on four control centers. As such, these stylized facts, while oversimplified, provide a powerful mechanism for understanding human choices regarding the environment.

The positive and negative manipulation of the ecosystem at RPP/RPA is a "macro-level" choice, based upon some desired products at P1/A1. The flows FPM+/FAM+ and IPM+/IAM+ reflect demand-side considerations. The supply-side is shown as RPP/RPA and TP/TA; it is here that the size and the character of the productive "plant" is determined. The various product flows are partly a function of the ecosystem—one does not grow artichokes near the Arctic Circle, nor do we find caribou in the tropics. But within these general constraints, man constructs a social and economic system to permit him to "make a living" with some minimal level of effort.

Our interest in resource management ought to include a careful study of how different societies have structured this choice process. We know that the pastoral herders of east Africa have innovated an institutional structure for managing livestock in an extremely severe and variable ecosystem. If one suffers unexpected losses these are made up by other members of the group—with the total contribution from others diminished by the extent to which the stricken individual was guilty of poor judgement (Swift, 1977). Under traditional management arrangements herds would move when the water source was depleted—water, not vegetation was the binding constraint. Under this regime the vegetation was, in essence, protected by the ephemeral nature of the water in tanks and shallow wells. Livestock production was largely driven by the needs of domestic consumption and status to be derived from owning livestock. As external markets opened up with the advent of colonialism this locally driven system became subject to the new relative prices imposed from outside of the system (Bromley, 1982a). Livestock now had value apart from status and local consumption, and hence cash could be earned by accumulating ever larger numbers. As the numbers increased it became obvious that water was the binding constraint and, as is to be expected, investments in deeper wells and more tanks began to be made-- capitalized from outside or from a nascent merchant class (Swift, 1977). Before long one found more sophisticated wells, fences, cattle owners, wage herders, vaccination and hence more cattle, merchants, and overgrazing. A system of control that had operated with a modest degree of "success" over a very long period of time in the most fragile of ecosystems was broken by colonialism and external markets. In the sense of Figure 6.2 there were now two social systems attempting to use the single ecosystem. Decisions were being made at the four control centers with one particular set of tastes, preferences, and values in mind, but now there are two competing imperatives operating at the various control points. Little wonder that there is tension, conflict, and environmental degradation.

In mountain ecosystems, we see a stable pattern of institutional arrangements and control decisions that are fashioned to operate a food system across a range of ecotypes (Netting, 1977; Rhoades and Thompson, 1975). For certain parts of the ecosystem we find institutional arrangements that locate resource-use decisions in the family or the individual. In terms of Figure 6.2 it is the individual or the family that is operating at the various control centers. For other parts of the ecosystem such control resides in collective decisions. In the Swiss Alps the valley bottoms are held in private hands and decisions there are highly individualized. In the summer pastures (the alp) this is not the case. Here, collective decision making prevails and so different processes are employed at the control centers. We find a similar situation in Nepal. The essence of these systems is variable control as a function of the season of resource use--since the nature of the resource being used is a function of the season.

What we see in any system--but especially obvious in those in which different resources are under differential control--is the design of social arrangements to permit the capture of the largest possible net social dividend from different parts of the ecosystem. The approach developed here would enhance the study of these arrangements and processes by focusing attention on the real (as well as monetary) valued effects. The framework presented in Figure 6.2 is a reminder that no decision made at a control center is made in isolation from decisions made at the others.

In conclusion, a thoroughgoing economic perspective on man and the ecosystem would, of necessity, focus on several levels of institutional arrangements. The highest and most abstract level is concerned with matters of ultimate social control and the means for arbitrating disputes among competing claimants. At the next level we find a more basic institutional structure. In terms of the above model, it is here that the basic configuration of control centers is determined. One important decision problem is that of ultimate control over natural resources-- that is, who is empowered to make allocative choices? Within this basic structure then, we finally encounter the operating rules where labor and capital allocations are made, where land is devoted to crop A rather than to B, where certain agricultural practices are chosen, and the like.

We do not need to enter the debate as to whether or not people are universally interested in "profit." It is quite enough to recognize that human effort carries an implicit cost in the form of foregone leisure, and that individuals uniformly attempt to conserve on their effort. Social organizations reflect the results of that process. The environmental problem is, in essence one of constantly watching for instances in which individuals and groups seek to shift certain costs to the ecosystem to avoid having to bear those costs directly. As tastes and preferences change, and as the technical means grow to shift ever more serious costs, the challenge to social innovation becomes greater. Some doubt that man is smart enough to avoid self destruction. Vested interests in the status quo, expressed primarily at the control centers in Figure 6.2, present a more serious threat than lack of knowledge. Careful study of the nature of the decisions made at the control centers is the obvious way to understand how vested interests influence resource use. And, from there we can begin to channel efforts to correct abuses--whether merely nuisances, or serious threats to human survival.

REFERENCES

Brockway, Lucile H. 1979. Science and Colonial Expansion: the Role of the British Royal Botanic Gardens. *American Ethnologist* 6:449-65.

Bromley, Daniel W. 1982a. *Economic Issues in Forestry as a Development Program in Asia.* Madison: University of Wisconsin, College of Agricultural and Life Sciences, Center for Resource Policy Studies, Working Paper No. 16, March.

Bromley, Daniel W. 1982b., Land and Water Problems: An Institutional Perspective. *American Journal of Agricultural Economics* 64:83(4-44).

Bromley, Daniel W. 1978. Property Rules, Liability Rules, and Environmental Economics. *Journal of Economic Issues* 12:43-60.

Geertz, Clifford. 1963. *Agricultural Involution*, Berkeley: University of California Press.

Kent, Noel J. 1983. *Hawaii: Islands Under The Influence*, New York: Monthly Review Press.

Loomis, Robert S. 1976. Agricultural Systems. *Scientific American* 235:99-105.

Netting, Robert McC. 1977. *Cultural Ecology*. Menlo Park, Ca.: Cummings Publ. Co.

Norgaard, Richard B. 1981. Sociosystem and Ecosystem Coevolution in the Amazon. *Journal of Environmental Economics and Management* 8:238-54.

Rhoades, Robert E. and Stephen J. Thompson. 1975. Adaptive Strategies in Alpine Environments: Beyond Ecological Particularism. *American Ethnologist* 2:535-551.

Swift, Jeremy. 1977. Pastoral Development in Somalia: Herding Cooperatives as a Strategy Against Desertification and Famine. in *Desertification: Environmental Degradation In and Around Arid Lands*, ed. by Michael Glantz, Boulder, Co.: Westview Press.

Part 3

Multidisciplinary Problem-Oriented Approaches

7
Range Management—Attempts to Build a Multidisciplinary Profession

Fee Busby

Rangeland is a major land resource of this country and the world. Depending upon whose definition of rangeland one uses, rangelands occupy between 40 and 45 percent of the land area of the United States and between 45 and 55 percent of the land area of the world (Williams et. al., 1968, and Heady, 1982). Large expanses of rangeland are found in Africa, Australia, Europe, Asia (particularly in the Soviet Union and China), South America, and North America. About 70 percent of the land area in the seventeen Western United States is classified as rangelands (Klemmedson et. al., 1978).

It is very appropriate for rangeland and range management topics to be included in a work titled Natural Resources and People. Such inclusion is also surprising because recognition of rangeland as a resource and range management as a unique discipline is the exception among most groups rather than the rule. The fact this chapter is included in this book is a positive sign of the growth and development of the discipline of range management and the recognition of rangelands as a unique and important resource. The purposes of this chapter are to: (1) define rangeland and range management, with particular emphasis on how these definitions have changed during the developmental period of the discipline, (2) trace the development of the discipline from its "official" beginning in the late 1800s to the present, (3) assess the state-of-the-discipline in the early 1980s and (4) "crystal ball" the future of rangeland resources and rangeland resource management into the early years of the twenty-first century.

Rangelands and Range Management Defined

The first true textbook on range management was written in 1943 by L. A. Stoddart and A. D. Smith. The title of the text was Range Management. These authors revised the text in 1955, and Smith and T. W. Box (Stoddart passed away in 1968) provided a third edition in 1975. This textbook has been the mainstay of range management education for forty years. Because of the long standing respect for this text and the continuity of authorship over this long period of time, I am convinced that changes in these three editions accurately reflect changes in thought the discipline has had about itself.

One interesting aspect of the 1943 edition of Range Management is Stoddart and Smith felt no need to define "rangeland". The two authors assumed everyone who would be interested in the text would know what rangeland was. The authors do make statements that are helpful to us in understanding their thinking in 1943. From the preface:

> The West is a land of livestock grazing. Roughly the 100th meridian marks the division between the area of cultivated crop production in the East and the area of range land in the West. Despite the many large and important irrigated farm sections and the occasional important dry farm lands, western United States is largely uncultivated. It is characterized by precipitation generally too low for crop production unless supplemented by irrigation and soil too shallow and rocky or too alkaline for successful crop production . . .. Essentially, then, these western states are range states not from choice but from necessity. Range is their heritage, and they will always be dependent upon it.

The idea that rangeland is a western resource is further indicated by the authors fifth chapter which discussed characteristics of nine major vegetation types or grazing regions--all occurring west of a line from central Texas through North Dakota. Mention is made that these same vegetation types extend into Mexico and western Canada.

Stoddart and Smith do define range management in their 1943 text: "Range management is the science and art of planning and directing range use so as to obtain the maximum livestock production consistent with conservation of the range resource." The authors add two additional thoughts in the preface and introductory chapter that are helpful to us in assessing how the discipline viewed itself. First, the authors claim that:

> Defining range management is not easy although it includes nothing incomprehensible. Rather, the difficulty arises from the fact that it does not comprise a specific field of knowledge but is based on many and widely different fields.

Stoddart and Smith use this as justification for defining range management as a "science and art", arguing that range management is a science because it embraces a body of scientific principles and an art in the sense that range management is the application of these principles.

Second, the authors discuss the 1940s as the "age of conservation", but express concern about the term "conservation" because it implies disuse. According to the authors:

> Resources may be classified as replaceable, as, for example, growing things, or as nonreplaceable, as, for example, minerals. In the case of the latter, disuse except as immediate necessity demands can be justified, whereas, in the case of the former, disuse is waste. This reasoning lead to the selection of the title <u>Range Management</u> for this book in preference to "Range Conservation", because the aim of the range guardian is maximum use, so long as that use is compatible with protection from permanent injury.

To summarize, in 1943 Stoddart and Smith indicate that the range management discipline had the following thoughts about itself: (1) rangeland was primarily a western United States resource, (2) use of rangeland was restricted (not suitable for cultivation) because of climatic and physical characteristics of the range environment, (3) the culture and economy of the western states was largely dependent on rangeland resources, (4) the primary use of rangelands was for grazing of domestic livestock, (5) range management was a science in that it is based on a body of scientific information and an art since information has to be applied, and (6) rangelands should be used to sustain long-term productivity.

The 1955 edition of <u>Range Management</u> also omits a definition of rangeland. The definition of range management changed slightly in wording, but not in meaning. However, the chapter on range vegetation types or grazing regions was changed to include the southeastern United States. Native forages produced in association with southeastern pine forests and on coastal prairies and marshes were included as rangeland in this revision. The authors argue such a classification is justified since those lands should be managed as range because the same plant physiology and community ecology principles which work on western rangelands work on the southeastern rangelands.

Thus, one change in the thinking of the range management discipline between 1943 and 1955 was the discipline and the principles it relied upon were seen to be applicable outside the seventeen western states. The major emphasis of the 1955 text remained livestock use of rangelands.

Substantial changes in how the range management discipline viewed itself occurred between 1955 and 1975. The 1975 edition by Stoddart, Smith, and Box does include a definition of rangeland, an indication the authors were convinced that people who had limited direct knowledge with the resource were studying the subject. The authors' definition reads:

> Rangelands are those areas of the world, which by reason of physical limitations--low and erratic precipitation, rough topography, poor drainage, cold temperatures--are unsuited to cultivation and which are a source of forage for free-ranging native and domestic animals, as well as a source of wood products, water, and wildlife.

This definition indicates great change in how the discipline of range management viewed itself in 1975 as compared to 1943. First, rangeland was thought of as a world resource and the authors changed the chapter on grazing regions to reflect this thought ("Grazing Areas of the World" versus the 1943 "Grazing Regions of the West"). The importance of rangeland climatic and physical characteristics and their effect on management and use was retained.

This definition of rangeland also indicated rangeland use was broader than domesticated livestock grazing. This was further emphasized by the new definition of range management provided by Stoddart, Smith, and Box in the 1975 edition:

> Range management is the science and art of optimizing the returns from rangelands in those combinations most desired by and suitable to society through the manipulation of the range ecosystem.

Significant changes indicated by this definition as compared to the 1943 and the 1955 definitions are a shift in emphasis from (1) maximization to optimization of uses and returns, (2) livestock grazing as the major use of rangelands to a combination of uses, and (3) planning and directing range use by the range manager to a decision making role by society. The authors discussed the reasons for these changes in the preface of the 1975 edition:

> In the more than 30 years since the appearance of the first edition of Range Management, there have been many changes. New facts have been uncovered, basic concepts have been refined and tested by

experience, and investigative techniques have been perfected. But even more important than the technical changes are the shifts in emphasis among the various rangeland products. Nonconsumptive uses, though not new, have become even more important. With increased human populations and greater demands for rangeland products, the need for clear understanding and greater knowledge of range ecosystems remains as vital as before. Nevertheless, no new conceptual framework differentiates the field of range management now from then. Basically, range management deals with the use of land of low potential productivity maintained under extensive systems to produce water, red meat, wildlife, timber, and recreational opportunities in such a way that the basic resources, soil and vegetation, remain unimpaired.

Rangelands did not really change from 1943 to 1975. However, people's and society's attitudes toward rangeland changed. Telecommunications and the ability to travel brought attention to the fact there were no additional areas of land to move to if we did a poor job of taking care of what we had. This idea was first expressed in the preface of the 1955 edition of Range Management.

American ranchers, after some hundred years of intensive use of the western range, are only now realizing that there are no new frontiers and that present resources must be made to last us forever.

Ranchers and farmers learned this lesson first because they were no longer able to move elsewhere if their current place didn't work out. By 1975, almost everyone understood this, and this understanding has had a great influence on rangeland use and management.

Historical Use of U.S. Rangelands and Development of Range Management

Historical use of rangeland must be approached from two perspectives: (1) the pattern of actual use that has occurred on these lands, and (2) the pattern of legislation that has been passed in an effort to direct use or respond to changes in use. Dana (1956) discussed four major periods in our country's history that had profound effects on rangeland use and management.

1. Acquisition of the Public Domain. The United States acquired land from the late 1700s until 1867 through cession from states, purchase, compromises with foreign nations, and war. Not counting Alaska, the federal government obtained through these methods 1.4

billion acres of land. Alaska added an additional 365 million acres. Generally speaking, the acquisition of land occurred in an east to west pattern.

This was also a period of inattention to the land because the population of the country was small and was concentrated in the eastern half of the country. The major use of rangeland resources during this period was harvest of wildlife through hunting and trapping. The latter activity had a significant impact on beaver (almost to the point of extinction) and other fur-bearers.

2. Disposal of the Public Domain. One of the original intentions of our federal government was to sell land to raise cash for the treasury. This intention was not particularly successful because people didn't have to buy land--they simply moved west beyond the federal land offices and claimed free land. The federal government proved adept, however, at bartering the public domain--exchanging land for settlement and development. The federal government provided land grants to soldiers for service in the Revolutionary War and the War of 1812, to support schools and other institutions, to encourage railroad development, to pay for work such as reclamation of swamps and construction of wagon roads, and to encourage numerous other activities.

An additional effort to encourage settlement and development of the public domain was a series of Homestead Acts designed to assist anyone who wanted to farm. The first such Act was passed in 1862 and provided that eligible individuals and families could claim 160 acres of land. Later Acts increased the acreage that could be claimed to 640 acres. The homesteader could gain the land free by living on it and cultivating it for five years. The idea was good, but the effort did not work well in the western range states because the people who wrote and administered the Homestead laws applied acreage limits suitable to the humid east. A 160 acre farm in the Mississippi Valley was adequate and possibly generous. However, a farmer or rancher in the Great Plains (Oklahoma on the south to North Dakota on the north) and the Mountain States needed much more (2,000-50,000 acres) for a ranch. Nowhere west of the 98th meridian was 640 acres a workable agricultural unit. The Homestead Acts prevented western settlers from obtaining enough land to meet their needs for an economic unit (Hibbard, 1939).

However, the settlers proved to be innovative in their approach. They simply homesteaded the quality land along the streams, and then claimed the water that flowed down the streams as their supply of irrigation water. Few higher elevation mountain lands or dry desert and foothill lands were claimed--at least not between the western slope of the Rocky Mountains and central California. This settlement pattern provided a marvelous use opportunity for those who were lucky enough to have claimed land on a stream bottom. Since they controlled the water, they used all of the surrounding desert, foothill, and mountain range for free. This settlement pattern, a ready supply of cattle from Texas (herds had built up during the Civil War), sheep from California and Oregon, the near elimination of buffalo, moving Indians to reservations, and a railroad system to move surplus animals and wool to market, allowed the beginning of the western range livestock industry.

3. <u>Exploitation of the Public Domain</u>. (We now call it the "tragedy of the commons".) For the first five years following the Civil War the major livestock enterprise in the U.S. was herding cattle north from Texas to the railroad shipping points in Kansas. Initially it was thought cattle could not survive in the northern part of the western U.S. because of the long, cold, and snowy winters. However, by the early 1870s several individuals had observed that large expanses of prairie grassland, foothill, and desert range were free of snow for most of the winter. When snow was fairly deep, many ridges and other areas would blow free of snow and livestock could survive until snow melted from other areas. Vegetation growth on the privately owned meadows and highly productive public domain areas allowed a high level of productivity from the cattle. Market prices were fair, but low costs of production (free land and forage, cheap labor, and no financing) were the factors that made cattle raising profitable in the 1870s and 1880s.

The origins of the western sheep industry were in California and Oregon. Early settlers in these two states (including the Spanish who dated from the 1500s in California) raised large numbers of sheep. The sheepmen determined that it was best to herd sheep to fattening and market points in the midwest. Experience gained from herding sheep to market indicated to the sheepherder that the ranges of Idaho, Nevada, Utah, Montana, Wyoming, and Colorado could support sheep year round and sheep ranches were established.

The sheepmen had two advantages over the cattlemen. First, they were accustomed to living in sheep camps and following their flocks. They often did not need permanent headquarters. This greatly reduced costs of production for the sheepherders. Second, early cattlemen and sheepmen moved their animals from the foothills and deserts to the mountains in the spring to graze new grass growth. Since sheep were more easily moved, the sheepmen usually won the race to the better feed. There was a great overestimation of how many animals could be grazed on an area by both the cattlemen and the sheepherders. The unfortunate result

of all this overestimation of what the land could produce, the eagerness to make a profit, and the competition between sheepmen and cattlemen for forage was an exploitive use of the western range.
H. L. Bentley of Abilene, Texas offered the following observation in 1898:

> Men of every rank were eager to get into the cow business. In a short time every acre of grass was stocked beyond its fullest capacity. Thousands of cattle and sheep were crowded on the ranges when half the numbers was too many. The grasses were entirely consumed; their very roots were trampled into the dust and destroyed. In their eagerness to get something for nothing, speculators did not hesitate at the permanent injury, if not the total ruin, of the finest grazing country in America.

Similar stories were told across the western U.S. in the late 1800s and early 1900s.

An important aspect of the settlement and exploitation period is indicated by Bentley--"speculators". The Homestead Acts did not prevent a rancher with a large number of cowboys or sheepherders from requiring that each employee claim homesteads for themselves with the intent of signing them over to the boss. Large land holdings were put together in this fashion. Some of these were controlled by absentee landlords whose only interest was profit. These landlords put pressure on their managers to build livestock numbers above what was reasonable. However, as modern range managers now know and appreciate, the range environment must not be ignored. Beginning in 1884 there were a series of exceedingly harsh winters. Don Biggers (1901, pp 22, 24-25) described the situation:

> In the winter of 1884 began a series of most disastrous years ever known to the cattle industry . . ..When a blizzard would sweep over the country the cattle would drift before it, and it was then no uncommon sight to see great herds of cattle rolling southward, nothing to eat, nothing to drink, pelted by sleet and covered with snow; while around them the pittiless (sic) blizzard seemed to howl in fiendish glee . . ..
> The winter of 1886 was very severe and in the spring of 1887 occurred, beyond a doubt, the most awful die-up ever known in the United States. From the Canadian borders to the Rio Grande the range country was covered with carcasses . . . . When the blizzards came the cattle would drift south until they came to the southern line of fence. Unable to go further they would move back and forth, pressing close to the fence or stand in

clusters suffering from cold, hunger and thirst, and trampling out every vestige of grass. One would fall or lie down and others would tumble over it, and soon there would be a heap of dead along the line of fence. Over these bodies the snow drifted and sifted between them, soon forming a solid frozen mass, over which hundreds of living cattle walked, tumbled over the fence and drifted away. This awful spectacle was to be repeated again in 1894.

This series of harsh winters and large die-offs of grazing animals brought adjustment and some stability to the range livestock industry. Land and livestock speculators were wiped out and the large ranches were broken up into smaller, more manageable units. Private lands were fenced and progressive ranchers began harvesting hay for winter feed from native meadows. The harsh winters proved to everyone animals could not survive year round without attention. Hay production and winter feeding became "necessary evils" for most ranchers.

However, the damage had been done to much of the western range. The native vegetation of many western rangelands had been depleted by overuse such as that described above by Bentley. And at the same time, forestry and dryland cultivation practices were causing serious water and wind erosion problems. (Craddock and Pearse, 1938) described the floods that occurred frequently in parts of the western United States between 1890 and 1905. Several of these floods caused damage to residential areas which had been built in the mouths of canyons or out in the valleys along stream channels, to cultivated croplands, and, in some cases, to human life. Jardine and Anderson, 1919, reported the loss of eighteen inches of top soil from a large mesa at 9,000 feet elevation in the Wasatch Mountains above Ephriam, Utah. Most of this soil ended up mixed with rocks and boulders on the cropland near the mouth of Ephriam Canyon at 4,300 feet elevation.

Dust storms became a common occurrence in the western U.S. as a result of poor grazing, timber harvest, and cultivation practices. These storms reached a peak in occurrence in the Great Plains during the early 1930s. The intensity and extent of wind erosion was increased by a severe drought which occurred over much of the western U.S. at this time. Wind erosion was so severe over such a large expanse of land that Hugh Hammond Bennett, an influential conservationist of the period, told a congressional committee meeting in Washington, D.C. regarding the dust cloud they saw outside, "There goes Kansas!" (Smith, 1966).

The result of actions by Gifford Pinchot, Theodore Roosevelt, Hugh Hammond Bennett, and numerous others in response to these secondary impacts on western resources (the primary impact was the destruction of protective plant cover by grazing, logging and cultivation) was the enactment of three laws and the establishment of three agencies to bring order to the rangelands and forest lands of the western U.S. In 1891 and in 1905 Congress acting under the leadership of Pinchot and Roosevelt, established the Forest Reserves and the Forest Service to manage and protect the higher elevation forest and rangelands that had not previously been claimed by homesteaders. Congress acted because everyone agreed these high elevation lands were not suitable for cultivation and thus did not need to remain available for homesteading.

Lower elevation desert and foothills that had not been placed in private ownership through the Homestead Acts were not given protection until 1934 when Congress passed the Taylor Grazing Act and created the Grazing Service. This organization was combined with the General Land Office in 1946 to form the Bureau of Land Management.

Control of grazing was accomplished by both the Forest Service and Grazing Service in approximately the same way. Both agencies recognized that the grazing land they controlled had a significant economic value to the people who lived in the immediate area. Therefore, initial grazing regulations required a person own base property near the location of their public land grazing areas--no base property, no grazing. This action eliminated the migratory sheep operators because they did not have base property. The number of animals any individual was allowed to graze on Forest Service and Grazing Service lands was limited to what the rancher could feed with his private holdings during the time the animals were not on federal land. The result of this congressional and agency action was that the numbers of domestic grazing animals using western rangelands being dramatically reduced, particularly after the remaining uncontrolled public domain lands were put under the control of the Grazing Service in 1934.

Gaining control of who could graze on the National Forest and Grazing Service lands and how many livestock would be allowed to graze were significant positive steps in the management of rangelands in the eleven western "public land" states. Privately owned lands in the region also benefited from the overall reduction in numbers of grazing animals because the private land owners no longer had to sacrifice their private lands because someone else had used their adjacent public lands.

In addition to this general benefit to privately owned rangelands, in 1935 Congress established an agency to help farmers and ranchers apply conservation practices on their privately owned lands. The agency, which was initially known as the Erosion Service and later became the Soil Conservation Service, was totally different from the Forest Service and the Grazing Service in its approach. This agency did not control any land. Its mission was to provide technical assistance to those private land owners who would accept such assistance. Local Soil Conservation Districts were organized to govern the actions of the federal agency.

Thus, by 1935, the federal government had created three agencies to oversee or provide technical assistance to all land resources in this country. Because 40 to 45 percent of our land resources are classified as rangeland, it is not surprising that all three of these agencies devoted considerable time and effort to rangeland management.

  4. <u>Conservation and Management of Rangeland</u>. The first range managers were individuals whose formal education was in allied disciplines. There was no organized body of knowledge upon which they could rely. In fact, most of what we thought we knew about managing land and forage resources had been proven wrong during the exploitation period. At its beginning in the early 1900s, the range management profession literally had to admit that everything we had tried to transfer from a more humid Europe and the eastern U.S. would not work in the arid west. The need for new knowledge was great and research programs were established by federal agencies (particularly the research stations of the Forest Service and the Agricultural Research Service) and by state land-grant universities. Three specific research achievements have, in my opinion, contributed the most to our understanding and practice of range management:

    a. <u>Relation of Plant Cover to Protection from Soil Erosion</u>. The first range experiment station was established by the Forest Service in 1914 in the Wasatch Mountains at Ephraim, Utah. Research conducted at this station clearly indicated that soil erosion could be greatly reduced by reestablishing plant cover on depleted range (Sampson and Weyl, 1918). This work and similar work is the foundation for most range management activities that are practiced today--manage the plant cover to protect the soil resource.

    b. <u>The Relation of Physiological Characteristics of the Plant to the Effect of Grazing Use</u>. Sampson (1914) was one of the first range researchers to recognize plant physiology as being important in influencing the affect grazing would have on a plant. However, it was the work of McCarty (1935) that established a firm understanding that plant energy storage could be depleted by excessive or too frequent defoliation. Once the plant's energy stores were depleted, the plant would die or be severely stunted in growth.

c. <u>The Relationship of Plant Succession to Grazing Use</u>. Clements (1928) and Weaver (1930) introduced the idea that plant communities change and the rate and degree of such change is related to the intensity and season of grazing. This concept led to an understanding of why many heavily grazed areas changed in plant species composition (tall grass prairie to short grass prairie) and became less valuable for grazing.

I'm certain that some range managers who read this will disagree with my classifying these three research contributions as being the most important in the development of the range management discipline. I will agree that there have been many other valuable contributions made by many managers and scientists. But it is upon these three research accomplishments that many of today's range management activities are based.

For instance, it is upon these principles that management plans are based. The seasons and kinds of use are manipulated to accommodate plant physiological characteristics and the need to balance competition among plant species within a community. The concept of resting an area from use for a given period of time is designed to give plants an opportunity to restore energy reserves. The purposes of range improvement practices such as brush and weed control, range seeding, and mechanical soil treatments is to increase productivity or change what is produced through manipulating succession. The commonly used range classification schemes are built around an understanding of successional patterns.

Range mangement has been termed by some as "applied ecology". This is a good description because range management must work with environmental characteristics of the landscape and the interactions that occur between these characteristics. Ecological principles are based on the work of a number of disciplines. This is also applicable to range research. Fredrick Clements was a well respected botanist at the University of Nebraska and the Carnegie Institute. Clements was a particularly good observer of the landscape and made most of his contributions as an ecologist. His observations and explanations of what occurred on prairie rangelands of the Great Plains might be thought of as the birth of range management.

A. W. Sampson, who was one of Clements students at Nebraska, also made substantial contributions to the management of rangelands. Many of Sampson's contributions were based on the plant physiology expertise he developed during his Ph.D. program. The definitive work on the relationship between plant cover and erosion was contributed by scientists with a background in hydrology and engineering. Truly, the foundations of range management were contributed by people from many disciplines. A full understanding and appreciation that "everything is connected to everything else" is a requirement for a successful range manager.

The development of the range management discipline has created a demand for knowledgeable people to apply the research information. Courses in range management were taught by some western U.S. colleges and universities in the early 1920s. Curricula and degrees were offered in the 1930s. These courses and curricula were taught in Forestry, Agronomy, and Animal Science Departments. The first Range Department was not established until 1947. Other full Departments have been added since that time, but many remain as sub-units of allied disciplines. This causes some problems in that range management programs within Animal Science Departments are viewed as having a domestic livestock forage producing emphasis. Those programs offered by Agronomy Departments are sometimes viewed as having a cultivated agriculture perspective. The advantage of such educational programs is that new graduates are entering the profession with a wide variety of ideas and concepts. However, it is also possible that the range discipline may not have an adequate opportunity to help its young professionals in such programs understand who they are and what the discipline is about.

Today, range management courses are taught at over one hundred junior colleges, colleges, and universities. All of the land-grant universities in the seventeen western states offer degrees in range management. Most other schools in this region offer courses if not degrees. A degree in range management is offered at the University of Florida and courses in range management are taught at Lincoln University in Missouri. Programs in range management are offered at several schools outside the United States.

Sampson (1954) discussed the curriculum needs for a student majoring in range management:

> The management requirements . . . clearly call for a broad knowledge in both the sciences and the arts. It calls for a knowledge of the biology of both plant and animal life. Specifically, a curriculum should include English and public speaking; botany embracing systematics, physiology, ecology, and genetics; chemistry--inorganic and organic; mathematics--trigonometry, college algebra, and

statistical analysis; engineering--topographic surveying and mapping; general geology; soil science; economics--theoretical and applied; sociology and philosophy--at least one course of each; zoology--general and applied, including wildlife management; agronomy; animal husbandry; forestry--in regions of commercial timber growth; and range management courses adequately covering vital subjects, including six weeks or so of summer camp and/or guided field inspections.

Clearly, the range management student must have a multidisciplinary background. The problem, however, is that too many range managers have become generalists--knowledgeable of many subjects but masters of none. The advantage such a person should have in the world of work is the ability to talk and work with people from a number of disciplines--to make everyone's knowledge more useful. I don't think the range management education process has helped many students capitalize on this advantage. Housely (1952) may have been on the right track when he wrote:

> Too often, we have not recognized the need for selling range management. If the technical side of the field is to contribute to the objective of wise range land use on a nation-wide basis, new discoveries must be brought home to the people who use and manage the range resource . . . .
> Techniques for selling range management/like techniques of any other kind of salesmanship, are limited only by the imagination of the salesman. Qualified technicians and experienced ranchmen need not limit their writing to technical and semi-technical journals, or to government bulletins. Their contributions to popular style periodicals have already improved the accuracy and usefulness of the range information in that area. Other popular selling methods in recent years have included show-me trips and a wide variety of contests . . . .
> Range land administrators have not always seen the need for selling as well as administering. The value of selling in this sphere of range work is twofold: first, it can make the job easier by showing the scientific reasons for administrative actions, and convincing stockmen of the need of actions; and second, it can result in the passing along of information which

> will be of value to the ranch operator in handling his own land to the best advantage . . ..
> Selling range management is not like "selling iceboxes to Eskimos". Any sincere range technician or rancher who knows from experience what he is talking about, and who will talk about it in the language of the range country will find that he can do a satisfying job.

Unfortunately, I think that Housley has underestimated the problems associated with selling. Formal training in salesmanship might be helpful, but no school offering a degree in range management has required such courses in their curricula. Agency in-service training sessions now include such topics, but earlier exposure to such topics in school should pay the individual and the profession great benefits.

The American Society for Range Management, the professional organization of the discipline, was formed in 1948. Membership in the Society included those who worked for the federal and state agencies charged with managing or providing assistance in managing rangelands, researchers, teachers, consultants, and ranchers. Representatives of many disciplines were involved in organizing the Society. The following objectives, like the definitions and discussions found in early textbooks, emphasize the use of rangeland for grazing. The Society established these objectives in 1948.

> To foster advancement in the science and art of grazing lands management; to promote progress in the conservation and greatest sustained use of forage and soil resources; to stimulate discussion and understanding of scientific and practical range and pasture problems; to provide a medium for the exchange of ideas and facts among Society members and with allied technologists; and, to encourage professional improvement of its members.

In 1971, the Society changed its name to the Society for Range Management to better reflect the world-wide nature of the resource and the discipline. At the same time the objectives were changed to read:

> To develop understanding of rangeland ecosystems and of the principles applicable to the management of range resources; To assist all who work with range resources to keep abreast of new findings and techniques in both the science and art of range management; To improve the effectiveness of range management to obtain from range resources the products and values necessary for man's welfare; To create a public appreciation of the

economic and social benefits to be obtained from
the range environment; and, To promote
professional development of its membership.

The major changes occurring in the Society's objectives
(and supposedly the discipline's perception of itself)
between 1948 and 1971 are (1) classification of rangelands as "ecosystems", (2) an emphasis on multiple
products and values of rangelands rather than only
livestock grazing, and (3) recognition of the attention
that must be given to the "public's" understanding of
the economic and social benefits to be obtained from
rangelands. The first change was of great technical
importance to the profession, but the latter "social"
change has probably had more far reaching impact on the
practice of range management.

Current State of the Discipline of Range Management

From the early 1900s to present, the discipline of
range management has developed. The accomplishments
appear to be many including the generation of an
organized body of knowledge based on research and
experience, the development of a cadre of profes-
sionally trained people, the development of management
practices to apply the knowledge in a practical way,
and the establishment of a professional Society which
allows the many disciplines involved in range management to work together. But what are the on-the-ground
results of this growth and development? How well has
the discipline done at managing our rangelands?

There are some who think that the discipline has
done a terrible job. Fradkin (1979) writing in the
Audubon magazine asserts that little progress has been
made in improving the quality of the land from the
deteriorated condition prevalent in the first third of
this century. Recent legislation seems to indicate
that Fradkin and others with similar beliefs are
correct or at least have the ear of Congress. For
instance, in 1960, Congress passed the Multiple Use and
Sustained Yield Act which required the Forest Service
and in 1964, the Bureau of Land Management to manage
lands for the sustained yield of several products and
values; in 1964, Congress passed the Wilderness Act
which allowed designation and protection of areas
because of their unique ecosystem characteristics; in
1969, Congress passed the National Environmental Policy
Act which stated national environmental policy and
required environmental impact statements (EIS) on
federal actions significantly affecting the environment; in 1971, Congress passed the Wild and Free
Roaming Horse and Burro Act which provided protection
to wild horses and burros grazing western rangelands;

in 1973, Congress passed the Endangered Species Act which outlined procedures for identifying and protecting plant and animal species that might be threatened by man's actions; in 1974, Congress passed the Forest and Rangeland Renewable Resources Act and in 1977, the Soil and Water Resources Conservation Act which required the federal agencies to evaluate the condition and management needs of all lands in the U.S.; in 1976 Congress passed the Federal Land Policy and Management Act which increased the Bureau of Land Management's responsibility for managing resources under its control; and in 1978, Congress passed the Public Rangelands Improvement Act which decreed that greater attention must be given to the management and improvement of public rangelands.

All of these Acts have had an influence on how rangelands in this country are managed. All have had "for the good of the land and society" as their purpose. However, one law and one action involving that law has had, I think, a greater impact on rangeland management than the others. In 1974, the Natural Resource Defense Council (NRDC) sued the Bureau of Land Management for "doing an inadequate job of managing the public rangelands under its control". The suit was brought under the National Environmental Policy Act. NRDC won and the Bureau was required by court order to write 212 localized EISs describing its grazing management program. This result was significant for at least three reasons:

1. The EIS process allowed any interested party to enter into management discussions with the Bureau. No longer were such discussions held just between the Bureau range managers and the effected rancher. Ranchers had to be part of this EIS dialogue and they were often forced into discussions with individuals and groups they had little understanding of or respect for. It is my opinion that everyone learned from this interaction. Those concerned about the rangeland environment learned that ranchers had a legitimate place on the range and a substantial responsibility for the day-to-day management of the resource. Ranchers learned that "environmentalists" had legitimate concerns about the land and its use. Some of the more open minded ranchers found that environmentalists even had useful ideas.

2. Often local parties (including Bureau of Land Management personnel) found that the BLM and the EIS process were unable to resolve problems. Rather, the draft EIS was issued by the agency, comments were received from the public, and a final EIS was issued. Initially, the Bureau tried to use the EIS to make sweeping grazing management decisions on all individual allotments. However, this proved to be inappropriate since many allotments were already being managed in a

proper manner or problems such as wildlife migration routes were larger than one allotment. After several different approaches to developing the EISs, the Bureau is now using a process that emphasizes long-term local input and cooperation. The EIS is used as a data gathering document. Once the EIS is finalized, local people begin the job of evaluating how to best balance multiple use demands and resource capabilities. This approach to management represents a healthy, cooperative attitude between the federal landlords, the ranchers, and the many other publics who want a say in how rangeland resources are used.

3. Loss of the court suit by the Bureau brought public and political attention to the condition of a large portion of our rangeland and to the lack of sufficient range management support and manpower for the Bureau of Land Management to do an adequate job of management. For the first time in the history of our country, rangelands and range management were topics of conversation for people other than ranchers and range managers. Not everything said was positive--or true--but the resource and the discipline seems to have benefited from the exposure.

The NRDC grazing suit also created problems for the range professional--particularly the Bureau range conser- vationists and ranchers. The suit was not specifically about the quality of management and use the Bureau and ranchers had provided over the years, but rather about the quality and adequacy of the agency's EIS process. However, NRDC had to introduce in court evidence that grazing was a great enough federal action to require that the agency should include grazing as part of its EIS program. The best way for NRDC to do this was to present evidence of where the Bureau's grazing management had failed. The Bureau's defense was examples of where their management had succeeded. NRDC won the court case and the agency was required to do EISs on their grazing program. Almost everyone interpreted this to mean that NRDC's evidence was true and the Bureau's evidence was false. In my opinion, grazing management was given a black eye because of faulty interpretation of the results of the court suit.

Nowhere was this more harmful than in the agency itself. There were a few Bureau of Land Management employees--some in range conservationist positions--who were against livestock grazing. Each had his or her own favorite range use or value. Many of these people used the NRDC court order as reason to chastise highly competent agency range conservationists for supposedly having done a poor job of grazing management. This resulted in the agency often not putting range conservationists in leadership positions on the EIS teams. Bureau employees whose own personal persuasions seemed to agree with the results of the court order were placed in such leadership roles. The result of such action was a very demoralized core of range conservationists within the agency and unnecessary battles with ranchers and others outside the agency. Fortunately, the good managers proved to be the individuals with the good ideas and the needed approach to communication.

It would be unfair to conclude this section without hearing from the other side and looking at the best data on range conditions available. While those outside the range profession were eager to criticize past Bureau of Land Management actions and results, many practitioners of the profession such as Box (1978) argue that "rangelands are in better condition today than at any time in this century". Table 7.1 includes the data Box used to support his claim. These data include all federal lands. Thus, any improvement that occurred on Forest Service lands between 1905 and 1936 are included in the 1936 data. Using successional theory to support his position, Box argued that the ranges that had been overgrazed prior to management were released from excessive grazing pressure with the establishment of the Forest Service and Grazing Service, had responded through successional change, and then stablized in "fair" condition.

Table 7.1 Percentages of all federal land in three condition classes

Year	Percent by Condition Class		
	Good or Excellent	Fair	Poor or Bad
1936[a]	16	26	58
1966[b]	18	49	33
1972[c]	18	50	32

[a] Data adapted from depletion categories in Senate Document 199 (1936). Moderate Depletion was used to represent good condition; material Depletion, fair condition; Severe and Extreme Depletion, poor to bad condition.

[b] Data adapted from Pacific Consultants (1968).

[c] Data from Forest Report No. 19, USDA Forest Service (1972).

For instance, the grass component in a sagebrush-grass range probably had been depleted by overgrazing. The sagebrush component had increased in composition because animals did not graze it as heavily. This mix of plant species would be rated as poor condition. When grazing pressure was reduced, sagebrush was the dominant species and increased in vigor or health. Grass species recovered slowly because they had to compete with the sagebrush for moisture, nutrients, and space and continue to be grazed by remaining animals. An equilibrium between the sagebrush and grass developed and the range condition stabilized. This mix of plant species is rated as fair condition as compard to excellent condition range which resembles the grass dominated plant community which existed before excessive grazing. The dominance of sagebrush prevents the community from returning to this excellent state. Thus, without long periods of time elapsing for the successional process to occur or without intensive management actions applied to speed the process, range condition remains stabilized in fair condition with sagebrush dominating the community.

Box and most range managers would like to see less range classified as poor or bad and more classified as excellent or good. However, given the limited financial resources that have been available to take the action needed to speed succession, most of the range profession is proud to have helped reduce the amount of poor or bad condition range by almost 50 percent during the thirty-six years represented by Table 1.

Today the approach to range management is multi-disciplinary and those with and without technical expertise share in the decision making process. This is true on public lands because of legal directions that have been provided by Congress and the courts. But it is also true on private lands where the direction has come from the market place. In all areas where private land ownership dominates, most ranchers look to all of the resources occurring on their land as a possible source of economic gain. Charging fees to hunt, camp, hike, or sight-see is common. By taking advantage of such economic opportunities ranchers are listening to the public and determining what mix of products and values are most appropriate for them to produce on their private land.

The Future of Rangelands and Range Management

Writing about the future is risky business because those who read such writing may have a different opinion and ridicule you and your thoughts. On-the-other-hand, if you push your thoughts far enough into the future it is likely that no one can ever prove you wrong; and, except in rare instances such as George Orwell's <u>1984</u>, it is unlikely what anyone will remember what you predict. However, I think it necessary that this chapter look toward the future.

I have no doubt that rangelands will be important to the future of mankind. It is a trite, but true saying, "they're not making any more land". Space exploitation has so far not provided us any alternative habitats for mankind to use for food production and other uses. We and future generations will have to make do with the land we have today. Since about 45 percent of the world's land is classified as rangeland, we will rely on these lands for the products and values they can produce and that society needs. Paramount among future needs of society and which can be partially provided by rangelands are mineral and energy supplies, water, red meat, and open space.

Large supplies of mineral and energy resources lie under rangelands in this and other countries. Until some breakthrough occurs in nuclear energy or alternate sources of energy, we must assume that the mineral and energy supplies underlying rangelands will be extracted in one way or another. Fortunately, strip mining and disturbed land reclamation practices have been developed so that only small acreages will ever be disturbed at any one time and disturbed lands can be reclaimed. Thus, the direct impact on rangelands of obtaining mineral and energy supplies should be minimal.

However, the indirect impacts of mineral and energy development in rangeland areas may be substantial. Most of this impact will be due to an increase in population--the people necessary to extract the minerals and energy supplies, to process the raw materials, and to service the increased population. This is particularly true in arid and semi-arid environments where water is a scarce, if not limiting resource. Range and forest watersheds are the initial source of the water supplies in such ecosystems. Management actions will have to be taken to control the amount, quality, and timing of water yield from these watersheds. Depending upon local goals and needs, this may involve modifying the plant community for either slower or more rapid runoff, applying soil treatments to increase water percolation into the soil, modifying the plant community or constructing structures for managing blowing snow, and manipulating plant species to control loss of water through evaporation and transpiration. There will be pressure to make more water available to the consuming public through watershed management principles and practices.

There will also be pressure to divert water from irrigated agriculture for use by industries, cities, and people. Irrigation water that remains available to agriculture will probably be used for producing cereal and vegetable crops suitable for direct human consumption. Feed grains and hay for livestock will become more scarce and expensive. This situation will become much more serious as it becomes economically unfeasible to pump water from the Ogallala underground water formation (western Texas, Oklahoma, Kansas, and Nebraska) and use it to irrigate feed grain crops. Lands irrigated with Ogallala water are now our major source of feed grains for livestock. At some time in the future water pumped from the Ogallala formation will probably have to be used to produce food stuffs that can be directly consumed by humans or will be used for industrial or municipal uses.

All of this means that feed grains for livestock will become limited. Feedlot feeding of animals will not be profitable. Animals will graze on the range for longer periods of time. "Grass-fat" meat will become the rule rather than the exception. This scenario also means that there will be fewer market animals available per year because off-spring which remain on the range to fatten will take the place of productive females.

Genetic engineering may help overcome this situation. For instance, an animal capable of going for long periods of time without water, producing an off-spring ready for slaughter in one year, and providing multiple products would be a great contribution of science and technology.

Despite these predicted changes in livestock production, I believe the demand for meat products will be strong because there will be more people. We will rely upon range forages to produce the bulk of our meat supply because such production is energy efficient. Nutrients and fiber contained in range grasses, forbs, and shrubs cannot be used directly as food by human beings. Range forage must be converted into human food by a grazing animal. We can then utilize the meat in our diets and other products (wool, hides, hormones) for clothing, medicine, and other uses. As our human population grows and food supplies become more strained each resource must be used in the food chain in the best possible way. Rangelands will have a place.

Finally, rangelands by their very nature are open and uncluttered with human developments. People want and need open space for their own well being, or as a minimum, people want to know that there are open spaces and wild things in the world. Wild animals will always be an important component of rangeland ecosystems. If energy becomes a more expensive item in our budget, recreational travel that involves long distances may become less available for a higher percentage of our population. Should this happen, then only those who live near to rangeland areas and the wealthy will be able to directly partake in the open space values and recreational opportunities provided by the rangeland environment. However, all will benefit from the knowledge that the open space provided by rangelands exists.

Recreational and other human uses of the land must be properly managed. Livestock caused damage to the range landscape during the first fifty years of range use in this country. Part of the damage has been repaired. We will have gained little as a society if we now allow off-road vehicles, campers, wildlife populations, water managers, and others use the land in an improper fashion.

The challenge of range managers in the first years of the twenty-first century will not be unlike the challenges faced by range managers during the first half of this century. First, we will see great advances in science and technology that can--that must be used to advance the understanding and management of rangelands. Second, we will experience increasing demands from society for rangeland goods and services. However, society exerts its pressure through many interest groups, each group often wanting something different. The range manager must listen to Housely's (1952) arguments for doing a better job of salesmanship. As a person educated in a number of disciplines, the range manager of the future must be able and willing to help others contribute their knowledge and ideas to the proper management of the world's rangelands.

SUMMARY

Rangelands are an important land resource of the world because of (1) the amount of rangeland and (2) the multitude of products and values that man obtains from rangelands. It is this multiple use nature of rangeland and the complexity of the range environment that makes range management a multi-disciplinary profession. I have documented in this chapter several changes that have occurred in this discipline and have tried to explain why these changes occurred. Finally, I have tried to "crystal-ball" the future to determine what role rangelands and range management will serve in the twenty-first century. All of this leads me to conclude that the management of rangelands was not as urgent or as challenging in the past as it is at the present or as it will be in the future.

REFERENCES

Bentley, H. L., "Cattle Ranges of the Southwest: A History of Exhaustion of Pasturage and Suggestions for its Restoration," U.S. Department of Agriculture Farmers Bulletin 72, 1898.

Biggers, D. H., History That Will Never Be Repeated By L. Franks (pseud), High-Grade Printing Office of Biggers, Ennis, Texas, 1901.

Box, T. W., "The Arid Lands Revisited: 100 Years After John Wesley Powell," 57TH ANNUAL FACULTY HONOR LECTURE, Utah State University, Logan, 1978.

Clements, F. E., Plant Succession and Indicators, H. H. Wilson Company, New York, N.Y., 1928.

Craddock, G. W., and C. K. Pearse, "Surface Runoff and Erosion on Granitic Mountain Soils of Idaho as Influenced by Range Cover, Soil Disturbance, Slope, and Precipitation Intensity," U.S. Department of Agriculture Circular 482, 1938.

Dana, S. T., Forest and Range Policy--Its Development in the United States, McGraw-Hill Book Company, New York, N.Y., 1956.

Fradkin, P. L., "The Eating of the West," Audubon, 81:94-121, 1979.

Heady, Harold F., Rangeland Management, McGraw-Hill Book Company, New York, N.Y., 1975.

Hibbard, B. H., A History of the Public Land Policies, Peter Smith, New York, N.Y., 1939.

Housely, R. M., Jr., "Is Science Enough," Journal of Range Management, 5:302-304, 1952.

Jardine, J. T., and M. Anderson, "Range Management on the National Forests," U.S. Department of Agriculture Bulletin 790, 1919.

Klemmedson, J. O., R. D. Pieper, D. D. Duncan, W. F. Mueggler, and M. J. Trlica, "Research Needs on Western Rangelands," Journal of Range Management, 31:4-8, 1978.

McCarty, E. C., "Seasonal March of Carbohydrates in Elymus ambiguus and Muhlenbergia gracilis and Their Reaction Under Moderate Grazing Use," Plant Physiology, 10:727-738, 1935.

Pacific Consultants, "The Forage Resource," A Report Produced for the Public Land Law Review Commission, University of Idaho, Moscow, 1968.

Sampson, A. W., "Natural Revegetation of Range Lands Based Upon Growth Requirements and Life History of the Vegetation," Journal of Agricultural Research, 3:93-148, 1914.

Sampson, A. W., "The Education of Range Managers," Journal of Range Management, 7:207-212, 1954.

Sampson, A. W., and L. H. Weyl, "Range Preservation and Its Relation to Erosion Control on Western Grazing Lands," U.S. Department of Agriculture Bulletin 675, 1918.

Smith, F. E., The Politics of Conservation, Harper and Row, New York, N.Y., 1966.

Stoddart, L. A., and A. D. Smith, Range Management, McGraw-Hill Book Company, New York, N.Y., 1943.

Stoddart, L. A., and A. D. Smith, Range Management, Second Edition, McGraw-Hill Book Company, New York, N.Y., 1955.

Stoddart, L. A., and A. D. Smith, and T. W. Box, Range Management, Third Edition, McGraw-Hill Book Company, New York, N.Y., 1975.

USDA, Forest Service, "The Nation's Range Resources--A Forest-Range Environmental Study," USDA Forest Resources Report 19, 1972.

U.S. Senate, "The Western Range," Senate Document 199, 74th Congress, 2nd Session, U.S. Government Printing Office, Washington, D.C., 1936.

Weaver, J. E. "Underground Plant Development and Its Relation to Grazing," Ecology, 11:543-557, 1930.

Williams, R. E., B. W. Allred, R. M. DeNio and H. E. Paulsen, Jr., "Conservation, Development and Use of the World's Rangelands. Journal of Range Management, 21:355-360, 1968.

8
Desertification: Anatomy of a Complex Environmental Process

*Michael H. Glantz
and Nicolai S. Orlovsky*

The phenomenon known as desertification received widespread attention recently, as witnessed by the creation of the United Nations Conference on Desertification (UNCOD) in Nairobi in 1977, mainly as a result of the impact of extended drought in the West African Sahel in the early 1970s. That drought led to the loss of human lives and livestock and widespread environmental deterioration. Although many recent articles, papers, and reports from many countries begin with comments on the role of the Sahelian drought in the growing interest in the desertification issue, there remains significant disagreement within and between the disciplines (as well as between countries) as to what constitutes desertification (see, for example, Glantz, 1977; U.N. Secretariat, 1977; Quintanilla, 1981; Zonn, 1981). The Sahelian drought was neither the first manifestation of the desertification phenomenon nor the only reason for scientific interest in it. In fact, A. Aubreville, a French scientist, popularized the term desertification in his report in 1949 (Aubreville, 1949), and others, such as Le Houérou (1962), have discussed the phenomenon since the late 1950s.

The 1977 Nairobi conference did serve to draw attention to the phenomenon (U.N. Secretariat, 1977). It described desertification as

> ...the diminution or destruction of the biological potential of the land, and can lead ultimately to desert-like conditions. It is an aspect of the widespread deterioration of ecosystems, and has diminished or destroyed the biological potential, i.e., plant and animal production, for multiple use purposes at a time when increased productivity is needed to support growing populations in quest of development. Important factors in contemporary society--the struggle for development and the effort to increase food production, and to adapt and apply modern technologies, set against a back-

ground of population growth and demographic change--interlock in a network of cause and effect. Progress in development, planned population growth and improvements in all types of biological production and relevant technologies must therefore be integrated. The deterioration of productive ecosystems is an obvious and serious threat to human progress. In general, the quest for ever greater productivity has intensified exploitation and has carried disturbance by man into less productive and more fragile lands. Overexploitation gives rise to degradation of vegetation, soil and water, the three elements which serve as the natural foundation for human existence. In exceptionally fragile ecosystems, such as those on the desert margins, the loss of biological productivity through the degradation of plant, animal, soil and water resources can easily become irreversible, and permanently reduce their capacity to support human life. Desertification is a self-accelerating process, feeding on itself, and as it advances, rehabilitation costs rise exponentially. Action to combat desertification is required urgently before the costs of rehabilitation rise beyond practical possibility or before the opportunity to act is lost forever. (U.N. Conference to Combat Desertification, in Reining, 1978, p. 3.)

The conference also served to bring together representatives of many countries whose landscapes had been directly or indirectly affected by desertification. The usefulness of the conference varied from country to country. For some countries, such as the People's Republic of China, it served to direct the attention of national policymakers toward arid lands research and to elevate such research to one with a national priority. The Soviet Union's State Committee for Science and Technology (GKNT) established, with the UN Environmental Program (UNEP), international training courses on various aspects of desertification and on ways to identify and combat it (Zonn, 1981). In the United States, and in other countries, attention of national policymakers was directed toward this form of environmental degradation and a Plan of Action was drawn up to assess desertification in a national context (Sabadell et al., 1982; Biswas and Biswas, 1980).

Desertification has been of particular interest to climatologists in their attempts to understand climate variation and change on both short and long time scales (Hare, 1983). With increasing pressure on governmental decisionmakers to allow populations to move into the climatically defined marginal areas, the implications of natural variations in climate have become even more important in decisions relating to the use by society of its land in these desertification-prone regions. One can easily assert that there will always be climatic deserts. However, man-induced extensions of these deserts or the creation of desert-like conditions in areas where they had not existed can and must be avoided. The climatological communities at the national level and at the international level (through, for example, the World Meteorological Organization's World Climate Program and the U.N. Environment Program's World Climate Impacts Program) have, in general, made the identification of the climatological and meteorological aspects of desertification one of their most important priorities. Yet, research along these disciplinary lines, alone, will not provide the full knowledge about this phenomenon that is required in order to combat it effectively.

Desertification is acknowledged to be a complex phenomenon requiring the expertise of researchers in such disciplines as climatology, soil science, meteorology, hydrology, range science, agronomy, and veterinary medicine, as well as geography, political science, economics, and anthropology. It has been defined in many different ways by researchers in these and other disciplines, as well as from many national and bureaucratic (institutional) perspectives, each emphasizing different aspects of desertification, with some definitions emphasizing aspects that are usually not attributed to desertification.

A review of the desertification literature shows a great diversity among definitions (some say confusion; e.g., Carder, 1981). This broad mix of definitions (meanings attributed to the concept) can lead to miscommunication among researchers within disciplines as well as between disciplines, among policymakers, and most important, between researchers and policymakers within the same country as well as between countries (see IGU, 1975, passim). An analysis of the definitions of desertification should prove useful in developing an improved understanding of the phenomenon, of how it is viewed from different disciplines and countries (and bureaucratic units), and whether progress in combatting it has in fact been as slow as many observers suggest (e.g., U.N. General Assembly, 1981).

In the following sections more than 100 existing definitions of desertification were used as the basis for discussion, as they are often what is seen and used by decisionmakers. (References cited in this paper include only some of these definitions.) In the last section it is argued that the concept of desertification also applies to higher rainfall regions than those cited by contemporary researchers.

DESERTIFICATION: WHAT IS IT?

Some researchers consider desertification to be <u>a process</u> of change, while others view it as <u>the end result</u> of a process of change. This distinction underlies one of the main disagreements on what constitutes desertification. Desertification-as-process has generally been viewed as a series of incremental (sometimes stepwise) changes in biological productivity in arid, semiarid, and subhumid ecosystems. It can encompass such changes as a decline in yield of the same crop or, more drastically, the replacement of one (maybe equally productive or equally useful) vegetative species by another, or even a decrease in the density of the existing vegetative cover. Desertification-as-event is the creation of desert-like conditions (where perhaps none had existed in the recent past) as the end result of a process of change. To many, it is difficult to accept incremental changes as a manifestation of desertification.

In fact, both of these views represent different aspects of a broader concept of desertification. Thus, seemingly different statements such as "the creation of desert-like conditions in areas once green," "encroachment of desert-like conditions," or "the intensification of desert-like conditions", as well as less drastic projections like "changes in soils and in climate" or "the land becoming less fit for range and crops," can be encompassed by the concept of desertification.

Form of Change

Within the dozens of existing definitions of desertification, many words are used to describe the phenomenon, some of which complement each other while others appear to be contradictory. A point on which they all agree, however, is that desertification is viewed as an adverse environmental process. The negative descriptors used in these definitions of desertification include: deterioration of ecosystems (Reining, 1978), degradation of various forms of vegetation (Le Houérou, 1975), destruction of biological potential (UNCOD, 1978), diminution of biological potential (UNCOD, 1978), decay of a productive ecosystem (Hare, 1977), reduction of productivity (Kassas, 1977), decrease of biological productivity (Kovda, 1980), alteration in the biomass (U.N. Secretariat, 1977), intensification of desert conditions (Meckelein, 1980; WMO, 1980), and impoverishment of ecosystems (Dregne, 1976).

Each of these terms suggest change from a favored or preferred state (with respect to quality, societal value, or ecological stability) to a less preferred one. Also, depending upon the particular definition, the condition of vegetation, or moisture availability, or soils, or atmospheric phenomena is described. Other descriptors used in these definitions connote a movement or a transfer of characteristics of a desert landscape into an area where such characteristics had not existed. Extension, encroachment, acceleration, spread, and transformation: if one combined each of these negative and transfer descriptors with all the other factors cited in the existing definitions, the concept of desertification would encompass most kinds of environmental changes related to biological productivity (see Rozanov, 1981).

What is Changed

Different definitions focus on changes either in soil (e.g., salinization), or vegetation (e.g., reduced density of biomass), or water (e.g., waterlogging), or air (e.g., increased albedo). Most of them, regardless of primary emphasis, also describe changes in biological productivity, with comments related to the type, density, and value of vegetation.

Type of vegetation comments center on changes from desired (or accepted) species to less desired (or less accepted) ones. Such comments include a reduction in the proportion of preferred species having an economic or societal value, the lowering of yields of an existing preferred species, or a major ecological change such as species replacement.

Changes in the density of the vegetative cover is an important factor acknowledged by many authors in their definitions of desertification. As density decreases, for example, the risks of wind erosion, water erosion, and the adverse effect of increased solar radiation on bare soils are increased dramatically. Surface albedo (reflectivity), also enhanced by a reduction in the vegetative cover, is a major contributor to desertification processes.

With respect to the value of vegetation, a few researchers have explicitly referred to "lower useful productivity" (Johnson, 1977), "reduced productivity of desirable plants" (Dregne, 1976), "sustained decline in the yield of useful crops" (U.N. Secretariat, 1977), and "loss of primary species" (Rapp et al., 1976). However, the concern with the value of vegetation in desertification processes is not shared by all. Some researchers have dismissed the value concern, by suggesting that any type of vegetation that holds the soil in place is of value in the combat against desertification, whether or not it has an economic value.

As a final comment on what desertification is, it is important to note that disciplinary and institutional biases might appear in any given definition of desertification. For example, a meteorological bias might require that a change take place in the meteorological parameters of a given region, so that they become similar to those for a desert region (e.g., high evaporation rates, aridity, increased rainfall intensity, etc.). As another example, Meckelein (cited in Kharin and Petrov, 1977), alluded to the disciplinary bases for desertification when he wrote that desertification could be characterized by the following components: <u>climate</u>: increasing aridity (diminishing water supply); <u>hydrological processes</u>: runoff becoming more irregular; <u>morphodynamic processes</u>: intensification of distinct geomorphological processes (accelerated soil erosion by wind and water); <u>soil dynamics</u>: desiccation of soils and accumulation of salt; <u>vegetation dynamics</u>: decline of vegetation.

Location of Change

There is no agreement on where desertification can take place. Many researchers identify arid, semiarid, and sometimes subhumid regions as the areas in which desertification can occur or where the risks of desertification are highest. Others imply that the areas prone to desertification might not be restricted to arid, semiarid, or subhumid regions by using such descriptive words as extension, encroachment, and spread of desert characteristics into non-desert regions. Still others (e.g., Mabbutt and Wilson, 1980, p. 11) refer to the intensification of desert-like conditions, suggesting that desertification can occur in desert-like areas. Many oppose this view, however, contending that desert-like conditions cannot be created in a desert. They assert that desertification can only occur along the desert fringes. According to Le Houérou, "desertization" can occur only in the 50-300 mm isohyet zone.

Reversibility

Few definitions explicitly refer to whether desertification is permanent. Le Houérou (1975), for example, explained briefly the conditions under which desertification might be reversible. Others have implied reversibility with reference to the higher costs of rehabilitation of desertified areas (as opposed to prevention). For example, Adams suggested that the "reversibility of desertification was a function of technology and the cost of rejuvenating an area...

[I]rreversibility should refer to a situation in which the costs of reclamation were greater than the return from a known form of land use" (IGU, 1975, p. 138). Still others implied irreversibility by referring to the end result of desertification as the creation of desert-like conditions.

Two additional important considerations relating to the permanence of desertification are (a) when desertification (as a process or event) might be reversed (i.e., the "time" factor), and (b) under what conditions (i.e., the "how" factor).

With respect to the time factor, desertification may be considered by some observers to be irreversible during a season or a few seasons but may be reversible on the order of decades; if not decades, perhaps centuries. Peel "saw great danger in the concept of irreversibility because it has no time limitations whatever" (IGU, 1975, p. 138). One author has drawn a distinction between temporary and permanent desertification (WMO Secretariat, 1982). Is it possible to distinguish between temporary desertification and, for example, seasonal environmental changes? Some have addressed this question by defining desertification as a sustained (as opposed to temporary) decline in biological productivity (Sabadell et al., 1982; U.N. Secretariat, 1977). Le Houerou commenting on "what is temporary?", noted that "while temporary fluctuations may be interspersed with more favorable conditions, such a condition of successive crises does involve a progressively deteriorating situation, possibly past a threshhold of irreversibility" (IGU, 1975, p. 27).

With respect to how desertification might be reversed, the reversal might occur naturally, once the contributing causes have been removed. Otherwise, human intervention might be required (Kassas, 1977) if there is a desire on the part of decisionmakers to reverse it in less time than might be required to do so naturally. Chinese scientists, for example, have recently suggested a program for reversing desertification in the People's Republic of China (Zhu and Shu, 1981).

DESERTIFICATION: WHY DOES IT OCCUR?

Some researchers consider climate to be the major contributor to desertification processes, with human factors playing a relatively minor supporting role. Other researchers reverse the significance of these two factors. For example, Le Houérou (1959) concluded that "on its edges the Sahara is mainly made by man; climate being only a supporting factor" (quoted in Rapp, 1974, p. 32). A third group blames climate and man more or less equally. For example, Grove has noted that "desertification or desert encroachment can result from a change in climate or from human action and it is often difficult to distinguish between the two" (Grove, 1973). Each of these views can be shown to be valid, at least at the local level, and on a case-by-case basis. This suggests that there is a region-specific bias to perceptions about desertification, one that spills over to the definitions. Debates about causes of desertification occupy a large part of the desertification literature and need only be summarized here.[1]

Climate

References to climate in these definitions relate either to climate variability, climate change, or drought. __Climate variability__ (a term that is usually undefined in these definitions) seems to refer to the natural fluctuations that appear in the statistics representing the state of the atmosphere for a designated period of time, usually on the order of months to decades. Fluctuations might occur in any or all of the atmospheric variables (such as precipitation, temperature, wind speed and direction, evaporation, etc.). A result of those fluctuations might be the alteration of an ecosystem, and this could eventually affect societal activities that had been developed to exploit the productivity of that ecosystem.

It is important to note that during the annual dry season the characteristics of the atmosphere in an arid or semi-arid area are like that of a desert-like region (low precipitation, high evaporation, high solar radiation, etc.), and if improper use of the land occurs during this period, degradation results (Aubreville, 1949). Thus, short-term fluctuations in climatic factors as well as seasonal dry periods, when combined with improper land-use practices, can give the appearance of the impact of a climate change when none may have occurred at all.

__Climate change__ refers to the relatively longer term changes that appear in the statistics that represent the average state of the weather. Typically, desertification is seen to be primarily a result of such natural shifts in climate regimes. It has been suggested, for example, that there has been a trend toward increasing aridity in the West African Sahel; a natural desiccation of the region that man can do nothing to stop. Usually cited as evidence for long-term climate changes in that area in the past are the fossil dune fields near the West African coast far from the active dunes close to the desert. The debate over long-term climate change in the West African Sahel continues.

Drought episodes have also been cited as a major cause of desertification since, during such extended dry spells desertification becomes relatively more severe, widespread, and visible, and its rate of occurrence increases sharply. Since the probability of droughts increases as one moves from the humid to the more arid regions, so, too, does the proneness to desertification. Land forms, soils, and vegetation are often transformed during such extended drought periods.

Human Activities

Cultivation, herding, and wood-gathering practices, as well as the use of technology have all been cited in the definitions as major causes of, and contributors to, the desertification process in arid, semi-arid, and sub-humid areas. Cultivation practices that can lead to desertification include land clearing practices, cultivation of marginal climatic regions, cultivation of poor soils, and inappropriate cultivation tactics such as reduced fallow time, improper tillage, drainage, and water use. For example, areas that might support agriculture on a short-term basis may be unable to do so on a long-term sustained basis. Even areas that are considered suitable for cultivation may become degraded if they are managed in a way that is inappropriate to the ecological and climatic setting.

Rangeland use that can lead to desertification includes excessively large herds for existing range conditions (leading to overgrazing and trampling) and herd concentration around human settlements and watering points. Government policies toward their pastoral populations can also indirectly lead to desertification by, for example, not pursuing policies that encourage herders to cull their herds, by putting a floor on grain prices and a ceiling on prices that pastoralists might receive for their livestock, and so forth.

Gathering firewood by itself or in combination with overgrazing or inappropriate cultivation practices creates conditions that expose the land to "otherwise benign" meteorological factors (such as wind, evaporation, precipitation runoff, solar radiation on bare soil, etc.), thereby contributing to desertification.

The use of technology in arid, semi-arid and sub-humid environments is the result of the policymakers' desire for economic development. Thus, deep wells, irrigation and cash crop schemes, even the reduction of livestock diseases such as sleeping sickness (trypanosomiasis), each in its own way, can increase the risks of an area to desertification processes. It has been shown that desertification can result from road building, industrial construction, geological surveys, ore mining, settlement construction, irrigation facilities, and motor transport (Rozanov, 1977).

In sum, most researchers accept that both climatic and human factors are involved in the desertification process with a few observers noting that the two factors are so entwined that to separate them as to primary and secondary contributors would be a fruitless endeavor.

BROADENING THE CONCEPT OF DESERTIFICATION

Perhaps the most unfortunate aspect of the concept of desertification is that the concept of desert is a part of the term. This has tended to bias most descriptions of desertification toward the climatically defined dry margins of hot deserts. Thus, desertification, while originally described as a process of degradation toward a desert-like end state, has become tied to arid and semiarid regions. Yet it can be effectively argued that this may be too narrow a definition of desertification. It may be instructive to review the original use of the term.

As noted earlier, Aubreville discussed desertification at great length in his 1949 report entitled Climats, Forêts et Désertification. This report has appeared in the references of a large proportion of the contemporary scientific literature on desertification. However, as a result of discussions with many of these authors and from the contents of their articles in which Aubreville has been cited, it appears that very few have read his work. His report, when compared to the scores of contemporary definitions, raises, among other issues, the issue about where desertification can take place.

Broadly speaking, most of these contemporary definitions relate desertification to what might be viewed as the desert fringes. For example, a UNEP report identified types of deserts as rainless, runoff, rainfall, and man-made, with man-made deserts defined as "parts of the semiarid steppe country (rainfall 200-350 mm/yr) that have been transformed into deserts due to overexploitation [desertification]" (1975, p. 1). Aubreville, however, explicitly referred to the tropical forest of Africa delimited by the 700 to 1500+ mm precipitation isohyets (lines of equal precipitation), noting that "These are real deserts that are being born today, under our eyes, in the regions where the annual rainfall is from 700 mm to 1500 mm (Ce sont de vrais déserts que naissant aujourd'hui, sous nos yeux, dans des pays oùil tombe cependant annuellement de 700 à plus de 1,500 de pluies)" (p. 332). Thus the view of desertification given by Aubreville, who is considered by many as the father of the concept, would have no place in desertification studies today because it fails to meet the "desert fringe" criteria identified in most contemporary definitions.

Aubreville viewed desertification primarily as a process, but also referred to it as an event (the end state of a process of degradation). He described how forested regions were transformed into savanna (he called this "savannization") and savanna into desert-like regions. One of Aubreville's central concerns was the rate of destruction, resulting from human activities, of Africa's tropical forests. He noted that cultivation, deforestation, and erosion were so entwined as to lead to the destruction of the vegetative cover and soils in the forested regions of tropical Africa where "the desert always menaces, more or less evident, but it is always present in the embryonic state, during the dry and hot season" (le désert menace toujours, plus ou moins evidement, mais il est toujours present, à l'etat embryonnaire, dans la saison seche et chaude). Savanna would result. Continued disregard for the fragility of the savanna would result in the creation of desert-like conditions.

Aubreville's research findings are directly relevant to contemporary efforts to identify, understand, and combat desertification processes. The reincorporation of his research into the desertification discussions is not a call to discard other definitions. It is a call to broaden our thinking about what constitutes desertification as a process and where that process might occur, including consideration of the proper methods needed to combat it. Thus, if desertification can be identified by some of its component sub-processes, such as soil erosion, deforestation, overgrazing, or cultivation in marginal areas (determined, for example, by soil characteristics or by the amount of rainfall), then one could argue that there is a great deal of research activity underway that relates directly as well as indirectly to desertification, without explicitly having desertification in its title (Riquer, 1982).

Questions have been raised about the lack of agreement regarding the meaning of desertification: Are the regional biases and distortions in the definitions important? How do the different disciplinary and/or scientific definitions affect policymaking? Does the conceptual confusion and/or ambiguity lead to bad policy or does it enable agencies to do new and useful things?

Regional, disciplinary, and institutional biases and alterations in the definition of desertification are important. They can be said to represent a recognition of, and an interest in, the desertification concept by people whose research activities may not be encompassed by existing definitions, but whose research interests may in fact be analogous to research underway in core desertification studies. These researchers have modified the general descriptive definitions of desertification to include related processes in regions with which they are familiar.

The existence of more than one hundred definitions of desertification (and this list appears to be continually growing) should not discourage those interested in researching various aspects of desertification. First, there are central definitions from which most other definitions are derived. Secondly, desertification is a highly complex phenomenon involving complicated interactions between the atmosphere, the land, the vegetation, and people, their livestock, and land use practices. Different images come to mind when the term desertification is used, with researchers typically elevating one element or another above the rest. Often what distinguishes one definition from the next is the emphasis on what are perceived to be the primary and secondary factors in desertification. For example, the World Meteorological Organization (WMO) cites meteorology and climate as important factors; the Food and Agriculture Organization (FAO) cites soils; the Clark University study for the U.S. Agency for International Development cites human factors; COSPAR (as well as the Remote Sensing Institute in South Dakota) recommends the use of satellite imagery as the best way to monitor the process; yet others, skeptical of what remote sensing can do, suggest land-based monitoring networks.

As another example, researchers on desertification in the United States appear to be divided as to whether there is (or for that matter can ever be) such a process of degradation in the United States. To some of these people, desertification is seen as a Third World problem. This view surfaced frequently during hearings held in various cities throughout the American West with regard to a U.S. Department of the Interior draft assessment of desertification in the United States. Many farmers and ranchers expressed their beliefs that the desertification concept was one that was created for political reasons by bureaucrats in Washington, who were in fact unfamiliar with the American West. These same ranchers and farmers, however, acknowledged that they did have to cope with environmental problems such as wind and water erosion, deforestation, heavy grazing pressure, and so forth.

The diversity of views about desertification shows that additional disciplines and countries, as well as institutions, are becoming involved with the assessment of a variety of processes of degradation that have collectively been referred to as desertification. The broadened application of the concept can be seen in a recent U.N. study on financing the Plan of Action to

Combat Desertification (U.N. General Assembly, 1981, p. 7), which noted that antidesertification programs and projects

> ...affect food production, soil erosion, water systems, and other fragile ecosystems, such as range lands, pastures, rainfed crop lands and life-supporting natural balances. As such, antidesertification projects are, thus, aimed at a variety of developmental goals including agricultural and rural development and social ecological development, which are high on the priority list of development plans.

With a large variety of definitions, it does become possible, however, for policymakers to choose the one that best fits their needs or interests. The same is also true for decisionmakers in various agencies who often need to find, modify, or create a definition of desertification that meets their agency's administrative or jurisdictional needs. The UNCOD definition has been considered very general and therefore has provided little guidance for operationalizing the concept. Various U.N. agencies have drawn up their own plans of action to combat desertification.

The WMO, through its Commission for Agricultural Meteorology, has chosen to acknowledge the existence of many definitions. The Commission's Expert Meeting on Meteorological Aspects of Desertification (WMO, 1980) acknowledged that (a) the concept of desertification is difficult to define and that it may be impossible to find a single definition which is generally applicable in all regions and acceptable by scientists of all concerned disciplines; and (b) in each particular situation, the space and time scale considered should be specified and the factors of desertification indicated.

In sum, the acceptance of a broader conception of desertification, in addition to the specific working definitions of the concept designed to meet regional, disciplinary, or institutional needs, would shed a different light on understanding and combatting desertification. There is much research underway on soil erosion, range managment, deforestation, increasing biological productivity in arid lands and so forth. These research activities contribute to the combat against desertification processes, regardless of whether the term appears in the title of the program or project. Viewed in this broader context, it can be shown that there are many activities that contribute to an increase in our knowledge and understanding of the phenomenon known as desertification. Only in this broader conceptualization of desertification can we develop a more accurate assessment of how nations are faring in their "war" against desertification.

NOTES

1. In a recent book on drylands, the authors noted in a section on desert expansion and its causes that "There are two schools of thought about the mysteries of the expanding deserts: either the changes are due entirely to climate variation, or man is the cause, independently of the climate or in association with its variations." These authors noted that "man is the most common cause, sometimes in combination with climatic variations but generally on his own" (Adams et al., 1979, pp. 3-4).

REFERENCES

Adams, R., M. Adams, A. Willens, and A. Willens. 1979. *Dry Lands: Man and Plants*. New York: St. Martins Press.

Aubreville, A. 1949. *Climats, Forêts et Désertification de l'Afrique Tropicale*. Paris: Societe d'Editions Geographiques, Maritimes et Coloniales.

Biswas, M.R., and A.K. Biswas. 1980. *Desertification: Associated Case Studies Prepared for the UN Conference on Desertification*. London: Pergamon Press.

Carder, D.J. 1981. Desertification in Australia - A Muddled Concept. *Search* 12 (7): 218-21.

Dregne, H.E. 1976. Desertification: Symptoms of a Crisis. In *Desertification, Process, Problems, Perspectives*, ed. P. Paylor and R.A. Haney, Jr., Tucson: Univ. of Arizona.

Glantz, M.H., ed. 1977. *Desertification: Environmental Degradation in and around Arid Lands*. Boulder: Westview Press.

Grove, A.T. 1973. Desertification in the African Environment. In *Drought in Africa*, ed. D. Dalby and R.J. Harrison Church, Report of the 1973 Symposium, School of Oriental and African Study, University of London.

Hare, K. 1977. Connections between Climate and Desertification. *Environmental Conservation* 4 (2): 82.

_____. 1983. *Climate and Desertification: A Revised Analysis*. Geneva: WMO World Climate Program Publication 44.

IGU (International Geophysical Union) Working Group on Desertification. 1975. Proceedings of the IGU Meeting on Desertification, Cambridge University, 22-26 September. Cambridge, UK: Cambridge U. Dept. of Geography, mimeo.

Johnson, D.L. 1977. The human Dimensions of Desertification. *Economic Geography* 53 (4): 317-8.

Kassas, M. 1977. Arid and Semi-Arid Lands: Problems and Prospects. *Agro-Ecosystems* 3:186.

Kharin, N.G., and M.P. Petrov. 1977. *Glossary of Terms on Natural Conditions and Desert Development*. Materials for the UN Conference on Desertification, Moscow.

Kovda, V. 1980. *Land Aridization and Drought Control*. Boulder: Westview Press.

Le Houérou, H.N. 1962. Les Paturages Naturels de la Tunisie Aride et Desertique. Paris: Inst. Sces. Econ. Appl. Tunis.

_____. 1975. The Nature and Causes of Desertization. In Proceedings of the IGU Meeting on Desertification, Cambridge University, 22-26 September. (Also reprinted in M.H. Glantz. 1977. *Desertification.* Boulder, CO: Westview Press.)

Mabbutt, J.A., and A.W. Wilson, eds. 1980. *Social and Environmental Aspects of Desertification*, Tokyo: U.N. University.

Meckelein, W. 1980. The Problem of Desertification within Deserts. In *Desertification in Extremely Arid Environments*, Report of the IGU Working Group on Desertification in and around Arid Lands, 24th International Geographical Congress, Tokyo.

Quintanilla, E.G. 1981. Regional Aspects of Desertification in Peru. In *Combating Desertification through Integrated Development*, UNEP/UNEPCOM International Scientific Symposium, Tashkent, USSR, Abstract of Papers, 114-5. Moscow UNEPCOM.

Rapp, A. 1974. *A Review of Desertization in Africa: Water, Vegetation and Man.* Stockholm, Sweden: Secretariat for International Ecology.

———, H.N. Le Houerou, and B. Lundholm, eds. 1976. *Can Desert Encroachment Be Stopped? A Study with Emphasis on Africa.* Stockholm: Swedish Natural Science Research Council.

Reining, P., compiler. 1978. *Handbook on Desertification Indicators*, based on the Science Associations' Nairobi Seminar on Desertification. Washington, DC: American Association for the Advancement of Science.

Riquer, J. 1982. A World Assessment of Soil Degradation. *Nature and Resources.* 18 (2): 18-21.

Rozanov, B.G. 1977. Degradation of Arid Lands in the World and International Cooperation in Desertification Control. *Pchvovedenie* 8:5-11.

———. 1981. Principles of Desertification Diagnostics and Assessment. In *Combating Desertification through Integrated Development*, UNEP/UNEPCOM International Scientific Symposium, Tashkent, USSR, Abstract of Papers, 24-6. Moscow UNEPCOM.

Sabadell, J.E., E.M. Risley, H.T. Jorgenson, and B.S. Thornton. 1982. *Desertification in the United States: Status and Issues*, Final Report for the Bureau of Land Management and Department of the Interior, Washington, DC.

UNCOD (U.N. Conference on Desertification). 1978. *Round-Up, Plan of Action and Resolutions.* New York: United Nations.

U.N. General Assembly. 1981. Development and International Economic Co-operation: Environment. Study on Financing the Plan of Action to Combat Desertification, Report of the Secretary General. Rept. A/36/141. New York: United Nations.

U.N. Secretariat of the Conference on Desertification. 1977. Desertification: An Overview. In <u>Desertification: Its Causes and Consequences</u>. New York: Pergamon Press.
UNEP (UN Environment Program). 1975. <u>Overviews in the Priority Subject Area Land, Water and Desertification</u>, Nairobi: UNEP.
WMO (World Meteorological Organization). 1980. Expert Meeting on Meteorological Aspects of Desertification, December 1980. Report of the Meeting, point 2.4. Geneva: WMO.
WMO Secretariat. 1982. Unpublished draft by N.G. Kove. Geneva: WMO.
Zhu, Zhenda, and Liu S. 1981. Desertification and Desertification Control in Northern China. <u>Desertification Control</u> 5:13-9.
Zonn, I.S., ed. 1981. <u>USSR/UNEP Projects to Combat Desertification</u>. Centre of International Projects. Moscow: GKNT.

9
Impact Ecology: An Assessment Framework for Resource Development and Management

C. P. Wolf

INTRODUCTION

    This chapter has its origin in the U.S. Man and the Biosphere (MAB) Program, whose overall research task is usefully stated by Bennett (1981:30): ". . . to investigate the social systems which govern the human use and abuse of resources and the consequences of this." My involvement in MAB was focused on Project 10, "Effects on Man and His Environment of Major Engineering Works," which calls attention to the human ("socio") side of sociotechnical systems as well as to the physical technologies employed in serving human purposes and to the consequences of their application on both natural and built environments. The 1976 National Program Statement for Project 10 expressed this sense of purpose:

> Meeting the physical requirements of human populations and human settlements will require engineering and construction works of unprecedented scale. Equally, it will subject those peoples and habitats to exceptional social and environmental stresses. The problem of MAB Project 10 is to find ways of providing for human needs while preserving human values, including those of environmental protection and enhancement. Experience with development planning over past decades has demonstrated the inadequacy of traditional engineering and economic solutions. Human problems are more complex, and human possibilities more diverse, than such efforts have allowed. The "humanistic coefficient" must be factored into development planning, as integral rather than incidental to needs assessment and their satisfaction.

---

*I wish to thank Paul Opryszek, Norman Schwarz, and the editors for reviewing an earlier draft.

The purpose of U.S. MAB Project 10 is to provide planners, engineers, decision makers, managers, and publics with the criteria and knowledge useful to estimating and evaluating the potential impacts, intended and unintended, of major engineering works. It seeks to broaden the range of planning alternatives to include intermediate ("appropriate") technologies and nonstructural approaches, to environmental preservation as well as natural resource development. In carrying out this purpose a primary objective will be to develop and deploy comprehensive methodologies for the identification and analysis of long- and short-term impacts on people and nature of development policies, programs, and projects.

Specific problem areas were identified as follows:

1. Siting: The location of facilities and services is a problem endemic to any development scheme. "Engineering solutions" are no longer considered adequate for location decisions; public acceptance must be regarded and respected.
2. Displacement and Relocation of Populations: Much development planning is accompanied by population displacement and relocation. Frequently it is impossible to re-establish the social positions and relations of impacted persons, or to compensate them adequately for personal and social loss.
3. Equity: The dissociation of costs and benefits from project impacts is especially marked in the extreme case of population displacement. Questions of social justice--who benefits and who pays--arise in every case of development planning, however.
4. Evaluation of Effects: Methodologies for deciding whether assessed impacts are desirable or undesirable, and from whose point of view, are urgently required. Present weighting and ranking schemes appear unreliable and arbitrary.
5. Decision Strategies: The rules and requirements for rational choice under conditions of uncertainty appear highly problematic, yet the alternative to a rational decision model is a power model in which the legitimacy of decision makers is itself in question.
6. Prediction versus Outcome: The analytic problem for Project 10 is a predictive one, involving the use of anticipatory research in the assessment of long-term, higher-order

engineering impacts. Such predictions demand
repeated validation and, ideally, continuous
monitoring of quality of life indicators,
including indices of environmental quality.
7. Methodological Integration: These methodological concerns and the substantive problems to which they are addressed must be placed in a comprehensive and consistent framework of analysis. Especially pressing is the need for a comparative methodology to balance societal interests in the areas of energy, economy and environment.

Despite these good intentions, and a good beginning to test our objectives and approaches in one specific case--the proposed superport at Palau (Smith and Goodenough, 1977)--Project 10 was a nonstarter. It became an early casualty of the institutional instability and intellectual insecurity that has attended the U.S. MAB Program (and doubtless those of other countries) throughout its existence. The precarious value of interdisciplinary research was compounded by the uncertainties of international and interagency cooperation. The recent United States withdrawal from UNESCO, sponsor of MAB, underscores this on the level of macropolitics--although if previous experience with the International Labor Organization is any indication, this may be a temporary condition. Efforts towards developing and deploying a system of comprehensive and integrated assessment have continued in other contexts and guises, however (see Rossini and Porter, 1983). This chapter will survey and project those developments and their applications to resource management and related problems. First it is necessary to restate the nature and scope of those problems to which integrated impact assessment is offered as a potential, if partial, "solution."

THE "RESOURCES PROBLEMS"

Statement of the Problem

Many problem statements have been advanced, but usually they come down to questions of resource sufficiency and sustainability. A few writers, such as Julian Simon, believe that resource scarcity is a myth and that because of the advancement of science and its technological applications we are entering an "age of substitutability." Other writers point out that because of their spillovers and side effects, "technological fixes" are themselves part of the problem--in fact, the leading part; technological hazards and risks have replaced natural ones as the center of human concerns. In the language of the National Environmental Policy Act (NEPA), the problem can be phrased as one of achieving and maintaining "productive harmony;" other phrasings include "sustained yield," "design with nature," and now, "ecodevelopment." Following this line, Bennett (1981:23) identifies "the problem" as one of establishing balance between natural and social systems:

> In many existing socionatural systems, the human component has tended to enlarge its scale of control or intervention; this is what we know today as the environmental or ecological problem. (The direct result of technology plus increasing human population, this tendency has warped socionatural systems toward the human side, which in many cases means a destruction of natural diversity and the corresponding loss of automatically-operating checks and balances against deterioration, or changes which reduce potential productivity and source of support of component organisms). Clearly, the main objective of human intentions toward the planet must include a redressing of this imbalance and a restoration of true systemic in place of linear-causal. This is, in simple terms, the objective of MAB; that is, to perform research which will assist or guide this change in the role of the human component in socionatural systems.

By this reckoning, the problem is that cultural development has, by technological means, acquired the capacity of overwhelming natural systems and their defenses--ostensibly to human benefit, but ultimately to its detriment. While this is a way of expressing the long-term trajectory of cultural evolution (Redfield, 1975:12), only in very recent times has the magnitude of the human impact reached truly global proportions, e.g. through "geo-engineering." Having assumed and asserted dominion over nature, we place ourselves in the position of doing nature's work. Thus the "Father of Waters" becomes a Corps of Engineers management project, a "man-made river" (Belt, 1975). Thus the Colorado River in its present unnatural state is "primarily a product of the political process . . . rather than a natural phenomenon" (Fradkin, 1981). Just as "death is nature's way of telling you to slow down," the response of natural systems to environmental insult is negative feedback. It happens that expenditures for flood control and property losses from flood damage on the Missouri River ascend closely in parallel. In extreme instances, such as the explosion at Seveso, Italy, natural processes themselves become the carriers of technological threat, i.e. in the transport of dioxin (Whiteside, 1976).

The human response characteristically is technological intensification--a positive feedback that further distorts natural systems and magnifies environmental damage. Only rarely have we understood that we don't know enough to do nature's work and that the path of wisdom is letting nature take its course. This philosophy of "leaving alone"--the "no-build alternative"--is exemplified in the cases of shoreline protection against beach erosion, on barrier islands especially, and "natural" forest fires.

<u>The Containment Principle</u>. How far intervention strategies of environmental modification can safely proceed is formulated in the "containment principle"--"a requirement that the environmental effects of human activity be confined within areas dedicated to that activity" (Taylor and Humpstone, 1973:33). Its application is measured against the natural background level; ". . . one may say that man is significantly disturbing a natural balance when the amount of a chemical that he adds to the air or water is substantial compared with the amount in a natural cycle" (Taylor and Humpstone, 1973:50). Its objective is ". . . restoring the earth to a state of balance between natural and human activity" (Taylor and Humpstone, 1973:49). Implementing this strategy requires neither a change of mind nor of heart--except in the knowledge of consequences and an "ethic" of consequences (Parsons, 1968:157):

> We began by questioning two assumptions: that man is wise enough to determine how much man-made change the biosphere can support and that the way to environmental salvation lies through changing spiritual or ethical values. Discarding both, we have asserted that man has and should exercise the ability to insulate the biosphere from human activity. . . . (Taylor and Humpstone, 1973:165-66)

According to Taylor and Humpstone (1973:138), however, containment ". . . is the only strategy for which all the costs and consequences can be determined now and which can be carried out now using the knowledge we have." Later I will argue that the basis for accounting those costs and consequences is a system of comprehensive and integrated assessment, here called "impact ecology." The exceptions taken above--improving the knowledge and "ethic" of consequences--can be reconciled with the last statement quoted by exerting a restraint on human intervention policies and strategies in the face of ignorance and error, i.e. the scope of decisions and actions, especially the "irreversible and irretrievable commitment of resources" (NEPA) under conditions of uncertainty or, in Duhl's (1967) words, "what to do when you don't know the names of the variables." Acting responsibly under the containment principle would imply efforts toward the reduction of causal ignorance and the attribution and acceptance of public accountability on that basis.

Problem Analysis

It is apparent that to characterize the resource problem as technological or environmental is to speak elliptically. Above all, it is institutional--the cultural and behavioral forms by which collective decisions are made and collective actions are taken. No clearer proof is required than to consider the world's "food problem." By every admission the proved technology exists to satisfy food requirements, both quantitative and nutritional, at home and abroad, now and in the foreseeable future. Despite this, government agencies such as the U.S. Department of Agriculture continue to advocate ever-increasing agricultural productivity through application of emerging biotechnologies while at the same time attempting to curtail actual production. There are many good reasons for increasing the efficiency of resource allocations in the agricultural sector; however, absent institutional controls their cumulative impact tends to be counterproductive. In fact, the American "farm problem" is already overproduction-- more formally stated, ". . . persistent tendencies to overinvestment of capital (accompanied at times by some underinvestment), a persistent tendency to overallocation of manpower to agriculture, and a consequent persistent tendency to a level of output not planned for when the resource allocation was initially made. . ." (Clawson, 1972:vi)

Internationally, at a time when it seems that an era of chronic famine has descended on parts of Africa, increased production by means of a "green revolution" (see Brady, 1985) would appear an obvious solution. Again, such appearances are deceiving. The "food problem" is really a problem of rural poverty (Kastens, 1981:7), the solution to which lies in creating mechanisms for effective redistribution, not just increasing production. Institutional arrangements in agriculture have not been geared to serve this redistributive function, or for that matter to reward primary producers. This is not simply an institutional failure in the farm sector, of course; it reflects imbalance within the social system across all sectors and segments of society. By continuing to emphasize agricultural productivity gains as the problem solution, there is a

wholesale commission of "errors of the third kind"--
"the error, or probability, of having solved the wrong
problem, choosing the wrong problem representation, when
one should have solved the right problem, chosen the
right representation" (Mitroff and Featheringham, 1974:
383). Ackoff (1974:239) concludes, "the failures of
society and its institutions derive more from their
failure to face the right problems than from their failure to solve the problems they face."

This technologic-economic ("supply-side") bias in
problem definition has been noted repeatedly in other
areas of natural resource development and management.
In energy, for example, there is growing if grudging
recognition the importance of "nontechnical" factors:

> The committee would like to note that nontechnical
> constraints are considered to have a decisive
> effect in limiting the rate of exploration and
> exploitation of the nation's energy resources.
> Even if the drilling rate is made more effective
> and efficient through technology, substantial
> increases in this rate will not be directly
> reflected in a comparable improvement in the whole
> energy resource recovery system because of nontechnical restraints. (Ad Hoc Committee on Technology
> of Drilling for Energy Resources, 1976:ii)

More generally, in regard to "The complex of nonmaterial
factors that affect man's use of and demand for
resources," the Committee on Resources and Man (1969:
16) concluded:

> Although circumstances required the present Committee to bypass most aspects of such a study, our
> inquiries so strongly reinforce the need for it
> that we urge the formation of another group to
> study the various social, psychological, legal,
> medical, religious, and political aspects of the
> problems of resources and man that we have been
> forced to set aside.

It is not recorded that such a group was empaneled. A
major breakthrough did occur in one resource management
agency, however, when the Corps of Engineers decreed the
admissability of "nonstructural" alternatives. Though
lacking in engineering virtue, managing the nation's
water resources no longer required going out and building water control structures. Similarly, the "energy
crisis" managers did at least admit the possibility of
demand reduction through application of various conservation measures. It matters then how problems are perceived and defined in formulating alternative solutions.

In any case, to analyze resource problems and their proposed solutions, we first need to characterize the systems in relation to which the resources in question stand <u>as resources</u>. At a minimum, these systems are historical (time-dependent), functional, purposive, adaptive, complex, dynamic, and (under varying conditions) nonlinear. They are members of the class whose distinguishing characteristic Weaver (1948) described as "organized complexity." Correspondingly, system problems are characterized by a high degree of interrelatedness; less politely, Ackoff (1979:251) calls them "messes." As such, they require a thoroughly interdisciplinary attack. Because of the multiple perspectives and paradigms employed historically by the various disciplines, the result is that the phenomena of interest have been "overdetermined." In turn this creates an analytic problem of integration, both conceptual and methodological. In addition to systems analysis, systems <u>synthesis</u> is required to capture their relational properties.

Problem Solutions

Now, in the words of that old revolutionary, Nikolay Chernyshevsky, "What is to be done?" In the first place, it must be stressed that problem selection involves a normative stance, whether that of the value system of science or of the larger society. Just as there is a value basis there is also a value bias--we may select only those problems for which conventional solutions are available (indeed, that is the criterion of a "good" problem--one "ripe for solution"--within the paradigm of "normal science" (Kuhn). Ideally the search for method is driven by the problem to be solved. However, one may venture that if conventional solutions were adequate, identified problems would not persist. Again, we might invoke the "do nothing" alternative, trusting that some technological fix will come along to rescue us from our current predicament. In the history of societal problems it is more usual that problems are superseded rather than solved. Yet the common perception today is that the continuation of present trends is a prescription for global calamity, and moreover that system problems require system solutions.

<u>The Systems Approach</u>. The response to perceived problems must combine both intellectual and institutional aspects, the latter including "politics" although often that is seen as part of the problem (e.g. lack of "political will") rather than its solution. The rise of the "environmental sciences" in response to the "environmental crisis" is a good example, taking the forms of

both intellectual and institutional development (Caldwell, 1983). Before deciding "What to do?" however, the prior question is "What to think?" We have said that the resources problem is a systems problem, indicating systems thinking (Emery, 1969) as the direction in which our thought processes should proceed. Hence the "systems approach" (Churchman, 1968) is a logical point of departure in the quest for coherence and problem analysis. Systems approaches lead directly to the "ecosystems complex" comprised of population, organization, environment, and technology (POET in the acronym put forth by Duncan, 1964), and to its applicability in particular settings, e.g. the Sahel (see Schölvinck, 1985).

The Ecosystems Approach. It is one thing to have a systems "perspective" or even an "approach." The analytic leverage gained, however, must point to some research directions and procedures that can be applied to the assessment problem. While some useful guides for application to environmental impact assessment are available in the literature of systems ecology (Institute of Ecology, 1971; Holling and others, 1978; Beanlands and Duinker, 1983), for present purposes the most relevant materials are those of cultural ecology. Steward's directives are instructive in this regard:

1. Analyze the interrelationships of the productive technology and the environment;
2. Identify the relevant environment as a function of the kind of knowledge that a cultural system had (has) of its ecosystem; and identify the behavior patterns associated with the technology in using the environment;
3. Ascertain the extent to which the behavior patterns entailed in exploiting the environment affect other aspects of culture. (Steward, 1955:41 quoted in Rose, 1981:8)

The ecosystems approach begins then by connecting "subsistence" (economic) activities with the resource base (environmental resources and "services") through applications of technology. In turn, economic activities are organized by cultural resources (values, institutions, organizations) and mobilized (motivated) by human resources (attitudes, abilities, affects). The detailing of these relationships under diverse conditions is the work of resource ecology, cultural ecology, psychological ecology, and related fields such as economic geography. Together they may be said to comprise the field of human ecology, broadly conceived; "social ecology" is a variant which emphasizes the organizational component. The much needed summation and integration of these various species of ecologies may be referred to under the generic heading of "impact ecology."

IMPACT ECOLOGY

Although Bennett (1973:230) classified an assortment of "impact" theorists within the intellectual and research traditions of cultural ecology, the term "impact ecology" was contributed by Opryszek (1981a, 1981b), following the lead of Murdock (1979), himself writing under the influence mainly of Duncan. Bennett was specifically referring to "a community study approach which views urban culture as having an undesirable 'impact' on small towns" (Bennett, 1985). He continues, ". . . one common issue pervades all 'impact' semantics . . . whether the notion of impact is applicable uniformly to all social situations involving an antecedent-consequent continuum." It is plain enough that what is being requested is a theoretical basis for integrated impact assessment, from which to systematize an operational methodology. Murdock and Opryszek believe that the field of human ecology provides that very basis. Conversely, through application in impact assessment, the notion of impact ecology lends a social relevance to the field of human ecology (for an earlier statement of this interest in the context of cultural ecology see Montgomery, Bennett, and Scudder, 1973).

According to Murdock, ". . . the major premises and concepts of human ecology, its conceptual and empirical traditions and the ecological research process are similar to those underlying the impact assessment process and environmental legislation and guidelines" (Murdock and others, 1982:4).

> The starting point for such an analysis is the conceptualization of impact events as consisting of the effects resulting from the adaptation of individuals and populations to environmental alterations. The area impacted is conceptualized as an ecosystem, and the major ecological factors operating within the ecosystem are those that make up the components of the ecological complex, population, organization, environment, and technology (Duncan and Schnore, 1959; Duncan, 1964). (Murdock, 1979: 558)

Included in the "impact event," then, are not only the effects on previous adaptations but the response of adaptive systems to those perturbations.

In Opryszek's view (1981b:abstract), impact ecology engages the problem of balance through an equilibrium assumption: ". . . the approach developed here advocates a general description of the local equilibrium before impact followed by a discussion of the theoretically and practically meaningful ways in which this equilibrium has been reinforced or undermined by the impact event." Again drawing on Steward, the impact assessment model contained in this formulation would appear as in Figure 9.1. Preimpact equilibrium is assumed as a matter of successful adaptation, although Bennett's (1976) notion of "ecological transition" can be interpreted as challenging that assumption. Rather than <u>assume</u> equilibrium, however, it can be hypothesized and <u>tested</u> by a "viability analysis" of existing (preimpact) conditions (see, for example, Reining and Lenkerd, 1980), such as the trend (nonproject) impacts of economic-demographic factors, e.g. industrial concentration and population aging, and their sociocultural counterparts, occupational succession and family continuity.

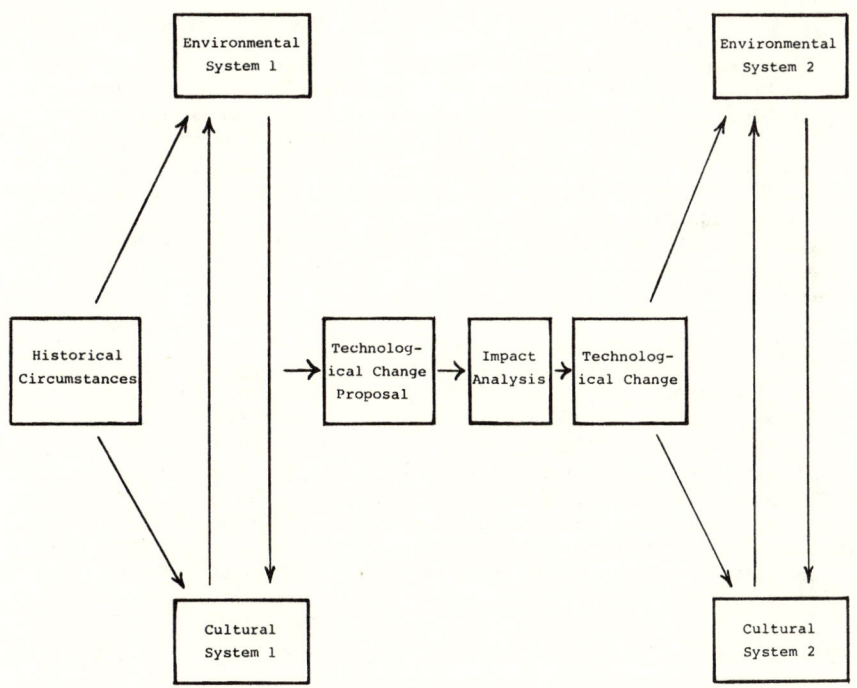

FIGURE 9.1 Cultural ecology and impact analysis
(Source: Honey and Hogg, 1978)

Opryszek's (1981b:4) impact ecology model actually combines both equilibrium and adaptation:

> The impact ecology model begins with two assumptions. First, population, organization, social and physical environments, and technology <u>combine</u> in a <u>balanced</u> way to produce a certain level of social activity, where "level of activity" is the most abstract inclusive notion of physical and intellectual behavior by a human population. Second, certain tradeoffs are possible between components of the ecosystem. . . .

The impact event is seen as "creating pressures upon certain input variables" such that "in an impact situation tradeoffs between variables are to be expected and attention is focused upon the balances between system components. The impact event is anticipated to especially affect the balance between organization and the differentiating social environment of the system" (Opryszek, 1981b:16). In any case,

> The general notion of the Impact Ecology theory and model is to evaluate the compatibility of a local ecosystem and some impact event. The broad questions posed are: Does change overwhelm the local social system (ecosystem) and endanger its viability, its equilibrium? Does change create, maintain, or aggravate any of the . . . types of equilibria? Is the old equilibrium and the newer activity(ies) viable, taken together as a unit? (Opryszek, 1981b: 16)

The notion of balance also provides an evaluative criterion by which the severity and adversity of impacts can be judged; "Adverse effects are detrimental impacts on a population in terms of creating an imbalance of any of the instrumental cultural functions thereby causing actual or potential maladaptation" (Honey and Hogg, 1977:26). Murdock and his associates (1982) have recently extended the impact ecology schema to the "back end" of the assessment cycle (see below), to impact evaluation, mitigation, monitoring, and management.

System Dynamics

Despite the appearance of linearity in Figure 1, we are really talking about a system of simultaneous equations in which the terms represent the mutual causal relations among components. Causal primacy has often been ascribed to "material" factors operating on "nonmaterial" ones; in his famous cultural lag hypothesis,

Ogburn (1966) termed the latter "adaptive culture."
Referring to preindustrial societies, these material
factors were construed as "environmental," e.g. climatic
(Huntington, 1959), and their causal influence was held
to be deterministic of the conditions of human existence. Thus, Steward (1938) and later Meggers (1954)
made ecological correlations between environmental types
and the extent of cultural development. As the ecological balance shifted from nature to culture, through the
development and deployment of technology, the direction
of causal flow reversed, from "environmental determinism" to "environmental modification." Ogburn (1956)
himself made the equation of "technology as environment." It is usual nowadays to consider "technology" as
the leading material cause, although with important
qualifications to be mentioned shortly.

The "Population Influx Hypothesis." Since Malthus,
the "population" component has been portrayed as exerting an environmental pressure amounting to "demographic
determinism." On a more intimate scale, Simmel (1956)
considered the size of a group as determining its social
form. Durkheim (1933) equated the quantity and quality
of relations in his distinction between "material" and
"moral density," later amplified by the Wilsons' (1954)
interpretation of social change as expanding "societal
scale." George Murdock (1949) further drew the morphological correlation between population size and political organization. These various strands were woven
together in Hauser's conception of a "social morphological revolution" (1969). The specific connection with
technology however is made in the "population influx
hypothesis," stated by Opryszek (1981b:14) as follows:

> . . . impact events induce a new population to
> move to or through the impacted area. This popula-
> tion influx is a major conduit of change, creating
> in many situations imbalances between ecosystem
> components. Characteristics of the population
> influx such as its size, composition, individual
> duration of stay, and activities engaged in reveal
> much of the impact event's effect.

This hypothesis was earlier asserted by Baldwin and
Poetsch (1977); their treatment may stand as something
of an informal test of its validity.

The approach described in this report is based on
the structural perspective of social organization
known as human ecology. It is assumed that there
are demographic bases for problems of so-called
sociocultural conflict or incompatibility and that
estimates of future population composition can be

> used as social indicators to anticipate these
> impacts in planning for their mitigation. (Baldwin
> and Poetsch, 1977:1-2)

The authors state further, "The fundamental premise of the methodology described in this report is that projections of population size and composition can be used as the basis for assessing possible sociocultural incompatibilities between existing residents and newcomers moving into communities that experience large-scale future developments" (Baldwin and Poetsch, 1977:17). Reasonably enough, they begin by assuming that "the greater the dissimilarity between the composition of these populations, the greater will be the potential for sociocultural conflict and the more intense these conflicts will be" (Baldwin and Poetsch, 1977:17).

Six economic-demographic indicators (age, sex, race, education, occupation, income) were selected to measure potential cultural differences between indigenous and immigrant populations and to identify potential "sociocultural problems." It was hypothesized that

> . . . populations with different structural characteristics also differ in: (1) service needs, such as those for housing, recreation, and education; (2) types of social organizations related to capacities for, or constraints on, reaping the benefits of rapid economic development and social changes (e.g., employment and income); and (3) attitudes, values, and cultural perspectives. (Baldwin and Poetsch, 1977:2-3)

Of these, "quantitative projections of population size and composition are more easily related to the first than to the third" (Baldwin and Poetsch, 1977:3). In fact, methodological development was concentrated almost exclusivley on those relationships. It was concluded--on what basis is not evident--that "The age differential between immigrants and indigenous residents is potentially the most important source of sociocultural conflict" (Baldwin and Poetsch, 1977:A-28), a finding not confirmed in Freudenburg's (1984) study of boom and control communities in western Colorado. He rejects "A straightforward 'compositionalist' argument--i.e., that the presumed 'social pathologies' of an energy boomtown are due to newcomers, perhaps because they are less bound by local norms than are the long-time residents. . . ." Rather, he locates the main source of conflict within adolescent society for reasons that "have more to do with the social worlds and the stages of personal development of the boomtown adolescents than they do with the kinds of facilities, services, and other logistical considerations that have been the primary focus of much past work in this area" (Freudenburg, 1984:701-703). Hence it would appear that the linkage between economic-demographic and sociocultural-psychosocial variables depends more on interpretation than on enumeration.

When it comes to the third "sociocultural problem" area, ". . . the impacts that population dissimilarities have on local attitudes and values have been the most difficult to identify in a generic way because the literature suggests that the tolerance for change varies by region and setting (e.g., rural, urban, etc.)" (Baldwin and Poetsch, 1977:17). Elsewhere it is held that ". . . normative differences between populations are the most difficult to forecast due to changes in public opinion" (Baldwin and Poetsch, 1977:12). The authors conclude, "Although demographic projection provides a valuable tool for estimating future social change, the knowledge about cause and effect is not sufficient to support the quantification of sociocultural impact. Therefore, the projections are used only as relative indicators and the assessments of sociocultural impact based on them are qualitative only" (Baldwin and Poetsch, 1977:3). Despite this negative finding, their view of such impacts as mediated by differential opportunities and abilities to gain access to and control over resources remains suggestive. Recognition of these "opportunity structures" and the social characteristics that provide differential access to them brings us to the fourth ecosystem component, "organization."

Technology as Organization. Earlier I said that to characterize the resource problem as technological or environmental is misleading; to that I would now add the adjective "demographic," referring to the population component. I said, "Above all it is institutional . . ." indicating by that the "organization" component of the ecosystem complex. Of course, the problem--and its "solution"--are all of those things; that is what it means to be a <u>system</u>. As they have been discussed here, the components are analytic structures, not physically separable even in principle (Levy, 1952), hence the question of causality in a mechanistic sense cannot arise. At the same time, the combination and composition of these "input variables" come together in the organizational component, and it is this term in the equation that has generally been neglected. Yet, as La Porte (1984:4) observes, "Technological developments can be viewed as a system of social and organizational relationships which, in a social sense, define the technology. In addition to being an intricate web of ideas, processes, and methods based on scientific work, 'technology' is intrinsically a human process." It is the instrumental means by which adaptations take place and which in turn engender further perturbations in the ecosystem complex.

The social construction of technology also calls attention to the symbolic dimension of cultural experience, and that brings us closer to the "more abstract" level of attitudes and values that eluded Baldwin and Poetsch's demographic analysis. It is this very quality that is often held against consideration of the organization component in its normative aspect. I remember very well the brief and faint struggles in OTA and EPA even to define the meaning of "environmental management," much less to exert the "social management of technology" (for which read "social control"). This is the realm of "intangibles" and "nonmarketables" and we may even say "ineffables." True, NEPA does accord federal recognition to "presently unquantified" environmental quality factors, but everyone knows we are playing a "numbers game," the harder the better. Certainly there is something to be said for the "quantification of concern" and its expression, e.g. in subjective landscape assessment indicators such as those dealing with amenities and aesthetics. Overall though, the stuff of common experience--those things we know and feel about ourselves and others--are factored out of the human equation, even though they are, as Durkheim remarked, "the most ordinary and the most important." The content of experience and our evaluation of it are etherealized; this is the true meaning of the "social discount rate."

In order to perform <u>causal</u> systems analysis, there must be some material connection between system elements. This "material" need not be interpreted in strictly physicalistic terms, however; the "symbolic" dimension also enters in the analysis of cultural systems. (If a physicalistic interpretation of symbolization were wanted, it would be akin to the psychologists' "stimulus.") For example, Dixon (1978:275) includes as elements of her "cultural ecology paradigm" the "cultural constructs which provide social integration through which large numbers of persons can live together (government, law enforcement, socializing institutions such as schools and churches, etc.)" and "knowledge which enables persons to function and survive in the cultural-ecological setting (science, leadership)." Nevertheless, the incorporation and assimilation of these elements in a system of comprehensive and integrated assessment remains unfinished business.

Nearly fifty years ago, a schism in the "Chicago School" divided the field of human ecology between quantitative positivists such as Hawley and later Duncan and "symbolic interactionists" led by Mead and Blumer. To say, as Lundberg did, "There is no difference between a man fleeing from a crowd and a newspaper blowing in the wind," became fighting words. Perhaps the pivotal

figure was Firey, however; despite his consideration of
"sentiment and symbolism" as ecological variables (1945;
see also Schmitt and Grupp, 1976), the center did not
hold. Later work (Suttles, 1968; Hunter, 1974) has not
fully repaired the intellectual damage; we continue to
suffer from disrelation and disarray of knowledge in the
field and struggle to surmount its disorder. One direction and orientation that effort has taken can be termed
the impact assessment "movement."

The Impact Assessment "Movement"

A notable feature of our generation is the effort
to be or become rational about resource development,
allocation, and conservation. Not that past generations
were seriously afflicted by "peasant irrationality" and
similar derangements; were that so, they (and we) hardly
could have survived thus far. Rather we have made a
conscious value choice to be explicitly and systematically--in a word (Talcott Parsons') "cognitively"--
rational in our attitudes and actions towards resources.

The Rationality Criterion.
By definition, the criterion of rationality is the appropriateness of selected
means to given ends, and on that reckoning there can be
substantial doubt over the rationality model's validity
as a general cultural value. No less than Albert Einstein observed that "perfection of means and confusion
of aims seems to be characteristic of our age." While
instrumental means have advanced rapidly, their detachment from valued ends threatens the very basis of their
rationality. The "confusion of aims" is a value confusion; the kind of rationality that excludes values
deprives itself of both realism and relevance. To quote
myself (Wolf, 1980:31-32), "there is a separation of
goals and actions that not only impedes progress towards
meeting national needs but actively undermines public
trust. It is to this condition that SIA (social impact
assessment) is ultimately addressed." Remedying it
requires both intellectual and values clarification--a
framework for addressing and expressing genuine social
concerns.

Just as means are relative to ends, what counts as
"resources" is relative to basic needs and higher aspirations, and to sociotechnical systems for converting
those resources to human purposes and uses. In Firey's
(1960:27) words, "Indeed, it is only insofar as a habitat has been made valuable by the culturally available
beliefs and techniques of a people that it contains any
resources at all." This relativity of resources provides a social criterion for rational decisions and
actions, i.e. enhancing the "quality of life" and its

various components, including economic well-being and environmental quality. Yet resource policy and planning are seldom informed and animated by a social goal orientation. What should be the starting point of policy formation and program planning usually enters in the category of "residual impacts." "People problems," as the President's Commission on the Accident at Three Mile Island (the Kemeny Commission) called them, persistently emerge as the most urgent and difficult concerns of resource management, however. If it seems that people are "in the way," perhaps that is because they are not perceived, and do not perceive themselves, as beneficiaries of resource development and management. In any event, paying attention to social purposes as well as to social consequences is a priority agency item of SIA.

There is a legitimate question as to how rational we can be in regard to resource management or indeed any policy analysis and planning exercise. Lynton Caldwell (1963), the principal architect of NEPA, has taken the position that significant improvements can be achieved by becoming comprehensive in our perception of and perspective on the environment, human as well as natural. Single-valued logics, such as economic cost-benefit analysis, must be encompassed within this wider framework of integrated impact assessment. The interdisciplinarity of this enterprise is again self-evident, and this is as true of SIA as of the other species of impact assessment (economic, environmental, technology, and risk assessment primarily; see White, 1979).

Let us be clear that the resources in question are cultural resources (institutions, artifacts, and their associated meanings) and human resources (abilities and potentialities) as well as natural resources. Considering and counting the former two as integral parts of our total resource endowment, e.g. "human capital," is one of the major social innovations of our time, ranking with the discovery of "the environment" as an object of generalized concern, the recognition of "the public" as distinct from the electorate, and the invention of "the future" as something we can better know and shape.

Why these intellectual and social innovations occurred at just this point in time is a problem for the sociology of knowledge. One can speculate that problems are perceived when things are getting better, not worse. On the "discovery" of the environment as a social problem, for instance, Albrecht (1983:541) believes ". . . there is ample evidence that the environment in some ways may have been in better shape at this time than in some immediately preceding period." The case of the (domestic) "poverty problem" is even clearer: poverty becomes a focus of public attention when it becomes less general, rather than being the general condition. The "War on Poverty" was declared after the economic recovery and prosperity of the 1950s shrank poverty into underclass "pockets" existing in the "impacted areas" (in the dental sense) of early deindustrialization. On the other hand, despite the warnings of Hubbard and Schumacher, energy was a problem we didn't know we had until gas lines formed after the OPEC embargo in the fall of 1973. Similarly, precipitating events such as publication of <u>Silent Spring</u> and the Santa Barbara Channel oil spill seem fortuitous rather than formative in launching the "environmental movement" of the 1960s. For whatever reasons, however, cognitive rationality has increasingly become the prevailing criterion of resource policy formation and its implementation.

How it comes to occupy that status and rank is more apparent. As an organized professional interest and political commitment, the effort to rationalize natural resource development and management began in the late 1950s and early 1960s with an early form of economic impact assessment, cost-benefit analysis. While technological rationality had been exercised for some time previously under the rubric of "value engineering," bringing considerations of economic efficiency into relation with those of technical feasibility marked a major departure. The economic valuation of public goods represented a significant broadening of the criteria under which public investments were to be judged in the "public interest," although to apply the market test to public expenditures seems perverse if the sphere of legitimate governmental operations is restricted to essential but unprofitable ("diseconomic") areas by the standard of market economics, e.g. infrastructure investments. The limits of "national economic efficiency" were soon exceeded when this economistic standard was applied beyond weapons systems acquisition to the provision of health and human services (Wildavsky, 1974).

With the advent of the modern "environmental movement" in the 1960s and its culmination in the passage of NEPA, environmental concerns emerged on the public agenda as potential and sometimes actual competitors with economic efficiency objectives. The environmental impact assessment process mandated under NEPA elevated environmental quality to at least parity in such areas as wetlands preservation and endangered species. More generally, multiobjective competition took the form of "benefit estimation" of environmental policies and programs weighed against economic costs (Roberts and Sievering, 1977; see also Swartzman, Liroff, and Croke, 1982). Efforts were mounted on the part of public agencies such as the Council on Environmental Policy and the Environmental Protection Agency to demonstrate a favorable cost-benefit ratio in the enforcement of environmental quality standards, e.g. in the contribution to

GNP of a pollution control technology industry. This is still perverse by social well-being criteria, and still playing the economists' "dirty game." Legislation and litigation gave environmental quality criteria standing in their own right, however, and spawned an environmental impact assessment "industry" with its own constituencies and interests. By broad construction, the "human environment" mentioned in NEPA came to include people.

Social Impact Assessment

While environmental impact assessment has focused mainly on the biophysical properties of natural environments, SIA is concentrated on the distinctively human side of human environments. SIA is about "people impacts"--what we are doing to folks or failing to do for and with them where they live, in families and communities, as a consequence of implementing policies, instituting programs, and constructing projects. Unlike the more familiar "evaluation research," which gauges the effectiveness of policies, programs, and projects already in operation, the task for SIA is anticipatory research. It seeks to place the analysis and attainment of socially valued outcomes on a more rational and reliable basis. Its aim is to develop and deploy the models and methods for what futurist Alvin Toffler has called "anticipatory democracy."

The analytic problem of SIA can be modestly stated as learning to make public (and private) decisions that will look good in 50 years, after the evaluative criteria by which they are judged today have changed. This "need to know" has arisen because of the unwanted and untoward impacts of planning approaches that looked good at the time but didn't turn out so good--combined storm and sanitary sewers, the bulldozer approach to urban renewal, and so on and on. "Nobody told us it would be like this!" is the familiar lament--something La Porte (1984:19) has termed "deferred regrets." Knowing now, as best we can, what we would expect to know then is another way of stating the problem. Philosophers have disputed the proposition of "knowing before you know" for generations, but at least we can know more than we do now and act better on what we do know. Who the "we" is also needs clarifying, since it turns out there are multiple publics holding multiple objectives and employing multiple criteria of evaluation. A further complication is that all these factors can be expected to change over time. That is all we are trying to do.

Allowing for value changes, perhaps the best guide to the future is what we want it to be. If getting "from is to ought" is a commission of the "naturalistic fallacy," the reverse proposition--"from ought to is"--

is a legitimate exercise in normative planning. Why are we doing or proposing these things?--whether resource development, environmental protection, historic preservation, neighborhood revitalization, or whatever is at issue. The only valid answer can be: because they are deemed "good" under some criteria of social value applied to some recognized social need. In the case of SIA, the "why" question resolves to some notion of "social well-being" or "quality of life"--what it is, how do we know when we have it, and how can we get more of it. Although SIA partly grew out of the sense of frustration over plans gone wrong or awry, its constructive use in achieving desirable futures is its chief social value.

In the past, most SIA work was focused on physical projects in rural areas, e.g. water resources development. Today greater emphasis is being placed on social planning in "built" (e.g. urban) environments. (Naturally these too have physical, economic, and environmental components, as in the construction and financing of housing units and the conversion of agricultural land to residential use.) "Software" applications, e.g. to health care delivery systems, demand and deserve increased assessment efforts. Although SIA began at the federal level, its gradual extension to regional, state and local levels is both feasible and desirable. In fact, SIA can and must be conducted at every appropriate scale, from local to global. International development of SIA is an especially pressing concern (see Derman and Whiteford, 1985).

The "bottom line" question for SIA is: "Who benefits and who loses?" (were a proposed action to be implemented). Since often these are not the same people, the dissociation of costs (or risks) and benefits creates a problem of equity. Just what the incidence and distribution of social costs and benefits may be in any particular impact situation is a matter for assessment. Getting them together, so that those who reap the benefits also bear the burdens, is a matter of social justice and social policy. SIA cannot prescribe what social values "ought" to be in this instance, any more than expert judgment generally can be said to reflect public preferences. It can only attempt to determine what the equity impacts would be were one or another planning alternative to be adopted. Here again, rationality must include values, although there can be no purely rational means for deciding what weight and rank should be assigned to various publics and their preferences.

What you do in SIA is assess the social impacts. If this seems to belabor the obvious, it must be said that how assessments are done varies widely. SIA is a "multimethod" approach, and its analytic tasks require assessors to draw freely but selectively from the full range of social research methodologies and techniques. Moreover, every impact situation has unique features, and general methodologies must be specified to those circumstances and tailored to their dimensions. While no "one best way" has (or can) be devised to fit all circumstances and cases, there is growing professional consensus and methodological convergence on what may be described as the "main pattern" of assessment steps (see Table 1). Essentially this is a "rational problem solving" schema closely resembling many others in technology assessment, decision analysis, and related fields. It should be noted that inputs at each step are the outputs of preceding ones; in the case of scoping, the input is the statement of work requested by the sponsor. The "value added" at each step are the analytic operations performed by means of associated impact methodologies.

The "main pattern" approach presented here is only the second level of detail; up to ten levels have been defined. Although detailing the fine structure of this schema is a very considerable undertaking since there is exponential growth along the edges, progress is nevertheless being made. A comprehensive, codified, and consolidated framework is still years--but not light-years--away. Because the framework is open-textured, incremental gains and selective applications are possible. Special treatments of this framework include:

- o Theory analysis
- o Empirical analysis
- o Case analysis
- o Issues analysis
- o Institutional analysis

- o Cultural analysis
- o Political analysis
- o Legal analysis
- o Value analysis
- o Community analysis

These represent the contexts in which applications of the main pattern are made to substantive assessment topics. The latter can be classified in various ways:

- o By assessment scale (local to global)
- o By resource areas (natural, cultural, and human) and subareas (e.g. land, water, air, visual, scenic resources)
- o By type of proposed action (e.g. lake restoration, robotics, farm policy)

As a generic framework, the main pattern is potentially applicable to any assessment topic and task, at any assessment level or scale. Thus far specific applications are being made in the cases of emerging agricultural production technologies and high-level nuclear waste repositories, but that is only a beginning. In the end, we expect to have on line computer-assisted systems loaded and updated for all major areas of application, e.g. outer continental shelf development, and specified and calibrated for site-specific applications as those arise in particular impact situations. This is an ambitious program; however, the challenges at hand and in prospect would seem to require nothing less.

SUMMARY

In this chapter I have argued that the field of impact assessment may offer a solution to the "resources problems," considered as a problem of balances between social and natural system components. The chapter began with a brief account of one early and unsuccessful effort to develop and deploy this approach through the U.S. Man and the Biosphere Program. Attempts to restate the problem, exemplified in the "containment principle," showed a need for both knowledge and an ethics of consequences. Further analysis suggested that appropriate problem solutions require a systems approach, represented here by the "ecological complex" notion of Duncan. Its principal components--population, organization, environment, and technology (POET)--can be systematically related under the heading of "impact ecology." Theoretical, methodological, and institutional development of this schema in various fields and specialties has occurred over the past generation; their convergence and coalescence now can be said to constitute an impact assessment "movement," in which a rationality criterion is asserted for policy choice and project selection as well as review and appraisal. The emergence of the field of social impact assessment illustrates both the problems and the possibilities of the assessment field generally.

REFERENCES

Ackoff, Russell L. "Beyond Problem Solving," pp. 237-39 in Anatol Rapoport (ed.), General Systems: Yearbook of the Society for General Systems Research, 19. Washington, DC: Society for General Systems Research, 1974.
⎯⎯⎯⎯. "The Future of Operational Research is Past," pp. 241-52 in Brian Gaines (ed.), General Systems: Yearbook of the Society for General Systems Research, 24. Louisville, KY: Society for General Systems Research, University of Louisville, 1979.
Ad Hoc Committee on Technology of Drilling for Energy Resources. Drilling for Energy Resources. Washington, DC: National Academy of Sciences, 1976.
Albrecht, Stan. "Environment," pp. 536-61 in Melvin L. DeFleur (ed.), Social Problems in American Society. Boston: Houghton Mifflin, 1983.
Baldwin, Thomas E. and Roberta Poetsch. An Approach to Assessing Local Sociocultural Impacts Using Projections of Population Growth and Composition. ANL/EES-TM-24. Argonne, IL: Energy & Environmental Systems Division, Argonne National Laboratory, August 1977.
Beanlands, Gordon E. and Peter N. Duinker. An Ecological Framework for Environmental Impact Assessment in Canada. Halifax, NS: Institute for Resource and Environmental Studies, Dalhousie University, 1983.
Belt, C. B., Jr. "The 1973 Flood and Man's Constriction of the Mississippi River," Science, 189 (29 August 1975), 681-84.
Bennett, John W. "Microcosm-Macrocosm Relationships in North American Agrarian Society," pp. 207-33 in Michael Micklin (ed.), Population, Environment, and Social Organization: Current Issues in Human Ecology. Hinsdale, IL: Dryden, 1973.
⎯⎯⎯⎯. The Ecological Transition: Cultural Anthropology and Human Adaptation. New York: Pergamon, 1976.
⎯⎯⎯⎯. "Social and Interdisciplinary Sciences in U.S. MAB: Conceptual and Theoretical Aspects," pp. 17-39 in Ervin H. Zube (ed.), Social Sciences, Interdisciplinary Research and the U.S. Man and the Biosphere Program. Washington, DC: U.S. Government Printing Office, 1981.
⎯⎯⎯⎯. Personal communication, 25 January 1985.
Brady, N. C. "Toward a Green Revolution for Africa," Science, 227, 4691 (8 March 1985), 741.
Caldwell, Lynton K. "Environment: A New Focus for Public Policy?" Public Administration Review, 23, 3 (September 1963), 132-39.

_____. "Environmental Studies: Discipline or Metadiscipline?" The Environmental Professional, 5, 3/4 (1983), 247-59.

Churchman, C. West. The Systems Approach. New York: Dell, 1968.

Clawson, Marion. "Foreword," pp. v-vi in Glenn L. Johnson and C. Leroy Quance (eds.), The Overproduction Trap in U.S. Agriculture: A Study of Resource Allocation from World War I to the Late 1960's. Baltimore, MD: Johns Hopkins University Press, 1972.

Committee on Resources and Man, National Academy of Sciences (ed.). Resources and Man: A Study and Recommendations. San Francisco, CA: W.H. Freeman, 1969.

Derman, William and Scott Whiteford (eds.). Social Impact Analysis and Development Planning in the Third World. Boulder, CO: Westview, 1985.

Dixon, Mim. What Happened to Fairbanks: The Effects of the Trans-Alaska Oil Pipeline on the Community of Fairbanks, Alaska. Boulder, CO: Westview, 1978.

Duhl, Leonard J. "Planning and Predicting: Or What to Do When You Don't Know the Names of the Variables," Daedalus, 96, 3 (Summer 1967), 779-88.

Duncan, Otis Dudley. "Social Organization and the Ecosystem," pp. 36-82 in Robert E. L. Faris (ed.), Handbook of Modern Sociology. Chicago: Rand McNally, 1964.

Durkheim, Emile. On the Division of Labor in Society. Tr. by George Simpson. New York, Macmillan, 1933.

Emery, F. E. (ed.). Systems Thinking. Baltimore, MD: Penguin, 1969.

Firey, Walter. "Sentiment and Symbolism as Ecological Variables," American Sociological Review, 10, 2 (April 1945), 140-48.

_____. Man, Mind, and Land: A Theory of Resource Use. Glencoe, IL: Free Press, 1960.

Fradkin, Philip L. A River No More: The Colorado River and the West. New York: Alfred A. Knopf, 1981.

Freudenburg, William R. "Boomtown's Youth: The Differential Impacts of Rapid Community Growth on Adolescents and Adults," American Sociological Review, 49, 5 (October 1984), 697-705.

Hauser, Philip M. "The Chaotic Society: Product of the Social Morphological Revolution," American Sociological Review, 34, 1 (February 1969), 1-19.

Holling, C. S. (ed.). Adaptive Environmental Assessment and Management. New York: John Wiley, 1978.

Honey, William D. and Thomas C. Hogg. "A Research Strategy for Social Assessment of Lake Restoration Programs." EPA-600/5-78-004. Corvallis, OR: Corvallis Environmental Research Laboratory, U.S. Environmental Protection Agency, February 1978.

Hunter, A. Symbolic Communities: The Persistence and Change of Chicago's Local Communities. Chicago: University of Chicago Press, 1974.

Huntington, Ellsworth. Mainsprings of Civilization. New York: New American Library, 1959.

Institute of Ecology. Optimum Pathway Matrix Analysis Approach to the Environmental Decision Making Process: Test Case: Relative Impact of Proposed Highway Alternatives. Athens: Institute of Ecology, University of Georgia, 1971.

Kastens, Merritt L. "Harvest of Hunger: How Government Meddling Threatens the World's Food Supply," The Futurist, 15, 5 (October 1981), 5-10.

La Porte, Todd R. "Technology as Social Organization." IGS Studies in Public Organization Working Paper No. 84-1. Berkeley: Institute of Governmental Studies, University of California, January 1984.

Levy, Marion J., Jr. The Structure of Society. Princeton, NJ: Princeton University Press, 1952.

Meggers, Betty J. "Environmental Limitation on the Development of Culture," American Anthropologist, 56, 5 (October 1954), 801-24.

Mitroff, Ian and Tom R. Featheringham. "On Systematic Problem Solving and the Error of the Third Kind," Behavioral Science, 19, 6 (November 1974), 383-93.

Montgomery, Edward, John W. Bennett, and Thayer Scudder. "The Impact of Human Activities on the Physical and Social Environments: New Directions in Anthropological Ecology," Annual Review of Anthropology, 2 (1973), 27-61.

Murdock, George P. Social Structure. New York: Macmillan, 1949.

Murdock, Steve H. "The Potential Role of the Ecological Framework in Impact Analysis," Rural Sociology, 44, 3 (Fall 1979), 543-65.

Murdock, Steve H., John K. Thomas, Don E. Albrecht, and Rita R. Hamm. "Toward a Conceptually and Methodologically Integrated Model of Socioeconomic Impact Assessment." Paper presented at the First International Conference on Social Impact Assessment, Vancouver, BC, 24-27 October 1982.

Ogburn, William Fielding. "Technology as Environment," Sociology and Social Research, 41, 1 (September-October 1956), 3-9.

Ogburn, William Fielding. Social Change: With Respect to Cultural and Original Nature. New York: Dell, 1966.

Opryszek, Paul. Impact Ecology: A Development and Application. Unpublished doctoral dissertation. Urbana: Department of Sociology, University of Illinois, 1981a.

_____. "Impact Ecology: A Reformulation of Human Ecology Theory for Social Impact Assessment." Paper presented at the 76th Annual Meeting of the American Sociological Association, Toronto, ON, 24 August 1981b.

Parsons, Talcott. "On the Concept of Value-Commitments," Sociological Inquiry, 38, 2 (Spring 1968), 135-60.

Redfield, Robert. The Primitive World and Its Transformations. Ithaca, NY: Cornell University Press, 1953.

Reining, Priscilla Copeland and Barbara Lenkerd (eds.). Village Viability in Contemporary Society. Boulder, CO: Westview, 1980.

Roberts, Howard A. and Herman Sievering. A Guide to Environmental Benefits Assessment in Economic Impact Studies. IIEQ Document No. 77/32. Chicago: IL: Institute for Environmental Quality, October 1977.

Rose, Dan. Energy Transition and the Local Community: A Theory of Society Applied to Hazelton, Pennsylvania. Philadelphia: University of Pennsylvania Press, 1981.

Rossini, Frederick A. and Alan L. Porter (eds.). Integrated Impact Assessment. Boulder, CO: Westview, 1983.

Schmitt, R. L. and S. E. Grupp. "Resource as Symbol," Social Science Quarterly, 57 (September 1976), 324-38.

Schölvinck, Johan B. W. "Interrelationships between Population, Resources, Environment and Development in Sub-Saharan Africa with Special Emphasis on the Sahel Region." Paper presented at the International Population Division Seminar, United Nations, New York, 16 May 1985.

Simmel, Georg. "The Number of Persons as Determining the Form of the Group," pp. 126-58 in Edgar F. Borgatta and Henry J. Meyer (eds.), Sociological Theory: Present-Day Sociology from the Past. New York: Alfred A. Knopf, 1956.

Smith, Deverne and Ward H. Goodenough. Social Impact Assessment of Major Engineering Projects: A Case Study Relating to the Proposed Superport in Palau. Unpublished manuscript, n.d. (1977).

Steward, Julian H. Basin-Plateau Aboriginal Sociopolitical Groups. Bureau of American Ethnography, Smithsonian Institution, Bulletin 120. Washington, DC: U.S. Government Printing Office, 1938.

Steward, Julian H. Theory of Culture Change: The Methodology of Multilinear Evolution. Urbana: University of Illinois Press, 1955.

Suttles, Gerald D. *The Social Order of the Slum: Ethnicity and Territory in the Inner City.* Chicago: University of Chicago Press, 1968.

Swartzman, Daniel, Richard A. Liroff, and Kevin G. Croke (eds.). *Cost-Benefit Analysis and Environmental Regulations: Politics, Ethics, and Methods.* Washington, DC: The Conservation Foundation, 1982.

Taylor, Theodore B. and Charles C. Humpstone. *The Restoration of the Earth.* New York: Harper and Row, 1973.

Weaver, Warren. "Science and Complexity," *American Scientist*, 36, 4 (Autumn 1948), 536-44.

White, Irvin L. "Interdisciplinarity," *The Environmental Professional*, 1, 1 (1979), 51-55.

Whiteside, Thomas. *The Pendulum and the Toxic Cloud.* New Haven, CT: Yale University Press, 1976.

Wildavsky, Aaron. *The Politics of the Budgetary Process.* 2nd ed. Boston: Little, Brown, 1974.

Wilson, Godfrey and Monica Wilson. *The Analysis of Social Change: Based on Observations in Central Africa.* Cambridge: Cambridge University Press, 1954.

Wolf, C. P. "Getting Social Impact Assessment into the Policy Arena," *Environmental Impact Assessment Review*, 1, 1 (March 1980), 27-36.

Part 4
Systems Approaches

10
Systems Analysis and the World Food System

Donella H. Meadows

Somewhere recently I heard a story about an airplane. The airplane is found in a field by members of a "less-developed" society. It is fully functional, grounded, and unguarded. The peasants look it over, discuss what it must be, and eventually hitch their oxen to it and use it as a cart to haul hay.

That image haunts me, because it expresses perfectly my feeling about the use of formal systems analysis. We have a powerful technology that could allow us to soar, to reach places we have never reached before. And we are using it with unawakened peasant mentalities for peasant purposes.

In this paper I will elaborate on this theme, with examples from the analysis of food and agriculture systems. I could as well have chosen energy or economics or urban design or almost any area of large-scale social-system analysis. The views expressed here will be unabashedly personal and biased; they will probably sound curmudgeonly. I have many complaints about the practice of systems analysis. But my complaints do not spring from basic objections to the analytical tools, the analysts themselves, or the policymakers, all of which I respect. As systems analysts, we ought to know that the system in which we ourselves are enmeshed--the systems analysis system--behaves like all others. Its problems arise not so much from the <u>elements</u> in the system but from their interrelationships, from the structure of the system itself. And the structure arises, as all social-system structures do, primarily from the world views, ideas, intentions, and self-imposed limitations of its participants.

Hence my tendency toward curmudgeonliness. It is extremely frustrating hauling hay with an airplane when you suspect that there may be something far more exciting possible. What I really want to do is talk about and try out flying, but there is scarcely the language to talk about it, and not many partners who are foolish/wise, naive/visionary, brash/adventurous enough to help. My whole reason for writing this is to find or encourage more partners.

I will proceed first by summarizing very briefly from both a pessimistic and an optimistic bias the state of the food-agriculture system, the system in which food is produced and delivered to consumers. Then I will ask and provide my own answer to the question: What has formal analysis contributed to our understanding of that system? My answer will be "not much", not nearly as much as is possible. I will list some of what I feel are the most crucial unanswered questions and then assess the appropriateness and potential of our analytical tools to answer these questions. And finally I will discuss the ways in which I believe we analysts could most make a difference, the kind of difference that comes from adding the idea of flight to the technical possibility of an airplane, the kind of difference that could produce a system in which every human being is nourished sufficiently and sustainably.

The Current State of the System
Every minute on this planet about 24 people die from hunger, 19 of them children. Every three days severe malnourishment kills as many people as did the Hiroshima bomb. At any one time as many as 1 billion people--one of every five of us--are in some way suffering or debilitated because of improper nutrition. And every year the human population adds about 80 million new mouths to feed.[1]

Food production on the earth has increased steadily and exponentially at 2-3% per year for decades, but that has had little effect on the number who are hungry. In some parts of Africa the food production increase is lower than the population increase; food per capita on the average is declining.[2] Even where production is outstripping population, the distribution of food, like income, is often becoming more inequitable.

And the increase in land productivity may be slowing. Yields are leveling off in the most technically developed countries such as the United States.[3] Oil price rises are reducing use of fertilizers, pesticides, and irrigation equipment. Vast areas of topsoil are lost to erosion and urbanization each year; the United States has lost 18 million hectares since 1945, an area the size of Nebraska.[4] More and more countries are dependent on imports, primarily from North America, for their basic food needs, and their ability to pay for those imports is threatened by the increasingly problematic international trade/aid/debt/monetary system. In the last decade in the oil-importing developing countries, real GNP per capita growth rates dropped by more than half, inflation rates more than tripled, and the real balance-of-payments deficit tripled.[5]

Farmers are squeezed for profit. In every market economy farm numbers are dropping and farm sizes and farm debts are growing.[6] During the last decade agricultural prices, both within nations and on the world market, have been fluctuating far more wildly than in any previous decade within memory.[7]

That is the pessimistic side of the picture.

On the optimistic side, since World War II at least 32 nations, with a combined population of 1.6 billion, have adopted major programs to end hunger within their borders and, by all statistical measures, have done so. They have included relatively rich nations and relatively poor ones, food importers and food exporters, with capitalist, communist, and socialist governments, with and without violence (examples include the Peoples' Republic of China, Taiwan, the Soviet Union, South Korea, Cuba, Costa Rica, Argentina, Portugal, Greece, and Sri Lanka).[8]

The amount of food that would be needed to provide a sufficient diet to all those now hungry would be about 40 million tons of grain--about 3% of the annual total world output.[9] That is almost exactly the amount by which grain used as animal feed was reduced in the U.S. in 1974 when the international grain price rose. There is far more than enough food grown in the world every year to feed everyone if it were equitably distributed. As much as five to ten times more food could be grown if the best technologies now known were more widely applied.[10] Many technologies are now in practice that combine high yields with low soil loss, low energy use, and little or no use of pesticides.[11] Only a few desert nations and city-states such as Singapore do not possess the basic water, soil, and climatic resources to feed their own people sufficiently and sustainably.[12]

As far as I know, all the statements above on both the optimistic and pessimistic sides are true. Most of them are widely agreed upon by the expert community. To me they add up to a picture of a system that is malfunctioning severely and unnecessarily. There seem to be the resources and technologies to feed everyone adequately and sustainably. Almost any one of the prevailing sociopolitical systems seems to be sufficiently organized to do the job. No one particularly wants anyone else to starve or farmers to go bankrupt or soil to wash into the ocean. Surely no person, group, or nation intends the overwhelming and intolerable actual state of the system.

And yet that state persists. It has persisted for decades in spite of dedicated efforts by public and private aid organizations, experts, UN conferences, and dozens of other well-meaning and high-powered policy interventions. The system continuously produces widespread hunger, underpaid farmers, uncertain prices, and eroding soil. And even if one argues cynically that the purpose of the system is not to produce adequate nutrition, prosperous farmers, and an enhanced resource base, but rather to produce well-fed rich people, prosperous middlemen, and political power, even those functions are not performed regularly, sustainably, or at the peak of the system's potential.

What Has Formal Analysis Contributed to our Understanding?

The use of formal analysis in food and agriculture systems has burgeoned over the past 15 years. There must be thousands of agriculture-based computer models and still more thousands of quantitative but not fully computerized analyses. The United States General Accounting Office has found a total of 71 active computer models for agricultural policy analysis in the U.S., 15 at the global level, 22 national, 12 single-commodity, and 8 on the management of food reserves.[13]

Clearly no one has a complete grasp of all models in the field in full technical detail. My own knowledge, on which the following generalizations will be based, comes from a random sampling of papers at international conferences, scuttlebutt in the halls of the USDA, IIASA, and some land-grant colleges, and familiarity with about ten global-scale models, about a dozen long-term national-planning models, a few discrete agriculture-sector models for the U.S. and Eastern and Western Europe, and a few crop-specific and field-level ecological models.

A quick scan of the titles of models described in the technical journals verifies my own general impression--most quantitative analyses done by food and agriculture models focus on the short term and on very small pieces of the total system. A sampling of titles tells the story:
- "An empirical model of the U.K. land market and the impact of price policy on land values and rents"
- "Composite forecasting of hog prices"
- "A model of fertilizer demand in the Asian rice economy"
- "An interregional intertemporal activity analysis model of the United States apple industry"
- "Decision models for California turkey growers"
- "Projections of demand and supply of wheat and rice in Pakistan, 1970-1985"

- "A programming model for the planning of the agricultural economy of Thailand"

Richard Ashley[14] has come up with the idea of characterizing any field of study by its "Warranted Queries"--the questions that are considered by the field's practitioners as legitimate to ask and possible to answer. The following are what I would identify as Warranted Queries in the field of agriculture-food systems analysis:
- What quantities of what crops are likely to be produced at what cost and using what inputs under given weather and policy conditions?
- What effect is that level of production likely to have on domestic and international markets, on consumers' demand, and on future production conditions?
- What policies and/or technologies and/or investments are required to bring about a given set of target conditions, usually stated in terms of production or profit, at a given target date, while minimizing cost (or maximizing producers' and consumers' surplus or absorbing or releasing labor or achieving some other specified objective)?
- If all current policies and conditions continue unchanged, what, very exactly, is likely to happen at specific future dates to output, prices, consumption, cropping patterns, farm income, farm debt, etc.?

These are all interesting questions, and quantitative analyses have provided some useful answers, which have sometimes been implemented and which have occasionally allowed national farm policy or specific industrial decisions to produce intended results. I certainly think there is a role for this sort of analysis. But I do not think this role should be the major one.

When I scan over the field of agricultural analyses, even the ones that purport to be comprehensive and long term, this is what I see:
1. They concentrate on easily quantified parts of the system, particularly those parts that can be measured in monetary units.
2. They are usually limited to one or at most two academic disciplines.
3. They require tremendous labor, both in data gathering and computation, to achieve relatively small improvements in precision.
4. They assume and reinforce the current social structure; they do not address or even raise the questions of large-scale goals or structural redesign.

5. They are virtually all complicated black boxes that the policymakers, and often the modelers, have to take on faith. One cannot understand fully how they produce their results. They do not inform or develop the intuitive understanding of their users. In fact they are condescending to users.
6. Many of them proceed from the paradigm that the future happens to us and at best we can foresee it and be prepared for it, not from the paradigm that we can produce the future we want.
7. They tend to focus one's attention on obstacles rather than opportunities, costs rather than benefits, impossible, intransigent properties of the system rather than points of real leverage. They discourage any action larger than marginal readjustments.
8. <u>They are not organized around and generally never mention the problem of hunger, the goal of sustainable human nourishment, the long-term viability of the agriculture resource base, the economic survival and human dignity of farmers.</u>

In short, the very good minds and powerful techniques of the analytical community are not being applied to the total system or to the really crucial questions that need to be asked. The profession as a whole is making Mitroff's "error of the third kind":[15] <u>asking the wrong questions</u>, questions that in their underlying assumptions and limitations cannot lead to the answers one really wants to find.

Persisting in this kind of error might be justifiable if the system under consideration were only mildly malfunctioning, if our net effect on the system were neutral, or if our tools were inadequate to asking and answering questions of the "right kind". None of these three conditions holds true. The system is generating widespread and direct human suffering, minute by minute. Even those players in the system who are currently benefiting from its performance are not secure in their benefits; the system is unstable and ultimately unsustainable. Our undeniably able assistance in helping subunits of that system optimize their own workaday goals within an unchanged structure is undoubtedly <u>contributing</u> to the larger problems of inequity and <u>instability</u>, not solving them. Insofar as system actors follow our advice, they may even be undermining the workaday goals themselves in a true tragedy of the commons.[16] In the long term we are not even helping our direct clients, much less humanity as a whole. And if anyone possesses the tools to do better, to understand the whole system and to improve its performance for everyone, we do.

Important Unanswered Questions
So what are the questions "of the right kind", and which of our tools are appropriate to the answering?

I think one of the most arrogant ways one person can impose on another is to dictate which questions are important to ask, rather than encouraging each person to question for him or herself. The world is full of such arrogance, however, and we analysts are not only experts at it, we are paid for it. We are probably more influential through the questions we ask and <u>legitimize by asking</u> than through anything else we do. Given that we already do that, then, how can we use our influence

- to ask and legitimize questions that other people, especially those whose voices seldom count, would like to ask;
- to ask questions that open, rather than close the way to creative new solutions; and
- to ask questions that we with our particular systems expertise can see to ask that others might not see?

Best of all, what questions might meet all three of these conditions simultaneously?

As a systems dynamicist, my natural tendency in framing questions is to group dynamic phenomena that are very common even in different social systems and that operate over similar time horizons, and to ask questions about why these phenomena occur, and how the socially "good" ones can be enhanced while the "bad" ones are repressed. When I did that for the world's food/agriculture systems, I came up with five distinct categories of "super problems", or "quandaries", or, as Russell Ackoff calls them, "messes",[17] all of which lead to questions. Here they are, intended not to be an exclusive list but as a stimulus for you to identify others.

Mess 1. Instability of Production, Prices and Income
This problem can take the form of commodity production cycles, randomly-fluctuating prices, insecure farm income, interruptions of supply, overproduction and gluts, and at the extreme, famine. It is a consequence of the fact that agriculture is influenced by many uncertain factors, chief among them the weather. The natural fluctuations can be either amplified or attenuated by socioeconomic systems; in many parts of the world they are amplified. Coping with this problem probably occupies 98% of the attention of agricultural policymakers (and hence analysts) in nearly every country.
Basic goals: acceptably low consumer prices, adequate and continuous supply, acceptably high and regular farm incomes.

Typical policy response: price-setting, subsidies,
   buffer stocks, land set-asides, future markets,
   rationing, export or import restrictions.
Time horizon: one to ten years.
Questions: What are the structural characteristics of
   food production and distribution systems that at-
   tenuate rather than amplify natural instabilities?
   How could systems be designed to enhance their
   resilience and robustness to random, uncontrollable outside factors?
   How could systems be designed so that the brunt of
   the instability does not fall on those least able
   to bear it?

Mess 2. Increasing labor productivity
   This phenomenon includes rural-urban migration,
increasing farm size, decreasing farm numbers, increasing farm capital stocks, and often (but not necessarily) worsening income distribution within the farm sector. The dynamic trend is pervasive, but the policy
focus changes from low-productivity countries (who are
often trying to promote the trend although at the same
time trying to provide rural employment and slow rural-
urban migration) to high-productivity countries (who
are beginning to worry about the capital and energy
inefficiencies accompanying this process and the "decline of the family farm").
Basic goals: efficient production, rural-urban migration at absorbable rates, relatively even
   distribution of farm incomes.
Typical policy responses: technology transfer mechanisms such as extension, rural industrial
   development, land reform or land zoning, capital
   subsidies, farm income subsidies, incentives for
   young farmers.
Time horizon: ten to fifty years.
Questions: Which factors of agricultural production
   are in fact limiting?
   Which agricultural technologies are actually
   appropriate in the industrialized and the non-
   industrialized nations?
   Which technologies will be appropriate 30 years
   from now?
   Why do farmers feel an overwhelming pressure to
   increase their productive capacity?
   What will ultimately constrain farm size expansion?
   Where increased labor productivity is in fact
   appropriate, what natural forces can be encouraged
   so that rural people can find or choose employment
   that is remunerative and challenging?

Mess 3. Interdependence
　　　As world technologies become more homogenous and basic resources become more geographically concentrated, single nations become less self-sufficient and more dependent on world trade and a healthy balance of payments. Under such conditions, agricultural products are viewed less as a means to meet basic human needs and more as commodities. Food can become either a trade-balancing instrument or a foreign policy instrument, leading to policies that might counteract policies designed to solve Messes 1 and 2.
Basic goals: balance of import-export payments, guaranteed supply of basic commodities, favoritism for or sanctions against particular countries.
Typical policy responses: export or import control, manipulation of domestic demand, boycott, cartel, currency revaluation, debt acquisition and refinancing.
Time horizon: ten to fifty years.
Questions: What are the real costs and benefits of food self-sufficiency?
　　What is the real impact of export crops on the domestic economy and on domestic nutritional sufficiency?
　　Who gains and who loses from trade restrictions? Could a trade system be designed that captures the theoretical gains of comparative advantage but that does not render farmers in Ghana or city-dwellers in Jakarta vulnerable to weather fluctuations in Kansas?

Mess 4. Hunger
　　　Though the world is producing more and more food, there is a significant fraction of the human population that never receives any entitlement to that food and therefore is chronically debilitated by hunger. Often the hungry are a socially-isolated group, discriminated against because of race, religion, age or some other characteristic. The problem can be approached either by direct transfer of food to the needy, or by efforts to help the needy grow or earn their own food.
Basic goals: Secure, sufficient nutrition for everyone, everywhere.
Typical policy responses: Food stamps, income transfers, food-for-work programs, school lunch programs, famine relief, soup kitchens, nutrition education, general development and employment efforts.
Time horizon: 50-150 years.
Questions: What structural characteristics of a society cause poverty and hunger to persist or even worsen during rapid material growth?

What obstacles systematically prevent the poor from feeding themselves?
Are there short-term measures that would end hunger quickly and that would enhance rather than interfere with long-term measures that would end hunger permanently?

Mess 5. Ecological constraints

The ecosystem is not much in the minds of policymakers; for that reason ecological factors are likely to be the most surprising future influences on agriculture.
Basic goals: A sustainable, recycling, highly-productive agricultural system that uses rather than abuses natural forces.
Typical policy responses: Agricultural research, land irrigation and drainage, education, incentives for soil conservation measures.
Time horizon: 20-200 years
Questions: Where do diminishing returns to various factors become too costly to overcome?
How much land is actually and preventably lost by poor management?
Is the world agricultural system becoming increasingly vulnerable because of decreasing genetic diversity or increasing pesticide and fertilizer addiction?
How much water, nitrogen, phosphate, energy, land can really be allocated to the agriculture system, given the earth's constraints and societal desires for other things beside food?

The Power of our Tools

To illustrate that we do have the capacity to deal with questions like these, let me describe some analytical efforts, one each from Messes 2-5, that give me hope. The examples I will use here are chosen because I happen to know about them and I have learned something from them. They may not be the best studies in the field, by any definition of "best", and indeed I have serious technical reservations about all of them (as I do about any model I have ever seen—what model is perfect?). But I think they will serve to point in the direction I wish to point: to give us glimpses of new possibilities.

In Mess 2, increasing labor productivity, Philip Budzik undertook a study of the Vermont dairy economy,[18] asking the questions, "Why are farm sizes increasing and farm numbers decreasing? Will any of the proposed state policies (property tax relief, subsidization of young farmers, zoning land for agricultural use only) improve the farm economy?" Through an ingenious combination of field investigation, familiarity

with the statistics of farm accounts, and simulation of the total system, Budzik came to some startling conclusions:
- the trend toward larger farm size has no economic justification; rather than economies of scale, the larger farms are experiencing rising costs per unit of product, and still they expand.
- farmers are being pushed unwillingly into expansion by forces <u>they create for themselves</u> in the classic operation of the market; that is, increased production lowers price, therefore decreasing profit, therefore requiring more production <u>even to maintain a constant income</u>, therefore further increasing production, lowering price, etc.
- the policies proposed to ease the burden of the farmers all make the problem worse; by increasing farm liquidity in the short run they allow faster expansion of production, forcing still more expansion in the long run.
- if there were just one policy--a reasonably-set upper limit on the amount of milk any farmer could market in a year--the number of farms would stabilize, average farm income would rise, the economy could settle at the economically most efficient size, and the cost of milk to consumers would actually be decreased.

Mess 3, interdependence, has been tackled by a coalition of Dutch agronomists and economists. They explored the dynamics of the international food system with a simulation model called MOIRA.[19] The model represents the agricultural economies of 106 nations and regions. For each nation the model simulates production and consumption of food, and government policies regarding domestic markets and participation in international trade. Six different income classes are recognized in each nation, and explicit account is taken of those classes that receive inadequate food; the number of hungry people is the primary output index of the model. A sophisticated, general-equilibrium, international trade model determines world market price and the extent to which governments can successfully implement their trade policies.

This model provides fascinating insights into the dynamics of the trade system. It shows the way a minor weather fluctuation in the USA or USSR can be amplified into a major economic disaster in Ghana or Bangladesh. It also sheds light on generic policy issues. For example, the authors conclude that reducing consumption in the rich countries and even direct food aid do little for the poor. The most effective thing the rich countries can do to end hunger is to absorb price fluctuations into their own domestic markets, to allow a steady and rather high international price (which stimulates production and also nonfarm income in the poor countries).

A model aimed directly at Mess 4, the persistence of hunger, was made by a group of Latin Americans headed by Amilcar Herrera at the Fundacion Bariloche in Argentina.[20] The model asks the question: "What is required and how long would it take to satisfy basic human needs for all people in the world?" Rather than trace out the implications of the current system, this model attempts to allocate resources, particularly public investment, in order to <u>optimize life expectancy</u>, which is affected in the models by the adequacy of nutrition, health care, housing, education, and income. It is assumed that there will be no major changes in international trade/aid relations take place, only that within each region (Latin America, Africa, Asia) government decisions are made with basic human needs as top priority.

The primary conclusion (which is spelled out in far more detail than I can do justice to here) is that basic needs could be met rather easily by the year 2000 in Latin America and Africa from indigenous resources and capital if the decision were only made to do so. Asia shows great improvement but still has serious problems, especially with food, even up to 2025, the end of the model's time horizon. The work explores just how far internal priority shifts within regions can solve problems and therefore clarifies where aid from outside can be most useful.

Yet another example, from Mess 5, environmental deterioration, comes from the work of Genady Golubev at the International Institute of Applied Systems Analysis.[21] This Soviet hydrologist has been drawing together data on the ecological impacts of agriculture, particularly on soil erosion and nitrification of groundwater, primarily from field-level studies all over the world. He uses no single comprehensive computer model, just chemical-balance equations and the outputs of several ecological models, combined with simple mathematical accounting.

He links knowledge at the micro-level to the macro-level impact of widespread adaption of various technologies in the world's major soil-climate regions. This is one of the few efforts I know to look at the long-term sustainability of agricultural technologies on a level congruent with the jurisdictions of policymakers. The results, while still tentative, indicate cause for immediate concern in some agroclimatic zones, including some of the most productive ones, and healthy margins of safety in others.

These four studies represent completely different methods, foci, time horizons, and degrees of detail. I do not believe all their results unquestioningly. But I hold them together in a mental file called "interesting and useful work", probably because they counter at least some of the problematic qualities of agricultural models I listed earlier. They focus on questions of major importance, they connect disciplines or viewpoints that rarely are brought together, they bridge macro and micro views, they emphasize goals and processes beyond purely economic ones, and above all they begin to overarch the system, to look at its total functioning over the longer term rather than the functioning of some small part for a short while. None of them is fully comprehensive, and in fact taken together they fill in some of each other's weaknesses. But they are <u>fruitful</u> analyses--they do not close off investigation by providing "The Answer"; they raise new questions, direct one's attention to new interconnections, and at the same time suggest policy directions that transcend conventional wisdom. They provide a hint of what could be done if we asked larger questions and fully applied our analytical tools to the answers.

When we think of our analytical tools, we tend to think of optimization routines, simulation languages, regression packages, and data bases. In a limited sense these are indeed our tools. Like good carpenters, we need to know how to wield them skillfully, and we need to know the best ones to choose for each different purpose. However, if we view these technical supports as our <u>primary</u> tools, if we identify ourselves with them, rank ourselves by our skill with them, and begin to see the world through them, we are not only underrating ourselves, we are also constricting our vision of what we can do. "If your only tool is a hammer, you treat everything as if it were a nail." Our technical tools lead us to see the short-term, operational, quantitative side of things, not the long-term qualitative side, or the individual richness and diversity, or the most feasible visions of how things could be redesigned to work better.

The most important tools of the carpenter are not hammers and chisels. They are the ability to perceive a human need and visualize a structure to meet that need, and the deep wordless knowledge of materials, stresses, joints, surfaces that allows that vision to be actualized. A hammer is no more a guarantee of a fine piece of furniture or a soundly-built house than an airplane is a guarantee of flight in a peasant society or an input-output matrix is a guarantee of a social design that will meet peoples' needs. Our <u>real</u> tools are those we talk about least and are least formally trained to use. They include:

1. <u>Our experience</u>. Our knowledge of the system derived from knocking about in it, our "gut feelings" and "hunches" about why people do what they do what they do under different circumstances, our wordless mental maps of how the world works.
2. <u>The scientific method</u>. We pay lip service to this but rarely use it rigorously. We delight in the surface characteristics of science such as precisely-written numbers and arid, objective-sounding prose, but we seldom take seriously the notions of listing alternative hypotheses, designing critical experiments for <u>disproof</u>, or exposing our work to any serious real-world test (as opposed to nearly meaningless statistical tests).
3. <u>The paradigm of systems</u>. The ability to stand back and see the whole, to identify the purposeful self-correcting or exponentially-amplifying cybernetic characteristics of the system, to see the information flows and their delays or distortions, to focus on relationships instead of individual elements, to see the patterns of behavior inherent in the system structure, and to create or design the condition that will release natural, effortless system behaviors that society deems good.
4. <u>Our intuitive abilities</u> to create visions, sense right and wrong, feel compassion, judge quality, select for importance, seek truth, sense how other people feel. We have been carefully trained as scientists <u>not</u> to use these abilities, as if they were somehow incompatible with, rather than complementary to, our abilities of reason and logic.

The computer and all its software trappings are merely ways to enforce explicitness, consistency, and rigor in the expression of our real tools. The numerical techniques we are so carefully taught are undeniably valuable aids when used only as such, to detect our illogical and self-deceiving assumptions and to train us to deal accurately with complexity. Combined with our real tools, they are more than adequate to the task of providing analyses that can inform, empower, and inspire people to make the world they want--at a minimum a world in which everyone is decently and reliably nourished.

How We Could Most Make a Difference

We already know how we as analysts could most make a difference, and many of us have said it clearly:

"When will we realize that quantitative tools are only as good as the qualitative concepts underlying them? When will we appreciate that quantity and quality are only opposite sides of the same coin and that neither is complete without the other?"[22]

"It is important to keep in mind that the objectivity of the institutional world, however massive it may appear to the individual, is a humanly produced, constructed objectivity. Typically, the real relationship between man and his world is reversed in consciousness. Man, the producer of a world, is apprehended as its product...Human meanings are no longer understood as world-producing but as being, in their turn, products of the 'nature of things'".[23]

"I need descriptions of the social world that <u>include</u> the human beings who contribute to the <u>regulated</u> aspects of the world and to its emergent aspects through the application of the system approach...That is, these descriptions need to include descriptions of the planner, and the systems creators, their accepting or rejecting clients, and the consequences of the relationships among them. For by the very fact of their creativeness, <u>those contributing to the analysis and design of social systems must be self-conscious about themselves as biased intervenors into social reality.</u>[24]

In a profound sense that has both scientific evidence and the wisdom of the ages behind it, <u>we are what we see ourselves to be.</u> We can see ourselves as well-meaning but basically powerless pawns in the system, at the mercy of clients and funders who insist on hiring us for trivial tasks and who are not likely to follow our advice, especially not if the advice differs from what they already thought. We can see ourselves as objective and uninvolved, purified by, and therefore limited to, the truth as revealed by social statistics. We can believe ourselves to be more knowledgeable about the system than anybody (and wonder why no one seems to listen to us). We can consider that the greatest things we have to offer our society are our quantitative tools and the precise-appearing numbers that emerge from them.

I would humbly suggest that seeing ourselves in these ways has resulted in the generally lackluster and unconstructive performance I believe our profession has delivered so far. And that those who do the brilliant and constructive work in our profession see themselves quite differently. Therefore the most powerful thing we can do is to see ourselves differently--that is always the most powerful way any actor embedded in a system can begin to transform the system. We can see ourselves as:

- those who are responsible not only to parochial, short-term interests but to all mankind, and those who are able to find ways in which parochial, short-term interests can be compatible with global, long-term well-being,
- those who simplify and clarify, rather than those who complicate and obfuscate,
- designers, questioners, visionaries of new system structures, rather than predictors or optimizers of the current structures,
- askers of the questions people really want to ask,
- listeners rather than pontificators,
- persons with hearts, values, beliefs, and moral stands, as well as persons with minds, machines, and mathematical algorithms,
- accountants for the vital qualitative aspects of social systems, as well as their quanitative aspects,
- integral parts of the system we analyze, with unique importance and responsibility as interpreters of the system to itself.

I am very much aware of the strong forces that prevent us from seeing ourselves that way and acting accordingly. Those forces include the necessity of funding not only ourselves but our colleagues and students, political credibility, the respect of our peers, academic tenure, the ability to publish, and many more. I struggle with those forces myself all the time, not always successfully. And in the process I have learned two things. One is that those forces are not as strong or perverse as I sometimes think. They are not really arrayed against analysis of the sort I am describing here. The other thing I have learned is that the real job before us as analysts is to break out of the system that confines us to offer so much less than we actually have to offer. That is our job not only because accomplishing it will make us better analysts. Far more important, in the process of confronting our own role in our own system and in learning to make the full contribution we can make, we will gain empathy for all others trapped within the pressures of social systems, including the farmers, the politicians, and the poor and hungry. If we can find our own way out of the system's traps, we may be able to pass our insights and experiences on to others. And that kind of transcendence of the system, which will ultimately lead to transformation of the system, is a way out of the world's current difficulties that I see as necessary, possible, and very desirable. All it takes is the willingness to see ourselves differently, to imagine the possibility of flight and to try out flying.

NOTES

[1] World Bank, World Development Report; Lewis Richardson, *Statistics of Deadly Quarrels*, Washington DC, 1980.

[2] Food and Agriculture Organization of the United Nations, *Agriculture: Toward 2000*, C79/24, Rome, July 1979.

[3] For basic data, see R. Gerald Saylor, "The Evolving Structure of U.S. Agriculture", Market Economics Department, Deere & Company, September 1978, p.19. For a review of the data and theories and an extrapolation into the future, see Yao-chi Lu, Philip Cline, and Leroy Quance, "Prospects for Productivity Growth of U.S. Agriculture", U.S. Dept. of Agriculture, Agricultural Economic Report No. 435, September 1979.

[4] Medard Gabel, *Ho-Ping: Food for Everyone*, Garden City, N.Y.: Anchor Books, 1979, pp. 128-129.

[5] See Lester R. Brown, *The Twenty-Ninth Day*, New York: W. W. Norton, 1978, p.135 and Ranvir K. Trehan, John G. Leigh, & Wayne R. Park, "Energy and Development", The MITRE Corp., MTR-79W00216, July 1979.

[6] See Lyle P. Schertz, *Another Revolution in U.S. Farming?*, U.S. Department of Agriculture, Washington, DC, 1979.

[7] For documentation and alternative hypotheses about why prices may be fluctuating, see Fred H. Sanderson "The Great Food Fumble", *Science*, May 9, 1975 and Leonard J. Brzozowski, "Grain Sales and Production Cycles" in *Analyses of Grain Reserves*, Economic Research Service, U.S. Department of Agriculture, ERS-634, Washington, DC, August 1976.

[8] Roy Prosterman, in the Hunger Project, *An Idea Whose Time Has Come*, 2015 Steiner Street, San Francisco, 1977, pp.20-21.

[9] This is a figure internationally agreed upon and often cited. I believe its source is the World Food Council.

[10] My own estimate from yield comparisons across whole farm economies of high and low yield ranges for similar crops in similar climates.

[11] See, for example, the USDA report on organic farming, 1980, and the many publications of Rodale Press.

[12] Land, Food, and People, FAO, Rome, 1984.

[13] Food and Agriculture Models for Policy Analysis, U.S. General Accounting Office, Washington, DC, CEO-77-87, July 13, 1977.

[14] Richard K. Ashley, "International Political Economic Considerations in Global Modeling" prepared for the Berlin Conference on Large-Scale Global Modeling, Science Center Berlin, July 1980.

[15] Ian I. Mitroff, "On the Error of the Third Kind" in H.A. Linstone & W. H. Clive Simmonds (eds.), Futures Research, Addison-Wesley, REading, Mass., 1977, p.45.

[16] Garrett Hardin, "The Tragedy of the Commons", Science Vol. 162, pp.1243-48, December 13, 1968.

[17] Russell Ackoff, Redesigning the Future, New York, John Wiley & sons, 1974.

[18] Philip M. Budzik, "The Future of Vermont Dairy Farming", DSD #45, June 1975, Resource Policy Center, Dartmouth College.

[19] H. Linnemann et al., MOIRA: Model of International Relations in Agriculture, North Holland, Amsterdam, 1979.

[20] A. Herrera et al., Catastrophe or New Society? IDRC-064e, International Development Research Center, Ottawa, 1976.

[21] See the following papers, all available from the International Institute of Applied Systems Analysis, A-2361, Laxenburg, Austria. Genady Golubev, Igor Shvytov & Oleg Vasiliev, "Environmental Problems of Agriculture", RM-78-32; Genady Golubev, "Nitrate Leaching Hazards: A Look at the Potential Global Situation", WP-80-89; Genady Golubev, "Agriculture and Water Erosion of Soils: A Global Outlook", WP-80-129.

[22] Ian I. Mitroff, op.cit., p.52.

[23] P.L. Berger & T. Luckmann, *The Social Construction of Reality*, Anchor Books, New York, 1967, pp.60 and 80.

[24] Donald Michael, "Planning's Challenge to the Systems Approach" in Harold Linstone & W.H. Simmonds, *Futures Research*, Addison-Wesley, Reading, Mass., 1977, p.95.

11
Ecosystems and Natural Resource Management

Frank B. Golley

INTRODUCTION

Ecology has been defined as the study of relationships between living organisms and their environment. Collections of living organisms and their environments are called ecological systems or ecosystems. The word, ecosystem, was coined by the English ecologist, Sir Arthur Tansley, in 1935 but until the early 1950's the concept was not used extensively. It entered common ecological terminology when E. P. Odum (1953) made it the central theme of his popular textbook, Fundamentals of Ecology. The ecosystem concept became a powerful research tool under the International Biological Program (IBP) when a comparative study of biological productivity was carried out world-wide (Worthington, 1975). The IBP program was organized on ecosystem principles and proposed to study ecosystems representing each of the world's major biomes--tundra, coniferous forest, deciduous forest, grassland, desert, and tropical rain forest. This study terminated in the early 1970's but led to the organization of another study of broader scope developed by UNESCO and called the Man and Biosphere program or MAB. MAB attempted to compensate for two shortcomings of the IBP, that of being too north temperate in orientation and of ignoring the problems of applied ecology. Man and Biosphere passed its tenth year of operation in 1982 (di Castri et al., 1984). During this period of substantial environmental concern, the US/NSF also began a program called Research Applied to National Needs (RANN), one part of which, under Philip Johnson, applied the ecosystem concept to large-scale regional studies. Unfortunately this program was terminated for political reasons before an adequate test of the ecosystem concept was made.
    Thus, over the past 20 years there have been a series of ecosystem studies which have expanded the concept and tested its application. These experiences provide a basis for reviewing the usefulness of the ecosystem concept in multidisciplinary research. In

this review I intend to, first, examine the ecosystem concept through its methodology, and then discuss various criticisms of the theoretical concept. Second, I will examine the application of the ecosystem concept to multidisciplinary projects.

THE ECOSYSTEM PARADIGM

The ecosystem concept is a complex and multifaceted idea which focuses on groups of biological entities and organizes them into a systems framework. It began as a point of view and was turned into a popular paradigm by E. P. Odum. At this point in time it involves two rather different approaches. One (termed here a scientific approach) focuses on methodology and is basically an analytical (or reductionistic) approach which seeks mechanistic explanations for phenomena observed in nature. The second involves development of inferences about systems from experience, observation, or from other scientific principles. These inferences may be derived from the reductionistic experiences of the scientist (that is, by induction) or be deduced from information or theory. Frequently inferences are developed by analogy. While this latter, philosophical approach to ecosystems is derived from scientific research in ecology, its statements, conclusions, and rules are not always amenable to proof since the evidence frequently comes from the agreement of statements with our intuition and experience. For example, E. P. Odum (1977) says that our understanding of ecosystems is "common sense".

Both of these forms of ecosystem studies have been influential in interdisciplinary work. Ecosystem science has probably been of greatest utility in environmental management. I will devote a major share of space to this approach. Ecosystem philosophy has had its greatest impact on development of policy, on politics, and in environmental philosophy and ethics. The Green movement, for example, bases many of its ideas on the ecosystem concept (Capra and Spretnak, 1984). I will deal with this aspect of ecosystem studies later in the text. Both the scientific and philosophical forms of ecosystem studies are relatively immature and they are closely coupled together. Indeed, there are many students of ecosystems that would probably feel uncomfortable with my division of the subject into two parts. Nevertheless, it helps to keep two quite different ways of thinking separate and helps us to understand how this method and point of view can be helpful in solving problems.

I feel that there are four subdivisions of ecosystem research which are relevant to this discussion. These are: (1) definition of the ecosystem, (2) description of the behavior of the ecosystem, (3) analysis of the system to develop a mechanistic explanation of the system behavior, and (4) understanding the system behavior in the context of its environment or, what I call, ecosystem synthesis. I call this sequence of definition, description, analysis, and synthesis the ecosystem method. Let us examine how the sequence is developed.

Definition

In the study of an ecosystem the first step is to define the object of study. While this step seems obvious and simple, in actuality it is exceptionally difficult. There are two problems. First, the environment is structured in gradients of change over space and time--the soil catena and the passage of the seasons are familiar examples. The living organisms which make up the biota are distributed along these environmental gradients with the result that there are seldom recognizable sharp divisions which can be used to separate one system from another. The boundary problem is a perennial issue in ecology. For example, recently O'Neil et al. (unpubl) proposed that boundaries are recognized by change in the rates of processes but they do not specify a rule to distinguish between significant and insignificant change in rates. Second, while a lake, a patch of forest, or a river is readily recognized as a system, an entire forest, the ocean, or a grassland is not because they are so large in size compared to our methods of observation. Spatially large landscapes must be sampled. Since ecosystem studies are usually complex, involving tens to hundreds of scientists, it is difficult and costly to take many samples of a geographically broad system such as a grassland. Thus, ecosystem ecologists tend to focus on one site, which is assumed to be representative of the undefined larger landscape system. These two problems, dividing a gradient up into separate objects of study and taking an adequate sample of geographically large objects, are very serious. However, ecosystem ecologists have tended to ignore them, taking "representative" samples at a convenient place and assuming homogeneity over space. One of the central questions of present day ecosystem studies is the significance of landscape heterogeniety. Until this question is satisfactorily answered we must recognize the conceptual nature of boundaries, the limitations of our methods, and the incompleteness of our representation of ecosystem structure.

Ecosystem Behavior

Once an ecosystem is identified and defined, we can take the second step. This step involves the description of the behavior of the ecosystem. I am using behavior in a special way here. By behavior I mean the system's translation of a set of inputs the system receives from its environment into a set of outputs to its environment. Behavior may be expressed in terms of flow of energy, materials, or information. Energy flow has been a popular study in ecosystem science and has led to a variety of interesting applications which will be discussed later. Energy is received from the sun and is partioned into two flows of concern to ecologists. First, the majority of energy is absorbed by the earth and powers the climates and ocean currents, and provides the temperature environment for life. The second is energy captured by green plants through photosynthesis that powers the metabolic activities of living organisms. This energy flow is called organic production and has been measured extensively (Lieth and Whittaker, 1975).

The movement of chemical elements through the ecosystem is another system behavior of great interest to ecologists. The geologic cycle of uplift, erosion, and sedimentation form the background for the ecological cycles from the environment to biota and back again. The biota have specific chemical requirements and their growth and development may be enhanced or reduced by the amount of nutrients available. The ecosystem receives the elements from precipitation of water, from the atmosphere, and from the substrate, takes them up in specific proportions and then gives them up again as the nutrients pass out of the biota through the course of metabolism or when death occurs.

The input and output of information is not well understood in ecosystem studies. Usually information is thought to be encoded in matter and energy and to function in the control of processes (Margalef, 1980). Development of an understanding of information as a system behavior is a matter for future research.

Whatever the behavior, the ecosystem scientist is concerned with describing this behavior over sufficient time so that a pattern is recognized. Long-term studies have shown that a rather long time scale must be used to define the central tendency of system behavior (Bormann and Likens, 1979). Variation from year to year may be quite large and a pattern or trend over five to ten years may be abruptly reversed in the next period. This time-scale problem is similar to the space-scale problem of landscape heterogeneity.

Some ecosystem ecologists profess to be interested solely in the system behavior and not in the object or the structure of the object. It has been suggested that a field-theory of ecology, in a sense similar to field theory in physics, might be more useful in understanding dynamic activity than our present approach. A field theory would treat what we conventionally identify as objects as positions in a network where flows are slower and would be exclusively interested in rates, directions, and controls of flows through system networks. As far as I know studies of this type are exclusively marine. All terrestrial ecosystem studies with which I am familiar assume an object exists somewhere at some time.

Ecosystem Analysis

Once the ecosystem behavior has been described it can be compared with that of other systems or with the system of interest at another time or place. Questions then arise. Why was that behavior observed under those conditions, why does the behavior vary, and so forth? These questions require us to go into the system, identify the most important or more relevant components, determine how these components are linked together, determine their behavior and develop mechanistic explanations that can be tested by further observation and experiment. These are called process studies and by far the largest part of current research on ecosystems is focused here.

An ecosystem may be made up of literally thousands of populations of plants, animals, and microorganisms and millions of individuals. Since it is frequently impossible to describe each population as a separate component, most students group populations together. At the broadest level these groupings have been called trophic levels. Trophic levels recognize the flows of food, and thereby energy and chemical nutrients, through the system. Initially three components were recognized: the producers or green plants, the consumers which consist of herbivores and carnivores and obtain their energy from food chains based on living tissues, and decomposers, which obtain their energy from food chains based on dead tissue (Lindeman, 1942). This simple organization has been heavily criticized as inadequate to represent the actual structural complexity in ecosystems and has been expanded in modern studies. A more common approach is to recognize groups of organisms which perform common functions, such as pollinating a particular tree or breaking down cellulose, as separate components. One representative of the group is then studied in detail and the knowledge gained is then extrapolate to the other members of the group. If we are concerned with a single feature of the group's behavior, this approach might be perfectly satisfactory. However, if the biology of individual species is important in understanding the system behavior, this approach may still be too general. Finally in a relatively simple system, such as a hot spring (Wiegert, 1977), each population can be studied and the system components then will represent structures familiar to the biologist. However, in some studies further subdivision to the biology of individuals may be necessary.

Whatever the method of decomposing the ecosystem, one will frequently end up with a web-like pattern showing how the various components are interconnected through flows of energy, chemical materials, and information. The next step in ecosystem analysis is to understand how each component translates the inputs it receives from other components and from the environment into outputs to other components and the environment. Knowledge of these component behaviors and the web of linkages provide the basis for experimentation (or for observing natural experiments) and developing answers to the questions raised at the whole system level. Naturally this experience leads to yet other questions and the process goes on and on until we have adequate understanding of the whole system and its parts.

Synthesis

Description of system behavior is not the end to an ecosystem study. It is also necessary to understand the significance of the behavior and to develop general statements about how ecosystems perform. Here this process is termed synthesis. Synthesis has taken two forms: the development of ecological models and the development of theoretical statements without models. There is, in addition, a large set of ideas about ecosystems which I have defined earlier as philosophical statements. These philosophical concepts are valuable in that they may create hypotheses which lead to scientific questions and because they stimulate thought. However, they are outside of the strictly methodological approach to ecosystems I am describing here.

Ecological modelling is a very active field of study and is applied in all the subdisciplines of ecology. At the ecosystem level it is used in two ways. First, models are used to design studies, control the research, organize the data and analyses and integrate the results of component process studies into a whole system study. Second, models are used to predict the system behavior under different conditions. The results from a model depend upon the model structure and much research has been devoted to bringing into ecological modelling techniques from other fields in systems analysis. Other ecologists have devoted time to developing mathematical representations of the ecological events they observe in an ecosystem analysis. These activities have resulted in a rich literature (Patten, 1975; Shuggart and O'Neil, 1979).

The development of explanatory concepts which address why a particular ecosystem behavior occurs is the object of the science. An explanation can be tested and if found to be consistent then it forms a rule which can be used in management or in policy development. An example of this type of concept is the response of an ecosystem to disturbance. Bormann and Likens (1979) have studied the behavior of a deciduous forest ecosystem in processing nutrient inputs from weathering soil and rainfall into outputs in streamflow. The ecosystem behavior has been observed following clear cutting of the forest. In this example, annual streamflow increased from 26 to 41 percent over the streamflow of uncut forests and the concentrations of dissolved substances and their export was decreased during the first three years of vegetation regrowth. This decrease is partly due to uptake of chemicals by the growing vegetation, but other factors are also operating. These other factors might include exhaustion of the chemical substrate and direct control of the loss by the vegetation. Thus, the overall behavior has a dynamic pattern over time that can be explained by understanding the behavior of the components of the system and their linked interactions. These watershed studies have been replicated in a number of different places because they are an excellent experimental approach to study of system behavior.

A CRITICAL ASSESSMENT

Ecosystem studies have been criticized from their inception, as is true of any scientific idea, and this criticism has shaped the development of the science. Here I will review a few of the criticisms to clarify how ecosystem concepts may or may not be useful in multidisciplinary studies.

As mentioned above, the definition of an ecosystem as an object has usually not been of deep interest to ecologists. The selection of a study site often is made on the basis of convenience and it is assumed that space is homogeneous and that results from the study site apply over this space. And further, it typically has been assumed that a few years of observations are sufficient to reveal the temporal dynamics of the system. Thus, we frequently find ecologists scaling up or extrapolating from a site to an entire landscape or biome and from a few to many years. This is true if the site is a hectare plot or a watershed. While the watershed is an advance over the plot since it does represent a bounded system as far as water is concerned, one watershed is not necessarily representative of another. Ecosystem science badly needs comparative studies (Wiebe, 1985) but unfortunately it is exceedingly difficult to mount such studies. They require teams of scientists and large amounts of financial and logistic support. Few supporting agencies appear to understand the method of ecological science well enough to fund teams over the time necessary to obtain reliable data. We thus become satisfied with the three year grant, or the PhD thesis period, as providing adequate time for ecological work. It is also difficult to publish the results of the second, third, and further replication of the first study, since all that changes through replication is our certainty about the mechanism or process. Since ecosystems can be very large and complex objects the rate of real advance in understanding may be agonizingly slow. But ecosystem scientists are as impatient as other scientists, and their perceptions about the requirements for success in the scientific culture in which they live frequently do not permit the process to unfold as it should. And thus, we do find studies that are inadequate in their dimensions and we find conclusions drawn from inadequate observations.

I have suggested here that ecosystem behavior consists of the input-output dynamics of systems exclusively. Critics have pointed out that the input-output dynamics of energy or materials hardly accounts for all of the interesting behaviors of a lake or a forest patch. Of course this is true, but I feel that the development of sound scientific underpinning to ecosystem studies requires us to confine our attention to these behaviors initially. System behavior expressed as flows of information may hold the key to bringing into ecosystem science other topics of interest or other points of view. I could imagine, for example, that a cultural perception about a resource might be viewed as an information control (just as rainfall could be a control) on an energy flow. However, this is pure speculation on my part. The consequences of restricting ecosystem studies to energy and material flows means that the ecosystem approach is less attractive in multidisciplinary work since it requires that all elements in the system be represented in energy or material terms. We will discuss this further below, but for now we should note that this restriction bothers biologists as well as social scientists.

Ecosystem studies have also been criticized for using abstract groupings, such as trophic levels, in the analyses. This process of aggregation is due to the large number of subobjects (the individuals) present in systems. Even in relatively simple ecosystems the individuals are grouped into abstract entities called species and the deciduous forest described above may contain hundreds of species. I think that this criticism stems more from the attribution of purpose to the abstract groups than it does to aggregation itself. Ecologists have tended to write and speak as if groups such as consumers and decomposers were real objects and had a collective behavior. Actually they are frequently speaking about the behavior of a single individual or a single species and attributing that behavior to a whole collection of individuals or species. This is obviously a false attribution, yet it is also the first step in construction of a hypothesis about system or component behavior. If we conclude that consumers (defined in a precise way) perform a specific behavior at a specific rate over space and time, then we can hypothesize that another consumer will exhibit the same pattern of behavior. This expected pattern can be tested by field and laboratory study and be confirmed or rejected. If the hypothesis is rejected we may conclude that there are two kinds of consumers. As we have already observed this process can go on and on. The important point in this process of disaggregation is to determine when the observed differences no longer matter in explaining the system behavior with which we began. Frequently ecologists argue about these matters because they have different ultimate questions and the point where differences no longer matter differs among them.

I mentioned above that ecosystem analysis leads to the recognition of a web-like structure. Many ecologists also interpret these patterns as hierarchical structures. A hierarchical structure in ecology does not imply control, as in social hierarchy, but rather suggests a ranked series with one level subordinated to another based on some specific character. For example, the producer trophic level may be disaggregated into trees, shrubs, herbs or into leaves, stems, roots, and litter. In turn, trees can be broken down into coniferous trees and deciduous trees, and so on. In my view, this hierarchical structure is purely a conceptual device that has no reality in fact. Rather, as I suggested above, the real structure of ecosystems is the food, energy, material and information webs, which link together the individuals in a bewildering network of relationships.

ECOSYSTEM PHILOSOPHY

Frequently in ecosystem studies theorists have erected complex systems that are not based on observation and test (that is, do not derive from analytical studies). Rather, they reason from the scientific theories of physics, chemistry, or information science, or reason by analogy with social, economic systems. Actually this form of deductive thinking has had a long history in ecological sciences and it is frequently called holistic thinking. Holistic concepts include the assertion that the whole is more than the sum of the parts, system stability is a function of feedback control, and a perturbed system returns to a steady state after the disturbance is removed. Ecosystem modelling has tended to reinforce this manner of thinking since the components in a computer model can be considered real objects with mathematical behavior and collectively they can produce behaviors that are unexpected (that is, that are counterintuitive). And we must admit that the conclusions drawn from these reasonings have frequently led ecologists to go back into the field and look more closely at nature.

Finally, the development of general statements (the philosophical approach) has probably been the part of ecosystem study most heavily criticized by ecologists. There are at least two reasons for this criticism. First, ecosystem studies have been able to test synthetic hypotheses with great difficulty. This is due to the difficulty and cost of carrying out a study, and the way in which the hypotheses have been formulated. Speculation has tended to run ahead of test. Second, ecosystem ecologists have reasoned about ecosystems from the perspective of physics when energy flow is of concern, chemistry when nutrient cycling is of interest, and systems analysis when control and stability were considered. This has given ecosystem ecology a peculiarly nonbiological character. It has especially not incorporated the theory of biological evolution in the concept.

An example of this tendency concerns the application of cybernetics to the concept of ecosystem stability. There has been a general feeling that ecosystems are stable in their structure and function. That is, even when confronted with environmental disturbance the system regains its integrity

over time and space. This conclusion fits a general
perception that nature is stable; equally, it conflicts with out experience of a constantly changing
nature. The problem is, first, that ecologists have
tended not to set up criteria of stability before
they examine a system. Nevertheless, they have
gone ahead and speculated why stability might be
maintained under disturbance. The concept of feedback is involved since the analysis of foodwebs reveals complex links of energy, materials, and information to and from components. It is postulated that
a balance of positive and negative influences flowing
between the components results in maintenance of a
stable pattern. The theory has been advanced, then,
that ecosystems are cybernetic systems, driven by the
flow of energy acting under the laws of thermodynamics, and cycles of chemical elements under the laws
of conservation of mass (Patten and Odum, 1981).
Other scientists have resisted this conclusion (Engelberg and Boyarsky, 1979; and Smith, 1982). Clearly
the matter is one of definition, as well as empirical
evidence.

In my view this immensely stimulating side of
ecosystem studies is philosophical or theoretical and
not analytic. That is, it results from thought about
the world and it is expressed in statements that are
not directly testable using the scientific method. By
saying this, I do not mean to denigrate these speculations but rather to place them in their proper
context. The analytic scientific method can be applied to a limited series of events in the world and
its results have limited application. Where it can
be applied it is extremely useful but we would be
misguided to think that the method can be applied to
all events and to think that any philosophical
thought resulting from doing this kind of science is
false because it can not be tested. These speculations may not be useful for analytical scientific
work, but they may be very useful for further thinking about the world and our role in it.

In summary, the point that I am making here is
that ecosystem studies as a scientific activity applies the scientific method to the study of the
behavior of such objects as lakes, forests and
oceans. The conclusions that come from this work
will fit the tested conclusions from other scientific
work. Therefore, ecosystem science can provide the
information required to manage the resources on which
humans depend. Ecosystem philosophy involves our
thoughts about nature at scales above the species.
The idea of the whole, for example, can help direct
our political and social actions. Both are useful in
their place.

APPLICATION TO MULTIDISCIPLINARY WORK

While ecosystem studies originated in biology and much of its theoretical development and language is biological, social scientists soon adopted the idea of an ecosystem and applied it to systems in which human beings are a dominant element (Moran, 1984). The extension of the concept into the social and geographical sciences is due, in part, to the systems element which brings physics into these subjects, as well as to the integrative nature of the concept. There is no intrinsic reason why humans, their built environments, and their processes can not be treated in an ecosystem context. However, inclusion of human beings makes the study of ecosystems much more complex, makes the dangers associated with abstraction more serious, and raises questions about how one treats culture, history, ideology and so forth. These problems may be illustrated by briefly considering four applications of the ecosystem concept to multidisciplinary studies. These include application to resource management, to environmental impact assessment, to planning and decision making, and to social science research.

The allocation of natural resources is a familiar ecological problem and ecosystem concepts can be useful in resource management (for example, Watt, 1966). The issue here is that several systems are using a common resource and the problem is how to allocate the resource among various interests and still maintain the resource. Ecological modelling has been used in these studies successfully. In wildlife management, for example, the biology of deer is reasonably well known and the statistics of population growth and hunting are fairly reliable. Therefore, it is possible to develop predictive models which describe the consequences of hunting strategies on the deer population. More sophisticated models can include the food and environmental conditions required by the deer and predict the consequences of environmental disturbance. These types of applications are routinely used by management agencies.

Environmental impact assessment became a common practice in the early 1970's when the National Environmental Policy Act was enacted by Congress. This was a period when the IBP was finishing and the concepts of ecosystem modelling were popular. Environmental impact assessment was often couched in the language and framework of ecosystem ecology because the ecosystem was broad enough to incorporate the problems and because it claimed to integrate a variety of kinds of information in one predictive system

(Erickson, 1979). In actuality, the ecosystem concept was an effective device to order information and guide descriptive studies. Where the assessment problem could be treated with a relatively simple model, these were useful in predicting outcomes (Cairns, et al., 1975). Indeed, the EPA utilizes these models to manage environmental problems today. And it was possible to bring together a number of disciplines and address a single problem using an ecosystem conceptual approach. This approach might range from group dynamic procedures to development of complex system models. In this application the environmental and biological factors are dominant and central, with the social factors forming the context or entering the process as controls on biological components. Environmental impact assessment has tended to be focused on short-term and geographically restricted problems and this has made the application of the ecosystem concept less controversial. The approach, blended with conventional system analysis, has also been used in global studies (OTA, 1982). Here the assessment is more negative, although the use of an ecosystem oriented approach to determine the impact of global nuclear was on the environment (Ehrlich, et al., 1983) has been quite effective and has withstood some scrutiny. On a regional scale the approach has also been useful as in the acid rain project in the northeastern US (Burgess, 1984) and the atmospheric carbon dioxide studies (Miller, 1981).

The ecosystem approach has also been used extensively in planning and decision making. Probably the best known application of this type is that of H. T. Odum (1971, 1983). Odum has developed a theory and a method which he calls energy analysis. The theory is based on thermodynamics and has a strong physical base. For example, Odum has proposed (Odum and Pinkerton, 1955) the maximum power output theorem as a central tenet of energy theory. This theorem states that systems develop to maximize power, not efficiency of energy use. Systems that maximize power grow at the expense of other systems. This appears on the face of it to be a restatement of competition theory but it has a purposive sense, in that Odum hypothesizes that systems evolve to maximize power or they do not survive. In energy analysis Odum uses a special symbology which allows the reader to quickly understand the general function of a compartment--these functions are those of ecosystems and computers such as producers, storages, amplifiers and so on.

Energy analysis has been used in a variety of studies at different scales, principally by Odum and his students and colleagues. Lugo (1978) has applied it to stress in aquatic systems, for example, and

Zuchetto and Jannson (1979) have applied it to agriculture on the island of Gotland, Sweden. In these applications the technique has been useful, especially when applied by those accustomed to thinking in its terms. This is because many problems do have a physical basis and can be analysed in energy terms. But, in addition, the technique allows one to contrast energy involved in long term, large scale processes, such as sedimentation, with those of an immediate nature, such as gasoline consumption by automobiles. In the south Florida study (Odum and Brown, 1975; and Zucchetto, 1975) for example, conversion of water use and water related or controlled activities into energy terms removes some of their water specific character and allows them to be judged on common grounds. Not only is this effective in comparative analysis but it also defuses controversy. In my judgement this approach was much less effective in evaluating the energy performance of countries or a large scale conflict such as the Viet Nam war (Odum et al., 1974) than those on regional or local scales.

The ecosystem approach has also been widely used in the social sciences. I suspect that this is partly due to its integrative claim and to the fact that it forms a bridge to biology. Recently Moran (1984) has edited a volume which examines the application of ecosystem concepts to anthropology and among these papers is a particularly useful critique by Smith (1984). Smith is most critical of the cybernetic view of ecosystems as "orderly, stable, homeostatic, functional, and antientropic." Basically Smith's criticisms are those discussed above, but what is relevant here is that he proposes that another kind of ecology, evolutionary ecology, has more useful theory to apply to anthropology.

Smith's comments are not unique and I suspect that they can also hold for other fields in the social sciences. But the criticisms miss a point, recognized by Smith but not prominantly featured in his paper. This point is that study of a human population parallels the study of any other biological population. While the human population is more complex and involves culture, history, and technology, in a fundamental sense all populations have characteristics in common. Thus, a theory developed for one population should have some application to another. Thus, foraging theory, niche theory, spatial optimization theory, life history strategies and others mentioned by Smith should be of considerable interest to anthropologists. However, if we are concerned with the environment of the human populations, that is, with all living beings and their environment in a specified space and time, then ecosystem studies ought to be relevant too. These ecosystem concepts should apply to human populations like any other, although the human population has a special and unusually dominant role. Gerald Young (1974) has applied the ecosystem concept in this sense to human ecology. Thus, in my view it is not a case of determining if one or another kind of ecology is most relevant to multidisciplinary and social problems, but rather of applying the appropriate kind of concepts to the problems at hand. In neither case is the theory mature enough to allow it to be applied indiscriminately.

CONCLUSION

In this appraisal of ecosystem and multidisciplinary studies I have first considered the method of ecosystem study and then, second, considered how it has been applied to multidisciplinary work. I have stressed method because I feel that the method is the heart of the matter, not ecosystem concepts, modelling, or descriptive data. I have suggested that the method of ecosystem study is essentially the scientific method applied to a particular kind of system, called ecosystem. While there may be some who deny that ecosystems exist, the reality of lakes, forests, fields, rivers and other natural objects is obvious. And if we are to live in an increasingly human dominated world, we must understand these objects from a scientific perspective, even though scientific understanding will not be enough to manage them effectively. It is important that we separate out the scientific concepts from the philosophical concepts because the test of their validity is different. Both are necessary. It is not a case of either-or.

In ecosystem studies this distinction is especially important because many of the scientists studying ecosystems have also made important philosophical statements. Part of the problem of transferring ecosystem concepts to other disciplines is that the practioners in the other field can not judge the validity of the ecosystem concepts expressed in these two forms. I feel that ecosystem science itself has been confused in some cases and has wasted effort. It might have been more effective if the science had proceeded according to the methods I have emphasized above. These methods are basically reductionistic, and apply scientific analysis to questions. Explanation of why a structure or function exists must not contradict our understanding of physics, chemistry, or biology. Ecosystem theory may not explicitly include the theory of these other levels, such as the theory of evolution, but it must not contradict them.

The final point deals with the specificity of the ecosystem concept. Clearly ecosystems include but are not the same as populations and individuals. Evans (1956) pointed out that an ecological system is a system made up of a living portion and its environment and therefore, there may be ecosystems of individuals, populations, communities and so forth. Evans' logical concept was seldom implemented. Rather, ecosystem has come to mean a community and its environment or any complex of communities and their environments. In this sense an ecosystem may refer to a watershed, a landscape, a waterscape, a region, a country, a continent, or the entire earth. Obviously a concept that has such broad application has more of a methodological or structural than a theoretical nature. I think that it is most useful to look for the explanatory theory appropriate to each particular kind of system and be content with focusing on the method of ecosystem study. Comparison of the results of using a common method can be valuable in understanding the behavior of natural systems of all kinds.

ACKNOWLEDGEMENTS

I wish to express my appreciation to Craig Loehle, Terri Jacobson, Carl Jordan, Monica Turner and other members of Georgia ecology discussion group for critical comments on the manuscript and on the ideas developed in this paper.

REFERENCES

Bormann, F. H. and G. E. Likens. 1979. *Pattern and Process in a Forested Ecosystem*. Springer-Verlag, N. Y.

Burgess, R. L. 1984. *Effects of Acidic deposition on forest ecosystems in the northeastern United States: an evaluation of current evidence*. SUNY, College of Environmental Science and Forestry, ESF-84-016.

Capra, F. and C. Spretnak. 1984. *Green Politics*. E. P. Dutton, Inc., N. Y.

Cairns, J. Jr., K. L. Dickson, and E. E. Herricks. 1975. *Recovery and Restoration of Damaged Ecosystems*. U. Virginia Press, Charlottesville.

di Castri, F., F. W. G. Baker, and M. Hadley. 1984. *Ecology in Practice*. 2 Volumes. Tycooly Int. Publ. Ltd., Dublin.

Ehrlich, P. R., J. Harte, M. A. Harwell, P. H. Raven, C. Sagan, G. M. Woodwell, J. Berry, E. S. Ayensu, A. H. Ehrlich, T. Eisner, S. J. Gould, H. D. Grover, R. Herrera, R. M. May, E. Mayr, C. P. McKay, H. A. Mooney, N. Myers, D. Pimentel, and J. Teal. 1983. Long-term biological consequences of nuclear war. *Science*, 222:1293-1300.

Engelberg, J. and L. L. Boyarsky. 1979. The noncybernetic nature of ecosystems. *American Naturalist*, 114:317-324.

Erickson, P. A. 1979. *Environmental Impact Assessment, principles and applications*. Academic Press, N. Y.

Evans, F. C. 1956. Ecosystem as the basic unit in ecology. *Science*, 123:1127-8.

Lieth, H. and R. H. Whittaker. 1975. *Primary Productivity of the Biosphere*. Springer-Verlag, N. Y.

Lindeman, R. L. 1942. The Trophic-dynamic aspect of ecology. *Ecology* 23:399-418.

Lugo, A. E. 1978. Stress and ecosystems, pp 62-101. In, J. H. Thorpe and J. W. G. Gibbons (eds) *Energy and Environmental Stress in Aquatic Systems*. Div. Tech. Info., Dept. of Energy. Conf-771114.

Margalef, R. 1980. *La Biosfera, entre la termodinamica y el juego*. Ediciones Omega, Barcelona.

Miller, P. C. (ed). 1981. *Carbon balance in northern ecosystems and the potential effect of carbon dioxide induced climatic change*. U. S. Dept. of Energy, Conf-8003118, UC-11.

Moran, E. F. (ed). 1984. *The Ecosystem Concept in Anthropology*. AAAS Selected Volume 92. Westview Press, Boulder.

Odum, E. P. 1953. *Fundamentals of Ecology, First Edition*. W. P. Saunders Co., Philadelphia.

Odum, E. P. 1977. Ecology - the commonsense approach. The Ecologist 7(7):250-253.
Odum, H. T. 1971. Environment, Power, and Society. Wiley-Interscience, N. Y.
Odum, H. T. 1983. Systems Ecology, an introduction. John Wiley and Sons, N. Y.
Odum, H. T. and M. T. Brown (eds). 1975. Carrying capacity for man and nature in South Florida. Report to the Department of Interior, National Park Service. Center for Wetlands, U. Florida, Gainesville.
Odum, H. T. and R. C. Pinkerton. 1955. Time's speed regulator: the optimum efficiency for maximum power output in physical and biological systems. American Scientist, 43:321-343.
Odum, H. T., M. Sell, M. Brown, J. Zucchetto, and L. Peterson. 1974. Models of herbicides, mangroves, and war in Viet Nam. In, The Effects of Herbicides in Viet Nam, Part B. Working Papers. National Academy of Science.
OTA (Office of Technology Assessment). 1982. Global Models; world futures and public policy. Congress of the United States (OTA-R-165). 120pp.
Patten, B. C. 1975. Systems Analysis and Simulation in Ecology, Vol. 3. Academic Press, N. Y. 601 pp.
Patten, B. C. and E. P. Odum. 1981. The cybernetic nature of ecosystems. American Naturalist, 118:886-895.
Shuggart, H. H. and R. V. O'Neil. 1979. Systems Ecology. Benchmark Papers in Ecology 9. Dowden, Hutchinson, and Ross, Stroudsburg.
Smith, E. A. 1984. Anthropology, evolutionary ecology, and explanatory limitations to the ecosystem concept, pp 51-85. In, E. F. Moran (ed), The Ecosystem Concept in Anthropology. AAAS Selected Symposium 92. Westview Press, Boulder.
Tansley, A. G. 1935. Introduction to Plant Ecology. G. Allen and Unwin, Ltd., London.
Watt, K. E. F. 1966. Systems Analysis in Ecology. Academic Press, N. Y.
Wiebe, W. J. 1985. Aquatic microbial ecology - research questions and opportunities, pp 35-50. In, J. H. Cooley and F. B. Golley (eds), Trends in Ecological Research for the 1980's. NATO Conference Series 1: Ecology. Plenum Press, N. Y.
Wiegert, R. G. 1977. A model of a thermal spring food chain, pp 290-315. In, C. Hall and J. Day (eds), Ecosystem Modeling in Theory and Practice. John Wiley and Sons, N. Y.
Young, G. L. 1974. Human ecology as an interdisciplinary concept: a critical inquiry. Advances in Ecological Research, 8:4-40.
Zucchetto, J. 1975. Energy, economic theory and mathematical models for combining the systems of man and nature. Case study, the urban region of

Miami. *Ecological Modelling* 1:24-268.

Zucchetto, J. and A. M. Jansson. 1979. Total energy analysis of Gotland's agriculture. A northern temperate zone case study. *Agroecosystems* 5:329-344.

Part 5
Problems, Needs, and Prospects

12
The Idea of Disaster in a Technocratic Age and Natural Hazards Research

Kenneth Hewitt

> ...I am compelled to fear that science will be used to promote the power of dominant groups rather than to make men happy.
> Bertrand Russell (1925)

Human communities have always suffered losses from flood, drought or storm. The argument I wish to develop here, however, is that the prevailing scientific view of these problems is a quite recent <u>invention</u>. By that I mean a partial and reconstructed view, carefully detached from previous ideas of natural calamity, and reflecting the singular social context of its origins. That may not seem unusual. Among scholars and in planning institutions there is a widespread feeling that any topic or view not actively developed in the most recent studies and literature must be outmoded if not actually worthless. Equally, there is an assumption that the major role here is played and can only be played by established researchers and major institutions in, especially, the wealthiest industrial nations. Yet, for the scientific community, a consistent forward movement is supposed to rest upon serious, logical considerations rather than mere fashion. It presumes more comprehensive and precise empirical bases, in turn coordinated with increasingly powerful general concepts.

Contemporary natural disasters research is certainly rich in the results of scientific enquiries, whether in geophysics or the psychology of stress. It may have internal coherence or at least conviction. That does not alter my sense that it capitalises rather arbitrarily upon scientific discovery. Indeed it accords with 'the facts' only insofar as they can be made to fit the assumptions, development and social predicaments of dominant institutions and research that has grown up serving them. Moreover my assessment of it leads me to believe that such developments have become the single greatest impediment to improvement in both the understanding of natural calamities and strategies to alleviate them. That is why I have felt

justified in devoting most of this chapter to a critique
of the underpinnings of the prevailing views in hazards
research. I shall also be more concerned with developments beyond my own field of geography, but as I think,
forming the decisive intellectual and institutional
milieu of its contribution to these problems. As such,
I may seem to stray far from the immediate interests of
those concerned with flooding or earthquake disaster or
weather-damage to crops.

Looking across the range of studies and actions
relating to natural hazards, I am suggesting that one
can recognise a convergence of opinion or approaches;
a sufficient consensus, to speak of a 'dominant view'.
Dominance is evident in the resources allocated; in the
numbers of highly trained personnel involved and the
volume of their published works; in the public visibility and acceptance of these works; and perhaps most of
all in the attachment to this view of the more powerfull institutions of modern states. In the work of any
sub-field or study, the dominant view might be revealed
by the literature quoted and emulated. It may appear
in the terminology used or the audience anticipated.
For example, the more visible work of geography or
sociology seems to me largely to express such dependency even when making useful innovations.

What will be described as the dominant consensus
has certainly not gone uncriticised. There has been
recurring dissent within and from outside the various
fields relating to natural hazards. Nor does the
view go unchanged. However it seems that this consensus
has gone forward resisting any fundamental criticism.
In large part, it merely shares here in the forward
rush and rapid shifts in fashionable methods that
beguile our minds in every discipline, while careful
reflection can seem almost immoral in the face of
practical needs. Intellectually, at least, the changes
have been cameleon-like exercises in superficial novelty,
absorbing, co-opting or ignoring dissent at will. Of
course, one must beware of giving this view the attributes of a thing or actor. Rather, we have the
convergence of a wide range of thinking upon a unified
perspective that constitutes what Thomas Kuhn has
called a 'paradigm' (Kuhn, 1962), or more specifically
what Edward Said calls "...an academic-research consensus
..." (1978, p. 275). For the dominant view of hazards
is not merely enshrined in rarified language and technical apparatus. It is fully symptomatic of the social
contexts in which it has arisen and that still form
its main points of reference. Its strength depends
less upon its logic and internal sophistications than
on being a convenient, productive 'world view' for
certain dominant institutions and academic spokesmen.
In other words, it is, above all a construct reflecting
the shaping hand of a contemporary social order. From

a socio-cultural perspective it is, therefore, itself a phenomenon requiring investigation as part of the so-called "social construction of knowledge" (Mannheim, 1952; Berger and Luckmann, 1967). Hence, behind the empirical and methodological detail of particular hazards or disciplinary concerns, looms the larger, and for social science the most fundamental of all research questions, self-conscious examination of the psychosocial underpinnings of thought, assumption and practice.

I shall not attempt here to review hazards research in a detailed fashion. In any case, there is no lack of reviews, including lengthy studies of the various geophysical conditions involved. My purpose is rather to examine the styles of argument, the uses of information and managerial assumptions that divide off the dominant consensus not merely from other research, but from the variety of possible viewpoints and concerns of hazards research. We will attempt to discover what is the common ground that channels and reflects basic motivations, or social contexts.

THE DOMINANT VIEW IN OUTLINE

The superficial features of the dominant view are not hard to discern, though it requires specialised, lengthy training to contribute to them. There is generally a straight-forward acceptance of natural disaster as the result of 'extremes' in geophysical processes. The occurrence and essential features of calamity are seen to depend primarily upon the nature of storms, earthquakes, flood, drought. It may be accepted that 'hazard', strictly speaking, refers to potential for damage that exists only in the presence of a vulnerable human community. Actual usage almost invariably refers to an objective geophysical process, like a hurricane or frost, as 'the hazard'. In turn, damage and human actions are defined by, or as responses to the type, magnitude, frequency, and other dimensions of these processes (e.g. ed. DeWitt Smith, 1957, Part I; Hewitt and Burton, 1971; ed. White, 1974; Sorensen et. al. 1975; UNESCO, 1978, Burton et. al. 1978, Ch. 2; eds. Grayson and Sheets, 1979).

Conceptual preambles and the development of a refined language of 'risk assessment' appear to have swept away the old, unpalatable causality of environmental determinism seen in, say, Huntington's work on storms (1945, Ch. 21). The sense of causality or the direction of explanation still runs from the physical environment to its social impacts. The most expensive actions and more formidable scientific literature recommending action, are concerned mainly with geophysical monitoring, forecasting and directing engineering or land use planning in relation to natural agents (National Academy of Sciences, 1980a, 1980b; Soloviev, 1978; Ang, 1978; ed. Yoshino, 1971).

Few researchers would deny that social and economic factors or habitat conditions other than geophysical extremes affect risk. The direction of argument in the dominant view relegates them to a dependent position. The initiative in calamity is seen to be with nature, which decides where and what social conditions or responses will become significant. Here is the geophysicist Bolt (1978, p. 156) discussing an especially 'bad year' for earthquake disasters:-

> Paradoxically, despite these grim statistics, 1976 had slightly less than the average number of large earthquakes ... (the) figures demonstrate that the misfortune of 1976 was not that more large earthquakes than normal occurred, but rather that more than usual occurred <u>by chance</u> in susceptible highly populated regions
> (my italics)

The implication always seems to be that disaster occurs because of the chance recurrences of natural extremes, modified in detail but fortuitously by human circumstances. Incidentally, my own field research on earthquake disaster areas leads me to believe that socio-economic conditions, through their expression in settlement patterns, land uses and building quality, play an overwhelming role in where and to whom damage occurs in most earthquakes (Hewitt, 1976; 1983; 1984). The geography of risk is usually treated as synonymous with the distribution of natural extremes such as large earthquakes, and with the natural features directly associated with them such as faults, flood plains, drought 'polygons', and avalanche tracks (see Geographisches Rundschau 1985, Fig. 2, pp. 64-65). Reference is made to past major disasters in assessing risk (Swiss Re, 1978). Some account may be taken of population density, or national economic 'levels', themselves measured and treated so as to seem commensurate with geophysical parameters (see Kantarovitch et. al. 1970; Burton et. al. 1979). The Soviet geographers Gerasimov and Zvinova, do speak of the difference between "the intensity of a disaster" and the "potential (i.e. geophysical) danger" which, they say, "remains the same" (ed. White, 1974, p. 243). However, even geographers have, for the most part, been content to treat the geography of hazards as synonymous with the spatial distribution and frequencies of geophysical extremes. The maps in Sections IV and V of ed. White, 1974 are examples (see also, Strahler and Strahler, 1973, pp. 218-225; Ayre, 1975; Berlin, 1980, vol. I).

In the dominant view, then, disaster itself is attributed to nature. There is, however, an equally strong conviction that something can be done about disaster by society. But that something is viewed as strictly a matter of public policy backed up by the most advanced geophysical, geotechnical and managerial capability. There is a strong sense, even among social scientists for whom it is a major interest, that everyday or 'ordinary' human activity can do little except make the problem worse by default. In other words, the structure of the problem is seen to depend upon the ratios between given forces of nature and 'advanced' institutional and technical counterforce.

One can summarise the bulk of the work and expenditures within the dominant view as falling into three main areas:-

i) An unprecendeted commitment to the monitoring and scientific understanding of geophysical processes, - geologic, hydrologic, atmospheric, - as the foundation for dealing with their human significance and impacts. Here the most immediate goal in relation to hazards is that of prediction.

ii) Planning and managerial activities to contain those processes where possible, through flood control works, cloud seeding, or avalanche defences, and where it is not possible, to physically rearrange human activities in accordance with the objective geophysical patterns and probabilities. That involves zoning, building codes and 'failsafe' artifacts. A remarkable unity of language has emerged here to discuss geophysical processes, physical planning and assessment of risks.

iii) Emergency measures, involving disaster plans and the establishment of organisations for relief and rehabilitation. The ability to put in place the insights developed by geophysical research and planning is important here. Study however is necessarily subordinate to action. Action is most commonly and directly put in the hands of military, or quasi-military organisations.
(Since most of the world's people and land areas have little access normally to the products of modern geophysical science and management technology, it is through emergencies that they become involved in the perspectives of the dominant view.)

In terms of research, the main areas of expertise are those of the physical sciences and engineering. However, social sciences play a substantial role, notably in studying 'crisis behaviour', and emergency measures; or in focussing upon places and groups singled out by the experience, expectation or existence of major natural disaster in their area (Disaster Research Group, 1961; eds. Baker and Chapman, 1962; eds. Grosser, et. al. 1964; ed. Brictson, 1966; Dynes and Quarantelli,

1968; U.S. National Academy of Sciences, 1970; Hewitt and Burton, 1971; ed. White, 1974; eds. Haas et. al. 1976).

There have been important social analyses that disagree more or less profoundly with the dominant view (e.g. Walford, 1878/79, Part II; Sorokin, 1942; Kendrick, 1956; Lifton, 1970; ed. Copans, 1975; McNeill, 1976; O'Keefe, et. al. 1976; Torry, 1978). However, in recent decades, social scientists have tended to concentrate increasingly upon direct socio-economic and behavioural relations of the three areas of the dominant view noted above. They ask how individuals or groups appraise the risks of occupying areas classified as typhoon coasts or flood plains. The results tend to be compared with geophysical knowledge of typhoons and floods. They ask how people respond to forecasts, requests to conserve water and hazard zoning legislation. They examine how people and institutions 'cope' when the volcano erupts or a crop is destroyed.

These interests seem entirely reasonable in themselves. They become less so as they are tributary to supposedly more sophisticated geophysical and engineering knowledge and techniques of emergency management. Moreover, by this narrow focus upon information that centers the problem upon natural extremes and damaging events we miss the main sources of social influence over hazards. But the bulk of hazards work by social scientists is focussed in that way. It serves to reinforce the 'geophysicalist' and technological reductionism of the dominant view.

INTERNATIONAL 'NETWORKING'

It is not unimportant how completely the funding and mobilisation of most disaster research depends upon the agencies of national governments or international organisations. A singular feature is the near universal adoption by them of the same concerns and supporting ideas. Some would say that the dominant view reflects particular ideological and group commitments. Yet the main concerns expressed in it are being pursued or sponsored by more or less identically named institutions in most states, universities and city administrations. The view appears at its sturdiest, and is most forcefully sponsored in multi-national cooperation and under the auspices of international agencies (c.f. Eijkmann, 1911; Armytage, 1965 Chapter 21).

Burton, Kates and White (1979, p. 212 e.s.) have criticised the "natural science" and technological preoccupations of relevant United Nations' studies. Nearly all the materials from UNESCO's 'Disasters Division' illustrate precisely the concerns and research categories of the dominant view. The reader might consult a publication on earthquake risk as one

of the more thorough, competent and convincing examples
(UNESCO, 1978). Moreover, that book reveals a unity
of language and mission in the work of participants
from Turkey, Switzerland and Japan, no less than from
the United States, Soviet Union and New Zealand. This
might seem to be a tribute to the unity of science.
In my opinion that is a secondary matter.

Rather, what these materials show is firstly that
the dominant view constitutes a technocratic approach.
That means, the work subordinates other modes and bases
of understanding or action to those using technical
procedures. More precisely, technocracy gives precedence in support and prestige to bureaucratically
organised institutions, centrally controlled, and
staffed by or allocating funds to specialised professionals. For social scientists it is important to
recognise that technocracy is not only or necessarily
an obsession with technology in the narrow sense of
engineering structures and machines (c.f. Mumford,
1967, 1970; Armytage, op. cit.). There are plenty of
forthright critiques of the 'technological fix'
approach to hazards management. They often fall short
of recognising the full scope of this phenomenon. In
other words, the "... social, economic and political
'people' factors involved in hazards reduction...",
that White and Haas (1975) emphasise, also can be and
usually are approached technocratically. My own argument amounts to saying that the 'natural science-
technological fix' approach to hazards is itself,
essentially, a socio-cultural construct. It reflects
a distinct, institution-centered and ethnocentric view
of man and nature. In other words, there is no inherent logic to scientific discovery nor its application
requiring us to follow this route it has in fact taken.

My sense of these developments as a socially constructed knowledge, is not, however, that commonly
expressed in 'perception' studies of hazards and environment. These tend to relate 'responses' to hazards to
individual awareness, attitudes and experience. I am
not concerned to turn the tables on the experts and
show that they are, in their way, as subjectively,
attitudinally limited as the laymen in flood plains or
people who buy homes astride an active fault. They
surely are limited as individuals. I do not find it
useful to reduce the problem to the way individual perceptions are shaped at the interface of sense experience
and personality.

We are concerned with the way 'thought follows
reality'. But the 'realities' here are not assumed
universals of the empiricist's sense data and their
psychological assimilation in individual acts of perception and cognition. Rather we are looking at
conditions that shape these pliable processes: the
conditions that influence what facts we are likely to

recognise and deem important; the acquired, accepted ways of interpreting them. These are matters of the social order. They relate to the societal means that shape learning and formal enquiry: that validate and communicate scientific discoveries and especially that govern their implementation. As such, they are integral to Marxian notions of economic control and ideology. And we owe some of the most penetrating modern expressions of how 'thought follows reality' in this sense to Marx and Feuerbach (Marx, 1964). Some of the more incisive criticism of hazards work in the dominant mode has also been Marxist (see edited Hewitt, 1983, chapters 5, 13 and 14). It seems to me, however, that like so much else in modern states, the dominant view of hazards differs little across the broadest spectrum of political affiliations. My own view of its social construction and implications is Weberian rather than Marxist. That is to say, I see here an expression of the way institutions, especially centralised, official and bureaucratically organised ones route their human and material resources into particular styles of work and practice (see Weber, 1947; Albrow, 1970). We have to consider how far the dominant view in hazards research represents an on-going and deepening example of what C. Wright Mills (1959) called 'the bureaucratic ethos'. That involves the channeling of scientists into a distinctive approach to 'facts', and a distinctive view of the nature of theory and practicality. Even in their most felicitous forms these tend to reflect mainly the organisation sponsoring research or the researcher's image of what the institution can and should do. Moreover, science and research itself, however practical in orientation, tend to be determining factors only at certain levels in these institutions, - rarely the highest, - and only in the outlook of a certain class of persons within them, - rarely those with the main powers of decision.

The dominant view suits very well institutions that carry out technical studies, develop technical plans, and train technical managers or favour research oriented to such projects. Moreover, 'technical' invariably means wedding science to technology, preferably in what is considered the most 'advanced' form. Therefore, it is a creature of the most powerful, wealthy and centralised institutions. Such, of course, is the style adopted most widely by dominant organisations of government, business and culture today (Habermas, 1973, Chapter 7). There is little hope of doing much about that.

However, in drawing attention to this truism, I suggest first, that natural calamity is one of the special and especially intractable problems for a technocracy. Here indeed, as the philospher Eric Dardel puts it, "...L'inopiné vient attaquer le savant dans

ses laboratoires ou il poursuit le dressage du temps..."
(19, p. 52). Secondly, many of those involved appear
unaware that they are doing anything but pursuing an
'objective', scientific and even a necessary research
strategy. Thirdly, we are in many ways stuck with a
form of technocratic strategy that is peculiarly archaic
and inflexible, at least from a socio-cultural or management perspective. Fourthly, I suggest that the
international system where the strategy is operating,
and the social and intellectual debates raging in the
most powerful states, themselves challenge the effectiveness as well as the truth of the dominant view.
There is no lack of recent studies that reveal its many
failings on the ground (see ed. Hewitt, 1983). Hence,
it becomes a major issue to discover and describe the
basis of the view's robustness within the technical context, as well as in relation to other, quite different
approaches to natural clamity.

AN "ENCLOSURE SYSTEM"

There is a close analogy between the dominant view
of hazards and Michel Foucault's description of how
'madness' came to be treated, indeed invented, by the
'Age of Reason' (Foucault, 1965). Natural calamity in
a technocratic society is much the same sort of pivotal
dilemma as insanity for the champions of Reason. Disaster in the Twentieth Century international system
involves comparable pressures upon dominant institutions
and knowledge, as did the 'crazed poor' in the social
and economic crises that formed the underbelly of the
Enlightenment. Madness and calamity are both subjects
of very disturbing experience. So too is the notion of
crime which Foucault has found to have a similar or
parallel history in modern times (1977). These appear
or have been made to appear as direct challenges to our
notions of order. They threaten to be interpreted as
"...a punishment for a disorderly and useless science..."
(op. cit., p. 32). They can be seen as clear limits to
knowledge and power, because they are initiated in a
way that seems uncontrollable by if not actually denials
of society. However, there is also a long history of
belief that each is a 'judgement' upon human activity,
a sentiment echoed in attitudes to environmental problems in the Ecology Movement today, for example, or to
the arms race among peace groups.

In each case, however, there has arisen a dominant
view that counteracts these difficulties with a positive
creed, an assertion of potency where the grounds for
conviction seem the least. It is exactly here that we
can see the benefits to a technocratic approach of
dividing off hazards. It is very convenient to treat
calamity as a special problem for advanced research in
the areas noted above, and this outweighs other consid-

erations. The problem is made manageable by an extreme narrowing of the range of interpretation and acceptable evidence. The resulting partial view has been achieved much as the 'great confinement' of the poverty-stricken and 'crazy' in the Eighteenth Century was to form the foundation for dominant perspectives on madness, crime and punishment - and the most severe criticism of them in our century (Rothman, 1971; Cooper, 1978). We are not only dealing with the substance of such questions, or with a particular philosophy and set of practical procedures. We are also dealing with a careful, pragmatic and disarming <u>placement</u> of the problem.

The language of discourse is often a good indicator of basic assumptions. Indeed, one of the surest indicators that one <u>is</u> confronting a dominant, socially constricted view, is that a critique requires most terms to be put in quotes to indicate the divergence of the usage. In hazards work one can see how language is used to maintain a sense of <u>discontinuity</u>, or <u>otherness</u> that severs these problems from the rest of man-environment relations and social life. That is most obvious in the recurrent use of words stressing the 'un'-ness of the problem. Disasters are <u>un</u>managed phenomena. They are the <u>un</u>expected, the <u>un</u>precedented. They derive from natural processes or events that are highly <u>un</u>certain. <u>Un</u>awareness and <u>un</u>readiness are said to typify the condition of their human victims. Even the common use of the word (disaster) 'event' can reinforce the idea of a discrete unit in time and space. In the official-sounding euphemism for disasters in North America, they are "<u>un</u>scheduled events".

What emerges <u>is</u> that 'hazards' are not viewed as integral parts of the spectrum of man-environment relations or as directly dependent upon them. We have abandoned that aspect of the earlier environmentalists from Strabo to Huntington. One does find philosophical introductions and conclusions locating 'hazards' within a panorama of human ecology and its diverse collections of adaptive problems. But they are described and dealt with as a separate problem.

We have noted the precedence given to specialised geophysical research and the geophysical processes each of its sub-fields concentrate upon. However, common features, found across the various specialisations, serve to reinforce the sense of separateness of disaster and its causes. In nearly all cases, attention is directed towards the occurrence or likelihood of discrete, sharp bouts of damage. Natural hazards may be acknowledged to include a continuum of damages from ordinary wear and tear by sun or wind, to major catastrophes. Human societies may be seen to exist in a continuous process of interaction with the habitat, and under conditions that ultimately link us to the entire system of relations in the biosphere. Yet, it is the temporally and spatially limited 'event' that is the specialty in hazards work, - a Sahel drought; Hurricane Betsy; avalanches.

This geophysical approach is supported by a well-entrenched logic. It identifies hazardous events in strong, step-like changes of geophysical measures that accompany disastrous damages. The changes may involve river levels, seismic shocks, wind gusts and so on. The picture of a pointer-reading swinging off the scale is one of science's contributions to the common stock of disaster imagery. Human vulnerability is, in turn, tied to these extreme 'pulses' in nature through such notions as 'damage thresholds'. My diagrams in Hewitt and Burton, 1971, Figs. 1 and 21 expressed this with forthrightness! (see also, eds. Haas et. al. 1977; Chapter 1).

What we also find ourselves dealing with here are notions of stability and instability. In Scheidegger's words:-

> ... evidently, if a prevailing status quo is preserved no catastrophe occurs. Therefore a catastrophe generally entails the <u>termination</u> of a stable state... (1975, p. 2)

He also considers 'stable' to be the 'normal' state. Though he expressly refers to geophysical stability, the sense of a break-down in a stable set of relations to the habitat is found equally in the social interpretations of these risks. Hazards are taken as natural events that destabilise or <u>violate</u> ordinary life and relations to the habitat. Research commonly takes the idea of failure in social systems as a fairly exact analogue of that in mechanical systems, - the result of an (exceptional) force that exceeds the strength of the material or structure. Haas and Ayre (1969) have expressed this more conscienciously than most:-

> It does not seem unduly farfetched to think of a human community, in its response to dynamic imput, as a second order system described by the system of coupled nonlinear equations,
>
> $[M]\{Y\}+[D]\{Y\}+[R]\{Y\}=\{F\}$
> where $\{Y\}$ is the response vector;
> $[M]$, $[D]$ and $[R]$ are matrices of 'mass', 'energy dissipation' and 'restoration...(etc.)..
> (p. 7)

This makes plain what is merely assumed in much of disaster research. Again, the implication is one of a threshold, below which stable, 'normal', orderly activities and human competence apply; above it, disorder, the unexpected, the unplanned. J.W. Powell summed up the position by calling disaster:-

> ... the impinging upon a <u>structured</u> community of an <u>external</u> force on a scale wide enough to excite <u>public</u> alarm, and to disrupt <u>normal</u> patterns of behaviour ...
> (quoted Lemons, 1957, p. 2)

The concern with rare, 'chance' events, directs our attention in other ways. The more severe occurrences, the 'worst-case scenarios' tend to become definitive or at least symbolic of the whole problem (Barton, 1969, Chapter 1; Bolt, 1978, Chapter 2; Burton et. al. 1979, Chapter 1). Certain kinds of disaster, especially those in major urban centers, or the very largest examples; that is, those that are <u>least frequent</u> and most extraordinary of all disasters, come to represent the whole problem by a sort of historical-geographical compression. One sees this happening in the way the plight of San Francisco, the 1906 earthquake disaster, its anticipated recurrence and the San Andreas Fault, come to be touchstones of seismic risk problems, even as many other disasters occur and are forgotten. Furthermore, destruction, impairment, and what must be restored by <u>outside assistance</u> tend to form the entire concern in <u>individual disasters</u>. And these descriptions commonly deal only with the most severely damaging aspects. Patterns of survival and evidence of 'stability' in structures, - which in most 'disaster zones' could be seen to involve by far the larger fraction of people and property affected, - are of little concern.

THE DISASTER ARCHIPELAGO

In practice, then, natural hazards have been carefully roped off from the rest of man-environment relations. The enclosure where they reside is variously labelled 'unscheduled events', 'emergency social situations', 'negative resources' or simply 'hazards'. Not only do such acts of definition isolate them. Not only do such problem-formulations sever their explanation from supposedly 'normal', 'predictable' events. Major allocations of resources to manage risk have mainly involved attempts to physically wall in the places and occasions of disaster. Flood control work exemplifies this attempted enclosure system.*

---

*Though the language is different, my concern here mirrors that of Gilbert White's much earlier formulation of the problem in flood responses, where he contrasted the narrow, confining emphases upon 'technological' solutions with a sense of a 'range of possible adjustments' (White, 1961). However, two decades or more later, the problem looms as less one of 'choice of use,' and more of intellectual and institutional frameworks that circumscribe (technical) choice in general.

Meanwhile, the dominant response to actual disaster is to invest and seal off the damage zone with military personnel and a network of officials, clearly demarcating it as a zone of exclusion from on-going (peaceful?) life. In many examples we find the authorities making huge efforts to keep the people in the 'disaster zone' from moving out, and others from moving in (Waddell, 1975; Erikson, 1976). Elsewhere, as in the 1980 Italian earthquake, we have a tremendous struggle to relocate people, against their will (c.f. Oliver-Smith, 1974; Torry, op. cit. Geipel, 1982). When there is a forecast we see in industrial states the growing civil defense strategy of massive total evacuation that leaves 'the hazard' in a no-man's land (Foster, 1980, Chapter 4). These may well be fair and desireable responses in some cases and within the possible options of given communities. They nevertheless serve to reinforce the 'otherness' of the source of disaster, and also to emphasize the blanket classifying of entire areas as 'disaster zones', although some or most of them are intact. Also, the problems of disaster victims often transcend the immediate event. Damage and death in disaster are highly correlated with poverty.

By these and other means, natural disaster is quarantined in thought as well as practice. The geography of disaster is an archipelago of isolated misfortunes. Each is seen as a localised disorganisation of space, projected upon the extensive map of human geography in a more or less random way due to independent events in the geophysical realms of atmosphere, hydrosphere and lithosphere. More specifically, each disaster is an unplanned hole or rupture in the fabric of productive and orderly human relations with the habitat or 'natural resources'.

The importance of isolating the problem in this way may not seem as necessary as in disease control, in the asylums or lazarhouses Foucault tells us they replaced in the Eighteenth Century and the carceral systems that grew up along side. There may not seem a logic to it like the 'Gulag Archipelago' of Soviet labour camps, and similar mechanisms devised to remove 'undesireable' elements from intercourse with the rest of society. But the analogy and covenience of this isolation is there, deep in the structure of technocratic thought and its precursors.

In each field that has entered into hazards research it seems that, sooner or later, great excitement develops about just how to classify and partition off the issues involved in the subject. However, this is rarely done in an open-ended, philosophical and curious way. Rather, it becomes a 'territoriality' question, a zoning regulation for these sorts of studies. Nowadays, to judge from the efforts of geographers, it most often takes the form of plausibly locating the hazards 'box' within a model or diagram of the components and lines of interaction in man-environment studies (Kates, 1971; Burton and Hewitt, 1974, Figure 12.2; Ayre, 1975, p. 12). A moment's reflection usually shows that these are not 'models' of reality at all, but <u>managerial devices</u> to show the relations among the <u>study areas</u> or dimensions currently fashionable in the discipline and related fields.

The diagrams themselves tend to resemble nothing so much as an organisation chart of a large bureaucracy. They often bear little or no relation to actual places or conditions, the material interactions or human experience involved. They are prescriptions for showing where academic and managerial categories fit together. However, it is not merely that reputations are made by this sort of activity. The placement of the problem is a necessary founding act whereby each specialty field demonstrates its coherence with the whole dominant view. It is an act that will be paid homage to as an intellectual demonstration at the start of each new study. This is important because hazards studies are rarely research in the full sense. Most arise out of particular calamitous events, or 'applications', commonly on behalf of, or as an assessment of public policy and the performance of particular agencies. The 'expertise', therefore, is invariably that of a discipline like seismology or cognitive psychology, or a technique in say, statistics or remote sensing. The 'research' is essentially an empirical study in which, oddly enough, what happens in every disaster, fits into the categories and assumptions currently fashionable in the advanced research community, or questions specified by an agency's responsibility (c.f. The disaster mission reports of The National Science Foundation or the earlier ones of U.N.E.S.C.O.: "Disaster Division"). These considerations of haste also encourage the encapsulating of the problem in an official-looking diagram or 'model' of man-nature relationships. Once we have located the hazards 'box', however impulsively, we can then concentrate upon it. We are at liberty to define parameters, revalidate properties, gather expensive data and seek cures or restraining devices, all within a technical <u>monologue</u>. Thus encapsulated, the problem appears neutralised, objectified. Past and present notions that seem technically obscure or unpalatable are defused. Most comforting of all, the forces involved, so charged with drama, emotion and blame in the everyday world, become subordinate to objective dimensions and impersonal dynamics. We and the agency are simply doing a job. The work can then develop as a <u>well-crafted</u> monologue. That is not only because the language is so specialised. We are now free to speak of hazards <u>alone</u>, as if all these 'events' and all that happens within each one belong not only to a separate domain, but to a single, albeit 'multivariate' reality.

'Monologue' is Foucault's word to express how society and its instrument Psychiatry closed themselves off from a <u>dialogue</u> with madness and its sources in the everyday world. The psychiatrist was to be Reason's priest, and not obliged to contemplate his own madness, nor his part in the social conditions that might drive others beyond those bounds where abnormality or passion were to be confined. So it is with hazards research in its mainstream. It has invented its problem field to suit to convenience. It does not reflect upon the extent to which the institutions it serves, the societies that have made such technocratic authority possible, could be part of the problem. It does not reflect upon the flaws in itself, except in relation to what is deemed sophisticated in the current fashions of the scientific community. It gathers data about people at risk, but may not engage in dialogue with them. For example, most disaster reports in the so-called Third World have been by persons who cannot speak the language of the area affected, or have no background in its socio-cultural composition.

However, none of this could alone sustain the dominant consensus. It could not leave so many feeling satisfied to treat hazards as a separate set of problems, if there were not a deeper level of scientific, or supposedly scientific understanding implicit in it. That underpinning of the justification for keeping hazards separate, of paying lip service only to relations to other man-environment relations, brings us back to the sense in which disaster is a specially intractable problem for scientific rationalism and technocracy. We cannot, in fact, divorce the development of the dominant view from the entire perspective of materialism and the social pressures upon materialist and secular institutions required to interpret and deal with unpalatable or apparently unmanageable material events. The formulations of the dominant view must be seen against the background of what can serve as acceptable explanations of natural disaster in a technocratic framework; as a strategy that allows us to 'save the facts' and ourselves!

THE CONVENIENCE OF ACCIDENTS

Conceptually and analytically, what the dominant view does, the perspective that all the related hazards work has converged upon, is to define the distinctive features of the problem through the language and apparatus of 'the accident'. Natural 'calamities' are, before anything else, severed from the rest of material life by being what the Oxford English Dictionary calls "unforeseen contingencies".

Toblin (1977) states:-

> ... (disaster) implies the occurrence of an
> <u>unusual</u> event which was <u>not</u> adequately <u>predicted</u>
> in time or place to allow measures to be taken
> for the protection of the threatened people
> and property...
>
> (p. 13, my italics.)

The Soviet geographers Gerasimov and Zvonkova (1974) note that:-

> ... Natural hazards derive from highly dynamic
> processes whose elemental essence consists in
> their <u>indefinite</u> and <u>equivocal</u> manifestations...
>
> (p. 243, my italics.)

We will not enquire here why Lenin, and from a quite different ideological perspective Sorokin, emphasised other socio-economic or socio-cultural interpretations, for this is the language of detente! Gilbert White (1974) is quite firm about it and also states clearly its other implication:-

> ...were there perfectly accurate predictions
> of what would occur and when it would occur in
> the intricate web of atmospheric, hydrologic
> and biological systems, there would be no hazard.
>
> (p. 3)

In such a view, the human ingredients are necessarily of a dependent or tangential nature, being responses and contingencies that stem from <u>un</u>anticipated damage by nature. To the extent that there are human conditions specifically affecting hazard, they are found to lie in the category so commonly invoked in accidents: 'human error'. The literature is full of reactions or conditions described as <u>un</u>informed, <u>un</u>sound, <u>un</u>planned, or impaired, irrational or arational.

Again, natural disasters are 'accidents' only in the socio-cultural implications of the dominant view; not for its geophysical focus or the technologies it would bring to bear on the problem. There is an important contrast brought out between these 'accidents' and the scientific possibilities for handling them. Once research is under way, then indeed the 'controls, mechanisms and models, take over the discussion. For it is refined statistical and geophysical techniques that alone are thought able to reduce these rare, high magnitude, uncertain events to some sort of rational description. The common run of humanity is considered to have poor or 'subjective' impressions of 'the hazard' and its occurrence. Likewise, their ability to survive it at all, seems puzzling. As one recent official document put it:-

> Although human beings, unlike other animals, can project themselves into the future and make plans to deal with future <u>uncertainties</u>, they are more apt to be oriented to the 'here and now'. Present satisfactions, pleasures and rewards far outweigh their future counterparts and particularly their <u>indefinite</u> or <u>uncertain</u> counterparts.
>
> (My italics)
> (Working Group of Earthquake Hazards Reduction, 1980)

Never mind the Saruman-like tone, the unsupported (unsupportable?) assumptions and an omniscience that would attribute such banalities to "human beings". This is a genuine, concerned (but technocratic) expression of what hazards are about and how people fit into them. The role of research is also placed carefully. We are apparently in the presence of a new kind of 'white-man's burden'! There is little evidence that it is taken to apply only nor mainly to North American or urban societies.

For a variety of reasons, the research literature strives to dissociate itself from the full implications of these emphases and some will no doubt feel I am developing an unfair caricature of it. 'Accident Research' has been at pains to rid itself of the view of accidents as 'accidental' (Haddon, et. al. 1964). The sociologists Quarantelli and Dynes (1972) have voiced the need for a "principle of continuity" built into disaster research, to avoid the sense of the bizarre, or the impression that crisis behaviour bears little relation to pre-existing conditions and human roles. North American hazards work has continued to shift its language towards more neutral terms, preferring to speak now of "risk assessment" of "probabilistic consequences" (eds. Whyte and Burton, 1980). Geographers have repeatedly returned to the notion that settlement patterns or human ecology are the proper context of hazards work.

These developments reflect genuine unease. I suggest, however, that the sense of, indeed the fundamental metaphysic of accident, is so entrenched in the dominant view that these efforts have largely amounted to window dressing, dealing with issues that do not penetrate beyond conceptual preambles. In the technocratic style of work there is a structure of assumptions, and a use of science and management that always situates natural calamity beyond an assumed order of definite knowledge, and of reasonable expectation. More importantly it places disaster outside the realm of everyday responsibility both of society and individual.

More important still, it makes assumptions about everyday life - about its being 'normal', 'stable', 'predictable' - that are in turn debatable. We shall return to that.

What we must now ask is how this accidentalism operates as a solution to the problem of explanation in a technocratic context. How have we, as scientists, managed to inform it with the appearance of logical necessity and technical sophistication?

THE PROBLEM OF EXPLANATION I: THE BREAK WITH THE PAST.

Viewed historically, and perhaps in relation to the sense of disaster among the vast majority of people who are today excluded from its monologues, the dominant view of hazards is decidedly odd. But the source of its oddness lies deeper than the expediency of a technocratic 'package'. Unlike virtually all past views of calamity, materialism, especially in its technocratic form, cannot readily attribute disaster to 'Acts of God' or to 'Acts of Man'!

The former is inadmissable in scientific, utilitarian thought. However, the question of 'Acts of Man' is more problematic. Obviously humans are involved. It is their vulnerability and misfortune that are the central concern. But the question of human action is the difficulty here. Action is not mere process. Properly defined, it refers to organised, deliberate attempts to bring about change or maintain a certain status (cf. Arendt, 1958). It is not a matter of spontaneous, impersonal, unmanaged change such as physical science sees in the workings of the atmosphere or lithosphere. Action constitutes the very domain of management and planning. Thus, action is comfortably spoken of in the exploitation of natural resources or government response to an actual disaster. The utilitarian assumptions of the dominant view cannot, however, contemplate human action as leading to destruction, to the collapse of institutions or dis-organisation of the space economy. Materialism assumes that human activity derives from self-interest' whose first rule is 'survival' or at least belongs to an underlying principle of adaptation. An activity that directly invites catastrophe would not be wilfully put in place, except, 'by accident'. To orchestrate devastation in a rational, materialist world is to be criminal or mad. War for some people is an exception, the domain of human action par excellence. Beyond that however, to argue that organised activities create disaster has been in a sense outlawed from rational discourse. It is portrayed as possible only by invoking 'conspiracy theories', and conspiracies again are supposed to be practiced by criminals and imagined by the paranoid. I would just note here that a great deal of evidence from

recent famines, earthquake or typhoon damages gives
the lie to the idea that 'Acts of Man' do not bear a
large responsibility for modern disasters, although it
is hardly necessary to talk of actual conspiracies to
make them happen.

It is also worth pausing to note how great is the
assurance of proponents of the dominant view not merely
of its superiority, but that it has totally discredited
the views that have prevailed in the past. The latter
are generally labelled as religious, cosmological,
magical or fatalistic. They are views that do not find
the source or explanation of calamity to lie in an
inherent potentiality of brute matter or its physical
processes. They generally appear to us to depend upon
non-material, magical and ethical imagery or direct
human agency to interpret disaster (see Eliade, 1954,
Chapter 3; Blum and Blum, 1963; Tuan, 1980). 'God' is
invoked, but rarely as an arbitrary actor with respect
to man. Even when speaking of divine wrath as the
immediate source of destruction, past societies invariably attribute this, in turn, to human responsibility.
This may be expressed as competition between religio-magical communities and the strength of their divine
sponsors or their faith. More often, calamities are
ascribed to the workings of a moral calculus in human
affairs. The ethical and societal aspects of human
behaviour are central. In the West and Islamic lands
until recently, the dominant view had been essentially
that represented by the Old Testament prophets. For
them, the message behind calamity or its threat is a
people become immoral, idolatrous or vain (Heschel,
1962, Chapter 9; Scott, 1968, Chapter 6).

I need hardly review the sorts of developments
that lead us to neglect and demean this enormous part
of the human experience. Even sympathetic studies tend
to present it as, at best, archaic. This entire cultural
past is laid aside as a tissue of what John Brill calls
"... original, childlike and primitive concepts ..."
(1965, p. 6). And the further removed historically or
geographically is a society from urban-industrialism,
the more usual it is for studies of disaster to find
its people 'fatalistic', 'subjective', and in the thrall
of 'mystical', 'arational' or at least 'pre-scientific'
notions (e.g. Kates, 1971: c.f. Torry, 1978). But it
is also an article of faith in the dominant view that,
by a sort of reverse logic, the further removed people
are from urban-industrialism and its technocratic forms,
the more completely they are at the mercy of an elementary biophysical struggle with the habitat. Part of the
justification for the technocratic monolgue is, of
course, that the vast majority of these societies seem
not to have the faintest idea of their thoroughly
Malthusian condition and the natural selection that
arbitrates it! Necessarily therefore, the technocrat

may presume to speak <u>for</u> these people, but can find little value in dialogue <u>with</u> them or learning from them. The parallel with the "professional imperialism" that Midgley finds in the international social work scene is compelling (Midgley, 1981).

The dominant view then, belongs to an historically special culture that seeks to interpret the world through its underpinnings in material phenomena and mechanism. Yet, disaster remains a difficult, perhaps a decisive test of such explanations. It is a delicate problem for the prevailing interpretations of nature and human development and the way they are appropriated by technocratic institutions. These interpretations tend to be uniformitarian, evolutionary, and normative. They articulate with a view of human life as essentially Progressive. Disaster, taken literally, however, suggests revolutionary change. "De l'avenir, l'imprévu accourt, dejouant toutes les prévisions ..." (Dardel, op. cit., p. 53). Flood, famine, pestilence suggest retrogression rather than Progress. Severe degradation of the habitat suggests devolution, even the threat of extinction.

These would not be such problematic questions, but for the recent history of the sciences that has propelled them from the dispassionate realm of natural philosophy into the main street and market places of modern states. The sciences are identified with, and most of their more visible public figures <u>want</u> to be identified with, predicting, controlling and reproducing natural forces at will, rather than merely understanding them. In the process the sciences have become integral to the power and authority of leading institutions.

Disaster interpretations in the past were related to landscapes ascribed to the works of the Almighty, the labour of men's bodies and work of their hands. Today's landscapes evidence the most striking changes through technocratic initiative. In the minds of those who promote and resist such changes, applied science is made firmly responsible for them. If blame for damaging events, the still widespread world of moral rather than material calculation, were to be ascribed to a particular source, then it could very well be turned upon the technocratic ethos. Moreover, when knowledge is mobilised for purposes of control, its failures and limits, especially if they result in human misery and disarray, become a threat not merely to its credibility as knowledge, but also as power.

Surely these are major considerations in the thrust to make natural extremes the cause, and accidents the human framework of disaster? The 'space of the accident' emerges as an expedient if not a "face-saving formula" (c.f. Hawkins, 1964).

THE PROBLEM OF EXPLANATION II: ON REMAINING CALM

Appeal to natural processes as cause is, however, a convenient scientific rationalization too. The processes involved can readily be set within scales of space and time that dwarf them into normalcy. Globally, or over short spans of 'geological time', the conditions in natural disasters come to appear commonplace. Catastrophist notions, - the idea that rare, extremely violent or unique events shape past and future, - have met with solid and apparently secure resistance in the geophysical and biological sciences. Neo-catastrophism, except in events as remote as the "Big Bang", meets with even less favour than Cuvier's ideas. Though their expertise may be applied to sets of extreme events, geophysicists can feel that the extremes are part of measurement continua. Such events as earthquake or volcanic eruption appear, in the end, as part of the inexorable development of the solid earth. The power of scientific thought has derived especially from discovering scales and perspectives where phenomena seem to fall into elegant and parsimonious forms, regardless of how far these scales and perspectives diverge from the compass of everyday human experience.

The pressure to concentrate upon the geophysical conditions in disaster is great when we consider how much more difficult such detachment is from their sociocultural significance. When our concern is with people, the sense of disorder, of 'worlds' threatened if not destroyed; of meaningless and arbitrary death, are less easily dispelled from disaster. Each challenges the belief in coherent development through conservative and lawful processes. Even when dismissed as emotional or subjective, disaster leaves its victims and many other observers feeling their world will never be the same again; that an unprecedented, revolutionary change took place - or ought to have taken place! And catastrophism actually has a strong psychosocial appeal as explanation for the powerless, and victims of great distress. The dominant views of disaster in the past dealt with all of this by firmly locating blame. Calamity was not divided off in its meaning from the rest of life. Whatever the price for material explanations, the destruction was not therefore meaningless or absurd in Camus' sense, as it tends to appear in the physical but accidental universe of the dominant view. It would be naive to imagine the legacy of such ways of thinking does not exert an enormous pressure upon our dominant institutions and the scientific ethos.

While this 'space of the accident' is not the only one where technocratic thought could place natural calamities, and while it has not been the only scientific view, it is a persuasive one for science and technology. It makes of disasters not a 'judgement' but an 'unplanned side-effect'. They become, not a limit but merely a 'frontier' of knowledge. They lie between the tamed and the wild, the controlled and the as yet uncontrolled.

Natural hazards, like disease, poverty, even death, become simply the unfinished business of our endeavours. We can then focus daunting technical equipment and expertise upon tasks technocracy understands: forecasting physical conditions; ever more complete containment of natural processes; educating government and the public; devising general, centrally controlled systems to protect those at risk, to zone 'high hazard' areas; redesigning installations and, if all else fails, organising relief on a grand scale. The hierarchy of expertise is thus preserved. The wealthiest, best equipped institutions can help and lead the less sophisticated or fortunate. Of course, whatever else may be done, there is no place for any sort of 'grass roots' input; no way for any but the 'experts' to break into the technical monologue. A 'citadel of expertise' has indeed been created here (c.f. Roszak, 1973).

UNCERTAINTY AND PREDICTION

We have been discussing this 'citadel', as it were, from the outside looking in. We have asked about the interface between society and science, as it influences the kinds of questions we are obliged to consider and the sorts of answers that will satisfy us. But these are considerations often far removed from the everyday preoccupations of science and technology. Few scientists would feel commitment to the dominant view were it not also informed with logical and technical features of some sophistication and intrinsic interest. This, from the inside looking out, comes first. That it touches base in plausible ways with human need, managerial concerns and the politics of support for scientific activity is, for most of us, someone else's work.

The scientific ingredient that most helps to maintain the dominant view is the thoroughly respectable notion of <u>Uncertainty</u> and related ideas. Uncertainty is the umbilical chord that grounds the otherwise gratuitous notion of the accident, the separate assessment of 'extremes', in a challenging and refined language. Elsewhere this ground involves the very frontiers of physical science. And it is a form of reasoning that has done more than anything else to transform social science, environmental science and most applications of scientific work in recent decades; namely through the use of statistical techniques and inference. Universally, the literature states that the fundamental problem with hazards, the ultimate reason why disasters occur, is that people have little or no way of telling when, where or to whom they may happen. The uncertainty thus identified is not just intrinsically important. It is used to specify what is and is not likely to improve our grasp of the problem. And it provides scientific credibility for the treatment of natural disasters as 'accidents'.

Uncertainty then, in the form of probabilistic reasoning about threatening natural processes and the occasions of major damages, defines the technical logic and challenge of the dominant view. Herein lies its concern with measurement of natural extremes, stochastic forecasting models and actuarial types of risk assessment. We are led to flirt with the fashionable spin-off of the enormous statistics and probability industry. Examples exploited by geographers include aspects of The Theory Games, Bayesian Decision-making, and various cognitive models designed to deal with uncertainty or imprecision in the 'perception of hazard'. The idea of 'bounded rationality' is an example currently in vogue (Gould, 1963; Critchley, 1976; Gibson, 1976; Kates, 1978; Burton et. al., 1979; Whyte and Burton, op. cit.).

Statisticians, whose job it is to recognise the basic nature of the data with which a field works, have been serving all areas of geophysical risk research through similar styles of analysis and probability models. The widespread application of 'extreme value statistics' is a case in point (Gumbel, 1958). A statistician has described what is at issue in seismic risk, for instance (Vere-Jones, 1973). He recognises three categories of risk: 'geophysical risk' meaning the probability of an earthquake of a given magnitude in a given location; 'engineering risk', the probability that a given structure will fail; and, third, 'insurance risk' meaning the probability that clients will make claims against a given policy. This nicely catches the flavour of hazards research as a concern with rare stochastically governed events. It also defines how they are 'accidents' in a seemingly rational sense.

The realm of accidents has long been a specialty of statisticians (Macguire, et. al., 1952; Haddon et. al., op. cit.; Gibson, op. cit.). There is a substantial body of purely geophysical research that examines large magnitude natural events as separate phenomena, using the same or similar probablility models as in accident research (Hewitt, 1979; Scheidegger, 1975). It shows how the events appear as random or nearly random points in time and space, or separated by 'recurrence intervals' of nearly random length. Evidently, if it is these events that <u>are</u> 'the hazard' a probabilistic definition of the <u>problem</u> seems unavoidable. And if it is true that human societies are unprepared or ill-prepared for these events mainly because of their rare and uncertain occurrence, then predictability has to be the essence of the problem of management. In the end, only improved knowledge of when natural extremes occur; a chipping away at the degrees of uncertainty, emerges as the rational solution. Hence, the colossal commitment to means of improved forecasting.

We need pursue the scientific and technical basis of this reasoning no further here. Indeed, the logic of using statistical models to describe larger magnitude geophysical events, or sets of disasters is not in question. It is the transference of the logic, the reduction of the interpretation of hazards largely to it, that I would call a face-saving and misleading formula. Impressive as the techniques may be in their home disciplines of statistical hydrology or seismology or in actuarial science, they serve to misrepresent the sources and significances of natural disaster except in very narrow technical contexts. Let me emphasise that the argument is not that uncertainty, in a general sense, has no meaning here. It can reasonably be seen as a major ingredient of these as of most human affairs today. Nor am I denying any value to striving to foresee future developments and risks. The problem is with the way the <u>source</u> of the uncertainties involved is described, <u>the kind</u> of prediction championed, and hence the severance of the interpretation of disaster from the rest of material life through these devices.

THE MYTH OF "ORDINARY LIFE"

Ultimately, the inadequacies of the dominant view arise less from what it says about disaster, than what it chooses to infer about the rest of human activity and its environmental relations. As we have seen, its essential interpretive structure involves treating everyday life and disasters as opposites.

In the dominant view, the on-going conditions that provide the setting for disaster are inferred to be 'stable', 'orderly' and 'predictable', or at least sufficiently so to be called 'managed' and even 'planned'. To employ the language of Burton et. al. (1979) this is the 'human-use-system'. It is typified by patterns of settlement and activity permitting effective and controlled use of natural resources. 'Hazard' arises from the intrusion into this activity of unforeseen, essentially independent natural processes of extreme and rare occurrence. The only on-going manifestation of hazard is incautious settlement on natural features or in zones where those extreme events recur. Thus, the meaning of everyday life is severed from that of disaster. Man's relations to nature are given two modes. One is 'normal, 'secure', <u>productive</u>. The other is 'abnormal', 'insecure' and the occasion of losses. Thus, the dominant view pursues its analyses as though the continuities and discontinuities, the sources of stability and instability in human affairs, are uniquely defined at the times and for the places where damaging extremes suddenly terminate what was assumed to be ordinary life.

Now few things have done more to furbish the imagery of everyday life with the epithets 'normal', 'ordinary', 'scheduled', than the statistical treatment of social and natural conditions. Increasingly, social and environmental scientists work with data of the kinds defined, standardised and gathered by government and other centralised institutions. Of course, statisticians know well that 'normal' social conditions are as much a fiction as the 'average man'. That does not prevent such constructs becoming the cornerstones of technocratic ideas of 'reality' or pivots for their models of it.

Together, these notions of 'normal life' on the one hand and statistical uncertainty of natural extremes on the other strongly bolster the 'accidentalism' of the dominant view. Everyday life appears therefore to affect disaster only fortuitously or by default. Conditions before and outside of the damaging event have no part in it.

Another important ingredient here is the way the type of prediction in the dominant view is of an official, technological and centralised sort. Even when asking about frost in New Guinea, drought in the Sahel, or earthquakes in remote Himalayan valleys, 'prediction' means that sort of forecasting served by the monitoring, data processing and mathematical expression that technocratic agencies provide. Such prediction is, in its turn, modelled from the sort of forecasting required in the day-to-day, clock-time regulation of industrial economies, machine technology and mass institutions. It is associated with those forms of social control peculiar to the productive and institutional forms of urban-industrialism. What appears as uncertainty in <u>that</u> context is taken to hold sway everywhere. Of course, one does not need that sort of forecasting to know that within the lifetime of given persons or social projects, in given areas, the sorts of destructive natural events that concern us are likely to occur, and what is likely to be damaged by them. Meanwhile, with respect to rare, extreme fluctuations on nature, technocratic sorts of prediction encounter the same difficulties and failures as its forecasting of the extreme swings and dislocations of economic and political kinds.

One might begin by pointing to the well-known difficulties of preparing, communicating and getting appropriate responses to technocratic forecasting. Far

more critical, however, is what is implied by making
technical prediction the essence of the problem. What
does it imply about 'ordinary life' and the means to
encompass and defuse hazard within it?

We can begin with Burton et. al.'s (1979, p. 19) view
that hazard arises from the interaction of "... natural
and social systems ...". But suppose for the moment,
we agree there would be no hazard if geophysical events
were wholly predictable? That must surely imply that
all aspects of the natural environment are either predictable or benign <u>except</u> the 'extremes'. Even more
debatable, it implies that <u>human life at all other times
and places is either predictable or irrelevant to our
subject</u>. It also implies that, if prediction of nature
improves, society automatically follows with adjustments
that remove risk to that level. Everyday life thus
comes to appear as a 'frictionless' process, readily
poured into whatever mould technology and the certain-
ties of nature require. It is not difficult to see why
some accuse this approach of a covert environmental
determinism (Waddell, 1977).

This approach also infers that persons and
institutions are uniformly and unambiguously committed
to removing known, manageable risks from everyone's
life, failing to do so only where the risk is highly
uncertain. There is a lot of evidence that human groups
and institutions are less fervent about equity and
social justice than that. In any case, it is an odd
view, given that improved prediction and control of
natural processes has so often had the effect of making
people more careless, acting on a false sense that
'risks from nature' have been dealt with.

Even were human affairs in no way responsible for
disaster or its forms, except by default, these assumptions about predictability would be debatable. Moreover, they lead us swiftly from the complex realm of
human ecology, to the inner sanctum of that 'new,
illiberal practicality' that C. Wright Mills described
as characteristic of this sort of technocratic, applied
science (op. cit.). Specifically it leads to that
dangerous transfer of the notion of 'predictability'
as a feature of scientific method, to the partial and
scientistic notion of <u>predicting</u> <u>society</u>, which is
tantamount to controlling it. This is not the stuff
of scientific enquiry but technocratic wishful thinking:
a rhetoric that sees society as running smoothly only
when fully predicted and managed by its 'experts'.

Moreover, what of that other, even larger body of
thought and literature, much of it also technocratic,
that describes <u>everyday life</u> in the Twentieth Century
as something <u>extraordinary?</u> Technological innovation
and risks, 'future shock' and unprecedented human
powers are some of the main stresses said to be involved. From that perspective it is natural disasters that

are in some ways 'ordinary', the age-old scourges of
civil societies signifying a kind of continuity in
human experience and predicaments. Here one might
explore Robert W. Kates' suggestion that, after all,
perhaps risk or hazard is conserved, merely being
shifted around by socio-economic change.

In such terms, the prevailing interpretation of
disasters described above takes on the quality of myth.
Of course, in a socio-cultural framework that is not
the condemnation it may appear. Careful examination
of the mythologies of the past shows them to express
and have been grounded in definite psychosocial contexts and predicaments. They are important evidence
of the way knowledge is a social construct. However
we usually call an example 'myth' when its relevance
has gone or it appears anachronistic in the context
being discussed. The dominant view of hazards is myth
in that sense too.

In the past, most myths actually reflected the
views and problems of particular classes or activities;
of Princes or Priests, farming or childbirth. I have
described the dominant view of hazards as such a
limited and partial perspective of technocracy. Nevertheless, mythologies are generally grounded in a Cosmic
or Genesis-type of myth that supposedly gives the
others overall coherence. The dominant view of hazards
also masquerades as though it were the equivalent of a
Cosmic myth, subsuming all other approaches in an objective and fundamental ground.

One does not readily or lightly abandon a dominant
view, whether myth, theory, paradigm or "academic-
research consensus". This is not accomplished on mere
grounds of logic or demonstration (c.f. Kuhn, 1962;
Polanyi, 1958; Chapter 1). Such procedures may help
the scholar to modify a view or convince those involved
to modify it. Geographers and other social scientists
have been trying to do that in the hazards field for
several decades. Indeed, I think the dominant view of
hazards has arisen out of sufficiently rich founding
statements by scientists to embrace all but the most
radical proposals. But, as Whitehead said of "the
philosophy of organism", these rich grounds are lost in
aspects that "... subsequent systematizations have put
aside" (1929, p. v). For instance, as the hazards work
of geographers has been gradually absorbed into the
dominant view, the rich possibilities deriving from the
ideas of human ecology and geographic diversity have
also been lost.

ALTERNATIVE VIEWPOINTS

In contrast to the three features of the dominant
view singled out earlier, it seems to me that a social
science perspective should recognise:-

i) The important degree to which natural hazard is <u>not</u> explained by, nor uniquely dependent upon the geophysical processes that may initiate damage;

ii) The important degree to which human awareness of and responses to natural hazards are <u>not</u> dependent upon the geophysical conditions, whether their mechanisms, frequency or past experience of them. Rather hazard is seen to depend more upon concerns, pressures, goals, risks and, above all, orchestrated social changes that are tangential to, if not wholly indifferent to the particular society-environment relations where disaster has occurred. Perhaps more crucial still, effective or ineffective means to avoid or reduce risk are found to depend upon the on-going organisation and values of society and its institutions.

iii) the important extent to which natural disaster, its causes, internal features and consequences are <u>not</u> explained by conditions or behaviour peculiar to calamitous events. Rather they are seen to depend upon the on-going social order, its everyday relations to the habitat and the larger historical circumstances that shape or frustrate these matters.

These emphases do not arise from trivial or minor aspects of hazards and their human contexts. If they have validity, it has a profound bearing not just on the kind of social and environmental understanding geographers or anthropologists might contribute; but the general significance to be placed upon these problems.

In isolation, of course, in the absence of the dominant view described, our emphases would also create an unbalanced view. It would be absurd to suggest that events associated with flood or earthquake in no way reflect the nature of these geophysical processes. It would be indefensible to argue that the disruptions occasioned by disaster produce no distinctive, even unique crisis phenomena. And there are a number of important aspects of hazard that can be helped by improved geophysical forecasting. Nor are any foreseeable human actions going to remove the need to bring outside emergency assistance to ill-equipped victims of natural calamities.

However, the burden of what we find happening in recent disasters and their societal preconditions requires the social scientist to consider seriously whether the dominant view has not got the whole problem

of disaster back-to-front. My own view, and the one I
see supported in an increasing number of case studies
is that:-

i) Most natural disasters or most damages in
them, are <u>characteristic</u> rather than accidental features of the places and societies where
they occur.

ii) The risks, pressures, uncertainties that bear
upon awareness of, and preparedness for
natural fluctuations actually flow mainly
from what is called 'ordinary life', rather
than the rareness and scale of those
fluctuations.

iii) The natural extremes involved are, in a human
ecological sense, more expected and knowable
than many of the contemporary social developments that pervade everyday life.

There is a good deal of evidence that the settings
where recent disasters have occurred, are suffering
extraordinary socio-cultural change and environmental
impacts in an on-going way (e.g. Hewitt, 1976, 1977,
1978, 1982, 1983a, 1983b, 1984).
Are these transformations, in and due to social
circumstances, more manageable, expected, or certain
for the victims of disaster than natural extremes?
What is more characteristic of the Sahel and to
be expected by its long-time inhabitants; recurrent
droughts or the recent history of political, economic
and social change? What are more certain along the
San Andreas Fault, occasional large earthquakes, or
the sprawling developments of its so-called, 'post-
industrial' society?
A careful look at a century or two of history in
the 'hazard prone' regions of today, generally shows
the sorts of geophysical processes associated with
disaster to be entirely likely even inevitable. In
any sizeable group of inhabitants there are those who
know the processes have occurred and can occur again.
However, I am using certainty and uncertainty here in
a broad biosocial sense, in terms of cultural reproduction, rather than the technological prediction discussed
above. In most places and segments of society where
disasters are reported, the natural events are about as
certain as anything within a person's lifetime, or at
least that of himself, his children and grandchildren.
One of the few real <u>advantages</u> we have with these risks
is that the large task of being ready for them can be
accomplished incrementally, <u>because</u> they are relatively
rare events! Or should a sane social order disregard
the likelihood of massive destruction, simply because

it is not quite sure on which day of which year in the next decade or two, it will occur? Is it, as Brecht's Philosopher suggests:

> ... because people know so little about themselves that their knowledge of nature is so little use to them. (They) can cope with earthquakes, but not with their fellows.
> (Brecht, 1965, p. 31)

In hazards research, at least by social scientists, even for earthquakes it is our 'fellows' with whom we are required to cope first, and earthquake processes second. That is to say, the risks have to do with the economics of housing and real estate; the location of employment and services; the availability of insurance; the development of land or zoning and building codes, and, over all these, the distribution of wealth, power and choice in a society and between societies. Here again one must resist a technocratic fiction.

Are people unaware and poorly prepared because natural extremes are rare and unpredictable? Are they indifferent to the possibility of flood or earthquake because preoccupied with "present gratifications"? Or is it because the everyday conditions of work, life support, social and mental security, or the artificial environment require all of their risk-avoiding and risk-taking energies? Do 'laymen' appear 'poorly adapted' because the socially narrowed world of technocratic or academic specialists leave us incapable of recognising the realities with which other persons and groups must deal?

Surely, in the urban-industrial, commercial societies for which the dominant view is tailored, most people simply have not the time or means to prepare for and recover from natural disaster. It has become as difficult for individuals and families to set aside time, resources and worry to guarding against these things as to care for their aged parents, the chronically sick, the handicapped, mentally deranged, the unemployed, and all the other 'abnormal' and, especially, 'un-productive' elements of the human condition.

Moreover, one of the characteristic impacts of modernisation is to weaken and eventually destroy the traditional arrangements whereby extended family, village, 'tribe', reciprocal duties of lord and people, absorbed and dealt with such problems. This is surely a major aspect of the process that puts the poverty-stricken; the beggars, orphans, amputees, victims of famine and flood on the streets of cities in 'developing countries' as it did in Europe and North America until 'institutions' were created to hide them in. Such social developments flow from that most fundamental of all geographical and human ecological processes of modernisation, <u>alienation from the land.</u> And therefore, from nature and the 'man-environment relations' that must develop to deal with natural extremes. These developments are integral to the unavoidable vulnerability of 'ordinary' folk to natural calamity; to the futility of their developing a sophisticated knowledge of the risks even if they had the leisure for it, and, in the end, to the responsibility that indeed rests firmly upon centralised, technocratic institutions and hazards research.

There are natural forces and some damages in most disasters that lie beyond all reasonable measures any society could make to avoid them. What I believe to be definitive of the disasters I have examined is, however, that most of them would not be disasters, and many of the damages would not, indeed <u>do not</u> occur except as a direct result of characteristic and vulnerable human developments. These developments record mainly the mismatch between the requirements of sensitive, secure environmental relations at the local or regional levels, - more exactly in certain segments of society and activity at these levels, - and the demands of those extensive geographies of power and economy that technocratic strategies have grown up with, and mainly serve.

In order to explore that, the range of phenomena that form the mainstream of the social sciences becomes of direct interest. The common concerns and competence of human geography, human ecology and anthropology are of intrinsic interest to the understanding of hazard, rather than fortuitous matters arising only, and in special ways, when there is the impact of natural extremes or their threat. If society in its everyday and on-going development is integral to 'risks from nature', then questions of social order become central matters of research and discussion. The exercise of political and economic power appear basic to vulnerability, to the management and the redistribution of risk by institutional means. However, if social scientists treat these matters in terms of 'impersonal, objective' forces, of natural extremes and crisis responses, their social science itself must become a major part of the problem, for it hides much that is of the greatest social significance in hazards.

There are also serious implications for the evaluation of crisis management too. The dominant view serves to justify the channelling of a disproportionate share of resources and expertise into projects that are only indirectly or not at all concerned with the human misfortunes involved. Whatever its intrinsic interest, the enormous commitment to geophysical monitoring and prediction deals with a peripheral rather than a central ingredient of disaster. The dominant view also supports forms of official response to disaster that are often guaranteed to see that those whose need is greatest will be heard, understood and helped the least. Relief and reconstruction are often disproportionately focussed upon restoring, and more than restoring the infrastructural arrangements of the more powerful institutions of the economy, the state and international system, rather than direct responses to the needs of victims. This is particularly evident in the internal and foreign aid components of disaster response in the so-called Third World.

Nevertheless, any attempt to actually abandon technocratic approaches may be doomed to failure. Apart from the fact that the dominant institutions and allocations of resources are largely technocratic in character, the problems we have to deal with have grown and require or are forced to require these institutions. Most contemporary scholarship is also more or less powerfully influenced by technocratic ways of working. They might even be subsumed under a technocratic framework, - if it were not of the sort described above. Most of us utilise the same sorts of data and methods found in the dominant view. However, the perspectives brought to bear and the evidence that influences us most do not square with the dominant view. We need a new consensus. That consensus is unlikely to do much about the grosser misconceptions of the dominant view or to be intellectually honest and scientific unless enquiry is much more independent of the pressures and interests of technocratic institutions. It is also unlikely to improve matters unless, in due course, it can influence these institutions at least to adopt frames of reference, more aware of their own serious limitations in face of these problems, and of the on-going predicaments of those who most often suffer disaster and are least equipped to deal with it.

Of singular importance for geographers and anthropologists is the sense in which the dominant view is unashamedly indifferent to history and to human and environmental diversity; the way it becomes more abstracted and irrelevant to human predicaments the farther removed they are from urban-industrial centers and processes. When looking at hazards in a cross-cultural context, and disasters in non-Western, non-industrial contexts one begins to have the suspicion that the authority of the dominant view derives from much the same source as Said (1978) sees in the European view of "The Orient". It involves an invented geographical vision that is powerful:-

> ... a) because a white (sic.) specialist with highly refined scientific techniques could do the sifting and restructuring, and b) because a vocabulary of sweeping generalitiies ...

> referred not to a set of fictions but rather
> ... (in classical empiricist terms) ... to a
> whole array of seemingly objective and agreed
> upon distinctions ...   (p. 233)

CONCLUDING REMARKS

To summarise, I find much that is fascinating and useful in work that falls within the dominant view. In criticising it, I have criticised most of my own past work which largely pursued the dominant perspective. Yet, I believe that this perspective which natural disasters research is in the grip of, is the single greatest impediment to improvement in its quality and effectiveness. The perspective functions as though 'objective', 'general' and rigorous, but its rigor and generality are achieved through an extreme, opportunistic narrowing of interpretation and empirical interest. This involves a covert environmental determinism and the language of the accident. Yet it serves to conceal both a particular <u>metaphysic of enquiry</u> and <u>politics of management</u>. The former involves the face-saving formula of a 'natural sciences' style of analysis. The latter relies on a sort of <u>habeas corpus</u>, whereby disaster is appropriated and severed from its roots in the rest of material life. Behind that is a view of management whose obsession is with 'normality' in the productive functions of society. Moreover, technocratic thought never for a moment pauses to question how, or even if, those functions require and depend upon a centrally planned socio-economic order, or whether that is always or necessarily more sophisticated. Hence, to that order goes precedence in the treatment of disaster. The point is most obvious in so-called Third World 'peripheral' areas (c.f. Waddell, 1975; Tiranti, 1977; Torry, 1978; Hall, 1983; Watts, 1983). Discussions of the Irish 'Potato famine' reminds us too that there is a certain structural recurrence in these relationships of development, dependency and centralised power (Woodham, Smith, 1962; Gibbon, 1975; Regan, 1983). But the obtuseness of the dominant view is no less evident in the socio-economic ramifications of natural hazards in the so-called First World, the 'affluent' or central states (Erikson, 1976; Stern, 1976; Jackson and Mukerjee, 1974).

In sum, the geophysicalism of the dominant view is hidden within the assumptions that natural calamity is essentially the break-down of the productive functions of society, and, as crisis, essentially an infringement upon the centralised ordering of space, - or, in remoter areas, an indicator of what happens when you lack the benefits of this order. The restoration of productivity and reimposing of 'normal' relations become the main prescriptions of crisis management, relief and reconstruction. The ability to predict or contain natural processes in a technocratic framework become the main goals for disaster prevention. Now, I question whether this recognises some major, often the major ingredients of disaster. Because it fails to do so I think it fails to effectively deal with hazards problems. In particular, it fails to recognise how the roots and occurrence of contemporary disasters depend upon the way "... normal everyday life turns out to have become abnormal, in a way that affects us all (Brecht, op. cit.). A significant and recurring result, from the environs of the San Andreas Fault, to the Sahel is that what is best for dominant view is often far from best for the victims of disaster. Meanwhile, the continuing burden and changing forms of damage from natural processes create a growing sense that the very expensive research and management strategies supported by the dominant view become more and more like King Canute commanding the waves.

ACKNOWLEDGMENTS

This is a slightly modified version of Hewitt, (1983a). I wish to thank, in particular Ian Burton, Jerry Hall, Lynn May and George Morren, Jr. for their comments and suggestions concerning earlier versions of this. I want to thank Jo-Anne Horton for careful preparation of the manuscript.

REFERENCES

Albrow, M. 1970. Bureaucracy. New York: Macmillan.
Ang, A. H-S. 1978. US-Southeast Asia Symposium on Engineering for Natural Hazards Protection. Rep. Nat. Sci. Foundation Univ. Illinois, Urbana.
Arendt, H. 1958. The human condition. Chicago: University of Chicago Press.
Armytage, W.H.G. 1965. The rise of the technocrats: a social history. London: Routledge & Kegan Paul.
Ayre, R.S. 1975. Earthquake and tsunami hazards in the United States: a research assessment. Inst. Behavioural Science, Univ. Boulder, Colorado.
Baker, G.W. and D.W. Chapman (eds.) 1962. Man and society in disaster. New York: Basic Books.
Barton, A.H. 1969. Communities in disaster: a sociological analysis of collective stress situations. New York: Doubleday.
Berger, P. and T. Luckmann 1967. The social construction of reality. Garden City: Doubleday.
Berlin, G.L. 1980. Earthquakes and the urban environment. Boca Raton, Florida: CRC Press.
Blum, R. and E. Blum 1963. The dangerous hour: the lore and culture of crisis and mystery in rural Greece. London: Chatto & Windus.
Bolt, B.A. 1978. Earthquakes: a primer. San Francisco: W.H. Freeman.
Brecht, B. 1965. The Messingkauf dialogues, (transl. J. Willet). London: Methuen.
Brictson, R.C. (ed.) 1966. Symposium on emergency operations. System Dev. Corp. Santa Monica, California.
Brill, J. 1956. The chance character of human existence. New York: Philosophical Library.
Burton, I. and K. Hewitt 1974. Ecological dimensions of environmental hazards. In Human ecology. F. Sargeant (ed.), II, 253-84. Amsterdam: North-Holland.
Burton, I., R.W. Kates and G.F. White 1978. The environment as hazard. New York: Oxford University Press.
Cooper, D. 1978. The language of madness. Harmondsworth: Penguin.
Copans, J. (ed.) 1975. Sécheresses et famines du Sahel. Paris: Maspero.
Curry, L. 1964. The random spatial economy: an exploration in settlement theory. Ann. Assoc. Am. Geogs 54, 138-46.
Dardel, E. 1946. L'Histoire: science du concret. Presses Universitaires de France, Paris, 139 p.
Disaster Research Group 1961. Field studies of disaster behaviour. National Academy of Sciences-National Research Council, Washington, D.C.

Dynes, R.R. and E. L. Quarantelli 1968. Group behaviour under stress. Society and Social Research 52, 416-29.
Eijkman, P.H. 1911. L'internationalisme scientifique. The Hague: W.P. van Stockum.
Eliade, M. 1954. Cosmos and history: the myth of the eternal return. (transl.W.R.Trask). New York:Harper.
Erikson, K.T. 1976. Everything in its path: Destruction of community in the Buffalo Creek Flood. New York: Simon and Schuster, 363 p.
Foster, H. 1980. Disaster planning: the preservation of life and property. New York: Springer-Verlag, 275 p.
Foucault, M. 1965. Madness and civilisation, (transl. R. Howard). New York: Mentor Books.
Foucault, M. 1977. Discipline and punish: the birth of prison, (transl. Alan Sheredan). New York: Random House, 333 p.
Geipel, P. 1982. Disaster and Reconstruction. George Allen and Unwin, London, 202 p.
Geographisches Rundschau 1985. Naturrisiken, (Special Issue), v. 37, no. 2. Kiel: Westermann.
Gerasimov, I.P. and T.V. Zvonkova 1974. Natural hazards in the territory of the USSR: study, control and warning. In White (1974, pp. 243-53).
Gibson, S.B. 1976. The use of quantitative risk criteria in hazard analysis. J. Occup. Accidents 1, 85-94.
Gould, P.R. 1963. Man against his environment: a game theoretic framework. Ann. Assoc. Am. Geogs 53. 290-7.
Grayson, P.K. and P. Sheets (eds.) 1979. Volcanic activity and human ecology. New York: Academic Press.
Grosser, G.H., H. Wechsler and M. Greenblatt (eds.) 1964. The threat of impending disaster: contributions to the psychology of stress. Cambridge, Mass.: M.I.T. Press.
Gumbel, E.J. 1958. Statistics of extremes. New York: Columbia University Press.
Habermas, J. 1973. Theory and practice, (transl. J. Viertel). New York: Beacon Press.
Haas, J.E. and R.S. Ayre 1969. The western Sicily earthquake of 1968. Washington, D.C.: National Academy of Sciences.
Haas, J.E., R.W. Kates and M.J. Bowden (eds.) 1977. Reconstruction following disaster. Cambridge, Mas.: M.I.T. Press.
Haddon, W., E.A. Suchman and D. Klein 1964. Accident research: methods and approaches. New York: Harper & Row.

Hawkins, D. 1964. *The language of nature: an essay in philosophy of science*. San Francisco: W.H. Freeman.

Heschel, A.J. 1962. *The prophets: an introduction*. New York: Harper & Row.

Hewitt, K. 1970. Probabilistic approaches to descrete natural events: review and theory. *Econ. Geog.* 46, (2), 332-49.

Hewitt, K. 1976. Earthquake hazards in the mountains. *Natural History* LXXXV. 30-7.

Hewitt, K. 1977. Desertification, development and the 'Admirals' of Manchar Lake, Pakistan. *Economic Geography*, v. 53, no. 6, October, 363 p.

Hewitt, K. 1978. Some dimensions of seismic risk in mountain regions. Chapter One, pp. 12-68 in ed. P.H., D.C. *Society and Environment - The Crisis in the Mountains*, U. of Auckland.

Hewitt, K. 1980. Review: 'the environment as hazard'. *Ann. Assoc. Am. Geogs 70* (2). 306-311.

Hewitt, K. 1982. An interpretation of the geography of earthquake risk: settlement and change in Basal Zone Ecotones, in, *Proceedings of the Third International Conference: the social and economic impacts of earthquakes and planning to mitigate their impacts*, (National Science Foundation - Washington, D.C.), Chapter I, pp. 15-41.

Hewitt, K. 1983a. The idea of disaster in a technocratic age, chapter 1 in ed. Hewitt K. *Interpretations of Calamity*, London: George Allen and Unwin, pp. 3-32.

Hewitt, K. 1983b. Climatic hazards and agricultural development in the Indo-Pakistan subcontinent, Chapter 10 in ed. Hewitt K. *Interpretations of Calamity*, London: George Allen and Unwin.

Hewitt, K. 1983c. Seismic Risk and mountain environments: the role of surface conditions in earthquake disaster, *Mountain Research and Development*. vol. 3, no. 1, pp. 27-44.

Hewitt, K. 1984. Ecotonal settlement and natural hazards of mountain regions. *Mountain Research and Development*, vol. 4, no. 1, pp. 31-77.

Hewitt, K. and I. Burton 1971. *The hazardousness of a place: a regional ecology of damaging events*. Univ. Toronto, Dept. of Geog. Res., Publn. no. 6.

Huntington, E. 1945. *Mainsprings of civilisation*. New York: Wiley.

Jackson, E.L. and Mukherjee, T. 1974. Human adjustment to the earthquake hazard of SanFrancisco, *in* ed. White (1974). pp. 160-166.

Kantarovich, L.V., G.M. Molchan, V.I. Keilis-Borok and E.V. Vilkovich 1970. *A statistical model of the basic seismic effects*, (transl. J. Findlay). Izvestia Earth Physics, no. 5, 85-102.

Kates, R.W. 1971. Natural hazard in human ecological perspective: hypotheses and models. Econ. Geog. 47, 438-51.

Kates, R.W. 1978. Risk assessment and environment hazard. Scientific Committee on Problems of the Environment (SCOPE), Rep. no. 8. Chichester: Wiley.

Kendrick, T.D. 1956. The Lisbon earthquake. London: Methuen.

Kuhn, T. 1962. The structure of scientific revolutions. Chicago: University of Chicago Press.

Lemons, H. 1957. Physical characteristics of disasters: historical and statistical review. Ann. Am. Acad. Pol. and Soc. Sci. 309, January 1-14.

Lifton, R.J. 1970. History and human survival. New York: Random House.

Maguire, B.A., E.S. Pearson and A.H.A. Wynn 1952. The time intervals between industrial accidents. Biometrika 39, 168-80.

Mannheim, K. 1952. Essays on the sociology of knowledge, P. Keskemeti (ed.). London: Routledge & Kegan Paul.

Marx, K. 1964. The economic and philosophical manuscripts of 1844, transl. M. Milligan, D. J. Struik (ed.). New York: International Publishers.

McNeill, W.H. 1976. Plagues and peoples. Garden City, New York: Doubleday.

Midgley, J. 1981. Professional Imperialism. Social work in the Third World. London: Heinemann, 191 p.

Mills, C.W. 1959. The sociological imagination. Oxford: Oxford University Press.

Mitchell, K. 1974. Natural hazards research. In Perspectives on environment, I. Mannors and M. Mikesell (eds.). Commission on College Geography, Assoc. Am. Geogs Publn. 13.

Mumford, L. 1967 and 1970. The myth of the machine. New York: Harcourt, Brace & World.

NAS (National Academy of Sciences, US) 1976. Earthquake prediction and mitigation options for USGS and NSF programs (Newmark report. Washington, D.C.

NAS 1980a. The atmospheric sciences: national objectives for the 1980s. Steering Committee for the Atmos. Res. Rev., Comm. Atmos. Sci.; Ass. Math. Phys. Sci., Nat. Res. Council, Washington, D.C.

NAS 1980b. US Earthquake observations: recommendations for a new national network. Comm. Seismol. Nat. Res. Council, Washington, D.C.

O'Keefe, P., K. Westgate and B. Wisner 1976. Taking the naturalness out of natural disaster, Nature 260, 15 April.

Oliver-Smith, A. 1977. Disaster rehabilitation and social change in Yungay, Peru. Human Organization 36, 5-13.
Polanyi, M. 1958. Personal knowledge: towards a post-critical philosophy. New York: Harper & Row.
Quarantelli, E.L. (ed.). 1978. Disasters: theory and research. London: Sage.
Quarantelli, W.L. and R.R. Dynes 1972. When disaster strikes. Psychology Today 5, 66-70.
Roszak, T. 1973. Where the wasteland ends. Garden City, New York: Doubleday.
Rothman, D.J. 1971. The discovery of the asylum: social order and disorder in the New Republic. Boston: Little, Brown.
Said, E. 1978. Orientalism. New York: Random House.
Scheidegger, E. 1975. Physical aspects of natural catastrophes. New York: Elsevier.
Scott, R.B.Y. 1968. The relevance of the prophets. (revised edn.). New York: Macmillan.
Smith, de W. (ed.) 1957. Disasters and disaster relief. Ann. Am. Acad. Pol. Soc. Sci. 309.
Soloviev, S.L. 1978. Tsunamis. In Unesco (1980, pp. 118-39).
Sorokin, P.A. 1942. Man and society in calamity. New York: Dutton.
Strahler, A.N. and A.H. Strahler 1973. Environmental geoscience: the interaction of natural systems and man. Santa Barbara, California: Hamilton.
Swiss, Re. 1978. Atlas of seismicity and volcanism. Kummerly-Frey, Switzerland: Swiss Reinsurance Company.
Toblin, J. 1977. Disaster prevention and control in the earth sciences. Impact of Science on Society 27, 131-9.
Torry, W.I. 1978. Natural disasters, social structure and change in traditional societies. J. Asian Afr. Studs 13, 167-83.
Tuan, Yi-Fu 1980. Landscapes of fear. New York: Pantheon Books.
Unesco 1980. The assessment and mitigation of earthquake risk. Paris: Unesco.
Vere-Jones, D. 1973. The statistical estimation of earthquake risk. Bull. NZ Soc. Earthquake Engng, September, 122-7.
Waddell, E. 1977. The hazards of scientism: a review article. Human Ecology 5(1), 69-76.
Walford, C. 1878-9. Famines of the world, past and present. New York: Burt Franklin.
Weber, M. 1947. The theory of social and economic organizations. Oxford: Oxford University Press.
White, G.F. 1961. The choice of use in resource management. Natural Resources J., 23-40.
White, G.F. (ed.) 1974. Natural hazards: local, national, global. Oxford: Oxford University Press.

White, G.F. and J.E. Haas 1975. <u>Assessment of research on natural hazards</u>. Cambridge, Mass.: M.I.T. Press.

Whitehead, A.N. 1929. <u>Process and reality: an essay in cosmology</u>. New York: Free Press.

Whyte, A.V. and I. Burton (eds.) 1980. <u>Environmental risk assessment</u>. SCOPE, Report no. 15. Chichester: Wiley.

Working Group on Earthquake Hazards Reduction 1980. <u>Earthquake hazards reduction: isues for an implementation plan</u>. Office of Sci. and Technol. Policy, Executive Office of the President, Washington, D.C.

Yoshino, M.M. (ed.) 1971. <u>The water balance of monsoon Asia</u>. Honolulu: University of Hawaii Press.

13
Summary and Critique: Interdisciplinary Research on People-Resources Relations

John W. Bennett

PROLOGUE

This chapter addresses the papers in this volume as a single body of literature concerned with what may be called "People-Resources relations" (P-R relations). The theoretical positions taken by each author are analyzed and then combined to ascertain what broad patterns of theory and method might be represented. All papers in the volume save one are included in this synthesis: the immediately preceding chapter by Kenneth Hewitt. We excluded this paper partly because it was published first elsewhere and was not an assigned piece; and also because it is cast in a different mode. It is a philosophical critique of how Americans think about certain environmental problems, and is concerned primarily with people rather than with resources. The "disasters" it contemplates are disasters happening to humans, not to Nature.

We shall, however, comment briefly on Hewitt's contribution in this Prologue. Despite its different mood, the paper contains ideas which are echoed in this chapter: an entirely coincidental matter, since I did not read Hewitt's paper until after this chapter had been completed. I believe that most of the papers in the volume would qualify as exemplars of what Hewitt calls the "dominant view" (even though he is speaking of human disasters, not P-R relations). Disasters, of course, might well be considered a specific instance of P-R relations, since they obviously include some sort of interaction between humans and Nature. Hewitt is concerned with the insufficiency of this conception: that our view of disaster considers humans as more or less innocent victims of natural processes which occur unpredictably. In contrast, Hewitt considers disasters as the products of social as well as natural forces, and hence, entirely predictable, if we could face up to our responsibility. Our current expertise seems unable to do this, and therefore lacks a coherent theory of how human needs and greed create vulnerabilities which make people subject to recurrent natural forces (e.g., persistent construction activities on flood plains). This is a mirror image of what we see in the P-R context of this book: that humans "impact" Nature, but without a clear theory of social responsibility for this.

Instead of acknowledgment of the social factors involved in disasters, Hewitt perceives an emphasis on technological correctives or protection. This, in turn, requires bureaucratic organization--including academic disciplines, like those described in this volume--as the vehicles of remedial action. The upshot is a "disaster industry" which affords employment for specialized professionals who produce research which feeds the asocial, technocratic "dominant view." Hewitt might well have added that this same type of research helps to create situations like Minamata, Donora, or Bhopal; i.e., more and better man-made disasters.

Still, as Hewitt (and all of us) point out, we continue to require specialization and expert knowledge. The growing complexity of the socionatural processes demands technical information; this takes disciplines and universities, institutes and knowledge industries. What is needed is some means to make these more responsible to social forces and environmental conservation. Uncertainty and risk, our current conceptual tools for assessing the human element, are almost totally inadequate since these concepts possess no clear theory of social causation or responsibility. Thus we victimize ourselves and Nature in the process.

These issues are echoed in C.P. Wolf's paper on the evolution of social impact analysis (SIA). In the broad sense, I would expect that Hewitt would consider SIA to be part of the disaster industry and to be created by the same mechanisms that create the illusion that our troubles with Nature are largely unforeseen catastrophes. However, Wolf clearly acknowledges the "institutional" nature of our engagement with natural forces, and echoes Hewitt's point (though indirectly) that the entire engagement is located within society, and therefore can only be solved with social means. SIA--or what Wolf broadens into "impact ecology"--is this socially-constituted means of dealing with this socionatural process.

Impact ecology, as Wolf admits, is not about resources, but people. It is the effect on people that counts, and in this element the Wolf analysis is subject to Hewitt's more basic criticism to the effect that so long as we make humans the primary object of concern, Nature is bound to suffer. SIA (or whatever one calls it) is in defense of humans, whereas environmental impact analysis is in defense of Nature. Is "impact ecology" in defense of both? Wolf's general theory, delineated in the early part of the paper appears to include concern for resources (Nature), but the latter half of the paper is preoccupied with people. How do the two fit together? In this ambiguity we find a fundamental contradiction of the environmental movement and its offshoots: no clear alternative to human-centered values has emerged, only eloquent verbal advocacy of such values, voluntary social action, and some regulatory administration in defense of resources. The great change of heart has not yet taken place, at least not on a civilizational basis, and the institutionalization of concern evinces stronger values for human troubles than for Nature.

What, then, are Hewitt's and Wolf's papers doing in this book, which is primarily concerned about physical resources and not humans as victims? The answer is implied: first, because there is no clear-cut, generally accepted value position which holds that humans may be sacrificed in defense of Nature. Second, because we know that in higher levels of theory, humans are also resources, and are also part of Nature. At this point we enter murky waters; the philosophical issues are beyond the scope of this volume.

Wolf does the present writer the honor of citing several of his writings on ecological matters, but I believe he misses two central points of these, namely that (1) humans do to Nature what they do to each other; i.e., they treat Nature with the same thoughtlessness that they treat fellow humans; and (2) that if a better balance is to be created in human-Nature relationships, it will require a change of values and a commitment to the Earth at least as strong as a commitment to human gratification (Bennett 1976; 1980). A third key point of the writer's is acknowledged by Wolf; namely, that human ecology is rooted in human behavior (Bennett 1980), although as noted previously, he phrases it as "institutionalization." However, since the concern in SIA work is inherently one-sided, there is no way for it to establish a socionatural interactive framework, either as a practical routine or as a research and theoretical protocol. But at least Wolf has it in mind.

We may now turn to a brief introduction to our main task: a review of the substantive papers relating to academic disciplines and interdisciplines.

INTRODUCTION

We proceeded as follows: all chapters were read carefully, and categories of analysis were established. These formed the basis for a tabulation of views and concepts. The chapters were considered to be specimens of general dialogue, not as individual productions to be criticized or defended in their own right. If the individual chapters are cited as emblematic of particular views, it is in the typological sense; we do not hold the authors personally responsible for any deficiencies--or accomplishments--described. This is necessary for the following reason:

The original concept of the AAAS symposium featured disciplines as the basis of the presentations. That is, the presenters were selected by the editors because of their contributions to the general problem, and were asked to report on what their discipline, or field of study and endeavor, had to do with the People-Resources issues. They were not asked to construct their own multi-disciplinary or synthetic positions (although a few did anyway). Consequently, we can hardly hold them responsible for deficiencies which may be traceable to the parochialism of particular approaches. Moreover, everyone is to some extent the prisoner of the institutional system of universities, government bureaus, and other molders of our patterns of social and intellectual action. As Fred Buttel pointed out in a perceptive letter to the writer after reading the first draft of this chapter, nearly every participant in the symposium is known as a broad-gauge scholar and analyst who transcends the conventional limits of his or her own fields. At the same time, Buttel noted, these people are also known as excellent specialists in their own disciplines. Since the 1960's, activity in the social sciences and applied fields has become remarkably fluid, even though the university structure remains rigidly oriented around the old-line disciplines. Consequently, to hold disciplines fully responsible for our frustrations in solving the world P-R problem, is to neglect the fact that we would be much worse off if outstanding and flexible disciplinarians had not struck out into uncharted waters.

This may be. However, the writer acknowledges a bias: he is still inclined to emphasize that disciplines do impede a collaborative and imaginative attack on the complex issues of the environment and society for the simple reason that they insist on training students in narrow channels, usually leaving more unorthodox approaches to the student himself, who often pays a high price for maverick behavior. Of course there are other issues: we have not yet found a good or consistent way to train people in specialized expertise cast in some larger "interdisciplinary" framework. Attempts at interdisciplinary programs in "human ecology" have generally failed; universities did not encourage them for the simple reason that the old-line departments opposed them, or quietly sabotaged them.

But once again: we really cannot accuse our writers of the faults of their disciplines or fields since we asked them to use them as the basis for their analysis. Consequently our criticisms in this chapter are rhetorical and not personal.[1]

In the most general sense, the chapters may be considered to represent the basic dilemma of research on large ecological themes: that disciplines or specialized approaches contain only small slices of information derived from very large, complex real-life wholes. Each author, in his own way, notes that greater wholes must become the subject matter of the study of people-environment relations, yet each author is constrained to approach the problems with concepts and rhetoric from his own domain (or, as in the case of Meadows and Wolf, to have to depend on these domains for data). This may be put another way: that the overall impression given by these chapters is the very considerable ignorance our collective scholarly effort has of the overall complex system of human use of the environment--an ignorance which each author, whether directly or by implication, has commented on. Again the dilemma: while everyone recognizes holistic ignorance, it is the very disciplinary traditions of parochial scholarship which create this ignorance--or at least make it difficult to dispel it.

We are indebted to the Glantz/Orlovsky chapter for providing an example of the confusion resulting from segregated disciplinary attack on a large and complex P-R problem: desertification. The authors mention "more than one hundred definitions" of desertification, each of these derived from different special interests and disciplines: climate, human factors, animals, soils, natural vegetation, range management and so on. Moreover, the concept is fraught with values: some believe the U.S., for example, has no "desertification" since this is a Third World phenomenon, caused by primitive resource practices. In the face of such fragmentation, Glantz/Orlovsky nevertheless seem optimistic: "there are many activities that contribute to an increase in our knowledge and understanding of the phenomenon known as desertification."

So the issue is typical: on the one hand, a buzz word, "desertification," drifts through the scientific fraternity, with each local chapter defining it to suit its particular expertise. Then literary attempts at synthesis are made, in order to straighten out the apparent confusion and contradiction. Practical remedial measures are established, but these are usually limited to particular disciplinary definitions, depending on the persons selected to head up the effort. These fail, or have limited effect. Work then proceeds on other factors, experimenting with different definitions and outcomes. Meanwhile the physical process continues without letup since the forces causing the degradation are essentially institutional; i.e., economic and political--whereas the "definitions" generally relate to specific physical effects, technologies, or special local manifestations. However, because some effort is apparently being made to do something about it, optimistic and hopeful pronouncements begin to appear in the professional literature.

The original symposium featured the idea of world resources; that is, how disciplines view the relationships of humans to the global environment. All the authors are certainly aware that the problems are global, but there is no serious attempt to deal with the world context in some general theoretical sense. Mention is made in Dahlberg's chapter of the "world systems" approaches of Wallerstein, Braudel, and others, but no author has attempted to explore the possible relevance of such weltgeschichtliche approaches to the global ecological problem. (This is a curious omission; we shall comment on it later.) Bromley/Szarleta, the economists, do comment on different systems of resource management as a cross-cultural problem, but neither they nor Moran, the anthropologist, specify possible ways and means this might be adequately researched, or how the resulting knowledge can be put to use. Buttel, the sociologist, introduces material related to Third World issues in his discussions of the Green Revolution and other aspects of resource development in Latin America; Moran describes the situation in Amazonia; and Meadows is certainly addressing herself to the world food problem. But again, how can such knowledge be integrated and used to construct a general theory, based on solid empirical evidence, of people-environment relations on a global basis? All we have are the disciplinary approaches--yet these are specialized by topic, method, and theory. They are also very much a product of English-language thought patterns.

The original symposium also featured the term, "resources"--rather than "environment." This, too, probably constrained the authors, although not all undertake to define "resources." Resources presuppose human intentions, purposes, and transformation of physical substances. A science of people-resources relations is different from one of people-environment relations. The environment has, in most human history up to now, been viewed as a reservoir of raw materials--resources--for serving human ends, and only in tribal societies, with their limited population base, have such views coincided with conservationist strategies, or at least, minimal pressure on Nature. (However, there is little or no evidence in the ethnological record that any group of humans ever consciously and conscientiously sought to husband resources.[2] Most such instances refer instead to values or rituals which rationalize or validate existing minimal usage due to lack of population pres-

sure. Modest needs beget modest ideologies; it is a kind
of "low-level equilibrium trap" and humans have shown
little tolerance of it in the long haul.)
 Consequently, the authors present a generally
accepting--though critical--view of human use of the
environment. That is, the existence of human purpose
and need-want-satisfaction is taken as a given, and the
problem, then, becomes one of <u>restraining</u> these purposes, wants, and needs. As noted earlier, conservationist world views, the attitude of humility, and kindred values concerning a more modest posture <u>vis-a-vis</u>
the environment are not discussed. We believe this to
be revelatory of more than the constraints of the
assignment: the era of the idealistic Environmental
Movement is over (for the time being); the contemporary
mood is one of "management of the environment," or
"regulation of use"--not of transformations in the
nature and meaning of human activities. Where values
are mentioned, they usually refer to a causative element
in a theory of human institutional use of resources, and
their <u>substance</u> is not explored; that is, the question
of what <u>kinds</u> of value formations may be appropriate to
particular patterns of human action. Science cannot
solve problems which are matters of mind and spirit.

THEORETICAL CONSENSUS

 The general topic and focus of the book is on the
People-Resources Relationship, or "P-R relations." This
implies that the authors were asked to address themselves not to the "natural environment" in its pristine
or untransformed sense, but to the already-transformed
environment, or "resources." Still, the impact on
resources is, ultimately, an impact on Nature, so the
approaches merge in the long run. By and large, as we
shall see, the effort is concerned with <u>physical</u>
resources. Several chapters do note that social phenomena or states of being may also be considered to be
resources, but no paper developed this theme and none
attempt to treat social phenomena as a "natural" phenomenon to which humans respond. Instead, social phenomena
are viewed as causative or active elements, transforming
and impacting physical Nature. We shall examine the
issue at greater length later in the chapter.
 Now for some specific areas of theoretical consensus among the papers:
 1. <u>Social institutions, or sets of rules governing
human behavior accompanied by values and goals, are the
key factors in the human response to resources and the
physical environment</u>--and, by implication, one might
suppose, to the social process itself. That is, to
paraphrase the title of the paper cited earlier: human

ecology is human behavior (Bennett 1980). This proposition is so obvious that it hardly need be stated; it is, in fact, a standard tautology: human action vis-a-vis the environment is, simply, human action, and not some special "ecology."

2. The concept of system, or at least "holism," is the principal organizing frame for research on P-R relations. Only one author--Buttel--appears to explicitly reject systems approaches: he cites a paper by Andrew Vayda who criticizes systems analysis as productive of sterile and mechanistic analysis. However, Vayda was probably thinking of formal systems analysis, and not a general heuristic usage of the systems model. The stilted excesses of physical systems theorists are not what we need, of course, but we most certainly should explore world-systems theory and research for insights into how the present structure and process of international relations and competition stimulates the abuse of resources and threatens future generations. And an analysis of this largely econocentric world system necessarily partakes of systems theories and methodologies, since they do contain one vital element: a way of showing relationships between disparate phenomena--phenomena that are the specialties of the separate disciplines. Moreover, systems analysis, however pursued, constitutes the one major convergence on theory and method among environmental scientists since the heyday of the environmental movement in the late 1960's. It must be used and refined until we have something better. Social scientists have been especially doubtful about it because when pursued mechanistically, it appears to rule out voluntaristic social behavior. But this is not inevitable.

3. Research on P-R relations must necessarily be an applied science, even though theory is also important. This is nothing more than recognition of the fact that something is wrong somewhere in the relationship of humans to Nature, and that science should take an active role in penetrating the causes. This activist posture is a bequest of the environmental movement; before 1970, it is doubtful if most of the disciplines represented here would have seriously proposed that their main mission was to do something about ecological troubles. Take, for instance, the Bromley/Szarleta chapter, which explicitly proposes to substitute a more realistic and activist model of P-R relations for standard resource economics, which is oriented toward efficient and maximal use of resources to serve economic ends, perhaps especially profit. That is, Bromley/Szarleta seem to be saying that traditional resource economics is part of the problem, not the solution. Meadows takes a related position on systems analysis as applied to food prob-

lems. The point echoes Hewitt's argument, described earlier.

4. Research on P-R relations should move toward studies of broader systems and processes, in place of the dominant pattern of research on particular localized or "micro" cases. At the same time, micro-level studies are not to be discarded, but selected more carefully in relation to their representativeness as components of larger systems. Bromley/Szarleta, Berry/Johnson, and Moran are particularly eloquent on this point, although they use very different rhetoric to make it (more of this later). The issue is related to the mix of theory and application appropriate to the ecological problem: while much theory can be generated from micro-level studies, it may contribute little to the constructive analysis of large systems. An interpretation of causal relations in P-R nexi will be very different when viewed from the perspective of larger systems (or 'wholes'), since in the contemporary world, the use of resources is influenced by forces outside the locality. (E.g., resource abuse is not simply a matter of local ignorance, cupidity, or heedlessness, but may be required of local people as a matter of survival, by political and economic forces beyond their control--something illustrated in Dahlberg's concept of "industrial resource regimes" and exemplified in the Glantz/Krenz chapter on fisheries, where they show that the catch is influenced by everything from foreign exchange to international law.)

"Applied" orientations may be distinguished from "policy" orientations. While no author goes so far as to redefine his field as essentially a policy-generating science, there are some implications to this effect, especially in the applied multidisciplinary papers. But the absence of direct statements is probably significant: scientists in general are reluctant to claim the role of policy-makers, even though they may give occasional speeches which include a demand for a larger say in public affairs. In the background is the fundamental ambiguity as to just who has the power to control or direct human relations with resources. Contemporary institutions divide the responsibility in accordance with the principal of segregation of theory from purposive action. The environment is, fundamentally, a source of gratification or need-fulfillment; its presence is passive, subject to human will to transform and use. Industrial humanity is in a predatory posture toward the environment, seizing what it needs and wants. Thus policy is not environmental policy so much as it is human, or social policy. Holism may be a suitable scientific frame, but it is not the cultural frame, save for public conservationist groups who advocate institutional reform.

In the absence of direct policy statements, one may infer that scientific theory of P-R relations contains indirect policy declarations. Consider the following:

    A. Four of the authors explicitly avow that humans are part of Nature, and that there is in fact an interaction of humanity and the environment, even though humans do not acknowledge this in their institutions.

    B. Six of the authors--in different ways and degrees--feel that their own field of study, or its application, requires changes in order to accommodate a more conservationist understanding of P-R relations.

    C. Two of the authors explicitly criticize the tendency for humans to think in linear cause-effect or purpose-accomplishment terms, and acknowledge this proclivity as the root of our destructive attack on resources.

The picture is incomplete, and agreement is not total, but the indications would seem to be reasonably clear:

    5. <u>The theory of P-R relations is slowly evolving toward a normative position which acknowledges the need for a synthesis of policy and scientific concepts.</u>

VALUATIONAL POSTURES

Implications of something larger than scientific empiricism and theory there may be, but its expression, as already suggested, is ambiguous. To test the issue further, we examined the chapters to determine if the authors mentioned ethical or moral concerns in their views of P-R matters, and whether their texts could be interpreted as expressing either optimism or pessimism over the future of mankind. The results were inconclusive. Only one author--Dahlberg--could be understood to articulate a reasonably optimistic or upbeat view of a human capability to control their use of the Earth's resources; two more gave vague indications. Similarly, only one--Moran--could be interpreted as on the definitely pessimistic side. Three more gave vague indications of pessimism. Thus our tabulation suggests that there is <u>somewhat more pessimism than optimism</u>.

As to ethical or moral views, one author--Meadows-- appears to be genuinely disturbed at the callousness and lassitude with which problems of food inadequacy in human populations are handled. But five other authors show marginal or ambiguous concern with the ethical-moral issues lying behind P-R relations. Here again one might interpret this as an emerging consciousness of that fact that science cannot afford to take a passive or neutral position in these vital issues of survival, but the interpretation is tentative. However the seeming neglect of moral concerns must not be made to imply lack of concern. There is no doubt that all the authors are worried about the ecological crisis, and this is why they were selected to contribute to this symposium.

Closely related to the foregoing is the question of awareness of "structural" concerns. We use "structural" here in a vague neo-Marxist sense as referring to the distribution of survival necessities--or the proceeds of economic activity generally--among the groups and segments of human societies. Ideology is not the issue here: at stake is the genuine empirical question of "who gets what." That is, to what extent is the distribution of resources within human societies a legitimate topic for the construction of a science of P-R relations, on the basis of the assumption that deprivation equals demand equals pressure on resources? (And equally, one may assume that overconsumption equals demand equals pressure on resources.)

How do our authors fare on this issue? Five out of the ten papers show a degree of understanding that this is an issue, but none of the five single it out as a major question, nor do any of them attempt to integrate it into their explicit or implicit model of P-R relations. The issue is important enough to deserve more detailed analysis:

First, Berry/Johnson are aware of the problem of distribution, but to some extent they appear to regard this as a problem for micro-level research, and since they are (correctly of course) concerned that micro studies do not address the problem of global environmental problems, the issue gets shunted off into methodology. In other passages they are concerned with the stubborn difficulties presented by the desires and goals of people: "It is precisely because social, political and economic factors are so important, yet often seem so intractable and so slow of resolution, that preference for technological solutions to environmental hazards is so pronounced." Correct, and of course important, but the statement does not go on to ask why these factors should be so "intractable." It would seem that the reasons for this stickiness should be an intimate part of the analysis; but then, geographers cannot really be expected to deal with them. The main reason, of course, is that there is not only greed and overconsumption in the picture (which Berry/Johnson do acknowledge elsewhere), but also poverty.

Bromley/Szarleta concern themselves with processes that result in unequal distribution of resources--power, profit, "control centers," etc.--but do not explicitly discuss the consequences of these processes. Their use of the choice-exchange behavioral model (described later) converts the sense of inequity and consequent striving to reduce felt deprivation to a particular formula: "man must eat and must have access to certain materials and tools to facilitate that need, as well as to provide a range of creature comforts. It also is--or at least ought to be--obvious that man is a cost minimizer." That is to say, the minimization of costs may be relevant to larger theoretical concerns, but has nothing to do with desperate attempts to acquire what is needed and damn the costs, so to speak--as in revolutions, social movements, and so on. Who pays the costs? Who minimizes, who maximizes, under what circumstances of felt deprivation?

Golley, the biologist, on the other hand, gives more explicit recognition to the issue of distribution than all the rest except perhaps Meadows, who is openly indignant about the fact that food is not channeled to marginal and poor populations. Golley: "Both the capitalist and the Marxist societies perceive that inhomogeneous distribution of resources is undesirable; they differ substantially in their conception of how these imbalances should be changed. Clearly we are engaged in a world-wide debate on these fundamental problems." Fundamental they indeed are, and if so, should they not become an intimate part of the problem definition? However, Golley does not incorporate the problem and its causes in his model.

Moran is also aware of the issue, but his interests seem remote from the difficult and "intractable" problem of "inhomogeneous distribution." He is concerned with behavioral outcomes: e.g., "In all societies one can find individuals and/or institutions that serve to articulate these transformational rules of culture into a pattern of action toward Nature." True, but also toward other humans; and also in defense of one's needs, greed, and aspirations; and in recompense for one's real or relative deprivations. What role does ideology and anger play in the drive toward equity? Is this a problem of "rules of Culture," or a problem of human purposes? He also notes that the same "processes of unconscious simplification" and so on are found in both "urban-industrial settings" and "village-level populations"--again perfectly true, but who among these populations are getting what and why? From this social perspective sharp differences, not similarities, in human behavior or culture are to be observed.

We have already mentioned Meadows' concern with "inhomogeneous distribution" of foodstuffs, although she lacks any theory of why this is the case other than to note that we do not really study the problem as one of large global systems. Wolf is obviously concerned with what he calls "social purposes"--that is, what people need and want, and demand--but he digitalizes this, so to speak into his SIA methodology. All right as far as it goes, but like the others, it misses the issues of exploitation and deprivation on the way past. Dahlberg does speak of "exploitation," and distribution is somewhere in the general background of his thinking. However, it does not come across as a main point.

It is not a 'main point' for anyone--again, with the qualified exception of Meadows. Why is this so? It would appear to be a fundamental aspect of modern science: you avoid involvement in controversial social questions, because science cannot direct preferences. But this really cannot be a sound reason since the issue is a genuinely empirical one at root. Another possible explanation is the fear of being tarred with the Marxist brush--a more specific version of the above. Still another is the fear that the substance of the matter is really and genuinely "intractable;" i.e., simply not subject to prediction or explanation: the reactions of people to deprivation are not subject to scientific laws or even historical generalization.

So in essence, the missing piece in all of the chapters, and in the models the authors propose, is <u>relative deprivation</u>. Humans are driven by this socio-psychological mechanism; it is the source of the unpredictability and lack of fit between "objective" conditions and the response of people to these conditions. For example, what is hunger? Underlying Meadows' concerns is the difficulty of answering this question. Aside from the genuine below-threshold levels of nutritional need, hunger is relative to what people want, feel, think, and are told to feel and think. Science has grave difficulties handling matters like this. Hence the acknowledgment, but fundamentally marginal locus of the issue in these papers.

There are, of course, other considerations. Another neglected element in the picture is the geographically unequal distribution of physical resources. And since, as Bromley/Szarleta tell us, humans try to minimize costs, obviously the higher cost of delivering resources to resource-short locations at a distance will fix unequal distribution into the system. It certainly has, up to now. Is there a way around this? Perhaps new methods of international funding, ever-normal resource storehouses, and so on? The suggestions are legion; the issue suffers from no lack of attention in international writings. However, it does not surface in these papers. There is no attempt to build into the models a reality component that requires empirical planning of transportation, payments, definitions of needs, and the like. Or rather, just how correct is the economist's model of cost effectiveness as an explanation of why resources are abundant here but scarce there? And to what extent is cost a variable in the whole theory of P-R relations? Clearly, if we perceive the international economic market as the closest thing we have to a "world system," then economic or instrumental phenomena must play a very important role in our theory.

But there is open recognition by all of the authors the essentially global nature of the problems (it is this earth-centered orientation which probably lies behind the strong emphasis on applied approaches, the holistic-system conception, and the dominant concern over "impacts" of humans on Nature). Each author, in his or her own way, cites P-R problems in other countries and regions; these citations demonstrate an important type of scientific progress: the breaking out of the narrow continental limits of research, the participation of scientists in development and international resource and environmental agencies and conferences, the spread of cross-departmental and cross disciplinary courses of instruction in universities and institutes--all of which have grown since the days of the environmental movement.

THEORETICAL CLUSTERING

Our tabulations of the author's theoretical concepts and approaches yield two significant clusters of ideas which cut through the disciplines or different approaches--though they, too, are also derived from particular disciplines.

I. The first is represented mainly by Bromley/Szarleta for the integral discipline of economics, and by Wolf for the multidisciplinary or applied field of social impact analysis. Stated most simply, the model here is that known by the combined label of rational choice and social exchange (or "choice-exchange" model, for short).[3] While the origins of the model may not be immediately apparent from the texts of the papers, the indications are clear enough. Both papers go down the line on the main components of the model: the key factors involved in the human use-abuse of resources are choice, decision, values, goals, institutional rules, and systematic "control centers" (Bromley/Szarleta), vested interests, profit, and trade-offs. That is, human behavior in its instrumental aspects represents the heart of the human approach to the physical environment. Humans form purposes, then seek to fulfill these objectives by choosing among a set of appropriate strategies. Then, objectives often come into conflict, and compromise is required to achieve something. The system results in an accumulation of vested interests or power centers, and subsequently, interests of the environment itself becomes simply one factor among many that must be juggled in the social-behavioral process.

It is not difficult to understand why these two chapters emphasize this model: economics is largely, as a discipline, responsible for the emergence of the choice-exchange model in the social sciences. Social impact analysis is automatically embedded in the social behavioral area of choice and conflict resolution; it can entertain no other model of the process given its mandate and procedure. What is missing from the chapters is an acknowledgment of the possibility that the model is culturally relative: its applicability is a historic event, not a universal or constant in human behavior. That is, it arises in our civilization because of our emphasis on power-built institutions and macro-technologies.

The choice-exchange model is a powerful tool; it comes closer to describing the process of social-purposive behavior than any other. However, as previously noted, it is devoid of a theory of full human causation in the sense that it cannot handle the <u>intensity</u> with which things are desired or sought. "Values are taken as givens, not as social-emotional drives. And the origins of these drives in ideology, relative deprivation, and the like cannot be addressed in the theory as it stands. This can be especially serious in social impact analysis, where all positions at stake must be treated as approximately equal; that is, SIA necessarily subscribes to a pluralistic conception of culture, and thus (paradoxically) has difficulty making choices. Yet choices must be made. In SIA they are viewed as compromises, expedient outcomes, or practical accommodations based on bargaining. Since power is always a key factor in such decision processes, the fundamental issue of conservation of resources for the good of posterity is difficult to take seriously. The choice-exchange model of Bromley/Szarleta and others yields an imperfect decision procedure. It would seem that decision-making should be the heart of a P-R relational theory, but only Moran deals with this. And his approach is one-sided: he is concerned with rules or traditions that guide decisions (i.e., "culture"). Correct, so far as it goes, but what of spontaneous decisions made on the basis of social-emotional immediacies? When deprivation (real or relative) becomes acute, and people rebel and demand recompense, what rules guide them, and are rules really the important issue? It is in this sphere that we reach the cultural limits of the choice-exchange model: it tends to be shaped by a particular cultural milieu--it becomes the apology or ameliorative balm for that system, not its reform.

II. The second cluster or model is represented by the papers by Golley, Moran, Berry/Johnson, and Glantz/Krenz. It is a bio-social or "cultural ecology" model, since it strives to give emphasis to both physical and social systems. The authors probably agree with the choice-exchange behavior approach insofar as there is emphasis on values and institutions, but beyond this, the weight is put on <u>systems</u>: ecosystems and social systems; on the interaction between biological and physical-environmental factors and human activities. The model is also causal: it is the interplay between the physical environment and human activities and institutions which creates configurations of resource use and abuse. That is, the molding force is "culture"--meaning various second-level abstract constructs like "culture," "levels of social organization," or "institutions" which cause human behavior--whereas in the first model, it is human behavior which is viewed--at least implicitly--as causing or creating institutions and the P-R relational nexi.

When converted into applied orientations, the cultural-ecology model easily gives rise to a strong physicalism in terms of environment and resources: humans are seen as somewhat detached (although they "interact" with environment) and as causing impacts on Nature. The model contains, as do all models utilizing second-order conceptual entities derived from the "results" of behavior, some tautologies and contradictions, but this need not vitiate the positive orientation toward social problematic and application.

Golley's chapters may be singled out for special comment. Although they do not differ from the others in fundamentals, they contain a stronger emphasis on biological factors: the ecosystem. Ecosystems are more clearly distinguished from social systems; humans become an active force, distinct from Nature, and impacting upon Nature. Interaction between human and natural systems is acknowledged, but the specific processes of the interaction are not described. The human factor is included mainly in a plea for a choice of research topics which deal with the systemic processes in a human scale; presumably, in contexts chosen to represent key problem cases of human impact. Physicalism once more; but again, the problem-solving orientation of Golley's "new science" inevitably generates this perspective. Golley, though biologically-oriented, is also socially-conscious--perhaps more so than the other authors in this cluster.

It should be noted also that the cultural-ecology model shares the deficiencies of the choice-exchange approach insofar as it neglects the processes of relative deprivation and decision-making, although in different degrees. However, viewed from the standpoint of the choice-exchange model, the cultural-ecology approach is seriously deficient in its failure to work with a theory of human behavior. "Culture" becomes the substitute for a behavioral analysis; it gives the impression that it is not <u>people</u> who are the agents of environmental impact so much as their culture, or ways of doing things. Thus, components like goals, purposes, means and ends are not viewed as active or dynamic factors, but as standard givens. But culture cannot cause behavior, since culture is simply the descriptive corpus of ideas and actions existing at any particular period.

There are further problems with the cultural-ecology model concerning natural systems, or ecosystems. Humans may participate in ecosystems, but they do so out of will; they are not biologically-driven agents in natural food chains--at least, not in contemporary society. Consequently it is difficult to conceptualize the human-ecosystem interaction process; it tends to become abstract and general, not specific and concrete. This is the case because it is seen largely as a matter of the interaction of constructed second-order entities: culture, Nature, etc. For all its defects, the choice-exchange model gets closer to the behavioral process. Still, the cultural-ecology model, when informed by a keen sense of issues and causes, can serve useful ends, and it represents an advance, forged in the environmental movement, over the wholly human-centered approaches of an earlier era.

Where do the other chapters fit into these two clusters of theoretical principles? Buttel is hard to classify; his is a standard social-science or second-order abstraction approach, enhanced by his genuine concern for real problems in real world locations. He would probably fit into the cultural-ecology model. Busby's paper is entirely practical, applied; he is concerned with "management," not a general theory of P-R relations. He refers to range management as a "discipline" but it is in reality a multidisciplinary, problem-oriented approach, drawing its information from biology, geography, agronomy, anthropology or any field with something to offer. And "management" for him is not a matter of a science of human purposes, choice, decision, vested interests, and the like, but simply the gathering of technical and scientific knowledge about rangelands, and then hoping that it will be used intelligently. He is not concerned with theories of social process, or the larger questions of P-R relations.

The issue-oriented Glantz/Orlovsky chapter on "desertification" is the least theoretical of the entire set; no general model is defined because that was not their purpose in writing. However, the Glantz/Krenz chapter on fisheries makes an excellent point, neglected by other authors: that choices are determined by levels and degrees of integration in the world system: international, national, and individual. Dahlberg? He does not present a theory of P-R relations, but instead, a social-historical view of the human engagement with Nature. His paper provides the historical background for the book, and this is very much needed. His implicit model is, we think, the cultural-ecology approach of the geographers, anthropologists, and ecologists.

Before we leave matters of general theory, it is necessary to comment once more on the authors' conceptions of "resources." The tabulation yielded a variety of explicit and implicit definitions and the editors of the volume did not impose a single definition in their assignment. However, the physicalist emphasis is clear; it has already been discussed. Social resources are marginally recognized by only two authors (Golley and Dahlberg). Next to the physical emphasis, the notion that humans <u>define</u> or rather <u>create</u> resources in their goal-technology process is the most frequently expressed. Certainly all authors would accept this, whether they had occasion to say so or not. At this stage in our collective thinking, there really seems to be no better definition, and the doctrine of human-created "resources" out of passive natural substances is certainly acceptable. However, to be effective in a conservationist sense, it must be accompanied by ethical considerations as to the limits of this creative response with respect to posterity and the fate of the Earth. Without this normative prescription, the definition is simply a congenial elementary textbook concept.

SOME KEY ISSUES WITH THEORETICAL AND METHODOLOGICAL SIGNIFICANCE

1. The first issue is signaled by the critical stance toward their own fields taken by the authors; Bromley/Szarleta and Meadows are especially critical of economics, while most of the authors do display some awareness that more work needs to be done in their fields. Busby's historical account of the developing sophistication and coverage of range management is especially interesting and valuable. In general, the question of what constitutes adequate knowledge in the P-R field can be answered in three ways: <u>first</u>, acceptance that current disciplinary boundaries are appropriate and that the resulting views and corpus of information are reasonably complete and valid. <u>Second</u>, one might consider that while the information gathered thus far is incomplete, the methods and outlook necessary to collect it are valid and reasonably efficient. <u>Third</u>, one could assume that the knowledge possessed by a discipline is inadequate because the theories and methods of that discipline are inadequate.

As regards to the first possibility, we believe that Buttel, Busby and Wolf display such general acceptance of their fields, although as noted, Busby is mainly concerned with historical development. As regards the second position, we consider that Berry/

Johnson, Golley, Moran, Dahlberg, Glantz--fisheries--and Glantz/Orlovsky (possibly) are accepting on the whole, but also advocate change and development in their fields. Finally, two writers, as previously observed, Bromley/Szarleta and Meadows, feel that basic changes are needed in the concepts, aims, and methods of their fields of study. Their papers are really proposals for counter-disciplines; they would reform their fields of study.

Thus in general, there is a <u>vector toward a need for change and development in the disciplines and approaches described</u>. But at the same time, except perhaps for two papers, no radical rejection or revision is proposed.

2. Next, we shall consider the important idea of what we called, in our tabulation, "cultural knowledge" as a block against an adequate concept of P-R relations, as expressed by five authors (Berry/Johnson, Bromley/Szarleta, Glantz/Krenz, Wolf, and perhaps most articulately Moran). Each reflects a growing awareness of the fact that our civilization has created a mindset which makes it extremely difficult to think clearly about such matters as time, change, responsibility, conservation, and causation. Moran calls it "linear thinking," referring to the proclivity to formulate objectives and then do whatever is necessary to obtain them--thus proceeding through time like an arrow, never looking back, and never looking forward beyond the immediate goal. (We suppose that this pattern of thought might also serve, for Moran, as a surrogate for a choice-exchange behavioral model, but this remains to be seen.) The alternative to "linear thinking" would be circular, reciprocal, cyclical, or regenerative thinking, in which means and ends are always subject to a consideration of consequences far in the future, and where, above all, an attempt is made to calculate the ultimate cost-benefit ratios, with due consideration of ethical responsibilities for posterity (although Moran does not explore these wider implications, and Wolf only touches upon them--SIA is for the <u>present</u>, not the indefinite future). Other ways of putting the point, as in the Berry/Johnson chapter, concern the notion of power interests controlling resource use and impeding conservationist use, or the shielding of the existing P-R system of relations from the crucial issue of the future condition of resources. Glantz/Krenz emphasize "myths" about fisheries--especially the notion that it is an "economic" activity, to be judged like any other business--whereas in reality it is a complex P-R interaction process.

If "linear thinking" is to be singled out for criticism, then we might also focus on dichotomous thinking: Man and Nature; Conservationist <u>vs</u>. Exploiter; Doomsayer vs. Cornucopian; Culture and Environment; Positive vs. Negative Feedback; Static and Dynamic. Perhaps no conceptualization has so delayed regenerative or interactive thinking about P-R relations than the tendency to oppose or at least separate humans and natural phenomena--a tendency which is visible in every paper in this volume, despite the general insistence on holism and interaction. The oppositional mode prevails because our relations with the physical environment have gotten out of hand: since we are the aggressors, something must come to the defense of Nature; hence the dichotomy. The tendency to think in terms of goods and bads, blacks and whites, plus the emphasis on linear or purposive accomplishment, is self-reinforcing: to cope with degradation we must dichotomize humans and environment; to do something about it, we need to resort to linear thinking. Is there any way out of this circular cognitive trap? Insistence on interaction and reciprocal causation and so on is all to the good, but it is hard to see just how it can alter the forces which feed maladaptive behavior and thought patterns.

Many other examples of cultural blockage could be added: the parceling out of human awareness of the consequences of resource use by lack of knowledge or awareness of wider system components and effects; the "tragedy of the commons" mechanisms, or self-seeking behavior with social and environmental costs; the Bromley/Szarleta point about pushing off social costs onto the environment, in order to avoid political unrest or whatever; the inability of our educational system to teach people to think consecutively, in orderly steps of cause and effect, with due consideration of time; and the cultural emphasis on the here-and-now, or immediate gratification without regard for future consequences; the belief that "values" are things that just emerge in social life, and that no one has the responsibility, or the nerve, to try to create them and engage the nation in rational debate on their desirability.

Running through all these cultural blockages, in this writer's view, is the deficient temporal perspective of industrial and consumer culture. Time is measured almost exclusively by human purposes and the time it takes to satisfy them. Nature operates on very different time scales: some longer, some shorter--but generally the former. Regeneration of a forest takes much longer than it does to produce the benefits derived from harvesting it; yet these benefits are of short duration, and when achieved, cannot be repeated again with the same resources for a very long time, if ever. Consequently the gratification-oriented time perspective results in progressive depletion of natural substances (e.g., Glantz/Krenz point about the "myth" that fisheries are "economic"). We speak of "renewable resources," but in a literal sense there is no such thing--at least for short time spans.

And then of course there is the tendency to focus on disasters, crises, immediate problems, and to erect a bureaucratic apparatus to handle them--as if this procedure were really doing something about the future (Hewitt's chapter critiques it). The "future," in this crisis-oriented perspective, is simply the day after you react to the problem, but not the chain of consequences which may extend far ahead in time. And for all its desirability and need, Wolf's social impact analysis is little more than a stopgap means of responding to this kind of abbreviated temporal conception of human and environmental issues.

Acceptance of longer and ethically guided time perspectives implies, at least for the initial stages, some degree of control and regulation, of knocking heads together, of exhortation and alarm tactics--whatever method may be adopted by authorities who finally begin to run scared on the resources issues. While these loom as realities on some distant or really unforeseeable horizon, we are entertained by debates between the doomsayers like Paul Erhlich and the cornucopian theorists like Julian Simon. Clearly there is no consensus; still, the issue has been joined, and we are, in fact, on the threshold of the Great Debate over human and earthly survival--a debate which will carry on into the next century.

Aside from the cultural blockages, which are difficult to handle, we do need more history on human use of resources. Alone among the authors, Dahlberg shows awareness of this need. As a general criticism and also recommendation, the present writer would urge all of the authors to start attempting to handle historical data on resources and human intentions with the tools of their disciplines. It is a sure route to fresh new insights.

3. What happened to population? Its omission in these papers is probably due to the fact that the choice of disciplines did not include demography, and if any issue is conceived of in specialized and technical terms, it is demography. We would hesitate to accuse any of the authors of denying that population is an issue in P-R relations, but none of them, except perhaps Wolf, seems to have tried to incorporate it in their models or exposition. It functions in obvious ways as a cause of demand on resources, but it is also important in the context of social awareness of the ecological issues. As population increases in an urban-industrial world, smaller and smaller proportions of this population are directly engaged with transforming natural phenomena into resources, and consequently is unaware of the problems of degradation and impact. Thus, population tends to accentuate demand not only in terms of

basic needs, but also relative demands. Deprivation
becomes more acutely felt as more and more people are
deprived of the consumer goods they believe they need.
That is, environmental costs rise as social demands
increase both absolutely, in terms of number of consumers, and relatively, in terms of political and ideological demands for equity.

4. We may turn next to the issue of "social
resources." Since the environmental movement, and most
of the disciplines concerned with general ecological
matters, have strong physical and biological orientations, the "physicalism" of the general theory, as we
have called it, is of course comprehensible. Despite
such lip service, no contemporary theoretical model of
P-R relations possesses a detailed or convincing exposition of social phenomena as resources, or the view that
"social environment" should or can be considered in the
same frame of reference as the bio-physical side. The
closest we come to this is the systems approach, which
sees both social and bio-physical phenomena in some form
of interaction and feedback. But this is, on the whole,
'lip service,' as said above. Moran's concept of regenerative thinking, to replace linear forms, would of
course create a truly interactive model, if it could be
developed and applied.

But there is more than meets the eye here. There
_is_ a set of interdisciplines and disciplinary specialties which have developed a concept of human environments as something to which humans must respond and
manage. These fields are architecture, planning, and
environmental and ecological management--and in recent
years they have produced a considerable amount of
material. They are not represented in this book partly
because they were not well represented in MAB, which was
the patron organization for the symposium. They are not
represented for the additional reason that they are in
reality quasi-social-behavioral sciences, not environmental sciences. That is, they are not concerned with
resource scarcity, shortage, degradation, exhaustion,
pollution, and human needs in the same senses that the
ecologically-oriented fields represented in the book
are. They have developed out of contact, in the main,
with the ecologies; they are spinoffs of their own
fields, and utilize a terminology and battery of concepts that have little or no bearing on the problem of
world resources and human purposes.

The social sciences suffer from some of the same
limitations. Buttel candidly admits that sociology has
had little concern with P-R problems, despite its longstanding interest in what it called or calls "human
ecology"--a misnomer if there ever was one, since the
field is concerned almost exclusively with the distribution of social groups in urban space. In other writ-

ings, Buttel has also commended the pioneering work of
Walter Firey in the 1940s and '50s on the social management of resources, as influenced by culturally-styled
conceptions of entrepreneurship, property, and the like,
but his work was almost completely ignored by the mainline discipline (Buttel, correspondence). There is also
a shadowy contemporary field called "environmental sociology," and Buttel may be numbered among its adherents,
but the work is done mainly by rural sociologists and
has not had a significant impact on the academic discipline of sociology. Anthropology has more relevance to
P-R matters, because of its long-standing involovement
with biology and geography, something that is visible in
Moran's paper. Geography has done more with the problems of bringing human and physical phenomena together
in the same frame of reference than any of the social-behavioral sciences. As the present writer recently
pointed out in a MAB publication (Bennett 1982), the
social sciences cannot be expected to produce convincing
materials related to the human-resources interaction
nexus on a large scale until they transcend (as Moran
also makes clear) their exclusive micro-scale research
habit.

We thus have a confusing array of gaps and overlaps: anthropology studies the "cultural ecology" of
small-scale agrarian producers and tribal peoples, and
has evolved some interesting interactive propositions
and causal relations, but these do not address the problem of world resources and human needs. Food systems
research is concerned with global ecological-food problems but lacks a theory of social behavior and institutions which would help explain the puzzling ineptitudes
of transportation, markets, and the like. Ecology is
good on ecosystems, but has difficulty interpreting
these in the context of human purpose and effort. The
"world system" is generally ignored by everyone (except,
perhaps, by Glantz/Krenz, who emphasize international
factors in fisheries). Everyone is worried about population, but only demographers study it. And so on. If
one were to paste together these various ingredients
into a general science of P-R relations, it would be a
reasonably imposing one. However, no one has done it.
Kenneth Boulding recently made a heroic try, in his
Ecodynamics book (1980), and while it has many good
points, the fusion is incomplete, the chapters episodic
and on the whole basically expositions of slices of
separate disciplinary knowledge.

The present writer considers that one root of the
problem is the structure of institutions of higher
learning. As these developed in the 19th century and
into the 20th, they accepted the standard disciplinary
slices of knowledge as the basic frame of reference.
These slices are in most cases out of date; they repre-

sent a cognitive map about two centuries old, and mirror a period in scholarship when the main task was to <u>describe</u> the then relatively separate domains of reality. Now the problems have shifted: description, while important, is no longer the pressing need: we must now synthesize and integrate knowledge around today's relationships, processes, and larger systems. Yet the disciplines remain the basis of our knowledge industry, because they have come to be vested interests: interest groups which are reinforced by their power positions in the university. Until some more effective means is found to bring these disciplines together in cross-departmental institutes, not much will be done. Such institutes are of course emerging outside the university system, and government agencies charged with regulating the environment are beginning to create de facto interdisciplines--like social impact analysis. There is progress, but the universities are not doing as much as they should to further it.

PERSONAL VIEWS

It is only fair that the critic expose himself to criticism:
1. <u>Pessimism</u>. I am very pessimistic on the short run. I do not believe that things in the P-R world will get better soon; they will get much worse. <u>Humans rarely modify present practices in order to ward off future costs; they wait until the costs have to be paid. That is, there is a tilt toward immediate gratification in Homo sapiens behavior</u>. But possibly I am <u>optimistic in the long run</u>: I consider that humans will act constructively and alter their values when the dangers are clear and present. However, we must expect much suffering and environmental disruption before this materializes.
2. The field, obviously, has to be a <u>practical one</u>, one that deals with real social and historical issues. This is more than "application:" there needs to be <u>more concern with distribution of resources, and with deprivation</u>. The P-R issues must be set in a matrix of local and global social, political, and economic movements; human political ends need to be viewed in relation to resource needs, and vice versa. Therefore I would consider that world-systems approaches are essential--and yet these need to be integrated with intensive studies of key local processes and problems, insofar as these represent or symbolize the larger movements. The entire issue is complex and subtle: the environmentalist's concern with distribution and deprivation is not so much a matter of defending the rights of the deprived, but rather of understanding deprivation as a force for stim-

ulating demand, which in turn leads to pressure of resources.

3. I do not believe that academic disciplines can do the job of straightening out the human relationship to Nature--and to other humans: that is, a large reconstruction of the social and natural world as a single interactive entity is needed. I believe that disciplines are antique and outmoded; they desperately need reform and fusion. I agree with all the criticisms of their fields introduced by Bromley/Szarleta, Berry/Johnson, and Moran.

4. My preferred model of analysis of P-R relations is the choice-exchange model but augmented with such concepts as relative deprivation and decision-making. I select this as at least a provisional approach because it deals with what I also believe to be the most fundamental research need: to better understand why humans do what they do to Nature. I would also supply a stronger emphasis on institutions than is provided by all the authors except, perhaps Wolf, Bromley/Szarleta, and in a qualified sense, Glantz/Krenz. Institutions arise out of the choice-exchange nexus, and subsequently they guide choices and fix vested interests. They introduce lag into the system; they cause the deficient temporal perspective which plagues our environmental policies.

5. This augmented social-behavioral model also needs to be set into a matrix of systems analysis. More concretely, we need to identify the relevant systems--not assume that the methodology of systems will define them for us. Systems exist as we construct them, they are nothing more than the recognition of the fact that everything, in one way or another, is related to everything else. A systems approach is our only extant tool to proceed toward disciplinary fusion and focus on common problems. Systems analysis is difficult in this sphere since ecosystems are not the same as social systems, and must not be confused. Yet they are intertwined. Historical approaches are essential; as noted, the largest system level of the "world system" is probably largely equivalent, at this point in time, to the international economic market.

Historical approaches are one way to effect integration of the separate disciplinary contributions to P-R relations. Through history we can come to appreciate both the deficiencies of the separate disciplines, and also the extent to which our environmental disasters are socially generated. This, however, is purely descriptive knowledge: valuable, but lacking analytic precision. When we speak of "interdisciplinary research," or "multidisciplinary approaches" we are really speaking of combinations of specialists who acknowledge that the emerging historical reality of P-R relations are too complex for any one field to grasp. This awareness becomes instrumental as a matter of practical endeavor rather than basic research. The contrast between the two categories of papers in this volume is clear enough: it is the applied fields, represented by SIA, food relief, the amelioration of desertification, that are openly multidisciplinary. The disciplines, though often acknowledging the need for information from a variety of sources, give the impression that the solution to P-R problems can be found within the context of single fields. (But again--this may be an artifact of the assignment, as I noted at the beginning.)

It is also important to note that the applied fields are <u>multi</u>disciplinary, not <u>inter</u>disciplinary. The distinction is crucial: the applied fields are not concerned with research and knowledge which must be branded so a discipline can receive due credit. The applied approaches are problem-oriented, and their practitioners are obligated to obtain information bearing on the problem from any available source. Often this means that the practitioner foregoes disciplinary prestige to do what he can, with whatever information he can assemble, or whatever specialists he can persuade to join him. This in turn means that multidisciplinary efforts in the practical sphere are often not supported in the rear echelon by interdisciplinary research. The practitioner must try to make the linkages; scientists have shown less interest in this kind of work than they ought to. The rewards are not sufficient; also, the interdisciplinary research structure in academia is weak.

The structure is weakest between the physical disciplines on the one hand (biology, geology, soil science, etc.), and the social sciences on the other. In cases where development projects are in hand linkages often emerge; e.g., as in the construction of an irrigation project, where engineers, hydrologists, biologists, economists, and anthropologists may work together on feasibility or impact studies before or after construction. Again practical tasks bring specialists together. This kind of effort does, from time to time, produce broad-gauge individuals who seem able to master several fields of expertise, and who then may carry this true interdisciplinary-knowledge-in-one-head back with them into the academic setting. Michael Glantz may be such a person, but it is perhaps significant that Glantz does not work for a university, but a government agency concerned with problem-focused research.

There have been no dearth of unifying frames. Theory is easily come by; the environmental movement produced many, and the cross-departmental ecology programs of the 1970s strove to create such frames and incorporate them in the university structure. We have already commented on the exceedingly modest results. It takes more than impeccable logical constructions to create true interdisciplinary ecological theory. Such theory must be forged over a long period of time in the crucible of innumerable specialized inquiries in which two or more come together and painstakingly seek to translate the relevant variables into each other's language and measurements. And those disciplines which have a tradition of fusion--geography and anthropology in particular--need to strike out more vigorously than they have.

Having said this, I offer my own sketch of an interdisciplinary frame with all due modesty and brevity. I have no illusions that the fraternity will accept it as the unifying scheme for a joint effort, but in the general crisis we all need to speak our piece.

THE SOCIONATURAL SYSTEMS APPROACH

The approach requires adherence to systems theory as a heuristic frame of reference. The term "socionatural system" is my own (Bennett 1976; 1980; 1982, pp. 22ff). The underlying assumption is that all elements of the bio-physical world are interlocked with the human-social world, and are so to an increasing extent (the "ecological transition"). The first step is to define these systems of interaction between humans and the physical world, by tracing their history and emergence, and their present state, particularly as it concerns depletion, degradation, or sustained yield. Here are some preliminary candidates, based mainly on human activities in differing biomes:

Agricultural

1. Let us start with basic biomes:
    Humid tropical
    Dry tropical
    Temperate humid
    Arid and semiarid
    Deserts
2. Describe the various modes of agriculture associated with each.
3. Such biome-oriented agrisystems might be transacted by stages of technological and institutional development, with varying degrees of subsistence and market production. That is, each of the biome agrisystems would then be filled out with the specifications of particular adaptive social-behavioral and institutional factors; e.g.,

a) Desert development under conditions of low-energy technology, and the basic limitations to production this creates.
b) Desert development under conditions of high-energy technology, and the environmental degradation this may cause.
c) Likewise, for production and distribution institutions of collective or entrepreneurial types.

Extractive

The analytic mode would be similar to the above. Here are some concrete examples:

1. Sardine fisheries of the Pacific Coast, including the marine climatology, biology, the human settlements, industries, transportation systems, and so on that are dependent on sardine fisheries. (This is a good example since some research at the socionatural level has already taken place, although Glantz/Krenz do not comment on it in detail.)
2. Multiple-use resource systems like the timber-irrigation-recreation agriculture systems of Western North America.

Urban-Rural Systems

1. The central city and its physical resource needs.
2. City-Country relationships expressed in terms of food production and supply; physical resource allocation to different needs and interests.
3. Transportation and physical resource use.
4. Population concentration and dispersion and physical resource management.
5. Differential scales of demand and need and how these affect resource use.

Actually socionatural systems are empirical: wholly so. They are constructs created by human effort, and we need to understand them because we need to know precisely what we have done with the Earth. We know very little. And even when we begin to acquire information, we find it extremely difficult to relate it to policy, especially when human wants, configurated in institutional rules, and expressed in spontaneous demands, take on a "political" character. This is the fundamental problem that social scientists who wish to enter the field must focus on over the rest of this century. How can we re-order social organization so that we can become more flexible in our response to environmental crisis? The problem is identical for society itself: how can we control the paranoid-destructive forces emanating from the intersection of world economic systems with nationalism?

In the last analysis, the relationship of humans to the natural world mirrors the relationship of humans to humans: <u>we treat Nature much as we treat each other</u>. Let us hope this is not the enduring fate of mankind, but the characteristic of a particular civilization: the end product of the effort to conquer Nature that began in the Paleolithic. To paraphrase Nehru, it is time to practice that great idea: civilization.

NOTES

1. An outside reviewer felt that this chapter was too "negative;" i.e., that it failed to dwell on the positive and useful contributions made in the various chapters. The writer does not think this is wholly true, since favorable comments are made throughout. The level of comment is neither negative nor positive, but analytic, since the objective is to appraise the total effort and its parts as a sample of the rhetoric and thought patterns of the study of P-R relationships.

2. That is: as Edmund Leach noted, indigenous tribal people cannot be considered to be environmentalists or conservationists because they lack a sense of alarm over resource abuse, and hence do not "conserve" (Leach 1972). Historically, they simply used what they needed, and their low population size and density precluded any massive impact. Even so, there are some instances of considerable insult to Nature; e.g., the case of Plains Indians burning Western grasslands and depleting the already sparse tree cover in certain areas. (For a discussion, see Bennett 1976, pp. 78, 80, 151.)

3. The most readable essay on the approach, with particular reference to the use of choice and exchange concepts in social science, is found in Heath 1979.

4. The paired concepts, "instrumental" and "expressive" aspects of behavior or culture, come from Talcott Parsons (Parsons 1951). The writer has used the term "instrumental" to refer to those aspects of anthropological research which are concerned with survival and the maintenance of order and power and "expressive" of "interpretive" as referring to symbols, meaning, and identity. (Bennett 1976A). Obviously like all dichotomies, the distinction is analytically arbitrary, and in

real life we find an inextricable mingling of instrumental and expressive, insofar as we erect symbolic defenses for all actions, regardless of their function or purpose.

REFERENCES

Bennett, John W. <u>The Ecological Transition: Cultural Anthropology and Human Adaptation</u>. New York: Pergamon Press, 1976.
_____. "Anticipation, Adaptation, and the Concept of Culture in Anthropology." <u>Science</u>, 192 (1976):847-853.
_____. "Human Ecology as Human Behavior: A Normative Anthropology of Resource Use and Abuse," in I. Altman and others (eds.), <u>Human Behavior and Enviroment: Vol. 4, Environment and Culture</u>. New York: Plenum Press, 1980.
_____. "Social and Interdisciplinary Sciences in U.S. MAB: Conceptual and Theoretical Aspects," in E. H. Zube (ed.), <u>Social Sciences, Interdisciplinary Research and the U.S. Man and the Biosphere Program</u>. MAB Workshop Proceedings, University of Arizona, 1982.
Buttel, Fredrick. "Sociology and the Environment: The Winding Road Toward Human Ecology." To appear in a forthcoming volume on the social sciences and the environment, published by the International Social Science Council, Paris.
Heath, Anthony. <u>Rational Choice and Social Exchange</u>. Cambridge: Cambridge University Press, 1979.
Leach, Edmund. "Anthropological Aspects: Conclusion," in P. R. Cox and J. Peel (eds.), <u>Population and Pollution</u>. London: Methuen, 1972.
Parsons, Talcott. <u>The Social System</u>. New York: Harper, 1951.

14
Final Thoughts on Human Impacts on Global Resources

Frank B. Golley

In the original symposium this essay represented an ecologist's viewpoint of the human impact-global resource problem. Because it took a very broad view of the issue and proposed a different analysis and agenda, drawing from all disciplines, it has been placed in this final position. Thus, the essay represents a post script or final comment after the review of all chapters by John Bennett.

THE ECOSPHERE

Because of the variety of approaches and languages used heretofore we will begin with a restatement of definitions of the earth system and resources. We can view the planet earth as an ecological system called the ECOSPHERE. The ecosphere is composed of four spheres, the biosphere which is the collection of all living organisms, including man, the hydrosphere or oceans, the atmosphere and the lithosphere. These spheres provide the resources required by man and all other organisms. The first thing we will note about these spheres is that their distribution over the planetary surface is heterogenous. Some locations contain large quantities of resources required for life, other localities contain small quantities. These patterns of distribution are built into the very fabric of the planet. Solar energy falling on the spherical surface is received in disproportionate amounts and the redistribution of energy through the fluid media of the atmosphere and hydrosphere create the climates and ocean currents that so strongly influence life. The lithosphere is also dynamic, with the surface plates shifting and causing volcanism, earthquakes, and mountain building, which in turn create the mineral resources upon which modern society depends.

The biosphere responds to these patterns and forms a varied mantle over the surface with a rich, thick strata of living organisms dominating physical forces in equatorial rain forests to very sparse distributions of life in extremely cold or dry environments and in the ocean deserts. The biosphere is exceptionally responsive, forming living systems quickly even on volcanic islands isolated in the ocean. It is self-designing with continuous extinctions of no longer appropriate forms of life and development of new forms. The interaction of the biosphere with the atmosphere, hydrosphere and lithosphere has changed the nature of earth fundamentally so that the planet is, as far as we can tell, unique in the universe.

In this context, man is a member of the biosphere and follows the physical, chemical, biological and social laws which govern biosphere behavior. Of course, man is a unique species with special abilities to create built environments, social-cultural environments and patterns of thought. But uniqueness is a characteristic of every biological species. I have phrased it this way to emphasize man's ecological nature. The uniquely human character of expressing perception of natural reality in language and more abstractly through creative acts builds a uniquely human or humanized environment. There is a feedback between the human individuals and their environments (which include other humans) so that a consistent, even rational, system can be constructed that has little relation to the biosphere. As long as these humanized systems can be provided ecological services, such as clean air, water, food, and waste processing, then they can continue development within the wholly human creative mode. Where there is a close coupling between humans and the natural world, as in traditional societies, these tendencies are checked after a certain point through environmental feedback. This psycho-sociological ability of mankind allows man to operate in a unique way in the biosphere.

Human populations, like those of other species, are distributed unequally over the earth's surface. While these patterns are well known to literate people everywhere (high densities in China and the Indian subcontinent, low densities in America, Siberia, Australia), the reasons for the patterns are complex and special to each area. Clearly there is no single reason which explains the pattern of human population. Further, these patterns of distribution change quickly since man has a high capacity to reproduce, and through migration and transport of resources, can shift densities easily. In the recent past the trend has been toward higher densities but this has not always been true. Disease, war, environmental destruction all have caused long-standing declines in human population in specific regions of the earth.

Further, human population densities are not an entirely useful statistic with which to evaluate man's relation to resources. This is because human demand for resources varies between populations. Small populations can have as high a resource demand as large populations. For example, ten years ago it was estimated that the United States, which has about 5% of the population, used 42% of the world's production of aluminum, 40% of the molybdenum, 63% of the natural gas, and 33% of the petroleum (Meadows et al., 1972). And populations may be larger than the biological capacity of a local region to support that population. Japan is an example, since it has a small land mass and obtains its food from a very large area of ocean and through trade. These demand patterns also change rapidly.

HUMAN PERCEPTIONS

All that I have said so far is a generally acceptable factual and objective description of what exists. However, when we turn to man's perception and interpretation of these patterns, the analysis becomes more complex. Man assigns values to resources and populations. What is perceived, valued, compared, and how these comparisons are interpreted, are culturally controled. From an ecological perspective, culture is an adaptive mechanism through which man brings successful strategies of the past, interpreted through the filter of time and experience, into interaction with immediate events. Culture provides a way of understanding who and what we are, both individually and collectively.

Western cultural perceptions of man, resources and environment have been analysed by numerous writers. Among recent books are Bookchin (1983) and Worster (1977). Many authors choose a model where the perception of a population in a delimited area and time is described as a given and then this perception changes as a result of experience or feedback with resources, environmental change, other human populations, and the creation of technology. Among important formative factors are the Greek-Hebrew religious base of Christianity (White, 1967), the discovery of the new world by Europe, and the industrial revolution. Whatever the reasons, and they must be a complex set, modern Euroamericans perceive the future as one where technology will be used to solve problems in human, resource, or environmental parts of the total system. In general there is an optimism that man can create progress in the future. These twin ideas--progress and progress through the application of technology--characterize a large portion of the cultural perceptions of the time. However, persons in other cultures have quite different perceptions of man and resources. There is little cross-cultural understanding of these perceptions. Rather, the perceptions of strong and aggressive states seem to overcome the indigenous cultures that are adapted to a particular region.

We also happen to live in a period where a great deal of human attention is paid to the consumption of resources by different populations. Some of us interpret the inhomogeneous patterns of population distribution, resources, demand, and consumption as fair or unfair, as good or bad, as right or wrong. Since some humans are able to extend their social conceptions and committments beyond the family, community and tribe to other races, nations, and peoples, and even to consider all humans as one family, many institutions, including those of the United Nations, have been formed which seek to equalize populations, consumption and resource distribution, or to reduce the competition and aggression that is induced by these differences. Both Marxist and Capitalist societies perceive that inhomogeneous distribution of resources is undesirable; they differ substantially in their conception of how these imbalances should be changed. Clearly we are engaged in a world-wide debate about these fundamental problems. The debate takes many forms, is carried out in many different fora, and a consensus is difficult to obtain and seldom lasts very long. But the debate continues and that, in my opinion, is heartening!

AN ECOLOGICAL INTERPRETATION

An ecologist's interpretation of these patterns would lead, I think, to a recognition that human populations and demands far exceed available resources in specific habitats. However, there is a difference of opinion about the limits of resources on the ecosphere. Some would argue that there are limits to growth in an immediate sense. Others would argue that while there are limits in an ultimate sense, in that at some density there is standing room only, actually human adaptability is very great and we can expect that man will alter his population size, use of resources, and impacts on the environment before a seriously negative situation develops. Many current arguments reduce to these two positions. Does one or the other position have special merit?

Both positions reflect human experience. A population is limited by the complex of resources and the competition it must engage in with other populations for these resources. A complex interaction between species and resources takes place in a space that has resource parameters that define what can be the relative success or failure of species to live and reproduce. Similarly, ecologists have a dynamic concept of species interaction through both competition and mutualism. Individuals compete for resources, adapt to changing environments, and behaviorly adjust so that they survive and reproduce. Those unable to adjust do not reproduce and do not pass their traits to the next generation. These models suggest that individuals and populations are exceptionally adaptable and responsive. There is no reason to think that human beings are less adaptive than other organisms. The only problem with the model is that selection of the most fit traits involves loss of individuals (and possibly even the loss of species). Loss of individuals as a mechanism of adaptation is counter to our prevailing belief systems. Loss of the species is never discussed except in apocalyptic literature.

Thus, these ecological models raise several difficult problems when we think about global resources. Continually increasing populations or demands not only exhausts resources but it limits invention and technology, creates instabilities in human populations and causes the human environment to be disturbed or changed in fundamental ways. Alternatively, man might respond to these stresses and adapt by creating new patterns of resource use, which could lead to a local increase in resources per capita, with a decrease in poverty and resource deterioration. New patterns of resource use might involve new political configurations, new economic systems, new ways to preserve, conserve and use resources or a combination of all three alternatives. New patterns, however, assume the death of old patterns.

I think that most of us would find increasing poverty or increasing environmental deterioration unacceptable alternatives. Therefore, we must focus on new ways to use resources and to manage people. And thus, we come to an appreciation of the role of science and the humanities in global resource problems. Scientific research, while only one of several elements required, is fundamental to the global resource issue (Botkin, 1982). My objective is to suggest the character of a new science focused on the human-world crisis. While it may seem pretentious to describe a new science, I truly feel that science is essential in world-problem solving but that the sciences as they exist today are one part of the problem. What would be some of the key elements in a new science which would replace the plethora or disciplines that exist today?

CHARACTERISTICS OF A NEW SCIENCE

In order to address and solve the human-global resource problem a scientific approach is required that has the following characteristics. First, it must build upon the entire corpus of knowledge and not be restricted to that obtained by one group of scientists, one language group, or one national group. Our problems are world-wide and we require the insight, data, and experience from all societies and all sciences to address them. As scientists we must, somehow, rise above the restrictive concepts of tribe, guild, and myth which structure so much scientific interchange today and with good will, an open mind, and with trust try to communicate, understand, and work with colleagues from other cultures and disciplines (for an explanation of altruism in science see Hull, 1978). Often this need is expressed as the need for integration but integration can have a connotation of interaction imposed on a community for ideological reasons. Rather, integration must come from a commonly held concern for fellow humans and a deep willingness to interact with others. It is built upon and expands from the human concept of community.

Within my own scientific subculture, which intersects with biology, ecology and agriculture I have been impressed with the important role of competition in ordering scientific priorities. Recall the American agricultural establishment's attack on Rachel Carson and the idea that pesticide use could have harmful impact on crop production, the environment and human health. Twenty-five years of experience with these problems makes one ask why these scientists did not use a potential problem to improve their funding position, create jobs, and through increased scientific activity either show that pesticides did or did not impact the environment. Instead these scientists prevented study of an important phenomena and only retarded for a short moment society's desire to understand the interactions of these chemicals and biological organisms. Agricultural science used the same approach when confronted with organic farming and we have not yet seen the resolution of that issue. Why should an entire community of scientists take a position that is unobjective and, in retrospect, counterproductive?

These cases are merely examples of a general problem. Science appears to be used by scientists less to explore the unknown and find solutions to human problems, than to compete, obtain power, support existing structures, and maintain social order. Science rather than being the revolutionary activity it truly is, becomes transmuted into a culturally-conventional activity. The profound control of culture can be seen here--even the politically radical scientist expresses his or her radicalism within patterns that support the cultural order and his or her position as an individual seeking power and reward. For science to contribute to the global problems confronting mankind, we must overcome this cultural control and the disciplinary controls and find personal and social value in creating new solutions and new answers to questions based upon all spectra of knowledge.

The second characteristic is the ability to work at a variety of scales of place and time. The world-human systems can be arranged in a variety of hierarchies; each arrangement fits a purpose or objective of research (Pattee, 1973). Frequently science is organized to focus on one or a few levels of a hierarchy or one or a few dimensions in time. However, it is essential that we extrapolate across scales of space and time. What happens at one level of a hierarchy often depends upon events at another level. What happens in the present usually is influenced by history. We have a relatively poor ability to scale up or down the space-time continuum and this lack of ability seriously hampers our efficiency in harnessing science to problem solving.

I have been especially concerned with this problem in an attempt to apply ecological theory to rural planning (Golley and Mut, 1983). Here the issue involves organization of information about the production systems at the scale of a region (which is large enough to plan from the central government's viewpoint), and also at the scale of subregional political units, villages, and individual farms. If we concentrate too much on regional patterns individuals are treated as numerical units of income, production type, sex, age, etc. Of course, we know that individuals are not homogeneous units and further, we know that it is frequently the special attributes of an individual that creates special abilities to produce or respond. The individual is important and may provide the key to solution of the problem. Yet, on the other hand one can not contact, interview and incorporate every individual into a regional plan. So we resort to sampling, case studies, and so on. The results depend upon the hierarchical level emphasized by the researcher and the way the data are extrapolated to other levels of the hierarchy. The solution is to simultaneously view the problem at many levels of scale.

The third characteristic of a new science is a balance between analysis and synthesis. These two activities are fundamental in all scholarly pursuits, yet we seem to have placed much greater emphasis on the analytical than the synthetic activity. In popular phraseology, we must use the macroscope as frequently as the microscope. I am not certain why we have developed the analytical side so much more strongly. Surely it is due partly to a style of thinking that comes from Western European societies. It also confers a uniqueness and a status to individuals that gives them competitive advantage. Possibly it comes from the inherent structure of the human brain and our style of education. And of course, analysis is the primary activity of science.

However, the science I visualize would be a different kind of science in that it would balance both the analytic and synthetic. Meeker (1975) describes it thus using ecology as the example,

> "Ecology is an academic study that tries to do more than one thing, and that is why it is an embarrassment to many scientists, a threat to politicians, and a mystery to the news media and its followers among the general public. Indulgent and paternalistic critics of ecology call it a "soft" science to distinguish it from hardcore disciplines like physics and chemistry which are built on the linear rock of mathematical logic. No respectable scientific discipline, they feel, should attract a following among housewives, high school kids, and long-haired freaks, as ecology has done. Nor should a proper natural science concern itself with cultural ideologies, international and local politics, religion and art, as ecology sometimes has. It is bad enough that ecologists should mix together such disciplines as botany, zoology, meterology, geology, physics, and chemistry. Why can't ecologists just tend to their own gardens like other good scientists? There is an answer: ecology is a science more interested in wilderness than in gardens."

Wilderness in Meeker's sense is the real man-resource world and not a culturally, historically controlled concept of a garden. The study of wilderness may provide the balance we need to solve problems without reducing human freedom and destroying further the environment and human society. There seems to be no question that imbalanced use of analysis and synthesis creates an aberrant type of science, reduces the ability to communicate, and makes it less likely that a particular science or scientist can contribute to problem solving.

A fourth characteristic is that the new science will be systems oriented, developing consistent models of reality that, while simple and abstract, will faithfully reflect the nature of the world-man systems. The systems approach I am describing here accepts the view that nature-human systems are composed of myriad feedback loops in complex networks of relationships over time and space. Not all elements of these networks cannot be replicated in a model; yet, sufficient detail must be included, representing the real processes and relationships, so that the essence of the problem is captured. If this is done well, then I think the output will be consistent to the degree that people and nature are consistent rather than being linear, mechanized, simple cause and effect sequences.

The fifth characteristic flows from above. That is, the new science will produce practical, useful results. In a sense, the science will operate much like the carpenter who must build with hetergeneous materials around unexpected problems, yet follow an overall pattern and end up with a recognizable solution (Glassie, 1975). Unfortunately, the science of today frequently ends with only more questions and requests for more funding. Promise of closure is forgotten and new questions that arise are deemed more important than those originally asked. Or it is discovered that poor design requires a repeat of the study to make it definitive. These characteristics are familiar to those persons employing scientists and are immensely frustrating to science managers. But equally frequently, the research solutions developed under tight control are mechanical, predictable, unimaginative and merely discover what is already known.

These characteristics describe some, and only some, of the dimensions of a new and more useful science of world-human resource problems. It will help to make its dimensions clearer if we also outline an agenda for a new science.

AN AGENDA FOR A NEW SCIENCE

One of the first requirements in implementing an appropriate and useful world-man science activity is to select a geographic and temporal scale where man is part of the system. This is important because then man must be treated as a system component. If this is not done at the outset the scale may be too fine-grained and man is then treated as part of the system environment, impacting the system from outside. An appropriate level is, I feel, the landscape. Landscape is a word with many definitions, yet in most languages it conveys a sense of a large, but limited space in which many different types of plant, animal, and human systems can exist and interact (Naveh, 1982). Study of landscapes involves many disciplines. For example, a recent First International Congress of Landscape Ecology (Tjallingii and deVeer, 1982) brought together geographers, ecologists, planners, landscape architects, designers, agricultural engineers, and others. Landscape ecology seems to describe an appropriate set of scales for this work.

If a landscape system can be identified, then the next step requires that the behavior of the system be described. Usually this means the translation of a set of inputs by the system into a set of outputs. The mapping of inputs into outputs is then observed over sufficient time so that consistent patterns can be described. Inputs and outputs appear to be very mechanical elements but they are intended to include qualitative, quantitative, and nonmaterial phenomena. A change in attitude could be the output of a human social system responding to inputs from an environment. We need to understand that the modelling activity, while linguistically rigid, attempts to include all phenomena relevant to the question. The patterns of input and output tell us something about the stability of the system, its response to environmental changes and lead us to a set of questions and hypotheses.

Next, we turn to identification of the system components and their linkages one to another and then through observation and our prior knowledge we focus on those components that we think may strongly affect system behavior. Analysis of these components over time, under experiment, and after natural perturbations gives us an understanding of how they influence system behavior. Nonquantitative phenomena may function as controls on quantitative phenomena in the model. That is, only some of the quantitative alternatives are possible given the cultural, social, historical, religious, or philosophical constraints operating at that particular place and time. With appropriate experiments and statistical procedures we can define how much of the behavior we can explain and therefore decrease our uncertainty. This approach can be quite efficient since the effort fits what is needed to accomplish a given result.

If we can define system behaviors and we partly understand how certain components affect such behavior, we can turn to the study of extrapolation of behavior across space and time. We know little about extrapolation. On one hand, there are those who extrapolate freely from individual cases on the assumption that the geographic, cultural, and ecological differences are sufficiently minor that their influence on system behavior is secondary. On the other hand, there are those who are so strongly impressed with the individual nature of each component that they believe that no extrapolation is possible. In this latter case geographic, cultural and ecological relativity is so strong that we are told that we cannot extend the findings in any way. The new science finds a position between these extremes and studies the costs and benefits (in more than an economic sense) of moving across scales of time and space.

There are two final points in this agenda which concern the use of the results of a new science. First, we anticipate that these studies will create practical results and lead to effective decision making. We can be optimistic because the analyses will not be linear, crisis oriented, reactive and biased. In the approach I am sketching here, the process of decision making is within the study--it is part of the system of investigation--and the decision maker is as important as any other component. This is dangerous of course, since it identifies failure and inconsistency. Yet, failure, inconsistency, and inactivity must be identified to solve the man-world problem.

And finally, this research approach feeds back to and from the people within the system. The object is to help people, not use them. When the people and the research workers are part of the same system, they can understand relationships and communicate. This violates the objectivity of science in one sense, but it also focuses upon the need for a consistent, objective, and planned study by the scientists. The agenda becomes public, the needs are defined publically, and the approach and procedures are discussed openly. Science in this approach is limited to supplying objective analyses and syntheses to decision-makers, who may be the people collectively or their representatives. Decision-making, as always, is based in wisdom, which is something separate from science.

Naturally this sketch has described a utopian ideal of scientific work. Its construction is formed to counteract forces which stress and frustrate effective solution of man-world problems. I am not sure if the agenda can ever be effectively carried out if it was acceptable and was found fault-free. Nevertheless, I feel deeply as an ecologist that our present fractured and contradictory approaches have largely failed, and will continue to fail, even if resources can be found for addressing immediate problems. Only by understanding the fundamental weaknesses with the way we address problems and by outlining the characteristics and agenda of a much needed new science, can we hope to design new approaches to problem solving--ones which I think would have a much higher chance of success.

REFERENCES

Bookchin, M. 1983. *The Ecology of Freedom*. Cheshire Books, Palo Alto, Calif.

Botkin, D. B. 1982. Can there be a theory of global ecology? *Jour. Theoretical Biology* 96:95-98.

Glassie, H. 1975. *Folk Housing in Middle Virginia*. Univ. Tennessee Press, Knoxville.

Golley, F. B. and M. Mut Catala. 1983. Rural planning and the environment. unpublished mss.

Hull, D. L. 1978. Altruism in science: a sociobiological model of cooperative behavior among scientists. *Animal Behavior* 26:685-697.

Meadows, D. H., D. L. Meadows, J. Randers, W. W. Behrens III. 1972. *The Limits to Growth*. Universe Books, N. Y.

Meeker, J. W. 1975. Ambidextrous education or: How universities can come unskewed and learn to live in the wilderness. *The North American Review*, summer pp 41-56.

Naveh, Z. 1982. Landscape ecology as an emerging branch of human ecosystem science, pp 189-237. In, A. Macfadyen and E. D. Ford, eds. *Advances in Ecological Research*. Volume 12. Academic Press, N. Y.

Pattee, N. H. (ed.) 1973. *Hierarchy Theory, The Challenge of the Complex System*. George Braziller, N. Y.

Tjallingii, S. P. and A. A. deVeer (eds) 1982. *Perspectives in Landscape Ecology, Contributions to Research, Planning, and Management of Our Environment*. Center for Agricultural Publishing and Documentation, Wageningen.

White, L. Jr. 1967. The historical roots of our ecologic crisis. *Science* 155(3767):1203-1207.

Worster, D. 1977. *Natures Economy: The Roots of Ecology*. Sierra Club Books, San Francisco.

Index

Acid rain, 293
Adaptation,
  individual, 139, 141-142
  of the Latin American peasant, 151-152
Agricultural analysis,
  common characteristics of, 265-266
Agricultural labor,
  in Latin America, 145-147
  productivity of, 268
Agricultural prices, 263, 267
Agricultural production, 267
Agricultural productivity,
  in Africa, 83
  in Latin America, 150
Agricultural societies, 20-23, 179
  and resources, 21
  shift from pre-historic to historic, 22
  socio-political diversity of, 22
Agricultural specialization,
  in Latin America, 149
Agricultural systems,
  slash and burn, 69
Agriculture,
  ecological constraints to, 270
  increase in producers, 81
  intensification of, 82-83
  mechanized cultivation in, 81

Agriculture (cont'd)
  shift to, 20
  in the Sudan, 81
  in the United States, 236
  world interdependence of, 269
Amazonia,
  case study, 113-123
Analytic approaches. See Research, levels of analysis.
Anchoveta, Peruvian, 37-59
  catch, 38
  collapse of, 48, 53
  effect of El Niño on, 38
  fishmeal, 37, 45
  maximum sustainable yield (MSY), 56
  overfishing, 48
  relationship to guano, 39
  stock assessment, 44
Anthropology,
  environmental views in, 107, 108
  levels of analysis in, 107
  physical, 108
  and the resource problem, 16, 5, 157 (n3), 365
Applied science, 356
  multidisciplinary research in, 368
  vs. basic science, 13
Appropriate technology, 52, 232
Aubreville, A., 213, 222, 223

Bennett, J.W., 19, 111,
    231, 234, 240, 241,
    345, 365, 369, 371 (n2)
Berry, L., 71, 78, 79, 89,
    92, 351, 353, 357, 360,
    361
Biological potential,
    in arid, semiarid and
    subhumid ecosystems,
    216
  destruction of, 216
  diminution of, 213-214,
    216
Biological productivity,
    214, 216, 225
  changes in, 217
  decline of, 219
  efforts to increase, 81
Biomes, 110, 111, 122
Bromley, D.W., 174, 348,
    350, 351, 353, 355,
    356, 357, 360, 361,
    367
Busby, F., 359, 360
Buttel, F.H., 129, 130,
    133, 136, 148, 149,
    155, 157, 346, 350,
    360, 364, 365

Carrying capacity,
  increase of, 20
Catastrophism, 323
Choice-exchange model, 353,
    356, 357, 358, 359, 367
Climatology,
  and desertification, 214,
    215
Colonialism,
  effects of, 140, 143
Computer modeling, 16
Conservationist views, 12,
    27-29, 31, 33 (n1),
    348-349, 351
  in range management, 189
    204-205
"Containment principles,"
    235-236, 253
Costs and benefits,
  social, 251
Cost-benefit analysis, 248,
    249, 361
Crisis management, 334, 336

Cultural ecology, 107, 108,
    239, 340, 346, 357-358,
    359, 360, 365
  as a model, 76
  See also Steward, Julian
Cultural evolution, 15, 234
Cultural resources, 248
Cybernetics, 290-294

Dahlberg, K.A., 17, 24, 31,
    32, 134, 348, 352, 354,
    359, 360, 361, 363
Decision-making, 123 (n2),
    357, 358
  rational choice model,
    232
  use of the ecosystem
    approach in, 293
Deforestation,
  in the Amazon, 118
  causes of, 14
  as a subprocess of
    desertification, 223,
    225
Demographic patterns, 241
  among agriculturalists,
    21
  among hunter-gatherers,
    19, 33 (n2)
  world-wide, 274
Desertification, 77-80, 347
  in Australia, 79
  in China, 214, 219
  climatic causes, 219-221
  climatic effects, 215
  as a concept, 6
  definitions of, 213-225
  disciplinary views of,
    215, 218
  distribution of, 78-79
  human causes of, 215,
    219-222
  location of, 218
  in marginal areas, 214,
    222, 223
  as a multidisciplinary
    field, 368
  as a process, 222-223
  in rangelands, 221
  region-specific biases,
    220

Desertification (cont'd)
  reversibility of, 214, 218-219
  in the Soviet Union, 214
  subprocesses, 223
  in tropical forests, 222, 223
  in the United States, 78, 79, 214, 224
Development,
  the bottom-up approach, 73
  costs and benefits of, 71, 72, 73, 79
  export led, in Peru, 50. See also Fishing industry, Peruvian
  micro-scale and regional scale, 75-76
  theories of, 141, 143, 154, 157 (n7)
Development assistance, U.S., to Peru, 46
Development constraints, in the Third World, 143-144
Development, economic, 140, 179
  objectives of, 47
Development of energy, non-technical restraints, 347
Development projects,
  importance of scale, 71
  multidisciplinary nature of, 368
  problems of, 232
  role of social scientists in, 74
Disciplinary research, 93, 378
  adequacy of, 360-361
  critique of, 8, 346-348, 367
  questions in, 265
  specialization within, 12-13, 16
  strengths and weaknesses of, 4
  as a vested interest, 366
Disciplinary views,
  of desertification, 223, 224
  in geography, 67

Drought, 83
  and agriculture in the Sudan, 81
  and the economy of Sudan, 72
  in the Sahel, 77, 213, 220, 221
  in the western United States, 195

Ecological anthropology, 109, 136
Ecology,
  approaches used in, 282
  critique of, 287-288
  as a field of study, 239, 380
  models used in, 286-287, 290, 292
  and the resource problem, 365
Ecology, applied, 281
Economic development policies, 45-46
Economics,
  and the resource problem, 5
Economics, Third World, 140
Economies,
  "broad spectrum," 17
  "specialized," 17
Ecosphere,
  definition of, 373
  human effects on, 374
Ecosystem, 110, 172-173
Ecosystems,
  arid, 68
  behavior of, 284
  definition of, 281, 295
  determining scale of, 70
  inputs and outputs, 169, 179, 284, 286, 288, 382
  man's interaction with, 167, 359
  problems of boundary definition, 283
  of rainforests, 68
  of rangelands, 190-191, 201, 202, 207, 208
  response to disturbance, 287-288
  of the Rio Negro, 117, 118
  simplification of, 179

Ecosystems (cont'd)
  and social systems, 358
  stability of, 290
Ecosystem approaches,
  in the social sciences, 294
Ecosystem concepts,
  in anthropology, 108-109
  in multidisciplinary research, 281-292
Ecosystem production, 284
Ecosystem research,
  methodology of, 7
  subdivisions of, 282-283
Energy analysis, 293
Energy flows, 284
Environment,
  as a causal factor, 141, 323, 328
Environmental impact assessment, 292-293
Environmental impact statements (EIS), 82-84
Environmental sociology, 129
EPA (Environmental Protection Agency), 246, 249, 292
Erosion, 79, 217, 223, 225
  in the Amazon, 118
  in East Africa, 89
  in the humid tropics, 69
  and irrigation projects, 71
  in Kenya, 83
  in Latin America, 153
  on rangelands, 197, 199
  and vegetation, 217
Ethics, 360, 361
Ethnoscience-technoscience communication gap, 93
Ethnoscience, use of,
  in Nigeria, 91
ETMA (Environmental Training and Resource Management for Africa), 89-90

Famine, 236
Farming systems research, 154-155
Fisheries management, 39
  conflicting objectives, 46-50
  dominant interests, 49

Fisheries management (cont'd)
  effect of changes in national government on, 50-51
  effect of political changes on, 46
  individual factors in, 51-57
  international factors in, 40-46
  national factors in, 46-51
  use of analogues in, 58
Fishing industry,
  effect of environmental changes on, 55-56
  effect of factory ships on, 40-42
  overfishing, 54-55
  renewability of, 54-56
Fishing industry,
  Californian, 48, 50, 58
  collapse of, 42, 54
Fishing industry, Chilean, 43
Fishing industry, Mexican, 48
Fishing industry, Namibian, collapse of, 43, 54, 58
Fishing industry, Peruvian, collapse of, 42, 54
  decline of, 38
  effect of El Niño on, 57
  growth of, 37-38, 51
  overfishing, 44
  transfer of technology in, 43
Fishmeal, 47, 50
Food policies,
  in Latin America, 150
  in the Third World, 144-145
"Food problem", the, 236
Food production, 262, 263
Food systems,
  models of analysis for, 264-265, 270-273
  research problems, 267-270
Foreign exchange, 38
  as a means to development, 45, 47
Foreign experts, 49

Foreign investment, 40
Functionalism,
    criticisms of, 157 (n1)
    in sociology, 132
Future scenarios, use of,
    26-31, 233, 363, 375

Geography,
    and desertification
        research, 77-80
    levels of analysis in,
        70, 80-82
    physical and cultural
        perspectives, 67
    and the resource problem,
        5, 365
Glantz, M.H., 44, 58, 213,
    347, 351, 357, 359,
    361, 362, 365, 367,
    368, 370
Golley, F.B., 11, 354, 357,
    358, 360, 361, 379
Green Revolution, the,
    134, 135, 150, 236, 348
Guano Administration Company of Peru, 43-44,
    47, 53

Hewitt, K., 305, 306, 308,
    311, 316, 325, 331,
    343, 344
Holistic approaches, 73, 74,
    107, 290, 347, 350, 351,
    362
    in rural sociology, 156
    in the social sciences,
        136
Homestead Acts, 192, 194,
    196
Human action,
    definition of, 320
Human adaptation, 16, 108,
    109, 110, 119, 122,
    376-377
    the study of, 109-110,
        120
Human ecology, 107, 295,
    329, 333, 345, 346
Human environment, 248
Human resources, 239, 364
Human systems, 73, 118-120
Hunting and gathering
    societies, 16, 17-20,
    108, 179

Hunting and gathering
    societies (cont'd)
    adaptation of, 19
    complexity of, 33 (n3)
    technology of, 18

IBP (International Biological Program), 109,
    120, 122, 281, 292
    disciplinary biases in,
        109-110
Ideology, 354
IMARPE (Institute del Mar
    del Peru), 44-45, 48,
    49-50
Impact assessment, 240,
    241, 249. See also
    Social impact assessment.
    methodologies of, 232
Impact ecology, 344
Industrial resource regimes,
    14, 23
Industrial societies, 23,
    179
    biological limits of, 28-29
    and problems of disaster,
        332-333
    the relationship of academia to, 14
    and resources, 23, 25
    social and organizational
        limits, 29-30
    socio-political diversity
        among, 23
    specialization in, 23, 26
    temporal perspective, 362
    values of, 24, 375
Institutional structures,
    174, 175
    and agriculture, 236-237
    of education, 365
    effects of, 349, 367
    and natural hazards, 307,
        317
    and the resource problem,
        168-169, 236, 245, 347
    and science, 322
    and technological
        research, 309-310
Interdisciplinary research,
    110, 111, 273, 367
    approaches used in, 3

Interdisciplinary research (cont'd)
  difficulties of, 1-2, 233
  in ecology, 282
  a model for, 67, 76, 77
  need for, 378
  reasons for failure of, 346
  requirements of, 368-369
  in systems analysis, 238
Irrigation,
  environmental impacts of, 78
  from groundwater, 84
  Khasm el Gherba scheme, 72
  and riverine fish, 75

Johnson, D.L., 82, 84, 90, 91, 217, 351, 353, 361, 367

Krenz, M.E., 351, 357, 359, 361, 362, 365, 367, 370
Kuhn, T., 238, 304, 329
!Kung, 18-19

Labor,
  costs of, 166
  international division of, 139-140, 146
Labor productivity,
  in Vermont dairy industry, 270-271
Land grant colleges, 132-133, 156
  models of analysis used by, 264
Land grants, 192
Land productivity, 262
Le Houerou, 213, 218, 219
Levels of analysis, 114, 122, 123
  in anthropology, 107
  in geography, 70, 80-81, 82
  macro-level, 73, 88, 113
  macro-level/micro-level, 272-273
  micro-level, 73, 88, 113, 115, 351, 353, 365
  in sociology, 131, 132, 156

"Limits to growth" debate, 27, 376
Logic,
  binary, 118, 119, 120
  dichtomous, 361-362
  linear, 119, 361, 362
  non-linear, 119, 120
Long-term studies, 284

MAB (Man and the Biosphere Program), 5, 78, 110, 122, 253, 281, 364
  objectives of, 1, 111, 231, 234
Malaria, 86
Marginal areas, 79, 214
  expansion into, 82
Marxist societies, 354
Marxist theories, 131, 157 (n2)
Marxist views, 23, 57, 355
  in economics, 310
Meadows, D.H., 354, 355, 360, 375
Mills, C.W., 132, 156
Models,
  nested research on human ecosystems, 118
  non-linear, 119
  optimization, 119
MOIRA (Model of International Relations in Agriculture), 271
Moran, E., 107, 109, 113, 116, 117, 348, 352, 354, 357, 361, 364, 367
Multidisciplinary research, 3-4, 367
  among range scientists, 200, 206, 209
Multinational corporations, 139
  and natural disasters, 308

Natural disasters,
  as a concept, 315
  definition of, 305, 318, 322, 343
  environmental factors, 305
  human factors, 333

Natural disasters (cont'd)
  perceptions of, 311-312, 321
  socio-economic factors, 306
Natural disasters research,
  assumptions of, 303
  dominant view in, 304-308
  factors affecting, 7
  and prediction, 307
  social science perspectives in, 330
  technological orientation of, 308-309
Natural resources. See Resources
Nature,
  individual views of, 53
  man's relation to, 326
  need for change in view of, 31
  views of, 51-53, 309, 351, 374
  views of in natural hazards research, 306
  Western views of, 12, 234, 375
Neo-Marxist views, 353
NEPA (National Environmental Policy Act), 202, 203, 234, 236, 246, 248, 292
  critique of, 249-250
Nutrient cycling,
  in Amazonia, 111, 117

Odum, E.P., 109, 281, 282, 291
Odum, H.T., 109, 137, 293
OPEC (Organization of Petroleum Exporting Countries), 149
Orlovsky, Nicolai, 347, 359, 361

Pastoralists, 75, 81, 181-182
  and desertification, 79
  effects of agriculture on, 81
  and irrigation, 71
  resource exploitation by, 75
  and trade, 72

Peru,
  export-led development in, 45. See also Fishing industry, Peruvian
  Ministry of Agriculture of, 48
  Ministry of Fisheries of, 48, 51
  resource conservation and exploitation in, 48
Pesticides, 378
Petrochemical use,
  and agricultural production, 148-149
  in Latin America, 153
  worldwide, 147-148
Pollution, 178
Population. See also Demographic patterns
  as a causal factor, 243, 363-364
  within ecosystems, 285-286
  projections for, 244-245
  the study of, 294
Population growth,
  effects of, 142, 234, 377
  in Latin America, 152, 153
  on rangelands, 207-208
"Population influx hypothesis," 243
Population resettlement, 232
Poverty, 353
Probability models,
  in accident research, 325
Problem-solving,
  monologues and dialogues in, 317, 321
Public accountability, 236
Public domain lands, 191-196, 206

Rangeland,
  definition of, 188-191
  depletion of, 194-195
  exploitation of, 194
  productivity of, 198
  resources of, 191, 192, 207, 208
Range management, 359
  approaches to resource problems, 6

Range management (cont'd)
  development of, 190
  as a discipline, 199, 202
  and legislation, 196, 202-203
Rationality, 166-167
  bounded, 166-167, 325
  and resource use, 247-250
  and utility functions, 167
  conditions that define, 309
Research,
  analysis and synthesis in, 379, 383
  anticipatory, 232, 250
  comparative, 288
  importance of scale in, 381
  multi-method, 251
  predictive, 324-328
  quantitative vs. qualitative, approaches, 275
  tools needed for, 274
  use of extrapolation in, 382
Resilience. See Stability and resilience
Resource "control centers," 170-175, 180, 182-183, 353, 356
Resource degradation,
  in Latin America, 147
Resource economics, 165, 350
Resource management, 110
  ideological perspectives, 53, 57
  major problems of, 73-76
  use of ecosystems concept in, 292
Resource management training, 92, 93
Resource problem, the,
  global nature of, 356
  historical approaches, 367
Resource systems,
  multiple use, 370
Resources,
  allocation of, 171-172
  beneficiaries of, 248
  and colonialism, 180-181. See also Colonialism

Resources (cont'd)
  as common property, 41
  conservation of, 52
  definition of, 348, 360
  distributional problems of, 353-357, 366
  economic meaning of, 168-169
  effects of warfare on, 25
  exploitation of, 52, 354-355
  human impacts on, 174
  neg-resources, 177
  nonrenewable, 54, 179
  and non-resources, 169, 170
  over-exploitation of, 81, 82, 222
  over-exploitation in deserts, 214
  renewable, 54, 179
  varying demands for, 374-375, 376
Resource use,
  approaches to, 89-93
  effects of colonialism on, 23. See also Colonialism
  ethic of, 352
  factors determining, 2, 3
  historical, cultural, and institutional contexts, 13
  historical research on, 16
  and institutional structures, 167, 168, 171, 182-183. See also Institutional structures
  and natural hazards, 86-88
Risk assessment, 305, 307-308
  in natural hazards research, 319, 325
Rural planning, 379
Rural sociology,
  development of, 129, 133
  and the resource problem, 5
  in the Third World, 133

Salinization, 69, 85
  and irrigation, 85, 86

Sampling,
  aerial, 73, 115
  and random differences, 117
  representative, 114, 115, 122
  systematic, 113
Schistosomiasis, 86
Scientific empiricism, 352
Scientific rationalism, 317
Scientific uncertainty, 49
Sheep industry,
  in the United States, 193-194
Shifting cultivation, 108
Site-specific research,
  as an aim of MAB, 110
  in Amazonia, 113, 116
  validity of, 114, 122
Social goals, 248
Social impact assessment, 250, 344, 356, 357, 366
  methodology of, 252
  as multidisciplinary, 368
  resource concepts in, 6
Social sciences,
  limitations of, 364-365
  and natural hazards research, 307-308
Society,
  as a causal factor, 226 (n3), 344
Sociology,
  diversity within, 131
  levels of analysis in, 131, 132, 138, 156
Sociology of knowledge, 248-249
Socionatural systems, 118, 119
Solar energy, 373
  economic dimensions of, 168
Specialization,
  problems of, 14
Stability,
  within "disaster zones," 314
Stability and instability,
  of a habitat, 313
  in human affairs, 327
Stability and resilience,
  of physical systems, 68, 69

Stability and resilience (Cont'd)
  of resource systems, 84
  of society, 83
Statistics,
  and "normal life," 327
Steward, Julian, 107, 241, 243
Synthesis,
  in ecosystems research, 283, 286
  hypotheses derived from, 290
  as a research activity, 379, 383
System,
  as a concept, 350
  determining scale of, 70-73, 114. See also Levels of analysis
System behavior, 382
System components, 382
Systems analysis, 238, 350
  common characteristics of, 265
  components of, 240-247
  factors influencing, 261
  and the food problem, 261, 264, 265
  in geography, 81
  "Warranted Queries" in, 265
Systems approaches, 4, 238-239, 366, 380
  hierarchical ordering in, 379-380
  inclusion of social factors, 364
  identifying systems for, 367
  socio-ecological, 137-138
Systems models, 358
  critique of, 6-7
  monitoring, 89-92
Szarleta, Ellen, 348, 350, 351, 353, 355, 356, 357, 360, 361, 367

Technical advice, foreign, 44-45
Technological intensification, 235

Technology
  in arid zone development, 78
  as a causal influence, 243
  and desertification, 221
  determinants of, 17
  effects of, 234
  effects upon resources, 11
  and environmental hazards, 88
  as a human process, 245
  relationship to resources, 168-169
  relationship to values, 82
  "supply side" bias of, 237
  transfer of, 40, 43-45
Technology, agricultural,
  effects upon Third World, 81-82
Territorial waters, 40-42
Tragedy of the commons, 41, 79, 193, 266, 362
Tropic levels, 288
  components of, 285
Tropical forests,
  immigrants in, 113
  MAB research projects concerning, 111
Tropical soils,
  degradation of, 150

UNCOD (United Nations Conference on Desertification), 68, 74, 77, 78, 213, 214, 225
UNEP (United Nations Environment Program), 78, 88, 214-215
UNESCO (United Nations Educational, Scientific, and Cultural Organization), 233, 308-309, 316
U.S. AID (United States Agency for International Development), 78
U.S. Bureau of Land Management, 203-205
USDA (United States Department of Agriculture), 236
  models of analysis used by, 264
U.S. Forest Service, 196, 197, 202, 205

Values, 345, 349, 357, 362
Water allocation, 69
Water resources, 69
  and agricultural practices, 85
  research concerning, 84. See also Irrigation
  in the Sahel, 80
  in the Soviet Union, 85
  in the United States, 84, 85
Watershed studies, 287-288
Wolf, C.P., 247, 344, 354, 360, 361, 363, 367
World economy,
  effects on Third World, 139-140, 143-144, 146
World hunger, 262, 263, 355
  efforts to end, 263
  research questions, 269
  solutions, 272
World Meteorological Organization, 215